Quinto of Cambridge
34 Trinity St.
Cambridge
CB2 1TB
Tel: 358279
Cancelled GJC

£ 5 -
TM

20/45

NAVAL HISTORY

NATIONAL MARITIME MUSEUM
CATALOGUE OF THE LIBRARY
VOLUME FIVE

Naval History

Part One: The Middle Ages to 1815

LONDON   HER MAJESTY'S STATIONERY OFFICE

ISBN 0 11 880760 9*

Contents

Introduction

The fifth volume of the Library catalogue is concerned with Naval History from the Middle Ages to 1815. Its sequel – the next volume in the series – will continue the story into modern times.

Arrangement follows the general plan adopted in the previous volumes. The subject is treated chronologically and within each century there are subdivisions, classifying the material according to topic, area and period. Lists of general works conclude each chronological section. The arrangement is designed to facilitate the reader's search for appropriate material. In addition to printed books, the entries include a large number of references to relevant articles in journals and periodicals. All Library accessions up to the end of June 1974 have been included. Finally, since the arrangement of the entries has been subjective rather than alphabetical, the index has been made as comprehensive as possible.

As before, this volume could never have been completed without the advice and assistance of many people; in particular my colleagues in the Library – Colin Duffield, Mrs Maisie Morton and Mrs Elizabeth Wiggans – to whom I am extremely grateful.

Michael Sanderson *Librarian*

List of Plates

continued overleaf

Abbreviations & references

CMH	Cambridge Modern History.
CSP	Calendar of State Papers.
Devon Assoc. Jnl.	Devon Association Journal.
EHR	English Historical Review.
Essex Inst. Hist. Coll.	Essex Institute Historical Collection.
HMC	Historical Manuscripts Commission.
HMSO	Her Majesty's Stationery Office.
IHRBull.	Institute of Historical Research Bulletin.
JMH	Journal of Modern History.
Jnl. US Mil. Ser. Instit.	Journal of the United States Military Service Institute.
New England Hist. Reg.	New England Historical Register.
NRS	Navy Records Society.
Proc. Amer. Antiq. Soc.	Proceedings of the American Antiquarian Society.
Proc. Belfast. Phil. Soc.	Proceedings of the Belfast Philosophical Society.
Proc. Brit. Acad.	Proceedings of the British Academy.
Proc. Mass. Hist. Soc.	Proceedings of the Massachusetts Historical Society.
Proc. Roy. Irish Acad.	Proceedings of the Royal Irish Academy.
Proc. & Trans. Royal Soc. Canada.	Proceedings & Transactions of the Royal Society of Canada.
RHSTrans.	Royal Historical Society Transactions.
RUSIJ	Royal United Service Institution Journal.
Trans. Carm. Antiq. Soc.	Transactions of the Carmarthenshire Antiquarian Society.
USMag.	United Service Magazine.
USNIP	United States Naval Institute Proceedings.

anon.	anonymous.
Cmnd.	Command [paper].
n.d.	no date.
n.p.	no place of publication given.
n.s.	new series.
pls.	plates.
q.v.	quid videm, or which see.
repr.	reprinted.

Mediaeval

I. European waters

1. ALEXANDER, A.F.O'D.
The war with France in 1377.
IHRBull., vol.xii no.36 (February 1935), pp.190–192.

2. ANDERSON, *Dr.* Roger Charles.
The *Grace de Dieu* of 1446–1486.
English Historical Review, vol.xxxiv (1919), pp.584–586.
Based on information in the Calendar of Patent Rolls.

3. ANDERSON, *Dr.* Roger Charles.
English galleys in 1295.
The Mariner's Mirror, vol.xiv (July 1928), pp.220–241.

4. BAKER, *Sir* Sherston.
The office of Vice-Admiral of the Coast; being some account of that ancient office.
London; privately printed; 1884. xii, 140pp. 8vo.
'The only work which attempts to deal with the history of the office of Vice-Admiral . . . From the standpoint of the medieval historian, the author's reliance on spurious documents entirely deprives his work of any value whatever.' – Brooks: The English Naval Forces, 1199–1272, p.195. [q.v.]

5. BALLARD, A.
The Cinque Ports under Henry II.
English Historical Review, vol.xxiv (1909), pp.732–733.

6. BALLEINE, G.R.
A history of the island of Jersey from the cave men to the German occupation and after.
London & New York; Staples Press; 1950. 341pp., pls. (inc. foldg. map), illustr. 8vo.
Two chapters, (pp.57–81), are concerned with The Hundred Years War.

7. BÉMONT, Charles (1843–1939).
Le campagne de Poitou, 1242–1243.
Annales du Midi, vol.v (1893), pp.289–314.

8. BERKLEY, *Captain* George, RN (*d.*1746).
The Naval history of Britain, from the earliest periods of which there are accounts in history, to the conclusion of the year M.DCCLVI.
London; T.Osborne; 1756. 706pp., frontis., pls., maps. Folio.

9. BREE, John.
Cursory sketch of the state of the naval military and civil establishment, legislative, judicial and domestic oeconomy of this Kingdom during the fourteenth century with a particular account of the campaign of King Edward the Third in Normandy and France in the years 1345 and 1346 to the taking of Calais. Volume I. [*all published*].
London; for the author; 1791. xxxvi, 381, [22]pp. 4to.

10. BROOKS, Frederick William.
William de Wrotham and the office of the Keeper of the King's Ports and Galleys.
English Historical Review, vol.xl (1925), pp.570–579.
William de Wrotham (d.1217) held this office for the greater part of John's reign and did much to organize the English naval forces.

11. BROOKS, Frederick William.
The King's ships and galleys, mainly under John and Henry III.
The Mariner's Mirror, vol.xv (January 1929), pp.15–18.

12. BROOKS, Frederick William.
The Cinque Ports.
The Mariner's Mirror, vol.xv (April 1929), pp.142–191.
Discusses their importance in English mediaeval history.

13. BROOKS, Frederick William.
The Battle of Damme – 1213.
The Mariner's Mirror, vol.xvi (July 1930), pp.263–271.
In the summer of 1213, an English fleet surprised and destroyed a superior French force off Damme in the Zwyn estuary. This victory thwarted Philip Augustus's plans for invading England.

14. BROOKS, Frederick William.
The Cinque Ports' feud with Yarmouth in the thirteenth century.
The Mariner's Mirror, vol.xix (January 1933), pp.27–51.
This bitter feud arose principally over fishing rights.

15. BROOKS, Frederick William.
The English naval forces, 1199–1272.
London; A.Brown; [1933]. xvi, 228pp., frontis., pls. 8vo.
An important study. There are chapters on: naval armament in the 13th century; the King's ships and galleys; naval administration and the raising of fleets under John and Henry III.

16. BURLEY, S.J.
The victualling of Calais, 1347–65.
IHRBull., vol.xxxi (May 1958), pp.49–57.

17. CAMMIDGE, John.
The battle of Winchelsea.
Sussex County Magazine, vol.iv (1935), pp.476–479, 551–555.
  In August 1350 Edward III personally commanded his ships in action against a Spanish fleet off Winchelsea. Edward was victorious and his communications with Calais remained intact. The battle is also known as 'Les Espagnols sur Mer'.

18. CANNON, Henry Lewin.
The battle of Sandwich and Eustace the Monk.
English Historical Review, vol.xxvii (1912), pp.649–670.
  In the summer of 1217, Henry II's forces gained steadily against the barons who supported Louis of France's claim to the throne. In August a French fleet commanded by Eustace, was intercepted off Sandwich. The troop transports escaped but the supply ships were captured. Eustace was later executed and his head carried on a pole through the streets of Canterbury.

19. CAPPER, Douglas Parodé.
Moat defensive. A history of the waters of the Nore Command, 55 B.C. to 1961.
London; A.Barker; 1963. xi, 251pp., pls., maps & diagrs. 8vo.
  The early chapters are concerned with ancient and mediaeval times.

20. CIPOLLA, *Professor* Carlo M.
Guns and sails in the early phase of European expansion, 1400–1700.
London; Collins; 1965. 192pp., pls. 8vo.

21. CLOWES, *Sir* William Laird (1856–1905), *et alia.*
The Royal Navy. A history from the earliest times to the death of Queen Victoria . . . Volume. I.
London; Sampson Low, Marston; 1897. 698pp., frontis, pls., illustr. 8vo.
  Contains chapters on both the civil and military history of naval affairs for the periods 1066–1154, 1154–1399 and 1399–1485.
  For instance, there is material on:
(for 1066–1154): the naval aspect of William of Normandy's invasion & the Conquest; Sweyn of Denmark's attempted invasion in 1069; expeditions against Scotland in 1071 and 1091; the Court of Admiralty under Henry I and his expedition to Normandy in 1106; the wreck of the White Ship.

(1154–1399): Laws of Oleron; actions in the Mediterranean, 1190; King John's warships; the Cinque Ports and their ships; Black Book of Admiralty; naval developments under Edward III. Wars with France and Scotland; battles of Damme (1213), Sluys (1340), Winchelsea ('Espagnols Sur Mer'), (1350); La Rochelle (1372).

(1399–1485): Henry V and the Navy; The 'Libylle of English Polycie'; War with France and battle of Harfleur (1416).

22. COLTON, Robert Bell.
Annals and legends of Calais.
London; J.Russell; 1852. viii, 220pp., frontis. 8vo.
  The first two chapters describe Edward III's siege and capture of Calais, 1346–7.

23. COOPER, William Durrant (1812–1875).
The History of Winchelsea, one of the ancient towns added to the Cinque Ports.
London; J.R.Smith/Hastings; H.Osborne; 1850. viii, 264pp., foldg. frontis., pls., illustr. 8vo.
  Includes an account of 'Les Espagnols sur Mer' (29 August 1350) and the sack of Winchelsea by the French in March 1360.

24 DEGRYSE, Roger.
De admiraals en de eigen marine van Bourgondische hertogen, 1384–1488.
Marine Academie Medelingen, boek XVII (Antwerp, 1965), pp.139–225, illustr.

25. [EDWARD III, *King of England* (1312–1377).]
List of the fleet, 1322.
Archaeologia, vol.vi (1782), pp.197, ff.

26. FORMOY, Beryl Edith Rotherham.
A maritime indenture of 1212.
English Historical Review, vol.xl (1926), pp.556–559.
  William de Wrotham's reception and disposal of ships and goods captured from the Normans by English galleys, commanded by Geoffrey de Lucy.

27. FOWLER, Kenneth [*editor*].
The Hundred Years' War.
London; Macmillan; 1971. 229pp. 8vo.
  Includes chapters by H.J.Hewitt on the organisation of war and C.F.Richmond, on the war at sea.

28. GODMOND, Christopher.
A brief memoir of the campaign of Edward the Third in the years 1345, 1346, and 1347, ending with the surrender of Calais; with a defence or apology of Edward as to his conduct to Eustace de St.

28. GODMOND, *continued*
Pierre and other burgesses on the surrender of that fortress.
Gentleman's Magazine, (October 1837), pp.357–361.

29. GODOLPHIN, John (1617–1678).
Συνήγορος θαλάσσιος, a view of admiral jurisdiction. Wherein the most material points concerning that jurisdiction are fairly and submissively discussed. As also divers of the laws, customs, rights and privileges of the High Admiralty of England, by ancient records . . . whereunto is added by way of an appendix, an extract of the ancient laws of Oleron . . . With a catalogue of all the Lord High Admirals that have been in this Kingdome since King John's time, to the reign of His now most gracious majesty, K.Charles II.
The second edition corrected and ammended.
London; George Dawes; 1685. [lvi]; 230 + [20]pp. 8vo.
The first edition was published in 1661. The author was appointed a judge of Admiralty in July 1653 and held office until December 1659.

30. HAKLUYT, Richard (1552?–1616).
The Principall Navigations Voiages and Discoveries of the English nation . . .
London; G.Bishop, R.Newberrie . . .; 1599–1600. 3 volumes. 4to.
Includes: (i) 'The rolle of the huge fleete of Edward the thirde before Caleis.' (ii) 'The summe of expences layde out in the siege of Caleis. (iii) A note of Thomas Walsingham touching King Edward the thirde his huge fleete of 1100 ships, wherewith he passed over into Caleis anno 1360.' (iv) 'Libelles de politia conservativa Maris or the pollicy of keeping the sea.'
For details of other editions of Hakluyt held in the Library, see Volume I of the Library Catalogue: Voyages & Travel, entries 4–7.

31. HARGREAVES, Reginald.
The Narrow Seas.
London; Sidgwick & Jackson; 1959. xxvi, 517pp., fdg. map. 8vo.
Includes seven chapters (pp.24–168), on naval activities in the Channel in mediaeval times.

32. HEWITT, H.J.
The organisation of war under Edward III, 1338–62.
Manchester; University Press; 1966. 206pp., pls., map. 8vo.
There are details on the defences of the Channel against French attacks and a chapter on shipping and the movement of troops. An appendix lists the ships used to transport Henry of Lancaster's troops to Bordeaux in 1345.

33. HOLLOWAY, William.
History and antiquities of the ancient town and port of Rye in the county of Sussex with incidental notices of the Cinque Ports.
London; R.Smith; 1847. vii, 616pp. 8vo.

34. HUEFFER, Ford Madox (1873–1939).
The Cinque Ports: a historical and descriptive record.
Edinburgh & London; Blackwood; 1900. xiv, 403pp. pls. 4to.

35. JOHNSON, Charles.
London shipbuilding, A.D. 1295.
Antiquaries Journal, vol.vii (October 1927), pp.424–437.
Describes the building of galleys that the City of London had to furnish as their contribution to the extensive shipbuilding programme, which followed the outbreak of war with France in 1294.

36. JONES, Michael.
Two Exeter ship agreements of 1303 and 1310.
The Mariner's Mirror, vol.liii (November 1967), pp.315–317.
The agreements were for the supply of ships for the King's service against Scotland.

37. KINGSFORD, C.L.
The beginnings of English maritime enterprise.
History, vol.xiii (1928), pp.97–106; 192–203.

38. LA RONCIÈRE, Charles Bourel de (1870–1941).
Histoire de la Marine Française. Les origines.
Paris; Plon; 1899. 529pp., pls. 8vo.
Includes: The Normans; the Aragon War of 1285–91; conquest of Normandy and Poitou (1203–1242); Philippe Le Bel's blockade of England (1293–7); Flemish Wars 1299–1304 & 1315–18, and the opening campaigns of The Hundred Years' War.

39. LA RONCIÈRE, Charles Bourel de (1870–1941)
Histoire de la Marine Française: La guerre de Cent Ans. Revolution maritime.
Paris; Plon; 1900. 558pp. pls. 8vo.

40. LAUGHTON, *Sir* John Knox (1830–1915).
Studies in naval history. Biographies.
London; Longmans; 1887. 469pp. 8vo.
Chapter I (pp.1–29) is concerned with Jean de Vienne, Admiral of France, 1373–1396. It was originally published in the United Services Magazine, *October 1880.*

41. LEWIS, *Professor* Michael (1890–1970).
Spithead. An informal history.
London; Allen & Unwin; 1972. 208pp., pls. 8vo.
    The second chapter is concerned with the Middle Ages.

42. McKISACK, May.
The Fourteenth Century, 1307–1399.
Oxford; Clarendon Press; 1959. xix, 598pp., maps,
genealogical tables. 8vo.
    *Includes references to Isabella's and Mortimer's
invasion of 1326; the Hundred Years' War; 'Les
Espagnols sur Mer, (August 1350) and the battle of La
Rochelle (June 1372).*

43. MACPHERSON, David (1746–1816).
Annals of commerce, manufactures, fisheries, and
navigation, with brief notices of the arts and sciences
connected with them. Containing the commercial
transactions of the British Empire and other
countries from the earliest accounts . . .
London; J.Nichols & Son . . .; 1805. 4 vols. 4to.
    *Contains information on the Norman Conquest
(1066); Norwegian invasion of Orkney and the
Western Isles (1098), battle of Damme (1213), battle of
Sandwich (August 1217), Norwegian attack on Bute
(1231), Cinque Ports raids on French shipping (1242),
piratical outrages of the Norwegian Olaf in the Baltic
(1285), defeat of the French fleet in the Channel (1292),
the Easterlings depredations on the Scottish coast (1308),
attacks on English shipping by Calais-based ships
(1315), operations of Edward III's galleys off the east
coast of Scotland (1338), battle of Sluys (1340); siege of
Calais (1347); cruise of a Scottish squadron off the east
coast of Scotland (September 1357), French invasion of
the Thames (1379); the Earl of Arundel's attack on a
combined Flemish, French & Spanish convoy in the
Channel (24 March 1387) and the activities of Dartmouth privateers (1379–89).*

44. MANWARING, George Ernest (1882–1939).
[*editor*].
Document. The safeguard of the sea, 1442.
The Mariner's Mirror, vol.ix (October 1923),
pp.376–379.
    *A House of Commons ordinance for the provision of
eight ships with attendant barges and pinnaces, to be
maintained for the defence of the realm.*

45. MARSDEN, Reginald G.
Early prize jurisdiction and prize law in England.
English Historical Review, vol.xxiv (1909),
pp.675–697.
    Covers the early fourteenth to the sixteenth centuries.

46. MARSDEN, Reginald G.
The Vice-Admirals of the coast.
English Historical Review, vols.xxii (1907),
pp.468–477 & xxiii (1908), pp.736–757.

47. MARSDEN, Reginald G. [*editor*].
Documents relating to the law and custome of the
sea.
volume i. A.D. 1205–1648.
London; Navy Records Society; 1915. [volume
xlix] xl, 561pp. 8vo.
    *The documents include references to prizes; letters of
marque & reprisal; the Cinque Ports and piracy.
Pages 1–138 cover the period 1205–1485.*

48. MOORE, *Sir* Alan.
Accounts and inventories of John Starlying, clerk of
the King's ships to Henry IV.
The Mariner's Mirror, vol.iv (June 1914), pp.167–173.

49. MYERS, *Professor* Alexander Reginald [*editor*].
English Historical Documents, 1327–1485.
London; Eyre & Spottiswoode; 1969. lxviii,
1,236pp., foldg. genealogical tables. Large 8vo.
    *Includes: (i) The beginning of hostilities in the
Hundred Years' War, 1317. (ii) The battle of Sluys,
June 1340. (iii) The siege and capture of Calais, 1347.
(iv) French attacks on the English coast, 1403–04. (v)
French invasion of Wales in alliance with Owen
Glyndŵr, 1405. (vi) The English clear the Channel of
enemy ships, 1416–17. (vii) The building of a great
ship for the King at Bayonne, 1419. (viii) The capture
of the Bay Fleet, 1443.*

50. NEWTON, *Professor* Arthur Percival [*editor*].
The auditing of Navy accounts under Edward IV.
The Mariner's Mirror, vol.ix (February, 1923),
pp.56–58.

51. NICHOLAS, *Professor* L.
La puissance navale dans l'histoire. Tome i: Du
Moyen Age à 1815.
Paris; Editions Maritimes & Coloniales; 1958.
384pp., maps. 8vo.
    *There is material on the French monarchy and the sea
(987–1558); the command of the Channel (1215–17),
the navy under Philippe Le Bel (1285–1314); the
Hundred Years' War and the English landing at
Harfleur.*

52. NICHOLAS, *Sir* Nicholas Harris (1799–1848).
A History of the Royal Navy from the earliest times
to the wars of the French Revolution.
London; Richard Bentley; 1847. 2 vols. vol.i: xxvi,

52. NICHOLAS, *continued*
469pp., engr. frontis., illustr. vol.ii: 534pp., engr. frontis., illustr. 8vo.

Because of the author's death, only two volumes – tracing the Navy's history up to the reign of Henry V – were published. Sir William Laird Clowes wrote: 'Nicolas spared no pains in research; he was never satisfied until he had consulted the best contemporary authorities for details of every event . . .' (The Royal Navy. A history . . ., vol.i, p.vii).

The volumes include the following appendices: (i) Contemporary account of William the Conqueror's fleet. (ii) Wendover's and other chronicle accounts of the battle of Dover, August 1217. (iii) List of commanders, admirals and captains of the English fleets, 1189–1326. (iv) Commissions to Keepers of the seas, captains of the King's mariners and admirals. (v) Copies and translations of the King's mandates for impressing ships and men. (vi) Extract from Minot's poem describing Edward III's Flanders expedition, 1338. (vii) Extracts from various records giving the size, stores, armament and equipment of ships in the reign of Edward III. (viii) On the office and duties of admirals, the management of fleets ʼ . . . in the 14th century. (ix) Letter from Edward III to the Duke of Cornwall announcing the battle of Sluys. (x) List of English ships captured by the Spaniards off Brittany in August 1375. (xi) Indentures between the King's serjeant-at-arms & the masters of ships in 1394 & 1398. (xii) List of the Royal Navy, August 1417. (xiii) References to naval accounts in the reigns of Richard II, Henry IV and Henry V. (xiv) Commissions to admirals in the reigns of Richard II, Henry IV and Henry V. (xv) List of admirals, 1327–1422.

53. OPPENHEIM, Michael M. (1853–1927).
A History of the administration of the Royal Navy and of merchant shipping in relation to the Navy from MDIX to MDCLX with an introduction treating of the preceding period.
London & New York; John Lane; 1896. xiv, 411pp., cold. frontis., pls., tables. 8vo.

A brilliant work. The introductory chapter, (pp.1–44), is concerned with the organisation and administration of the Royal Navy prior to 1509.

54. OPPENHEIM, Michael M.
The Maritime history of Devon.
With an introduction by W.E.Minchinton . . .
University of Exeter; 1968. xxiv, 175pp., frontis. (port), pls., maps on endpapers. 8vo.

Oppenheim wrote this work in 1908 for inclusion in a then-projected volume of the 'Victoria History of Devonshire'. It includes a section (pp.4–23), covering the period from the Norman Conquest to the Tudors.

55. OWEN, *Sir* Douglas.
The Black Book of the Admiralty.
The Mariner's Mirror, vol.i (October 1911), pp.267–271.

56. PLATT, Colin.
Medieval Southampton. The port and trading community, A.D. 1000–1600.
London & Boston; Routledge & Kegan Paul; 1973. xvi, 309pp., pls., maps. 8vo.

Includes a chapter on the raid on Southampton by French and Genoese galleys in 1338.

57. POWICKE, *Sir* Maurice.
The Thirteenth Century.
Oxford; Clarendon Press; 1953. ['Oxford History of England' series.] xiv, 829pp. 8vo.

Contains references to the battle of Sandwich (1217); Henry III's expedition to Brittany (1230); the activities of Edward I's fleet off the east coast in 1296; the defeat of a Norman fleet by ships of the Cinque Ports off Cape Saint Mathieu; and the sack of La Rochelle (1293).

58. PRESTWICH, Michael.
War, politics and finance under Edward I.
London; Faber & Faber; 1972. 317pp., maps, illustr. 8vo.

Includes a chapter on the Navy (pp.137–150).

59. REID, W.Stanford.
Sea power in the Anglo-Scottish War, 1296–1328.
The Mariner's Mirror, vol.xlvi (January 1960), pp.7–23.

60. RICHMOND, C.F.
The Keeping of the Seas during the 100 Years War, 1322–1440.
History, vol.xliv (1964), pp.283–298.

Includes an important table – 'The sale of the King's ships, 1423–5' – giving details of the ships, their tonnage, origin, cost and date of sale.

61. RICHMOND, C.F.
English naval power in the fifteenth century.
History, vol.liii (1967) pp. 1–15.

62. RODGERS, *Vice-Admiral* William Ledyard, USN (1860–1944).
Naval warfare under oars, 4th to 6th centuries. A study of strategy, tactics and ship design.
Annapolis, Md.; US Naval Institute; 1939. xiv, 358pp., pls., foldg. maps, 8vo.

Chapter vii (pp.88–108) is concerned with the mediaeval wars between England and France. The Library also possesses a 1970 reprint of this work.

63. SENIOR, William.
Admiralty matters in the fifteenth century.
Law Quarterly Review, no.cxl (October 1919),
pp.1–10.

64. SHERBORNE, J.W.
The battle of La Rochelle and the war at sea, 1372–5.
IHRBull., vol.xlii no.105 (May 1969), pp.17–29.
 In June 1372, a fleet of armed merchantmen carrying English reinforcements to Aquitaine was intercepted and destroyed by Castilian galleys off La Rochelle. It proved to be England's worst naval defeat during the Hundred Years' War.

65. STENZEL, Alfred.
Seekriegsgeschichte in ihren wichtigsten abschnitten mit berücksichtigung der Seetaktik. Band II.
400 B.C.–A.D.1600
Hanover & Leipzig; Hahnsche Buchhandlung; 1909. xviii, 321pp., foldg. diagrs. 8vo.
 Includes the Norman Conquest of England, the battles of Damme (1213), Dover (1217) and Zierickzee (1300), The Hundred Years' War & the Hanseatic Wars.

66. TERRIER DE LORAY, *Le Marquis.*
Jean de Vienne, amiral de France, 1341–1396.
Paris; Soc.Bibliographique; 1877. ccxxii, 276pp. 8vo.

67. TINNISWOOD, J.T.
English galleys, 1272–1377.
The Mariner's Mirror, vol.xxxv (October 1949), pp.276–315.

68. TURNER, Barbara Carpenter.
Southampton as a naval centre, 1414–1458.
Paper in: *Collected essays on Southampton*, edited by J.B.Morgan & Philip Peberdy. Southampton Borough Council; 1958. pp. 38–47
 A second edition was published in 1961.

69. TURNER, *Mrs* W.J.Carpenter.
The building of the *Gracedieu, Valentine* and *Falconer* at Southampton, 1416–1420.
The Mariner's Mirror, vol.xl (January 1954), pp.55–72.

70. TURNER, *Mrs* W.J.Carpenter.
The building of the *Holy Ghost of the Tower*, 1414–1416, and her subsequent history.
The Mariner's Mirror, vol.xl (November 1954), pp.270–281.

71. TWISS, *Sir* Travers (1809–1897). [*editor*].
Monumenta Juridica. The Black Book of the Admiralty, with an appendix.
London; Longmans; 1871–76. 4 vols. vol.i: xciii, 491pp., foldg. pls. vol.ii: lxxxvii, 500pp., foldg. pls. vol.iii: lxxxvi, 673pp., foldg. pls. vol.iv: clii, 559pp. Large 8vo.
 The Black Book of the Admiralty is a unique source of maritime law containing the oldest sea-laws enforced in Great Britain and the earliest articles of war. The three supplementary volumes contain: the texts of other ancient sea codes including the Domesday of Ipswich, the Customaries of Oleron and Rouen, the charter of Oleron, the Consulate of the Sea, the Laws o, Amalfi and Gotland, and the Codes of the Teutonic Order of Livonia, of Danzig, Lubeck, Flanders and Valencia.

72. WARNER, *Sir* George F. [*editor*].
The Libelle of Englyshe Polycye. A poem on the use of sea-power, 1436.
Oxford; Clarendon Press; 1926. lvi, 126pp., pls. 8vo.
 '. . . "The Libel of English Policy" is remarkable as an early attempt to show the political and commercial advantages to be obtained by securing command of the sea'. – cf. editor's introduction.
 The poem's anonymous author was probably Adam de Molyneaux (or Molins), Bishop of Chichester.

73. WARNSINCK, Johan Carel Marinus.
De Zeeoorlog van Holland en Zeeland tegen de Wendische steden de Duitsche Janze, 1438–1441.
The Hague; Nijhoff; 1939. 40pp. 8vo.

74. WEIR, Michael.
English naval activities, 1242–1243.
The Mariner's Mirror, vol.lviii (February 1972) pp.85–92.

75. WILLIAMSON, *Professor* James Alexander.
The English Channel. A history.
London; Collins; 1959. 381pp., pls., maps. 8vo.
 Contains chapters on the Norman invasion and the Cinque Ports.

76. WRIGHT, *Reverend* R.F.
The High Seas and the Church in the Middle Ages.
The Mariner's Mirror, vol.liii (February & May 1967), pp.3–31; 115–135.

77. [Anonymous].
Account of the principal naval actions that have taken place in the Narrow Seas since the Conquest.
Naval Chronicle, vol.vi (1801), pp.123–124, 213–217, 288–290.
 Includes: the battles of Damme (1213), Sluys (1340) and La Rochelle (1372).

II. The Mediterranean

78. BOFARULL Y SANS, *Don* Francisco de.
Antiga Marina Catalana.
Barcelona; J. Jepús; 1898. 123pp., pls. 8vo.
Describes the Catalan Navy from the twelfth to the sixteenth centuries.

79. BRADFORD, Ernle.
The Mediterranean. Portrait of a sea.
London; Hodder & Stoughton; 1971. 574pp., pls. (some cold.), maps. 8vo.
A detailed history of the Mediterranean, containing chapters on the Crusades, the Knights of St. John, the fall of Byzantium and the Italian maritime republics.

80. BRADFORD, Ernle.
The Shield and the Sword. The Knights of St. John.
London; Hodder & Stoughton; 1972. 245pp., pls., maps. 8vo.

81. BRAGADIN, *Commander* Marc'Antonio.
Repubbliche Italiane sul mare.
Milan; Gazanti; 1951. 278pp., pls., illustr., maps. 8vo.
A comprehensive account of the rivalry between the maritime republics of Venice, Genoa, Pisa and Florence.

82. BROCKMAN, *Captain* W. Eric, RN.
The Two sieges of Rhodes, 1480–1522.
London; John Murray; 1969. 184pp., pls., illustr. 8vo.
Being the victory of the Knights of St. John over Mehmet the Conqueror, after a three-month siege in 1480 and their final defeat by Soleyman the Magnificent in 1522.

83. BROWN, Horatio.
Venice.
chapter in: *The Cambridge Modern History*, volume i, (Cambridge University Press; 1934; pp.253–287).
Discusses Venetian naval policy and organisation and the War of Chioggia, (1378–81).

84. CREASY, *Sir* Edward Shepherd (1812–1875).
History of the Ottoman Turks.
New and revised edition.
London; R. Bentley; 1877. xvi, 558pp. 8vo.

85. DELAVILLE LE ROULX, Joseph (1855–1911).
Les Hospitaliers à Rhodes, (1310–1421).
Introduction by Anthony Luttrell.
London; Variorum Reprints; 1974. [10], vi, 452pp. 8vo.

86. FERNANDEZ, Luis Suárez.
The Atlantic and the Mediterranean among the objectives of the House of Trastámara.
Chapter in: *Spain in the Fifteenth Century, 1369–1516. Essays and extracts by historians of Spain*, edited by Roger Highfield. (London; Macmillan; 1972, pp.57–79).
A survey of Castilian foreign policy, 1369–1420, with special emphasis on sea-power.

87. FISHER, *Sir* Godfrey.
Barbary Legend. War, trade and piracy in North Africa, 1415–1830.
Oxford; Clarendon Press; 1957. xii, 350pp., frontis., foldg. map. 8vo.
The first chapter is concerned with Barbary prior to the coming of the Turks.

88. GAVOTTI, *Contrammiraglio* G.
Guerra Navale Littoranea.
Rome; Senato; 1901. 2 vols. vol.i: 305pp. vol.ii: 303pp. 8vo.
Includes accounts of the Sixth Crusade (1249), the War of Chioggia (1378–81) and the fall of Constantinople, (1453).

89. GIBBONS, Herbert Adams.
The Foundations of the Ottoman Empire. A history of the Osmanlis up to the death of Bayezid I, 1300–1403.
London; Frank Cass; 1968. 379pp., frontis., (map), maps. 8vo.
First published in 1916.

90. GUGLIELMOTTI, P. Alberto.
Stora della Marina Pontifica nel medio evo dal 728 al 1499.
Florence; Le Monnier; 1894. 2 vols. vol.i: iv, 496pp. vol.ii: 556pp. 12mo.

91. HAKLUYT, Richard (1552?–1616).
The Principall Navigations Voiages and Discoveries of the English nation . . .
London; G.Bishop, R.Newberrie . . . ; 1599–1600. 3 vols. 4to.
Includes Richard I's rules and ordinances for his fleet during the Third Crusade (1189–1192). For further details see volume I of the Library catalogue: Voyages and Travel.

92. JURIEN DE LA GRAVIÈRE, *Amiral* Jean Edmond (1812–1892).
Doria et Barberousse.
Paris; Plon; 1886. 346pp. 12mo.
With a narrative of the rivalry between Genoa and Venice; the War of Chioggia (1378–1381); the fall of Constantinople (1453) and the siege of Rhodes (1480).

93. KHALIFEH, Mustaffa Ben Abdullah Haji (*d. 1657*).
The History of the maritime wars of the Turks.
translated from the Turkish . . . by James Mitchell.
Chapters I–IV.
London; Oriental Translation Fund; 1831. xiv, 80pp., 4to.
There are accounts of the expeditions to Amassero, Sinope and Trebizond (1459); Metylin (1461); Negropont (1467); Kafa and Azak (1475), Mota (1473) and Rhodes (1474).

94. LACY, A.D.
The siege of Rhodes, 1480.
History Today, vol.xviii (May 1968), pp.344–350, illustr.

95. LANE, *Professor* Frederic Chapin.
Venetian ships and shipbuilders of the Renaissance.
Baltimore, Md.; Johns Hopkins Press; 1934. x, 285pp., illustr. 8vo.
Includes chapters on the growth and management of the Arsenal and an appendix entitled: 'Doge Mocenigo's oration and the Venetian fleet, 1420–1450'.

96. LANE, *Professor* Frederic Chapin.
Navires et constructeurs à Venise pendant la Renaissance.
Paris; S.E.V.P.E.N.; 1965. [viii], 309pp., illustr. 8vo.

97. LA RONCIÈRE, Charles Bourel de (1870–1941).
Histoire de la Marine Française. Les origines.
Paris; Plon; 1899. 528pp., pls. 8vo.

98. LA RONCIÈRE, Charles Bourel de (1870–1941).
Histoire de la Marine Française. La guerre de Cent Ans. Revolution maritime.
Paris; Plon; 1900. 558pp., pls. 8vo.
Both these volumes include chapters on the Crusades.

99. LEWIS, Archibald R.
Naval power and trade in the Mediterranean, A.D. 500–1100.
Princeton University Press; 1951. xii, 271pp., maps. 8vo.
Discusses the relationship between naval power and commerce in the Byzantine, Moslem and Western worlds.

100. LOPEZ DE AYALA, *Don* Ignacio.
Historia de Gibraltar.
Madrid; Antonio de Sancha; 1782. xvi, 387, xlviii pp., foldg. engr. plt. 4to.
Pages 118–208 are concerned with the period, 1003–1502.

101. LOPEZ DE AYALA, *Don* Ignacio.
The history of Gibraltar from the earliest periods of its occupation by the Saracens comprising details of the numerous conflicts for its possession . . . until its final surrender in 1462 . . . translated from the Spanish . . with a continuation to modern times by James Bell.
London; W.Pickering; 1845. xx, 234pp., foldg. diagrs. 8vo.

102. MACPHERSON, David (1746–1816).
Annals of commerce, manufactures, fisheries, and navigation, with brief notices of the arts and sciences connected with them. Containing the commercial transactions of the British Empire and other countries from the earliest accounts to the meeting of the Union Parliament in January 1801 . . . In four volumes. Volume I.
London; J.Nichols & Son . . . ; 1805. xvi, 719pp. 4to.
Contains information on a seafight between the Venetians and a Norman fleet commanded by Robert Guiscard (1084); the war between Genoa and Pisa (1136–1138); Genoese naval power (1155); an engagement between a Venetian and a Greek fleet (1171); naval tactics in 1190; Richard I's naval battle with the Turks (1191); the Fourth Crusade (1201); the war between Genoa and Candia (1206); Catalan naval power in 1227; the Seventh Crusade (1270); a ten-day battle between four Catalan armed merchantmen and ten Genoese galleys (1331); the war between Genoa and Venice; the defeat of sixty Genoese galleys by a combined Catalonian-Venetian fleet (1365) and the fall of Constantinople (1453).

103. MANFRONI, *Professor* Camillo.
Storia della Marina Italiana dalla caduta di Constantinople alla battaglia di Lepanto.
Rome; Forzani; 1897. 534pp. 8vo.
Covers the period 1453 to 1571.

104. MANFRONI, *Professor* Camillo.
La battaglia di Gallipoli e la politica Veneta-Turco (1381–1420).
Offprint from: *Ateneo Veneto*, anno II, facs. 1–2 (1902). 72pp. 8vo.

105. MARKHAM, *Sir* Clements Robert (1830–1916).
The story of Majorca and Minorca.
London; Smith, Elder; 1908. x, 309pp., maps. 8vo.
The early chapters are concerned with the islands' mediaeval history.

106. POTTER, G.R.
The fall of Constantinople, May 29th 1453.
History Today, vol.iii (1953), pp.41–49.

107. ROBSON, J.A.
The Catalan fleet and Moorish seapower, (1337–1344).
English Historical Review, vol.lxxiv (1959), pp.386–408.

108. RODGERS, *Vice-Admiral* William Ledyard, USN (1860–1944).
Naval warfare under oars, 4th to 16th centuries. A study of strategy, tactics and ship design.
Annapolis, Md.; US Naval Institute; 1939. xiii, 358pp., pls., illustr., maps. 8vo.
There is a chapter on fourteenth century naval warfare in the Mediterranean.

109. RUNCIMAN, *Sir* Steven.
The fall of Constantinople, 1453.
Cambridge; University Press; 1969. xiv, 256pp., pls. 8vo.
In June 1452 war broke out between Mohammed II and the Byzantine Emperor Constantine XI. In the following April a Turkish force of some 80,000 troops and a large artillery train laid siege to Constantinople. Within the city Constantine had only 7,000 troops to garrison the thirteen miles of walls – the city's principal defences. He could expect no outside assistance because of his lack of naval forces. The city walls were subjected to continual bombardment, but the large Turkish fleet was denied access to the harbour by a heavy iron chain. Mohammed, however, ordered 70 smaller ships to be dragged overland from the Bosphorus to the Golden Horn, thereby completely blockading the city. Finally after a major Turkish assault on 29 May, Constantinople fell.

110. SEDDAL, Henry.
Malta: past and present, being a history of Malta from the days of the Phoenicians to the present time.
London; Chapman & Hall; 1870. xii, 355pp., foldg. map. 8vo.

111. SHEPHARD, Arthur MacCartney.
The Byzantine reconquest of Crete.
USNIP, vol.lxvii (1941), pp.1121–1130.
A general survey from the seventh century to the present day.

112. SHEPHARD, Arthur MacCartney.
The Naval history of Turkey.
USNIP, vol.lxviii (1942), pp.209–215 & 314–318.
From approximately 1200 A.D. to modern times.

113. SOTTAS, Jules.
Les Messageries Maritimes de Venise aux XIVe et XVe siècles.
Paris; Soc., Eds., Geographiques; 1938. 232pp., foldg. pls., illustr. 8vo.

114. VECCHJ, Augusto Vittorio.
Storia generale della marina militare . . . volume i. Seconda edizione.
Leghorn; R.Giusta; 1895. viii, 408pp., illustr. 8vo.
With chapters on the Norman conquest of Italy, the Crusades and the wars between the Italian maritime republics.

115. WIEL, Alethea.
The Navy of Venice.
London; J.Murray; 1910. xvi, 370pp., frontis., pls. 8vo.
A comprehensive history of Venetian naval affairs from the fifth to the late eighteenth century. It includes chapters on the Crusades, the development of the Arsenal, relations with Genoa and Constantinople and the wars of Chioggia (1378–1381).

PART TWO

The Sixteenth Century

I. The Early Tudors, 1485–1558

116. ANDERSON, *Dr.* Roger Charles.
Henry VIII's 'Great Galley.'
The Mariner's Mirror, vol.vi (September 1920), pp.274–281.
The Princess (or Virgin) Mary of 1515.

117. ANDERSON . . .
Armaments in 1540.
The Mariner's Mirror, vol.vi (September 1920), p.281.
A table listing Henry VIII's ships and their armament in February 1540.

118. ANSCOMBE, Alfred.
Prégent de Bidoux's raid in Sussex in 1514 and the Cotton Ms. *Augustus 7* (i) 18.
Trans., RHS, 3rd series, vol.viii (1914), pp.103–111.
See also entries: 120, 127, 134, 144.

119. ANTHONY, Anthony.
An alphabetical list of every [*sic*] the ships and vessels of the Royal Navy of England, anno 1546, the last of King Henry the 8th, who first formed a Royal Navy, sorted by their qualities: by Anthony Anthony, one of the officers of ordinaunce.
Naval Chronicle, vol.xxxix (June 1818), pp.38–39.

120. BASSELIÈRE, Jean.
Prégent de Bidoux.
Assoc. des Amis du Musée de la Marine Bull., no.iv (1939), pp.35–38.

121. BOULIND, *Dr.* Richard H.
Ships of private origin in the mid-Tudor Navy: the *Lartigue*, the *Salamander*, the *Mary Willoughby*, the *Bark Aucher* and the *Galley Blanchard*.
The Mariner's Mirror, vol.lix (November 1973), pp.385–408.

122. BREE, John.
Cursory sketch of the state of the naval, military and civil establishment, legislative, judicial and domestic oeconomy of this kingdom during the fourteenth century with a particular account of the campaign of King Edward the Third in Normandy and France in the years 1345 and 1346 to the taking of Calais. volume i [*All published*].
London; the author; 1791. xxxvi, 381, [22] pp. 4to.
Includes a list of the King's ships in the Thames, 1517.

123. BROOKS, Frederick William.
A wage-scale for seamen, 1546.
English Historical Review, vol.lx (May 1945), pp.234–246.

124. CALENDAR OF STATE PAPERS –
DOMESTIC & FOREIGN: Henry VIII.
vol.i [1509–14] – vol.xxi [1546–47].
London; HMSO; 1867–1920. 8vo.
Includes: [vol.i] The MARY ROSE. *[vol.ii] The Field of the Cloth of Gold. [vol.vii] Skeffingham's expedition to Ireland, 1534. [vol.xiv] fortifications and counter-invasion preparations, 1539. [vol.xvi] the defences of Calais, 1540–41. [vol.xviii] French expedition to Aberdeen, battle off Orfordness and the interception of the French fleet bound for Scotland, 1543. [vol.xix] the English occupation of Leith, the siege of Boulogne and naval operations in the Channel and Irish Sea, 1544. [vol.xx] Lord Lisle's fleet in the Channel, French attacks on the English coast and the loss of the* MARY ROSE, *1545. [vol.xxi] Naval operations against the French, May – June 1546.*

125. CALENDAR OF STATE PAPERS –
DOMESTIC: Edward VI, Mary, Elizabeth . . .
vol.i [1547] & vol.vii [Addenda, 1566–1579].
London; HMSO; 1856 & 1871. 8vo.
Includes: [vol.i] The Admiralty and Admiralty Court. [vol.vii] piracy off the Cumberland coast (April 1566), English admirals (1569–78) and vice-admirals (1571–75), foreign admirals (1568–1572), and the Admiralty (1575–79).

126. CALLENDER, *Sir* Geoffrey Arthur Romaine (1875–1946).
The evolution of seapower under the early Tudors.
History, vol.v (1920), pp.141–158.

127. CLOWES, *Sir* William Laird (1856–1905), *et alia.*
The Royal Navy. A history from the earliest times to the present. volume i.
London; Sampson Low, Marston; 1897. xiv, 698pp., pls., numerous illustr. Large 8vo.
There are descriptions of the blockade of Brest (1513), Prégent de Bidoux's raids on the English coast (1513–14), the Field of the Cloth of Gold (1520), the siege and capture of Boulogne (1544) and the loss of the MARY ROSE (1545).

128. CORBETT, *Sir* Julian Stafford (1854–1922) [*editor*].
Fighting Instructions, 1530–1816.
Edited with elucidations from contemporary authorities.

128. CORBETT, *continued*
London; Navy Records Society series vol.xxxix;
1905. xvi, 366pp. 8vo.
   *The first part is concerned with the early Tudors. It
contains Alonso de Chaves': 'Espejo de Navegantes',
(ca.1530) and the fleet orders of Lord Audley (ca.1530)
and Lord Lisle (1545).*

129. DAVIES, C.S.L.
The administration of the Royal Navy under Henry
VIII: the origin of the Navy Board.
English Historical Review, vol.lxxx (April 1965),
pp.268–288.

130. DERRICK, Charles.
Memoirs of the rise and progress of the Royal Navy.
London; H.Teape; 1806. [6], ii, 310 + [26] pp.;
engr. frontis. 4to.
   *Contains lists of the Navy in 1517, June 1521,
January 1548, January 1549, August 1552 and May
1557.*

131. [EDWARD VI, *King*, (1537–1553)].
Names of all His Majesty's ships, &c.
Archaeologia, vol.vi (1782), pp.218–220.
   The list is undated.

132. ELLIS, *Sir* Henry (1777–1869).
Account of an ancient drawing, reproducing the
attack of the French upon Brightlenstone in 1545.
Archaeologia, vol.xxiv (1832).

133. FOWLER, Elaine W.
English sea power in the early Tudor period, 1485–
1558.
Ithaca, N.Y.; Cornell University Press; 1965. [ii],
43pp., pls. 8vo.

134. GAIRDNER, *Professor* James.
On a contemporary drawing of the burning of
Brighton in the time of Henry VIII.
Trans., RHS, 3rd series, vol.i (1907), pp.19–31.

135. GIBBS, J.
Richard Cooper and the Spanish plate fleet of 1533.
Univ. of Birmingham Hist. Jnl., vol.viii (1959), pp.
101–103.

136. GLASGOW, Tom.
The Navy in Philip and Mary's War, 1557–8.
The Mariner's Mirror, vol.liii (November 1967),
pp.321–342.

137. GLASGOW . . .
Maturing in naval administration, 1556–1564.
The Mariner's Mirror, vol.lvi (February 1970),
pp.3–26 & 326; pls.

138. GOLDINGHAM, C.S.
The Navy under Henry VII.
English Historical Review, vol.xxxiii (1918), pp.472–
488.

139. GOLDINGHAM . . .
Warships of Henry VIII.
United Services Mag., vol.clxxix (1919), pp.453–462.

140. HENDRY, Frederic.
James IV and the Scottish Navy.
Aberdeen University Review, vol.vii (1920), pp.46–48.

141. HISTORICAL MANUSCRIPTS
COMMISSION:
Fifteenth report, appendix, part V. The manuscripts
of the Right Honourable F.J.Savile Foljambe . . .
London; HMSO; 1897. xiv, 190pp. 8vo.
   Contains references to the defence of Calais, 1557.

142. JOHNS, A.W.
Henry VIII and national defence.
Engineering, vol.cxiv (1922), pp.152–3, 168–9, 197–8
& 229–230.

143. LA ROGERIE, Bourde de.
Occupation de Serk par les Français en 1549.
Soc. Guernesiase Rept. & Trans. for 1938, xiii, pt.2
(1939), pp.178–185.

144. LAUGHTON, L.G. Carr (*d.*1955).
The burning of Brighton by the French.
Trans., RHS, 3rd series vol.x (1916), pp.163–173.

145. McKEE, Alexander.
King Henry VIII's *Mary Rose*.
London; Souvenir Press; 1973. viii, 346pp., pls.,
maps on endpapers. 8vo.

146. OPPENHEIM, Michael M.
A History of the administration of the Royal Navy
and of merchant shipping in relation to the Navy
from MDIX to MDCLX with an introduction treating
of the preceding period.
London; John Lane; 1896. xiv, 411pp., cold. frontis.,
pls., tables. 8vo.
   *A brilliant study. Includes chapters on the Navy prior
to 1509 and subsequently under Henry VIII, Edward VI
and Mary.*

147. OPPENHEIM . . .
Naval accounts and inventories of the reign of
Henry VII: 1485–8 and 1495–7.
London; Navy Records Society series vol.viii; 1896.
lvi, 349pp. 8vo.

148. RUSSELL, Joycelyne Gledhill.
The Field of the Cloth of Gold. Men and manners
in 1520.
London; Routledge & Kegan Paul; 1969. xiv,
248pp.; pls. 8vo.

149. SPONT, Alfred.
Letters and papers relating to the war with France,
1512–1513.
London; Navy Records Society series vol.x; 1897.
l; 219pp., cold. frontis., pls. 8vo.

150. STANDING, Percy C.
Henry VIII's Lord High Admiral.
United Service Magazine, vol.cxliv (1901), pp.448–
456.
That is, Sir Edward Howard (1477?–1513).

151. TENISON, E.M.
Elizabethan England: being the history of this
country 'In relation to all foreign princes.' From
original manuscripts, many hitherto unpublished;
co-ordinated with XVIth century printed matter
varying from royal proclamations to broadside
ballads.
Leamington Spa; privately printed; 1933–1961. 13
vols + portfolio. 4to.
*Includes accounts of the capture of Calais (January
1558), the battle of Gravelines (13 July 1558) and a list
of the Navy (29 May 1557).*

152. TOPHAM, John.
A description of an antient picture in Windsor
Castle, representing the embarkation of King Henry
VIII, at Dover, May 31, 1520; preparatory to his
interview with the French King Francis I.
London; J. Nichols; 1781. [ii], 42pp., fdg. engr.
frontis., engr. pl. 4to.
Includes details of the HENRY GRACE À DIEU'S
armament.

153. WEBB, John G.
William Sabyn of Ipswich: an early Tudor sea-
officer and merchant.
The Mariner's Mirror, vol.xli (August 1955), pp.209–
221.
*Sabyn commanded one of Henry VIII's ships during
the French War of 1512–13.*

154. WERNHAM, *Professor* Richard Bruce.
Before the Armada. The growth of English foreign
policy, 1485–1588.
London; Jonathan Cape; 1966. 447pp., maps,
genealogical tables. 8vo.
*There are chapters on seapower and trade, (1485–
1509), and Henry VIII's first war with France.*

155. WILLIAMSON, *Professor* James Alexander.
Maritime enterprise, 1485–1558.
Oxford; Clarendon Press; 1913. 416pp., frontis.,
illustr., maps. 8vo.
Includes a chapter entitled 'The Navy, 1485–1558'.

II. The Elizabethan era and the struggle with Spain

i. The Early Years, including the Revolt of the Netherlands

156. BLACK, *Professor* J.B.
Queen Elizabeth, the Sea Beggars and the capture of Brille, 1572.
English Historical Review, vol.xlvi (January 1931), pp.30–47.
The 'Sea Beggars' – Dutch privateers with commissions from William of Orange – captured Brille on 1 April 1572.

157. BLOK, *Dr.* Petrus Johannes (1855–1929).
De Watergeuzen in Engeland, 1568–1572.
Bijdragen voor Vaderland Geschiedenis en Oudheidkunde, 3rd series, vol.ix, (1896), pp.226–263.

158. BROOKE, Z.N.
The expedition of Thomas Stukeley in 1578.
English Historical Review, vol.xxxviii (1913), pp.330–337.
In 1578 Stukeley sailed from Civita Vecchia with a Papal fleet intent on the invasion of Ireland. His ships were so unseaworthy that he had to put into Lisbon. There he was persuaded to join the Portuguese expedition against the Moors, in the course of which he was killed at the battle of Alcazar.

159. CALENDAR OF STATE PAPERS – DOMESTIC: Edward VI, Mary, Elizabeth . . .
vols. vii [Addenda, 1586–1579] & viii [Addenda, 1580–1625].
London; HMSO; 1871–1872. 8vo.
Includes: [vol.vii] lists of English admirals and vice-admirals (1569–1578), references to victualling accounts (1570) and the Admiralty (1575–1579). [vol.viii] lists of English admirals, vice-admirals and rear-admirals (1581–1608) and material on Charles Howard, Lord High Admiral (1581–1606).

160. CLOWES, *Sir* William Laird (1856–1905), *et alia*.
The Royal Navy. A history from the earliest times to the present. Volume i.
London; Sampson Low, Marston; 1897. xiv, 698pp., frontis., pls., numerous illustr. Large 8vo.
There are descriptions of the blockade of La Rochelle (1573) and the Revolt of the Netherlands.

161. DURO, Cesáro Fernandez.
Armada Española desde la unión de los reinos de Castilla y de Aragón. Tomo II.

Madrid; Rivadeneyra; 1896. 532pp. 8vo.
Includes a chapter on Ireland and Flanders, 1579–1587.

162. EDMUNDSON, *Reverend* George.
The Revolt of the Netherlands *and* William the Silent.
Chapters VI & VII in: *The Cambridge Modern History. Volume iii. The Wars of Religion.*
(Cambridge University Press; 1907). pp.182–259.
Both chapters contain references to the 'Sea Beggars.'

163. GEYL, *Professor* P.
The Revolt of the Netherlands.
London; Williams & Norgate; 1932. 310pp., map on endpapers. 8vo.

164. GLASGOW, Tom.
Original guns of the Royal ship *Aid* – 1562.
The Mariner's Mirror, vol.lii (February 1966), p.77.

165. GLASGOW . . .
The origin of the first royal ship *Victory* – 1562.
The Mariner's Mirror, vol.liii (May 1967), pp.184–186.

166. GLASGOW . . .
The Navy in the first Elizabethan undeclared war, 1559–1560.
The Mariner's Mirror, vol.liv (February 1968), pp.23–37, pls.

167. GLASGOW . . .
The Navy in the French wars of Mary and Elizabeth I: part 3: The Navy in the Le Havre expedition, 1562–1564.
The Mariner's Mirror, vol.liv (August 1968), pp.281–296, pls.

168. HERWERDEN, P.J. van.
Oranje, Noord-Europa en de Watergeuzen.
Bijdragen voor Vaderlandsche Geschiedenis en Oudheidkunde, 7th series, vol. ix (1938), pp.211–219.

169. HISTORICAL MANUSCRIPTS COMMISSION:
[a.] The Ancaster Mss. Dublin; HMSO; 1907. xl, 594; viiipp. 8vo.
[b.] The De L'Isle & Dudley Mss. London; HMSO; 1936. lxxix, 547pp. 8vo.
Both volumes contain material on the naval aspects of the Revolt of the Netherlands.
[c.] The Foljambe Mss. London; HMSO; 1897. xiv, 190pp. 8vo.
Contains references to the Navy between 1583 and 1587 and the defence of Calais in 1557.

170. JONGE, Johannes Cornelis de (1793–1853).
Geschiedenis van het Nederlandsche Zeewezen.
Eerst deel.
Haarlem; A.C.Kruseman; 1858. xvi; viii; 805pp.
8vo.

171. LEWIS, *Professor* Michael (1890–1970).
The Hugenot Navy, 1568–1570.
The Mariner's Mirror, vol.xlvi (February 1960),
pp.67–68.
*The operations of the Hugenot and English corsairs
against Catholic shipping off the Guienne coast during
the Third French Religious War.*

172. MEIJ, J.C.A.de.
Het Beeld van de Watergeuzen in de Nederlandse
geschrijving.
Tidschrift voor Geschiedenis, vol.lxxxiii (1970),
pp.358–377.

173. MEIJ . . .
De Watergeuzen en de Nederlanden, 1568–1572.
Amsterdam; Noord-Hollandsche; 1972. xii, 362pp.,
frontis., pls., tables. 8vo.
*An important study of the 'Sea Beggars,' with
summaries in English and French. There is also a
comprehensive bibliography.*

174. MOTLEY, John Lothrop.
The Rise of the Dutch Republic.
London; W.W.Gibbings; 1892. 3 vols. vol.i: xx,
544pp. vol.ii: xvi, 568pp. vol.iii: xiv, 651pp. 8vo.

175. OPPENHEIM, Michael M.
A History of the administration of the Royal Navy
and of merchant shipping in relation to the Navy.
From MDIX to MDCLX with an introduction treating
of the preceding period.
London & New York; John Lane; 1896. xiv,
411pp., cold. frontis., pls., tables. 8vo.

176. PETRIE, *Sir* Charles.
The Hispano-Papal landing at Smerwick.
The Irish Sword, vol.ix (1969–70), pp.82–94, pls.
*The expedition landed at Smerwick in July 1579 and
built a fort. The Papal forces were reinforced by the
arrival of another expedition in September 1580, but
both surrendered two months' later.*

177. POWELL, J.W.D.
Description of the Royal Navy in 1580.
The Mariner's Mirror, vol.vi (March 1920), p.90.

178. READ, C.
Queen Elizabeth's seizure of the Duke of Alva's
pay-ships.
Journal of Modern History, vol.v (1933), pp.443–464.

178a. ROUND, J.H.
Queen Elizabeth and the Beggars of the Sea.
Athenaeum, no.3545 (1895), pp.455–456.

179. TENISON, E.M.
Elizabethan England: being the history of this
country 'In relation to all foreign princes.' From
original manuscripts, many hitherto unpublished;
co-ordinated with XVIth century printed matter
ranging from royal proclamations to broadside
ballads.
Leamington Spa; privately printed; 1933–1961. 13
vols. + portfolio. 4to.
*Volumes ii & iii include narratives of the projected
Spanish invasion of England in 1571; a list of the Royal
Navy in 1576–7; the Hispano-Papal landing at
Smerwick (1579–80); the defeat of the French fleet off
the Azores by Alvaro de Bazán (1582) and the battle of
Terceira, (July 1583).*

180. VERE, Francis.
Salt in their blood. The lives of the famous Dutch
admirals.
London; Cassell; 1965. xiv, 226pp., cold. frontis.,
pls., map. 8vo.
*The first two chapters are concerned with the 'Sea
Beggars'.*

181. VOGELS, F.
Eenige Amsterdamsche watergeuzen, 1568 – 1 April
1572.
Jaarboek van het Genootschap Amsteldamum, vol.xxix
(1932), pp.87–102.

182. WARNSINCK, Johan Carel Marinus.
Een mistakte aanslag op Enkhuizen in 1568.
Offprint from *De Gids*, July 1932. 25pp. 8vo.
*This is an account of the action off Enkhuizen, in
which a squadron of 'Sea Beggars' routed a much larger
Spanish force in the Zuyder Zee.*

ii. Elizabethan Privateering Voyages to the Caribbean, 1567–1586

183. ANDREWS, *Dr.* Kenneth Raymond.
The economic aspects of Elizabethan privateering.
University of London Ph.D. thesis; 1951.

184. ANDREWS . . .
Elizabethan privateering. English privateering
during the Spanish War, 1585–1603.
London; Oxford University Press; 1964. xv, 279pp.,
map. 8vo.
An important study.

185. ANDREWS . . .
Drake's voyages. A re-assessment of their place in
Elizabethan maritime expansion.
London; Weidenfeld & Nicolson; 1967. 190pp.,
maps. 8vo.

186. ANDREWS . . .
The aims of Drake's expedition, 1577–80.
American Historical Review, vol.lxxiii (1968),
pp.724–741.

187. AYDELOTTE, Frank.
Elizabethan seamen in Mexico and ports of the
Spanish Main.
American Historical Review, vol.xlviii (1942), pp.1–19.
  *Accounts of the trials by Inquisition of the survivors of
Hawkins' 1567–68 expedition.*

188. BOAZIO, Baptista (*fl.*1588–1606).
[General charts and four maps, to illustrate Sir
Francis Drake's voyage to the West Indies, 1585–6.]
Leyden; 1588 *and* London; 1589. One chart & four
maps – St. Augustine, Cartagena, San Domingo and
St. Iago – in contemporary colouring. Folio.
  *The chart and set of maps were published as a
collection with Walter Bigges': A summarie and true
discourse of Sir Francis Drake's West Indian voyage,
(London; 1588).*

189. BRY, Theodor de (1528–1595).
Collectiones peregrinationum in Indiam Orientalem
et Indiam Occidentalem . . . Americae pars VIII.
Primo descriptionem triam itinerum nobilissimi et
fortissimi equitis Francis Draken . . .
Frankfurt; T. de Bry; 1599. [First edition]. 99pp., 18
engr. pls., fdg. engr. map. Folio.
  *Includes accounts of Drake's voyages of 1577–80 and
1585–86. A copy of the second edition (Frankfurt; 1625)
is also in the Library. For more details on De Bry's
'Grands et Petits Voyages', see volume I of the Library
Catalogue:* Voyages and Travel, *pp.9–16.*

190. CALENDAR OF STATE PAPERS –
VENETIAN.
vol. viii (1581–1591).
London; HMSO; 1894. 8vo.
  Contains references to Drake's West Indian voyages.

191. CALLENDER, Sir Geoffrey Arthur Romaine
(1875–1946).
Fresh light on Drake.
The Mariner's Mirror, vol.ix (January 1923), pp.16–
28.
  *An examination of the historical value of Juan de
Castellaños' contemporary account of Drake's capture of
San Domingo (1–2 January 1586).*

192. CLOWES, Sir William Laird (1856–1905), *et
alia.*
The Royal Navy. A history from the earliest times
to the present. volume i.
London; Sampson Low, Marston; 1897. xiv, 698pp.,
frontis., pls., numerous illustr. Large 8vo.

193. CORBETT, Sir Julian Stafford (1854–1922).
Drake and the Tudor Navy. With a history of the
rise of England as a maritime power.
London; Longmans Green; 1898. 2 vols. vol.i: xvi,
436 pp., frontis., pls., maps; illustr. vol.ii: viii, 488
pp., frontis., pls., maps. 8vo.
  *A masterly study. There are chapters on Elizabethan
privateering in the Caribbean.*

194. CORBETT . . .
Papers relating to the Navy during the Spanish War,
1585–1587.
London; Navy Records Society series vol.xi; 1898.
lii, 363pp., frontis. 8vo.
  *The first section is concerned with Drake's 1585–6
expedition.*

195. DRAKE, Sir Francis (1540?–1596), *et alia.*
Sir Francis Drake revived, who is or may be a
pattern to stirre up all heroicke and active spirits of
these times . . . being a summary and true relation of
fourre severall voyages made by the said Sir Francis
Drake to the West Indies . . . collected out of the
notes of the said Sir Francis Drake, Master Philip
Nichols, Master Francis Fletcher, preachers . . .
London; Nicholas Bourne; 1653. 87 + 108 + 41
+ 60pp., frontis. black-letter text. 4to.
  *This famous work comprises the first collected edition
of Drake's voyages being: 'Sir Francis Drake revived
. . .' [the 1572–73 voyage] and: 'A Summarie and true
discourse of his West Indian voyage . . .' [the 1585–
86 voyage].*
  *The Library also posses a copy of the later edition,
which contains additional material by Nathaniel Crouch
(1632?–1725?) entitled: 'The English Hero: or Sir
Francis Drake reviv'd . . .' (London; C.Hitch &
J.Hodge; 1850. 186pp. 12mo.)*

196. DURO, Capitan Cesáro Fernandez.
Armada Española desde la unión de los reinos de
Castilla y de Aragon. Tomo. II.
Madrid; Rivadeneyra; 1896. 531pp. 8vo.
  *Includes a chapter on English privateering voyages,
1578–1587.*

197. GREEPE, Thomas.
The True and perfecte newes of the woorthy and
valiaunt exploytes, performed and doone by that
valiant knight Syr Frauncis Drake: Not onely at
Sancto Domingo, and Carthagena, but nowe at

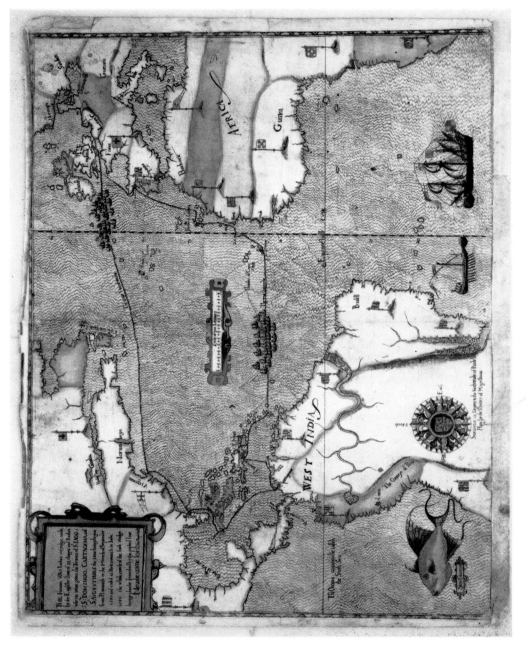

PLATE I: Baptista Boazio's: [General Chart to illustrate Sir Francis Drake's voyage to the West Indies, 1585–6]. Leyden and London; 1588–9

ORDERS,
Set dovvne by the
Duke of Medina, Lord general
of the Kings Fleet, to be obserued in
the voyage toward England.

Tranſlated out of Spaniſh into Engliſh by T.P.

Imprinted at London by Thomas Orwin for Thomas Gilbert, dwelling in Fleetſtreete neere to
the ſigne of the Caſtle. 1588.

197. GREEPE, *continued*
Cales, and uppon the coast of Spayne, 1587 . . .
Now reproduced in facsimile . . . With an
introduction, notes, and a bibliography of English
military books by David W. Waters . . .
Hartford, Conn.; printed for H.C.T.; 1955.
[*Americanum Nauticum* No.3]. 95pp., pls. (some fdg.).
4to.

198. HAKLUYT, Richard (1552?–1616).
The Principall Navigationes, Voiages, Traffiques
and discoveries of the English nation . . .
London; George Bishop, Ralph Newberie . . . ;
1599–1600. 3 volumes. black-letter text. 4to.
*Includes accounts by John Hawkins and Job Hortop of
the former's third voyage, (1567–68) and Drake's West
Indian voyages of 1572–73 and 1585–86.*
*For details of other editions of Hakluyt held in the
Library, see volume I of the Library Catalogue:
Voyages & Travel, entries 4–8.*

199. HAMPDEN, Janet *and* John [editors].
Sir Francis Drake's raid on the treasure trains: being
the memorable relation of his voyage to the West
Indies in 1572 . . .
London; Folio Society; 1954. 92pp.; woodcuts. 8vo.
A modernized version of 'Sir Francis Drake
revived . . .'.

200. HAMPDEN, John [editor].
Francis Drake – privateer. Contemporary narratives
and documents.
London; Eyre Methuen; 1972. 286pp., facsims.,
maps. 8vo.

201. HAWKINS, *Sir* John (1532–1595) *and Sir*
Richard (1562?–1622).
The Hawkins' voyages during the reigns of Henry
VIII, Queen Elizabeth, and James I. Edited with an
introduction by Clements R.Markham, CB, FRS.
London; Hakluyt Society [1st series, vol.lvii]; 1878.
liii, 453pp., pl. 8vo.
*Contains an account of Hawkins' disastrous 1562–3
voyage.*

202. HORTOP, Job.
The Rare Travailes of Job Hortop. Being a
facsimile reprint of the first edition, with an
introductory note by G.R.G. Conway.
Mexico; private published; 1928. xi, [24] pp. 12mo.
*Hortop accompanied Hawkins' third voyage (1567–
68). After the disaster at San Juan de Ullua, he was
amongst those who left the ships to avoid starvation and
returned to Mexico. Later he was seized and sent to
Spain, where he served in the galleys for twelve years.*

203. JAMESON, A.K.
Some new Spanish documents dealing with Drake.
English Historical Review, vol.xlix (July 1934),
pp.14–31.
*Refers to his 1585–6 voyage – especially the sack of
Cartagena.*

204. KRAUS, H.P.
Sir Francis Drake. A pictorial biography. With an
historical introduction by Lt. Commander David
W.Waters & Richard Boulind and a detailed
catalogue of the author's collection.
Amsterdam; N.Israel; 1970. viii, 236pp., frontis.
(port.), fdg. maps & facsims., illustr. 4to.
*Includes material on San Juan de Ullua, Panama and
Drake's 1585–6 voyage.*

205. LEWIS, *Professor* Michael (1890–1970).
The guns of the *Jesus of Lubeck*.
The Mariner's Mirror, vol.xxii (July 1936), pp.324–
325.
A translation of the Spanish inventory of the JESUS OF
LUBECK'S *guns and those of other English ships aban-
doned at San Juan de Ullua.*

206. LEWIS . . .
Fresh light on San Juan de Ullua.
The Mariner's Mirror, vol.xxiii (July 1937), pp.295–
315.
*Translations of two Spanish documents – (a) reports of
the auction of the captured English ships and (b) a letter
(dated 16 December 1568) to King Philip II from Juan
de Ubilla, the vice-admiral of Luxan's fleet.*

207. PURCHAS, Samuel (1575?–1626).
Purchas His Pilgrimes. In Five bookes.
London; Henrie Fetherstone; 1625. 4 vols. black-
letter text. Folio.
*Includes accounts of Hawkins' and Drake's West
Indian expeditions.*

208. UNWIN, Rayner.
The defeat of Sir John Hawkins. A biography of his
third slaving voyage.
London; Allen & Unwin; 1960. 320pp., frontis.
(port.), pls., illustr. 8vo.

209. WATERS, *Lt. Cmdr.* David W., RN.
The guns of the *Jesus of Lubeck*.
The Mariner's Mirror, vol.xxxvii (April 1950),
pp.156–157.

210. WILLIAMSON, *Professor* James Alexander.
The Age of Drake.
London; A. & C.Black; 1938. xi, 401pp., maps. 8vo.
*Copies of the fourth (1960) and fifth (1965) editions
are also in the Library.*

211. WILLIAMSON . . .
Hawkins of Plymouth. A new history of Sir John
Hawkins and of other members of his family
prominent in Tudor England.
London; A. & C.Black; 1969. [second edition]. xii,
348pp., frontis. (port.), pls., map. 8vo.

212. WRIGHT, Irene Aloha [editor].
Spanish documents concerning English voyages to
the Caribbean; 1527–1568. Selected from the
Archives of the Indies at Seville.
London; Hakluyt Society [2nd series, vol.lxii]; 1929.
x, 167pp., frontis., pls. 8vo.
    Contains documents relating to San Juan de Ullua.

213. WRIGHT . . .
Documents concerning English voyages to the
Spanish Main, 1569–1580.
I. Spanish documents selected from the Archives of
the Indies at Seville. II. English accounts. *Sir Francis
Drake revived* and others reprinted.
London; Hakluyt Society [2nd series, vol.lxxi];
1932. lxiv, 348 pp., frontis. (port.) fdg. maps. 8vo.

214. WRIGHT . . .
Further English voyages to Spanish America, 1583–
1594. Documents from the Archives of the Indies at
Seville illustrating English voyages to the
Caribbean, the Spanish Main, Florida, and Virginia.
London; Hakluyt Society [2nd series, vol.xcix]; 1949.
xcii, 314pp., frontis. (fdg. map), fdg. pls., maps. 8vo.

iii. The Armada Campaign, 1586–1588

215. ADAMS Robert (d.1595).
Expeditionis Hispanorum in Angliam vera descriptio.
Anno . . . MDLXXXVIII.
London; Robert Adams; 1588 [–90]. Engraved title;
10 double-page charts in contemporary colouring.
    *This celebrated series of charts, engraved by Augustine
Ryther, depicts the engagements between the English and
Spanish fleets. It was prepared as an accompaniment to:
Ubaldini's: Discourse concerninge the Spanish
fleete . . . [q.v.]*

216. ALLINGHAM, Hugh.
Captain Cuellar's adventures in Connacht & Ulster,
A.D. 1588. A picture of the times, drawn from contemporary sources. To which is added an introduction and complete translation of Captain Cuellar's
narrative of the Spanish Armada and his adventures
in Ireland.
London; Elliot Stock; 1897. 72pp., illustr. 8vo.
    Captain Francisco de Cuellar's ship – probably the LA

LAVIA *of the Levantine squadron – was wrecked off the
west coast of Ireland on the night of 24–25 September.
After many adventures as a fugitive in Ireland and
Scotland, de Cuellar eventually succeeded in reaching
home.*
    See also entries: 231, 269, 275.

217. ANDERSON, *Dr.* Roger Charles.
The Armada fireships.
The Mariner's Mirror, vol.vii (February 1921), p.60.
    A note on the ANGEL *of Southampton.*

218. ARMSTRONG, Edward.
Venetian despatches on the Armada and its results.
English Historical Review, vol.xii (October 1897),
pp.659–678.

219. BROUWER, *Dr.* J.
De Onoverwinnelijke Vloot in Juli/Augustus 1588.
The Hague; G.C.Visscher; 1888. 51pp. 8vo.

220. [BRUCE, John (1745–1826)].
Report on the arrangements which were made, for
the internal defence of these kingdoms, when Spain,
by its Armada, projected the invasion and conquest
of England; and application of these wise proceedings of our ancestors, to the present crisis of
public safety.
[Privately printed; 1798]. 98; [iv]; ccviii pp., engr.
frontis., engr. fdg. pl. small 4to.
    *This report, based on documents in the State Paper
Office, was prepared on Lord Melville's instructions for
the use of ministers during the Napoleonic invasion scare.*

221. BRUCE, R. Stuart.
Ships of the Armada at Shetland.
The Mariner's Mirror, vol.iv (March 1914), pp.92–93.
    A note on the loss of the GRAN GRIFON *on Fair Isle,
during the night of 9–10 August.*

222. CALENDAR OF STATE PAPERS –
DOMESTIC: Edward VI, Mary, Elizabeth . . .
vol.viii [1580–1625] & vol.xxii [July–December
1588].
London; HMSO; 1872 & 1936. 8vo.

222a. CALENDAR OF STATE PAPERS –
FOREIGN.
vol.xxi Pt.iv – vol.xxiii [January–December, 1588].
London; HMSO; 1931–1950. 8vo.

222b. CALENDAR OF STATE PAPERS –
VENETIAN.
vol.viii [1581–1591].
London; HMSO; 1894.
    *All the above contain numerous references to the
Armada.*

223. CALLENDER, *Sir* Geoffrey Arthur Romaine (1875–1946).
The real significance of the Armada's overthrow.
History, vol.ii (1917), pp.174–177.

224. CALLENDER...
The Naval campaign of 1587.
History, vol.iii (1918), pp.82–91.
Drake's celebrated destruction of Philip II's invasion fleet in Cadiz Bay, April 1587.
See also entries: 229, 261.

225. CHRISTY, Miller.
Queen Elizabeth's visit to Tilbury in 1588.
English Historical Review, vol.xxxiv (January 1919), pp.43–61.

226. CLOWES, *Sir* William Laird (1856–1905), *et alia*.
The Royal Navy. A history from the earliest times to the present. Volume i.
London; Sampson Low, Marston; 1897. xiv, 698pp., frontis., pls., numerous illustr. Large 8vo.
Includes an important chapter (pp.539–604) on the Armada campaign.

227. COLLINSON, *Major-General* T.B.
A warning voice from the Spanish Armada.
RUSIJ, vol.xix (1875), pp.285–333.

228. CORBETT, *Sir* Julian Stafford (1854–1922).
Drake and the Tudor Navy, with a history of the rise of England as a maritime power.
London; Longmans Green; 1898. 2 volumes. vol.i: xvi, 436pp., frontis. (port.), pls., maps, illustr. vol.ii: viii, 488pp., frontis., pls., maps. 8vo.
A masterly study, with important chapters on the Armada campaign in the second volume. A second edition, in smaller format, was issued in 1899.

229. CORBETT...
Papers relating to the Navy during the Spanish War, 1585–1587.
London; Navy Records Society series, vol.xi; 1898. lii, 363pp., frontis. 8vo.
Includes Drake's Cadiz expedition.

230. CORBETT...
Spanish reports and the wreck at Tobermory.
Scottish Historical Review, vol.viii (1911), pp.400–404.
Corbett argues that the SAN JUAN DE BAUTISTA *was the Spanish ship blown up in Tobermory Bay, Mull.*
See also entries: 246, 257, 258.

231. CUELLAR, *Capitan* Francisço de.
A letter written on October 4, 1589 by Captain Cuellar of the Spanish Armada to His Majesty King Philip II recounting his misadventures in Ireland and elsewhere after the wreck of his ship. Translated from the original Spanish by Henry Dwight Sedgwick, Jr.
New York; G.H.Richmond; 1895. xii, 109pp. small 8vo.
One of an edition limited to 500 copies.

232. DIGGES, Thomas (d.1595).
England's Defence. A treatise concerning invasion: or, a brief discourse of what orders were best for repulsing of foreign forces if at any time they should invade us by sea in Kent, or elsewhere. Exhibited in writing to the Right Honourable Robert Dudley Earl of Leicester, a little before the Spanish invasion, in the year 1588...
London; F.Haley; 1680. [vi], 16pp. 4to.

233. DURO, *Capitan* Cesáro Fernandez.
La Armada Invencible.
Madrid; Rivadeneyra; 1884. 2 volumes. vol i: x, 535pp. vol.ii: 539pp. 4to.
The standard Spanish history.

234. DURO...
La Marina de Castilla desde su origin y peigia con lo de Inglaterra hasta la refundicion en la Armada Española.
Madrid; El Pragesoni; [1894]. 542pp., pls. 8vo.

235. DYER, Florence E.
Burghley's notes on the Spanish Armada.
The Mariner's Mirror, vol.xi (October 1925), pp.419–424.

236. ELLIS, *Sir* Henry (1777–1869).
Naval expeditions, 1588–1603, with lists of the fleet.
Archaeologia, vol.xxxiv (1852).

237. FROUDE, James Anthony.
The Spanish story of the Armada and other essays.
London; Longmans Green; 1892. x, 328pp. 8vo.

238. GRAHAM, Winston.
The Spanish Armadas.
London; Collins; 1972. 288pp., cold. frontis. & pls., illustr. 8vo.

239. GREEN, Emanuel.
The preparations in Somerset against the Spanish Armada, A.D. 1558–1588.
London; Harrison; 1888. vi, 136pp., fdg. cold. frontis. 8vo.

240. GREEN, *Reverend* William Spotswood.
The Armada wrecks on the Irish coast.
Proc. Belfast Phil. Soc., for 1902–3, (1903), pp.59–63; map.

241. GREEN . . .
The wrecks of the Spanish Armada on the coast of Ireland.
Geographical Journal, vol.xxvii (1909), pp.429–451, map.

242. GREEN . . .
Armada ships on the Kerry coast.
Proc. Royal Irish Acad., vol.xxvii (1909), pp.263–269, map.

243. GUZMAN, Alonso Perez de, *7th Duke of Medina Sidonia* (1550–1615).
Orders set downe by the Duke of Medina, Lord General of the Kings Fleete, to be observed in the voyage toward England. Translated out of Spanish into English by T.P.
London; Thomas Orwin; 1588. [14pp.], black-letter text. small 4to.

244. HADFIELD, A.M.
Time to finish the game. The English and the Armada.
London; Phoenix House; 1964. 228pp., cold. frontis., pls., maps, illustr. 8vo.

245. HALE, John Richard.
The story of the great Armada.
London & Edinburgh; Nelson; [1913]. 350pp., cold. frontis., pls. (some cold.), maps & plans. 8vo.

246. HARDIE, R.P.
The Tobermory argosy; a problem of the Spanish Armada.
Edinburgh; Oliver & Boyd; 1912. 68pp. 8vo.
    The author identifies the Tobermory wreck as the SAN JUAN DE SICILIA, *a Ragusan ship. His evidence is supported by Professor Kostic's paper* [q.v.].

247. HARDY, Evelyn.
Survivors of the Armada.
London; Constable; 1966. xiv, 186pp., frontis., pls., maps. 8vo.

248. HART, Roger.
Battle of the Spanish Armada.
London; Wayland/New York; Putnam's; 1973. 128pp., frontis., illustr. 8vo.

249. HENRICX, Jan *and* CORNELIS, Jacob.
Despositions of two Dutch sailors who were in the Spanish Armada.
In: Historical Manuscripts Commission: Calendar of the Manuscripts of the most Hon. the Marquis of Salisbury . . . part III. (London; HMSO; 1889; pp.343–346).

250. HISTORICAL MANUSCRIPTS COMMISSION:
Fifteenth report, part V. The manuscripts of the Right Honourable F.J.Savile Foljambe . . .
London; HMSO; 1897. xiv, 190pp. 8vo.
    Contains numerous references to English preparations for counter-invasion and Queen Elizabeth's instructions to Lord Howard of Effingham, dated December 1587.

251. HUME, *Major* Martin A.S.
The year after the Armada and other historical studies.
London; Unwin; 1896. x, 388pp., frontis. (port.), illustr. 8vo.
    Includes a chapter on the evolution of the Armada.

252. HUME . . .
The defeat of the Armada. An anniversary object lesson.
The Fortnightly Review, vol.lxviii (1897), pp.286–296.

253. HUME . . .
Some survivors of the Armada in Ireland.
Trans., RHS (new series), vol.xi (1897), pp.41–46.

254. JERDAN, W.
Documents relative to the Spanish Armada and the defences of the Thames and Medway.
Br. Archaeol. Soc. Proc., vol.xvii (April 1920), pp.165–176.

255. KER, William Paton.
The Spanish story of the Armada.
Scottish Historical Review, vol.xvii (April 1920), pp.165–176.

256. KESTEVEN, G.R.
The Armada.
London; Chatto & Windus; 1965. 96pp., illustr. 8vo.

257. KOSTIC, *Professor* Veselin.
Ragusa and the Spanish Armada.
Balcanica (Belgrade), no.3 (1973), pp.195–235, maps, illustr.
    See also entries nos: 246, 273.

258. LANG, A.
The mystery of the Tobermory galleon revealed.
Blackwood's Magazine, no.cxci (March 1912), p.425, *et seq.*

259. LAUGHTON, *Sir* John Knox (1830–1915).
State Papers relating to the defeat of the Spanish Armada, anno 1588.
London; Navy Records Society series, vols.i–ii; 1895.

259. LAUGHTON, *continued*
2 volumes. vol.i: lxxxiv, 365pp. vol.ii: [vi], 418 pp.
8vo.
  An important primary source on the subject.

260. [LEIGH, Richard].
The Copie of a letter sent out of England to Don
Bernadin Mendoza, Ambassadour in France for the
King of Spaine, declaring the state of England . . .
This letter . . . by good hap, the copies thereof as
well in English as in French were found in the
chamber of one Richard Leigh a Seminarie Priest,
who was lately executed for high treason committed
in the time that the Spanish Armada was on the seas . . .
London; I.Vautrollier for Richard Field; 1588. [ii],
38[+3] pp. 4to.
  Includes contemporary details of the Armada's losses:
' . . . as well as in fight with the English Nauie in the
narrow seas of England as also by tempests and contrarie
winds, vpon the West and North coasts of Ireland. . . '.
  There are also in the Library copies of the French
edition, (1588) and the later English edition (George
Miller, 1641), in which the wording of the title differs.

261. LENG, Robert.
Sir Francis Drake's memorable service against the
Spaniards in 1587. Written by Robert Leng . . . one
of his co-adventurers and fellow-soldiers. Now first
edited from the original ms. in the British Museum
together with an appendix of illustrative papers, by
Clarence Hopper.
In: The Camden Miscellany, volume i. (London;
Camden Society; 1860; 54pp. 8vo.)

262. LEWIS, *Professor* Michael (1890–1970).
The Spanish Armada.
London; Batsford; 1960. [*British Battles* series].
216pp., pls. 8vo.

263. LEWIS . . .
Armada guns. A comparative study of English and
Spanish armaments.
London; Allen & Unwin; 1961. 244pp., fdg. tables.
8vo.
  An important study, which was initially published as a
series of articles in The Mariner's Mirror: *vols.xxviii*
(1942), pp.41–73; 104–147; 231–245; 259–290 and
xxix (1943), pp.3–39; 100–121; 163–178; 203–231.

264. McKEE, Alexander.
From merciless invaders. An eye-witness account of
the Spanish Armada.
London; Souvenir Press; 1963. 291pp., pls., maps on
endpapers. 8vo.

265. MALTBY, William S.
The Black Legend in England. The development of
anti-Spanish sentiment, 1558–1660.

Durham, N.C.; Duke University Press; 1971. [viii],
180pp. 8vo.
  Chapter IV (pp.76–88) is concerned with the
Armada.

266. MATTINGLY, *Professor* Garrett.
The defeat of the Spanish Armada.
London; Jonathan Cape; 1959. 382pp., frontis
(port.), pls. 8vo.

267. MAURA Y HAMAZO, *Duque de.*
El designio de Felipe II y el episodio de la Armada
Invencible.
Madrid; Ed. Cultura Clasica y Moderna; 1957.
284pp. 8vo.
  Includes an account of the Duke of Medina Sidonia's
career up to and including 1588.

268. MOOREHOUSE, Esther Hallam [*editor*].
Letters on the English seamen, 1587–1808.
London; Chapman & Hall; 1910. xvi, 318pp.,
frontis., pls. 8vo.

269. MORETON, Henry John, *3rd Earl of Ducie.*
An episode of the Armada.
Nineteenth Century, vol.xviii (September 1885),
pp.374–387.
  Cuellar's narrative.

270. NAISH, George P.B. [*editor*].
Documents illustrating the history of the Spanish
Armada.
In: *The Naval Miscellany*, volume iv. (London;
Navy Records Society series, vol.xcii; 1952; pp.
1–84; pls. 8vo.)
  Contains eleven Spanish documents relating to the
Armada's inception and departure; Petruccio Ubaldini's
narrative and a song, purported to have been written by
Queen Elizabeth after the Armada's defeat.
  See also entries: 215, 298.

271. NOBLE, T.C.
The names of those persons who subscribed towards
the defence of this country at the time of the
Spanish Armada, 1588, and the amounts each
contributed. With historical introduction . . .
London; A.R.Smith; 1886. xxxvi, 92pp. 8vo.

272. NOBLE, W.Mackneth [*editor*].
Huntingdonshire and the Spanish Armada. Edited
from original manuscripts.
London; Elliot Stock; 1896. viii, 62pp. 8vo.

273. NOVAK, *Professor* Viktor.
Učešće dubrovačke flote u španskoj nepobedivej
armadi.

273. NOVAK, *continued*
Zgodovinski časopis, 6–7 (1952–3), pp.604–615.
   The author claims that there were at least thirty-three Ragusan ships in the Armada.

274. Ó DANACHAIR, Caoimteu.
Armada losses on the Irish coast.
Irish Sword, vol.ii (1954–56), pp.320–331, map.

275. O'REILLY, *Professor* J.P.
Remarks on certain passages in Capt. Cuellar's narrative of his adventures in Ireland after the wreck of the Spanish Armada in 1588–89, followed by a literal translation of that narrative.
Proc. Royal Irish Acad., 3rd series, vol.iii (Dublin 1893–96), pp.175–217.

276. ORIA, Enrique Herrera.
La Armada Invencible. Documentos precedentes del Archivo General de Simancas . . .
Valladolid; Casa Social Catolica; 1929. [vi], 488pp. 8vo.

277. ORIA . . .
Felipe II y el Marques de Santa Cruz el la Empressa de Inglaterra. Según los documentos de Archivo de Simancas.
Madrid; Instituto Histórico de Marina; 1946. 176pp. 8vo.

278. PEARS. Edwin.
The Spanish Armada and the Ottoman Porte.
English Historical Review, vol.viii (1893), pp.429–446.

279. PIERSON, Peter O'Malley.
A commander for the Armada.
The Mariner's Mirror, vol.lv (November 1969), pp.383–400.
   Discusses Philip's reasons for appointing Medina Sidonia as commander of the Armada.

280. PINE, John (1690–1756).
The Tapestry hangings of the House of Lords: representing the several engagements between the English and Spanish fleets, in the ever memorable year MDLXXXVIII . . . Also an historical account of each day's action.
London; 1739. [iv], 24, [2] pp., 16 double-page engravings. Folio.
   These tapestries were made by Francis Spiering in about 1589 for Lord Howard of Effigham. Later sold to James I, they were hung in the House of Lords from 1616 until their destruction in the fire of 1834.

281. PRESSEY, *Reverend* W.J.
Echoes of the Armada, as heard in the archdeaconery records.
Essex Review, July 1926.

282. RICHMOND, *Admiral Sir* Herbert William (1871–1946).
The Invasion of Britain. An account of plans, attempts and counter-measures from 1588 to 1918.
London; Methuen; 1941. 82pp. 8vo.

283. RODGERS, *Vice-Admiral* William Ledyard, USN (1860–1944).
Naval warfare under oars, 4th to 16th centuries. A study of strategy, tactics and ship design.
Annapolis, Md.; US Naval Institute; 1939. xiv, 358pp., pls., fdg. maps. 8vo.
   Includes a lengthy chapter on the Armada campaign.

284. ROSE, *Professor* John Holland (1855–1942).
Was the failure of the Spanish Armada due to storms?
Proc. British Academy, vol.xxii (1936), pp.207–244.

285. SCHELTEMA, Jacobus.
De Uitrusting en ondergang der Onoverwinnelijke Vloot van Philip II in 1588.
Haarlem; Vincent Loosjes; 1825. 312pp. 8vo.

286. SCOTT, Thomas (1580?–1626).
The Second part of Vox Populi: or Gondomar appearing in the likeness of Matchiavel in a Spanish Parliament wherein are discovered his treacherous & subtill practises to the vaine as well of England, as the Netherlandes. Faithfully translated out of the Spanish coppie by a well-wisher to England and Holland.
Goricum; Asherus Janss.; 1624. Engr. title; iv; 60pp., woodcut illustrs. Small 4to.
   This political pamphlet about Prince Charles' escapade in Spain contains the earliest known reference to Drake's game of bowls.

287. STANHOPE, Philip Henry, *5th Earl Stanhope* (1805–1875).
On an anonymous letter to John Stanhope, reporting the dispersion of the Spanish Armada.
Archaeologia, vol.xxxviii (1860), p.246 *et seq.*

288. STÉNUIT, Robert.
Treasures of the Armada.
Newton Abbot; David & Charles; 1972. 282pp., illustr. (some cold.). 8vo.
   The first part of this book is concerned with the history of the Armada. The second relates the author's discovery and salvage of artifacts from the wreck of the GIRONA off Port na Spaniagh on the Antrim coast.

289. STORE, Lawrence.
The Armada Campaign of 1588.
History, vol.xxix (September 1944), pp.120–143.

290. TENISON, E.M.
Elizabethan England: being the history of this country
'In relation to all foreign princes.' From original
manuscripts, many hitherto unpublished; co-
ordinated with XVIth century printed matter
ranging from royal proclamations to broadside
ballads.
Leamington Spa; privately printed; 1933–61. 13
vols. + portfolio. 4to.
*Volumes V & VI include: Burghley's memoranda on
counter-invasion plans; fireships at Antwerp; Cadiz and
the Armada.*

291. THOMPSON, Henry Yates.
Lord Howard of Effingham and the Spanish Armada.
With exact facsimiles of the 'Tables of Augustine
Ryther' A.D. 1590 and the engravings of the
hangings of the House of Lords by John Pine A.D.
1739.
London; Roxburghe Club; 1919. 35pp., pls., charts.
Folio.

292. THOMPSON, I.A.A.
The Armada and administrative reform: the Spanish
council of war in the reign of Philip II.
English Historical Review, vol.lxxii (October 1967),
pp.698–725.

293. THOMPSON . . .
The appointment of the Duke of Medina Sidonia
to the command of the Spanish Armada.
Historical Journal, vol.xii no.2 (June 1969), pp.197–
216.

294. [THURSFIELD, *Sir* James R. (1840–1923)].
The Armada.
Quarterly Review, vol.clxxii, no.363 (July 1895),
pp.1–30.
*A review of Laughton's: State Papers relating to the
defeat of the Spanish Armada; Calendar of State
Papers relating to English affairs . . . in the archives
and collections of Venice . . . vol.viii, 1581–1591;
J.A.Froude's: English seamen in the sixteenth
century, and Robert Southey's: English seamen.*

295. TILTON, William Frederick.
The Spanish Armada.
Century Magazine, (July 1889), pp.204–220.

296. TILTON . . .
Die Katastrophe der Spanischen Armada, 31 Juli–8
August, 1588.
Freiburg; C.A.Wagner; 1894. 150pp., map. 8vo.

297. TILTON . . .
Lord Burghley and the Spanish Armada.
American Historical Review, vol.ii (1896), pp.93–95.

298. UBALDINI, Petruccio (1524?–1600?).
A Discovrse concerninge the Spanishe fleete inuading
Englande in the yeare 1588 and ouerthrow by her
Maties Navie under the conduction of the Right
honourable the Lorde Charles Howarde high
Admirall of Englande: written in Italian by
Petruccio Ubaldini citizen of Florence, and trans-
lated for A.Ryther: unto wch discourse are annexed
certaine tables expressing the several exploites and
conflicts had with the said fleete.
[London; A.Hatfield; 1590]. engr. title; [iv], 27pp.,
engr. pl. small 4to.
*The 'certaine tables' mentioned in the title are Robert
Adams' celebrated series of Armada charts [q.v.].*

299. UDEN, Grant.
Drake at Cadiz.
London; Macdonald; 1969. 96pp. 8vo.

300. WATERS, *Lieut.-Cmdr.* David W., RN.
The Elizabethan Navy and the Armada campaign.
The Mariner's Mirror, vol.xxxv (April 1949), pp.94–
138, pls., figs., tables.
A detailed study of the strategy of the campaign.

301. WERNHAM, Richard Bruce.
List and analysis of State Papers: Foreign series:
Elizabeth I.
London; HMSO; 1964–69. 2 volumes. 8vo.
Contains numerous references to the Armada.

302. WESTROPP, J.J.
Notes on Armada ships lost on the coast of Clare,
1588.
Royal Soc. Antiq., Ireland, 4th series, vol.ix (1869),
pp.131–133.

303. WILLIAMS, Jay.
The Spanish Armada.
London; Cassell; 1966. 153pp., cold. illustr. 8vo.

304. WINDEATTE, E.
Fitting out of two vessels against the Armada at
Dartmouth, 1588.
Devon Assoc., Jnl., vol.xii (1880).

305. WRIGHT, W.H.K.
Spanish Armada.
English Illustr. Mag., vol.v (1887–8).

306. [Anonymous].
Certain Advertisements ovt of Ireland, concerning
the losses and distresses happened to the Spanish
Nauie, vpon the VVest coastes of Ireland, in their
voyage intended from the Northern Isles beyond
Scotland, towards Spaine.

306. [Anonymous], *continued*
London; Richard Field; 1588. [xx] pp. Small 4to.
  Includes two tables of Spanish losses – warships and men.

307. [Anonymous].
Relacion de lo que hasta oy a los cinco de Septiembre de 1588 a las tres lorcias despues de medio dia, se ha sabido por las relaciones que on venido à Su Magestad, de la felice armada en que yra por general el Duque de Medina, en la conquista de Inglaterra.
Seville; Cosmé de Lava; 1588. Broadside. 1 sheet.

308. [Anonymous].
Relacion verdadera och Armada, que el Rey Don Felipe . . . mando juntar en el puerto de la ciudad de Lisbon . . . el ano de 1588 . . .
Madrid; Alonso Gomez; [1588]. [18pp]. 4to.

309. [Anonymous].
Asserte Ragioni d'Incerto Inglesa, del mal'euento della poderosa Armata Spagnuola nei Mari d'Inglitterra l'anno M.D.LXXXVIII.
Bergamo; Comin Ventura; 1593. [79] pp. 8vo.

310. [Anonymous].
History of the Spanish Armada . . . containing lists of its ships, land forces, moorings . . . and also of the . . . forces raised . . . for the defense of the realm.
London; R. & J.Dodsley; 1759. [iv], xi, [i], 60pp. small 4to.

311. [Anonymous].
The names of the nobility, gentry and others who contributed to the defence of this country at the time of the Spanish invasion, in 1588. With a brief account of their spirited and patriotic conduct on that occasion.
London; Leigh & Sotheby; 1798. 70pp. 8vo.

iv. The Last Years, including the Portuguese expedition, 1589, the Drake and Hawkins' voyage of 1595 and Cadiz, 1596.

312. ABREU, Pedro de.
Historia del saqueo de Cadiz por los Ingleses en 1596.
Cadiz; Revista Médica; 1866. [8], vi, 165pp.; pls. 8vo.

313. ANDERSON, *Dr.* Roger Charles.
Records – a list of the Royal Navy in 1590–1591.
The Mariner's Mirror, vol.xliii (November 1957), pp.322–323.
  An extract from a volume of eighteenth century transcripts in the Admiralty Library.

314. ANDREWS, *Dr.* Kenneth Raymond.
English privateering voyages to the West Indies, 1588–1595.
Cambridge; University Press; 1959. [Hakluyt Society, 2nd series, vol.cxi]. xxvii, 421pp.; pls. 8vo.

315. ANDREWS . . .
Elizabethan privateering. English privateering during the Spanish War, 1585–1603.
Oxford; University Press; 1964. xv, 297pp.; map. 8vo.
  An important study.

316. ANDREWS . . .
Drake's voyages: their contribution to English maritime expansion in the reign of Elizabeth.
London; Weidenfeld & Nicolson; 1967. 190pp.; maps. 8vo.

317. ANDREWS . . .
The last voyage of Drake and Hawkins.
Cambridge; University Press; 1972. [Hakluyt Society, 2nd series, vol.clviii]; xiv, 283pp. 8vo.
  This is an account of the expedition of royal and private ships, which left Plymouth in 1595 under the command of Drake and Hawkins with the aim of capturing Panama. The expedition ended in total failure; both leaders died and attempts to capture Grand Canary, Puerto Rico and Panama were repulsed.
  See also entries: 320, 325, 329, 336, 338, 340–2, 347, 349, 352, 358.

318. ARBER, Edward (1836–1912) [*editor*].
The last fight of *The Revenge* at sea under the command of Vice-Admiral Sir Richard Grenville on the 10–11th of September 1591, described by Sir Walter Raleigh November 1591, Gervaise Markham, 1595 and Jan Huygen van Linschoten in Dutch 1596; English 1598; and Latin, 1599.
London; Constable; 1895. [*English reprints series*]. 96pp. small 8vo.
  The REVENGE *was one of Lord Thomas Howard's small squadron, which encountered a Spanish fleet of fifty-three ships off the Azores. Grenville refused to turn from the enemy and was surrounded by a far superior force. The famous fight which ensued, raged from three o'clock in the afternoon until the following morning and at least fifteen Spanish ships were beaten off in turn,*

318. ARBER, *continued*
before the REVENGE *finally succumbed. Grenville himself was severely wounded in the battle and died two days later.*
See also entries: 321, 323, 334, 336–7, 345.

319. BOVILL, E.W. (*d.*1966).
The *Madre de Dios*. The taking of the carrack, [1592].
The Mariner's Mirror, vol.liv (May 1968), pp.129–152.

320. BRY, Theodor de (1528–1598).
Collectiones peregrinationum in Indiam Orientalem et Indiam Occidentalem . . . Americae pars viii. Primo descriptionem trium itinerum nobilissimi et fortissimi equitis Francisci Draken . . .
Frankfurt; T.de Bry; 1599. [First edition]. 99pp.; 18 engr. pls.; fdg. engr. map. Folio.
Includes an account of Drake and Hawkins' last voyage, 1595–96.

321. BUSHNELL, George Herbert.
Sir Richard Grenville; the turbulent life and career of the hero of the little *Revenge*.
London; Harrap; 1936. 342pp.; frontis.; pls.; maps. 8vo.

322. CALENDAR OF STATE PAPERS – DOMESTIC: Edward VI, Mary, Elizabeth . . . vols.iii [1591–94] – vol.viii [Addenda, 1580–1625].
London; HMSO; 1867–72. 8vo.
Includes: vol.iii [1591–4]: Naval operations in the Narrow Seas and the war with Spain. vol.iv [1595–7]: Essex's Calais expedition (1595); details of the naval forces of Essex in March 1596 and the Cadiz expedition (1597). vol.v [1598–1601]: The naval war with Spain. vol.vi [1601–3]: Naval administration and the war with Spain. vol.vii [Addenda 1580–1625]: The Drake-Norris expedition to Portugal (1589); lists of admirals, vice-admirals & rear-admirals (1581–1620) & lists of the fleet, 1588–1621.

322a. CALENDAR OF STATE PAPERS – VENETIAN.
vol.viii [1581–1591].
London; HMSO; 1894. 8vo.
Includes the Drake-Norris expedition to Portugal, (1589).

323. CALLENDER, *Sir* Geoffrey Arthur Romaine, (1875–1946).
The battle of Flores, 1591.
History, vol.iv (1919), pp.91–102.
Another name for the last fight of the REVENGE.

324. CLOWES, *Sir* William Laird (1856–1905), *et alia*.
The Royal Navy. A history from the earliest times

to the present. volume i.
London; Sampson Low, Marston; 1897. xiv, 698pp.; frontis.; numerous illustr. Large 8vo.

325. CORBETT, *Sir* Julian Stafford (1854–1922).
Drake and the Tudor Navy, with a history of the rise of England as a maritime power.
London; Longmans, Green; 1898. 2 vols. vol.i: xvi, 436pp.; frontis.; pls.; maps; illustr. vol.ii: viii, 488pp.; frontis.; pls.; map. 8vo.
A masterly study, with important chapters on the Portugal expedition (1589) and Drake's last voyage (1595–96).

326. CORBETT . . .
The Successors of Drake.
London; Longmans Green; 1900. xiv, 464pp.; frontis.; pls.; maps. 8vo.
A sequel to the above work, covering the years 1596–1603.

327. [DEVEREUX, Robert, *2nd Earl of Essex* (1566–1601), *et alia*.].
Opinions delivered by the Earl of Essex, Lord Burleigh, Lord Willoughby, Lord Burrough, Lord North, Sir William Knollys, Sir Walter Raleigh, and Sir George Carew, on the alarm of an invasion from Spain, in the year 1596, and the measures proper to be taken on that occasion.
[London; A.Strahan; *n.d.*]. lxpp. 8vo.

328. DRAKE, W.R.
Capture of the *Great Carrack* (1592).
Archaeologia, vol.xxxiii (1852).

329. DURO, *Capitan* Cesáreo Fernandez.
Armada Española desde la unión de los reinos de Castilla y Léon. Tomo III.
Madrid; Rivadeneyra; 1897. 522pp.; pls. 8vo.
The standard Spanish history, with chapters on the Drake-Norris expedition to Portugal (1589) and the Cadiz expedition (1596).

330. ELLIS, *Sir* Henry, (1777–1869).
Naval expeditions, 1588–1603, with lists of the fleet.
Archaeologia, vol.xxxiv (1852).

331. [G., T.P.].
The Royal Navy of 1599.
Naval Review, vol.xxxv (1947), pp.263–264.

332. GOLDINGHAM, C.S.
The Navy of Spain at the end of the 16th century.
RUSIJ, vol.lxiii (May 1918), pp.226–234.
There is a table of Spanish ships (1591–1600) and an account of their fates.

333. GOLDINGHAM . . .
The expedition to Portugal, 1589.
RUSIJ, vol.lxiii (August 1918), pp.469–478.

334. GOLDSMID, Edmund [*editor*].
The last fight of the *Revenge* and the death of Sir
Richard Grenville (A.D. 1591). Related by Sir Walter
Raleigh, Sir Richard Hawkins, Jan Huygen van
Linschoten, Lord Bacon and Sir William Monson.
Edinburgh; 1886. [*Bibliotheca Curiosa* series]. 66pp.
12mo.

335. GRAHAM, Winston.
The Spanish Armadas.
London; Collins; 1972. 288pp.; cold. frontis. &
pls.; illustr. 8vo.

336. HAKLUYT, Richard (1552–1616).
The Principall Navigationes, Voiages, Traffiques
and Discoveries of the English nation . . .
London; George Bishop, Ralph Newberie . . . ;
1599–1600. 3 vols. black-letter text. 4to.
   Includes accounts of the last fight of the REVENGE
   (*1591*); *the Earl of Cumberland's privateering expedi-*
   tions of 1589, 1590, 1591 & 1594; the capture of the
   MADRE DE DIOS (*1592*); *the final voyage of Drake &*
   Hawkins (1595–96); and the Cadiz expedition (1596).
   For details of other editions of Hakluyt held in the
   Library, see volume I of the Library Catalogue: Voyages
   & Travel, *entries nos. 4–8.*

337. HANNAY, David.
At Flores in the Azores.
New Review, vol.xvi (1897).

338. HAWKINS, *Sir* John (1532–1595) & *Sir*
Richard (1562?–1622).
The Hawkins' voyages during the reigns of Henry
VIII, Queen Elizabeth, and James I. Edited with an
introduction by Clements R.Markham . . .
London; Hakluyt Society [1st series, vol.lvii]; 1878.
lii, 453pp. 8vo.
   Includes an account of the 1595–96 voyage.

339. HENRY, L.W.
The Earl of Essex as strategist and military organizer,
1596–7.
English Historical Review, vol.lxviii (1953), pp.363–
393.

340. HEWITT, G.R.
Drake at San Juan de Puerto Rico.
The Mariner's Mirror, vol.l (August 1964), pp.199–
204.

341. HISTORICAL MANUSCRIPTS
COMMISSION.
Calendar of manuscripts of . . . the Marquis of

Salisbury . . . Parts vi–ix.
London; HMSO; 1895–1902. 4 vols. 8vo.
   Includes material on: Drake and Hawkins' last
   expedition (1595–96); the Cadiz enterprise (1596);
   Essex's expedition to Spain and the abortive Spanish
   Armada (1597); the threatened Spanish invasion of
   1599; Sir Richard Leveson's operations in Ireland and
   against Spain (1601–2); and the operations of Sir
   William Monson's squadron in 1602.

342. KRAUS, Hans P.
Sir Francis Drake. A pictorial biography. With an
historical introduction by Lt. Commander David
W.Waters & Richard Boulind . . .
Amsterdam; N.Israel; 1970. viii, 236pp.; frontis.
(port.); fdg. maps & facsims.; illustr. 4to.
   With an account of the Drake-Norris expedition
   (*1589*) *and the voyage of 1595–6.*

343. LATHAM, W.
A complete list of the Royal Navy of England in
1599.
Archaeologia, vol.xiii (1807), pp.27–34.

344. LAUGHTON, L.G.Carr. (*d.*1955).
The *Revenge*.
Yachting Monthly, vol.xiv (1913), pp.189–195; illustr.

345. LENDALL, R.
Sir Richard Grenville and the *Revenge*.
Geographical Magazine, vol.v (1878).

346. LLOYD, Howell A.
Sir John Hawkins' instructions, 1590.
IHR Bull., vol.xliv (May 1971), pp.125–128.

347. MAYNARDE, Thomas.
Sir Francis Drake his voyage, 1595, by Thomas
Maynarde, together with the Spanish account of
Drake's attack on Puerto Rico. Edited from the
original manuscript by W.D.Cooley.
London; Hakluyt Society; 1849. [1st series, vol.iv].
viii, 65pp. 8vo.
   A contemporary narrative of the disastrous Caribbean
   expedition of 1595–96. The author commanded a
   company of troops and was a member of the expedition's
   council of war.

348. MEYRICK, *Sir* S.R.
Report of the commissioners appointed to inquire
into the amount of booty taken at Cadiz, 1596;
with the charges preferred against Sir Anthony
Ashley.
Archaeologia, vol.xxii (1829).

349. MONSON, *Admiral Sir* William (1569–1643).
Sir William Monson's Naval Tracts. In six books
containing i. A yearly account of the English and

349. MONSON, *continued*
Spanish fleets during the war in Queen Elizabeth's time . . . ii. Actions of the English under James I . . . iii. The Office of Lord High Admiral of England . . . iv. Discoveries and enterprizes of the Spaniards and the Portuguese . . . v. Divers projects and stratagems tender'd for the good of the kingdom. vi. Treats of fishing . . . The whole from the original manuscript.
London; A. & J.Churchill; 1703. [vi], (163–560)pp. folio.
Includes accounts of the Drake-Norris Portugal expedition (1589); the Earl of Cumberland's privateering expeditions (1586–1598); the capture of the MADRE DE DIOS *(1592); Drake and Hawkins' last voyage (1595–1596); the operations of Sir Richard Leveson & Monson (1600–1602); and a list of privateers and their prizes (1585–1603).*

350. [MONSON . . .].
The Naval Tracts of Sir William Monson in six books. Edited with a commentary drawn from the State Papers and other original sources by M. Oppenheim.
London; Navy Records Society series, vols.xxii–iii, xliii, xlv & xlvii; 1902–1914. 5 vols.; pls. 8vo.
The first complete printing of Monson's manuscript.

351. OPPENHEIM, Michael M.
A history of the administration of the Royal Navy and of merchant shipping in relation to the Navy. From MDIX to MDCLX with an introduction treating of the preceding period.
London & New York; John Lane; 1896. xiv, 411pp.; cold. frontis.; pls.; illustr.; tables. 8vo.

352. PEREA, Jean Augusto y Salvador.
La catástrofe dramatica de Drake en Puerto Rico.
Ateneo Puertorriqueñó, vol.iv (July–Sept. 1940), pp. 214–223.

353. PURCHAS, Samuel, (1575?–1626).
Purchas His Pilgrimes. In Five Bookes . . .
London; Henrie Fetherstone; 1625. 4 vols. folio.
Contains contemporary narratives of the expeditions directed against Spain by Drake & Norris (1589) and the Earl of Essex (1597).

354. RALEGH, *Sir* Walter, (1552?–1618).
A Report of the truth of the fight about the Iles of Açores, this last summer. Betwixt the *Revenge*, one of her Maiesties shippes, and an Armada of the King of Spaine.
London; Wm. Ponsonbie; 1591. [facsimile reprint by the Scolar Press; 1967]. [28pp.] small 4to.
This account was reprinted in the Naval Chronicle, *vol.ii (1799), pp.474–485.*

355. ROWSE, Alfred Leslie.
Sir Richard Grenville of the *Revenge*.
London; Jonathan Cape; 1940. [*Bedford Historical* series]. 366pp.; frontis.; pls. 8vo.

356. SLINGSBY [*or* SLYNGISBIE], *Sir* William, (*ca.*1562–1634).
Relation of the voyage to Cadiz, 1596. Edited by Julian S.Corbett.
In: The Naval Miscellany. Volume i. (London; Navy Records Society series, vol.xx; 1902). pp.; (25–92); pls.; fdg. diagr. 8vo.

357. SOMERVILLE, *Vice-Admiral* Boyle.
The Spanish expedition to Ireland, 1601.
Irish Sword, vol.vii (1965–6), pp.37–57.

358. TENISON, E.M.
Elizabethan England: being the history of this country 'In relation to all foreign princes'. From original manuscripts . . .
Leamington Spa; privately printed; 1933–61. 13vols. + portfolio. 4to.
Volume viii includes material on the Azores voyage (1589); documents relating to Drake and Hawkins' defeat at Puerto Rico (1596), are included in volume ix.

359. WERNHAM, *Professor* Richard Bruce.
Queen Elizabeth and the Portugal expedition of 1589.
English Historical Review, vol.lxvi (1951), pp.1–26 & 194–218.

360. WILLIAMSON, George Charles, (1858–1942).
George, third Earl of Cumberland (1558–1605); his life and voyages. A study from original documents.
Cambridge; University Press; 1920. xx, 334pp.; frontis.; pls. 8vo.
George Clifford, third Earl of Cumberland, fitted out ten privateering expeditions to Spain and Spanish America between 1586 and 1598. He accompanied those of 1589, 1591, 1593 and 1598.

361. WILLIAMSON, *Professor* James Alexander.
Hawkins of Plymouth. A new history of Sir John Hawkins and of other members of his family in Tudor England.
London; A. & C.Black; 1969. [second edition]. xii, 348pp.; frontis. (port.); pls.; map. 8vo.

362. WILSON, *Sir* Thomas, (1560?–1629).
The State of England, Anno Dom. 1600.
Edited . . . by F.J.Fisher.
In: The Camden Miscellany, vol. xvi (London; Camden Society; 1938). viii, 47pp. 8vo.
Contains a list of the Queen's ships, with details of their tonnage, armament and complement.

III. The Mediterranean and the Ottoman Empire

363. ARGENTI, Philip P. [editor].
The expedition of the Florentines to Chios (1599), described in contemporary diplomatic records and military dispatches.
London; Bodley Head; 1934. 228pp.; pls. 8vo.
The Florentines failed to wrest Chios from the Turks, mainly because of inadequate preparations for the expedition.

364. AUSSEUR, *Capt.* J.P.
Galériens du XVIe siècle.
Neptunia, no.xcvii (1970), pp.2–7; illustr.

365. AUSSEUR . . .
La Marine du Grand Seigneur.
Neptunia, no.c (1970), pp.2–7; illustr.
A general survey of Ottoman naval activities during the period.

366. BEDFORD, *Reverend* W.K.R.
The great siege of Malta, 1565.
RUSIJ, vol.xlii (February 1898), pp.115–127; fdg. pls.
Following the loss of Rhodes in 1522, the Knights of St. John settled in Malta and continued raiding Turkish shipping from there. In May 1565, Soleyman the Magnificent laid siege to the island. The fortress of Saint Elmo fell, but Valetta resisted valiantly against over-whelming odds. Throughout the summer the Turks strove to complete the conquest, but finally raised the siege in September after the arrival of a Christian relief force.
See also entries: 367, 390, 392–3, 400.

367. BRADFORD, Ernle.
The Great Siege.
London; Hodder & Stoughton; 1961. 256pp.; pls.; illustr. 8vo.
Malta, 1565.

368. BRADFORD . . .
Mediterranean; portrait of a sea.
London; Hodder & Stoughton; 1971. 573pp.; pls.; map. 8vo.

369. BRADFORD . . .
The Shield and the Sword. The Knights of St. John.
London; Hodder & Stoughton; 1972. 245pp.; pls.; illustr.; maps. 8vo.

370. BRAGADIN, *Commander* Marc'Antonio.
Republiche Italiane sul mare.
Milan; Gazanti; 1951. 278pp.; pls.; illustr.; map. 8vo.

371. BRAUDEL, *Professor* Fernand.
The Mediterranean and the Mediterranean world in the age of Philip II. Translated from the French by Siân Reynolds.
London; Collins; 1972–73. 2 vols. 1,375pp.; pls.; illustr. 8vo.
A major work of scholarship.

372. BROCKMAN, *Captain* Eric, RN.
The two sieges of Rhodes, 1480–1522.
London; John Murray; 1969. [viii], 184pp.; pls.; maps. 8vo.
Repeated attacks on Turkish shipping by the Knights of St. John, prompted Soleyman the Magnificent to despatch an expeditionary force against their island fortress of Rhodes. The second Ottoman siege began on 28 July 1522, but was met by fierce resistance. However, assistance from the Christian powers did not materialise and the garrison finally surrendered on 21 December.

373. BROSCH, Moritz.
The height of Ottoman power.
Chapter iv in: *The Cambridge Modern History.*
volume iii. *The Wars of Religion* (1907). pp.104–139.
Includes accounts of the activities of the Barbarossas; the capture of Tunis (1569); and the battle of Lepanto (1571).

374. BUISSERET, D.J.
The French Mediterranean fleet under Henry IV.
The Mariner's Mirror, vol.l (November 1964), pp.297–306; pls.

375. BURY, *Professor* J.B.
The Ottoman Conquest.
Chapter iii in: *The Cambridge Modern History,*
volume i. (1934). pp.67–104.

376. CHACK, Louis Paul André.
Deux batailles navales: Lépante-Trafalgar.
Paris; Éditions de France; 1935. [iv], 349pp.; maps. 8vo.
The Ottoman attack on Cyprus in 1570 led to the formation of the Holy Alliance by Pope Pius V and Philip II of Spain. Don John of Austria was given command of the Allied naval forces and assembled a fleet of some 300 ships at Messina before sailing in search of the Ottoman fleet. The two fleets met off Lepanto on 7 October 1571 and the Turkish fleet was utterly defeated after a long bitter struggle. Thereafter, the Turks never regained their supremacy in the Mediterranean.

377. CREASY, *Sir* Edward Shepherd, (1812–1875).
History of the Ottoman Turks.
New and revised edition.
London; R. Bentley; 1877. xvi, 538pp. 8vo.

378. DAVIS, James C. [*editor*].
Pursuit of power. Venetian ambassadors' reports on
Spain, Turkey and France in the age of Philip II,
1560–1660.
New York; Harper & Row; 1970. xiv, 282pp.;
illustr. 8vo.
   Includes an account of the battle of Lepanto.

379. FARINE, Charles.
Deux pirates au XVIe siècle – histoire des
Barberousses.
Paris; Paul Ducrocq; 1869. ix, 377pp.; illustr. 8vo.

380. FISHER, *Sir* Godfrey.
Barbary legend. War, trade and piracy in North
Africa, 1415–1830.
Oxford; Clarendon Press; 1957. [xii], 349pp.;
frontis.; map. 8vo.

381. GUGLIELMOTTI, Alberto.
Marcantonio Colonna alla battaglia di Lepanto.
Florence; Le Monnier; 1862. 448pp. 12mo.
   *Marc'Antonio Colonna, (1535–1584), was second-in-
command of the Allied Fleet at Lepanto.*

382. GUGLIELMOTTI . . .
Storia della fortificazione nella spiaggia Romana
visarcite ed accresciute dal 1560 al 1570.
Rome; Monaldi; 1880. 531pp. 12mo.

383. GUGLIELMOTTI . . .
La Squadra permante della Marina Romana. Storia
dal 1573 al 1644.
Rome; Voghera Carlo; 1882. 486pp. 12mo.

384. GUGLIELMOTTI . . .
La guerra del pirati e la Marina Pontifica dal 1500 al
1560.
Florence; Le Monnier; 1895. 2 vols. 901pp. 8vo.

385. GUYON, *Capitaine* Marcel.
La flotte turque en Provence. L'hivernage à Toulon
(1543).
La Revue Maritime, vol.lv (July 1924), pp.21–22.

386. HERRE, *Dr.* Paul.
Europäische politik im Cyprischen Krieg, 1570–1573.
Leipzig; Theodor Weicher; 1902. 165pp. 8vo.
   *War broke out between Turkey and Venice in 1570,
when the latter refused to cede Cyprus. Nicosia and
Famagusta capitulated after lengthy sieges and the
Venetians finally abandoned the island in 1573.*

387. JENRICH, Charles H.
The Papal Navy.
USNIP, vol.lxxxix, no.727 (September 1963), pp.74–
79.

388. JURIEN DE LA GRAVIÈRE, *Amiral* Jean
Edmond. (1812–1892).
Doria et Barberousse.
Paris; Plon; 1886. 346pp. 12mo.

389. JURIEN DE LA GRAVIÈRE . . .
Les Chevaliers de Malte et la marine de Philippe II.
Paris; Plon; 1887. 2 vols. vol.i: xvi, 188pp.; fdg.
maps. vol.ii: 230pp.; fdg. maps. 12mo.

390. JURIEN DE LA GRAVIÈRE . . .
Les corsaires barbaresques et la marine du Soliman
Le Grand.
Paris; Plon; 1887. xii, 377pp.; fdg. maps. 12mo.

391. JURIEN DE LA GRAVIÈRE . . .
La Guerre de Chypre et la bataille de Lépante.
Paris; Plon; 1888. 2 vols. vol.i: xlvi, 198pp.; fdg.
maps. vol.ii: 262pp.; fdg. charts. 12mo.

391a. KHALIFEH, Mustaffa Ben Abdullah Haji.
(*d*.1657).
The history of the maritime wars of the Turks
translated from the Turkish . . . by James Mitchell.
Chapters i–iv.
London; Oriental Translation Fund; 1831. xiv,
80pp. 4to.

391b. LA RONCIÈRE, Charles de.
Une bataille de Navarin-Lépante ignorée.
La Revue Maritime, vol.clxviii (March 1906),
pp.405–410.
   *Kemal Rëis' defeat of a Venetian fleet at Modon (or
Navarino), December 1500.*

392. LOCHEAD, Ian C., & BARLING, T.F.R.
The siege of Malta, 1565.
London; Literary Services; 1970. 38pp.; illustr.
(some cold.). 8vo.

393. McGUFFIE, T.H.
The Great Siege of Malta, 1565.
History Today, vol.xv (1965), pp.539–548; illustr.

394. MANFRONI, Camillo.
Storia della marina Italiana della caduta di
Constantinopli alla battaglia di Lepanto.
Rome; Senato; 1897. xviii, 534pp. 8vo.

395. MARX, Robert F.
The battle of Lepanto, 1571.
Cleveland & New York; World Publishing; 1966.
128pp.; illustr. 8vo.

396. MERILLAU, Jacques.
Le quatrième centenaire de la bataille de Lepante, 7
October 1571.
Neptunia, no.civ (April 1971), pp.11–19; illustr.

397. [MIDGLEY, Robert (1653–1723)].
The history of the War of Cyprus. Written
originally in Latin.
London; J.Rawlins; 1687. [xviii], 370pp.; engr.
frontis. & map. 8vo.

398. MONDFELD, Walfram zu.
Der sinkende Halbmond. Die seeschlacht von
Lepanto im jahre 1571. Vorbereitung, schlachtge-
schelen, auswirkung.
Würzburg; Arena; 1973. 135pp.; illustr. 8vo.

399. NOBLE, *Lieut.* George Warwick, RCN.
The forgotten admiral; a study of offensive warfare.
Naval Review, vol.xliii (1955), pp.61–66.
 Khair-ed Din (Barbarossa).

400. [PERCIVAL-PRESCOTT, Westby &
NAISH, George P.B.].
The maritime siege of Malta, 1565.
Greenwich; National Maritime Museum; 1970.
32pp.; illustr. oblong 8vo.

401. PETRIE, *Sir* Charles.
Don John of Austria.
London; Eyre & Spottiswoode; 1967. 336pp.;
frontis.; pls.; maps. 8vo.

402. RODGERS, *Vice-Admiral* William Ledyard,
USN. (1860–1944).
Naval warfare under oars, 4th to 16th centuries. A
study of strategy, tactics and ship design.
Annapolis, Md.; US Naval Institute; 1939. xiv,
358pp.; pls.; fdg. maps; illustr. 8vo.
 *Contains an important chapter on the War of Cyprus
and the Lepanto campaign.*

403. ROSELL, *Don* Cayetano.
Historia del combate naval de Lepanto y juicio de la
importancia y consecuencias de aquel suceso.
Madrid; Real Academia; 1853. 256pp.; chart. 8vo.

404. ROSSI, Ettore.
Storia della Marina dell'Ordine di S.Giovanni di
Gerusalemme di Rodi et di Malta.
Rome & Milan; SEAI; 1926. 159pp.; pls. 8vo.

405. SEDDAL, Henry.
Malta: past and present, being a history of Malta
from the days of the Phoenicians to the present time.
London; Chapman & Hall; 1870. xii, 355pp.; fdg.
map. 8vo.

406. SERRANO, R.P.D.Luciano.
La Liga de Lepanto entre España, Venecia y la
Santa Sede (1570–1573). Ensayo historico a base de
documentos diplomaticos.
Madrid; 1918. viii, 396pp. 8vo.

407. SOTTAS, *Professor* Jules.
Les Messageries Maritimes de Venise aux XIVe et
XVe siècles.
Paris; Soc. Eds. Géographiques; 1938. 232pp.;
diagrs. 8vo.

408. TENENTI, *Professor* Alberto.
Piracy and the decline of Venice. . . . translated from
Venezia e i corsari, 1580–1615 (Bari, 1961), with an
introduction by Janet and Brian Pullan.
London; Longmans; 1967. xviii, 210pp.; pls.; maps.
8vo.

409. VAUGHAN, H.S.
The *Santo Cristo* of Lepanto.
The Mariner's Mirror, vol.x (October 1924), pp.324–
334, figs.

410. VERTOT, *L'Abbé de.*
The History of the Knights Hospitallers of St. John
of Jerusalem . . .
Edinburgh; A.Donaldson; 1770. 5 vols. 8vo.

411. WIEL, Alethea.
The Navy of Venice.
London; J.Murray; 1910. xvi, 310pp.; frontis.; pls.
8vo.
 *A valuable source of reference, with three important
chapters on the period:- 'ix. Venice and the Turks. x. The
War of Cyprus, 1521–1570. xi. Lepanto, 1571.'.*

IV. Events and operations elsewhere

i. Northern Europe

412. ANDERSON, *Dr.* Roger Charles.
Naval wars in the Baltic during the sailing ship era, 1522–1850.
London; C.Gilbert-Wood; 1910. 423pp.; diagrs. 8vo.
Includes accounts of the Northern Seven Years' War (1563–1570); the Russo-Swedish Wars; and the Wars of the Vasa Succession (1570–1610) and, in addition, tables of ships lost between 1563 and 1613.
A copy of the 1969 reprint (London; Francis Edwards), with a new introduction by the author, is also in the Library.

413. BÄCKSTRÖM, P.O.
Svenska Flottans Historie.
Stockholm; P.A.Nordstedt; 1884. 513pp. 8vo.
Two chapters cover the period 1521–1632.

414. ESPER, T.
Russia and the Baltic, 1494–1558.
Slavic Review, vol.iii (1966).

415. GARDE, Hans Georg.
Den Danske-Norske sømagts historie, 1535–1700.
Copenhagen; F.S.Mable; 1861. 346pp. 8vo.

416. HORN, G.van.
Bilder Från Nordiska Sjömarskriget.
Offprint from: *Tidskrift i Sjøvasendet, 1904–5.*, pp.26–29 & 493–507; 4 charts. 8vo.
The Swedish-Danish War of 1563–1565.

417. HORN . . .
Svenska sjötag under 1500-talet.
Stockholm; P.A.Nordstedt; 1908. 76pp.; pls. 8vo.
Includes the battles of Bornholm (30 May 1563) and Viborg (31 May 1564).

418. LIND, H.D.
Fra Kong Frederick den andens tid bidrag til den Danske-Norske sømagts historie, 1559–1588.
Copenhagen; Gyldendalsk Boghandel; 1902. 334pp. 8vo.

419. SVENSSON, S.Artur [*editor*].
Svenska flottans historia. Orlogsflotten i ord och bild från dess grundläggning under Gustav Vasa fram till våva dagar.

[volume i: 1521–1679].
[Malmo; A.-B.Allhelms]; 1942. 533pp.; pls (some cold.). 4to.

420. SZELAGOWSKI, *Professor* Adam.
Der Kampf um die Ostsee, (1544–1621).
Munich; Neue Deutsche Bücherei; 1916. 291 [+ 5] pp. 8vo.

421. TORNQUIST, *Lieut.* Carl Gustaf.
Utkast till Svenska Flottans sjö-tåg. Stockholm; A.J.Nordström; [1788]. 2 vols. vol.i: [iv], 175pp.; fdg. tables. vol.ii: 107 + 13pp.; fdg. tables. 8vo.
The first volume covers Sweden's naval history up to 1679.

422. VAMPELL, Otto.
Den Nordiske Syvaarskrig, 1563–1570.
Copenhagen; C.A.Reitzels; 1891. 203 [+ 5]pp.; chart. 8vo.

423. ZETTERSTEN, Axel.
Svenska flottans historia, åren 1522–1634.
Stockholm; J.Seligmanns; 1890. 511pp. 8vo.

ii. The Indian Ocean and Far East

424. ALBUQUERQUE, Afonso de (1453–1515).
The Commentaries of the Great Afonso Albuquerque, second viceroy of India. Translated from the Portuguese edition of 1774, with notes and an introduction by Walter de Gray Birch . . .
London; Hakluyt Society; 1875–1883. [vols.liii, lv, lxii & lxix]. 4 vols. vol.i: lx, 256pp.; pl.; maps. vol.ii: cxxxiv, 242pp.; pl.; maps. vol.iii: xliv, 308pp.; pls.; maps. vol.iv: xxxv, 324pp.; pls.; maps. 8vo.
Albuquerque was the founder of the Portuguese empire in the east. He was appointed Viceroy of Portuguese lands in Asia in 1506 and captured Goa in 1510. Thereafter, he secured gradual control of the Malabar coast, Ceylon, the Sunda Isles, Malacca and Ormuz, 1510–1515.

425. BALLARD, *Admiral* George Alexander, (1862–1948).
The War of the Arabian Sea.
The Mariner's Mirror, vol.xi (January 1925), pp.29–49.
Includes Lorenzo Almeida's three-day battle in the Chaul River (1508) and the destruction of the Gujerat fleet at Diu, in March the following year.

426. BALLARD . . .
Albuquerque's operations on the western seaboard
of India.
The Mariner's Mirror, vol.xi (April 1925), pp.116–
134.

427. BALLARD . . .
The maritime operations of Albuquerque after the
capture of Goa.
The Mariner's Mirror, vol.xi (July 1925), pp.251–275;
illustr.

428. BALLARD . . .
The century of Portuguese supremacy in the Indian
Ocean.
The Mariner's Mirror, vol.xi (October 1925), pp.370–
391.

429. BALLARD . . .
Rulers of the Indian Ocean.
London; Duckworth; 1927. xv, 319pp.; frontis.;
pls. 8vo.
Includes reprints of the foregoing four articles.

430. HAGERMAN, *Captain* George M., USN.
Lord of the Turtle Boats.
USNIP, vol.xciii, no.778 (December 1967), pp.65–
75; illustr.
During the Japanese invasions of Korea (1592–3 and
1597–8), they suffered a series of major naval defeats at
the hands of the Korean admiral Yi Sun-Sin. The
Korean fleet's success was largely due to the use of 'kwi-
suns' ('turtle-boats') – iron-clad warships built to Yi
Sun-Sin's own design.
See also entries: 432, 434–5.

431. NAMBIAR, *Professor* Odayamadath Kunjappa.
The Kunjalis – Admirals of Calicut.
London; Asia Publishing House; 1963. xii, 155pp.;
frontis.; pls. 8vo.
'The theme of this book is the hundred years' naval
war fought between India and Portugal in the sixteenth
century . . .'. (cf. preface). It is an expanded and
revised edition of the author's: Portuguese pirates and
Indian seamen, *published in India in 1955.*

432. SADLER, A.L.
The naval campaign in the Korean war of
Hideyoshi, (1592–1598).
Trans. Asiatic Soc. of Japan, 2nd series, vol.xiv (1937),
pp.177–208; illustr.

433. SANCEAU, Elaine.
Knight of the Renaissance. D. João de Castro,
soldier, sailor, scientist and Viceroy of India, 1500–
1548.
London; Hutchinson; [1949]. 236pp.; frontis.

(port.); pls.; maps on endpapers. 8vo.
João de Castro commanded the Portuguese fleet which
raised the siege of Diu in 1538. He returned to India
with another fleet in 1545, in the course of which he
relieved Malacca and Diu a second time.

434. SEARLES, *Lieut.-Cmdr.* P.J., USN.
The naval hero of Korea.
USNIP, vol.lv, no.7 (July 1929), pp.589–594; pl.
Namely Yi Sun-Sin.

435. UNDERWOOD, H.H.
Yi Sun Sin and the naval campaigns of 1592–1598.
Korean Survey, February 1958.

436. WHITEWAY, R.S.
The rise of Portuguese power in India, 1497–1550.
London; 1967. [second edition]. xvi, 357pp.; fdg.
col. map. 8vo.

437. WINDAS, *Lieut.-Cmdr.* J.M., USNR.
Kunjali: the great hereditary admiral of Calicut.
USNIP, vol.xcvi, no.814 (December 1970), pp.70–71.

A True
RELATION
Of
VERY GOOD SERVICE
Done by the
ANTILOPE

And some other ships, under the
Earle of *Warwicks* Command, at *Barwicke*,
Newcastle, and the *Holy Island*, the latter end
of *May*, and beginning of *Iune* last 1643.

Faithfully expressed in a Letter from a Gentleman of Quality, who was in the Service,
to a friend of his in London,

LONDON:
Iuly 4, Printed by *Elizabeth Purslow.* 1643.

PLATE III: Title-page of Sir William Batten's: *A True Relation of very good service done by the Antilope and some other ships, under the Earle of Warwick's command, at Barwicke, Newcastle, and the Holy Island . . . 1643.* London; 1643

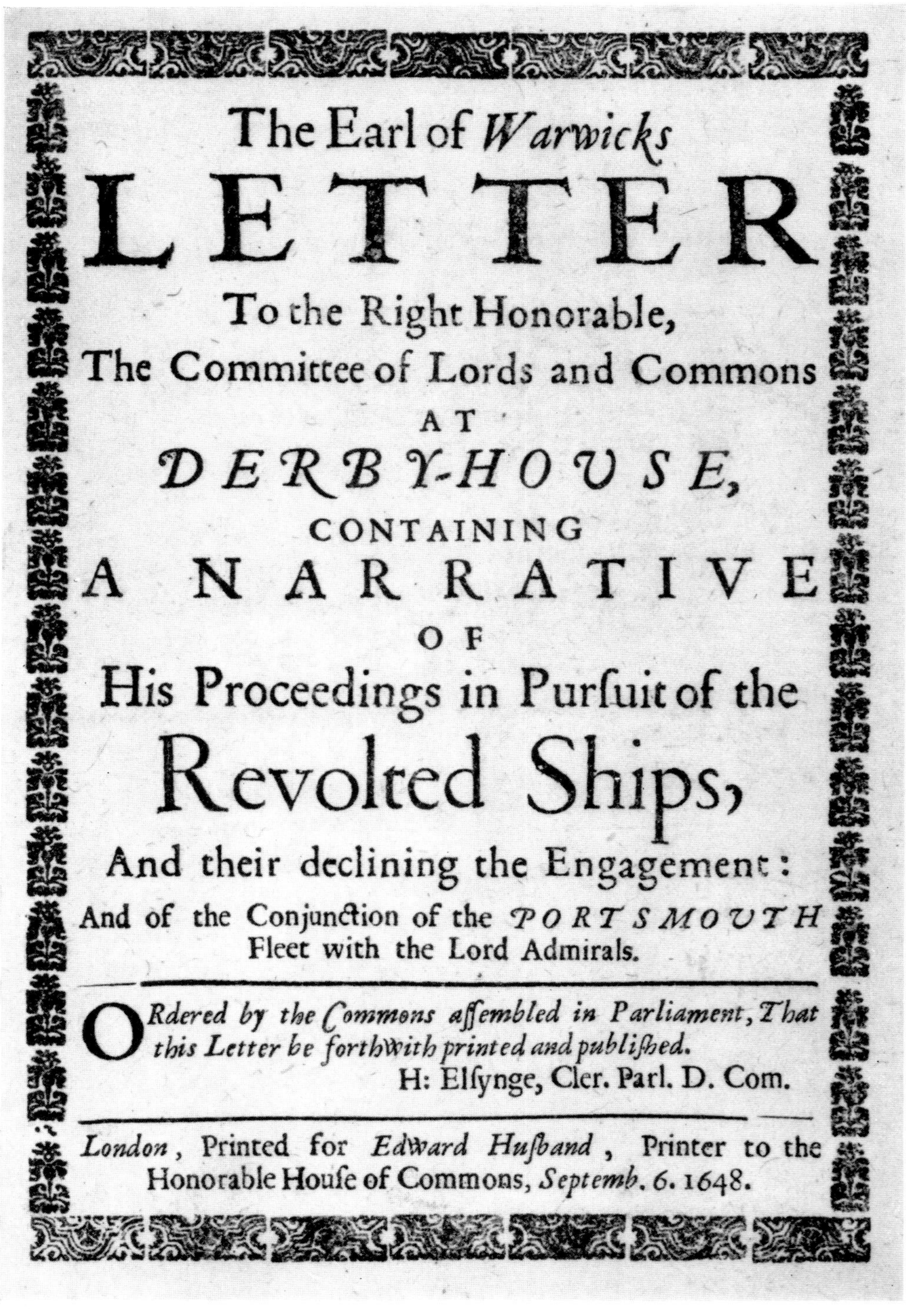

The Earl of *Warwicks*

LETTER

To the Right Honorable,
The Committee of Lords and Commons
AT
DERBY-HOUSE,
CONTAINING
A NARRATIVE
OF
His Proceedings in Purſuit of the

Revolted Ships,

And their declining the Engagement:
And of the Conjunction of the *PORTSMOUTH*
Fleet with the Lord Admirals.

*Rdered by the Commons aſſembled in Parliament, That
this Letter be forthwith printed and publiſhed.*
H: Elſynge, Cler. Parl. D. Com.

London, Printed for *Edward Huſband*, Printer to the
Honorable Houſe of Commons, *Septemb.* 6. 1648.

PLATE IV: Title-page of: *The Earl of Warwick's Letter to the . . . Committee of Lords and Commons at Derby-House, containing a narrative of his proceedings in pursuit of the Revolted Ships . . .* London; 1648

V. General works

438. ANDERSON, *Dr.* Roger Charles.
List of English Men-of-War, 1509–1649.
Cambridge; University Press for the Society for
Nautical Research; 1959. 36pp. 8vo.
See also entry no.450.

439. BARROW, John (1808–1898).
Memoirs of the naval worthies of Queen Elizabeth's
reign; of their gallant deeds, daring adventures, and
services, in the infant state of the British Navy. With
brief biographical notices of the respective
commanders.
London; John Murray; 1845. xvi, 496pp. 8vo.

440. BELL, Douglas.
Elizabethan seamen.
London; Longmans; 1936. x, 323pp.; frontis.; pls.;
maps. 8vo.

441. BEVAN, Bryan.
The Great seamen of Elizabeth I.
London; R.Hale; 1971. 319pp. pls.; 8vo.

442. BOULIND, *Dr.* Richard H.
Tudor captains: the Beestons and the Tyrrells.
The Mariner's Mirror, vol. lix (May 1973).;
pp.171–178.

443. BOURNE, H.R.Fox.
English seamen under the Tudors.
London; R.Bentley; 1868. 2 vols. vol.i: xiv.;
304pp.; maps.; vol.ii: x, 314pp. 8vo.

444. BRIDGE, *Admiral Sir* Cyprian Arthur George.
(1839–1924).
Did Elizabeth starve her seamen?
Nineteenth Century, vol.l (1901), pp.774–789.

445. CLOWES, *Sir* William Laird (1856–1905), *et
alia.*
A History of the Royal Navy from the earliest times
to the present day. Volume i.
London; Sampson, Low, Marston; 1897. xiv.;
698pp.; frontis.; pls.; numerous illustrations. large
8vo.

446. CROWSON, Paul S.
Tudor foreign policy.
London; A. & C.Black; 1973. xiv, 288pp. 8vo.

447. DURO, *Capitan* Cesáro Fernandez.
Armada Española desde la union de los reinos de
Castilla y de Aragon. Tomos iii–iv.

Madrid; Rivadeneyra; 1896–97. 2 vols. 8vo.
*The standard Spanish history, based on original
sources.*

448. DYER, Florence E.
The Elizabethan sailorman.
The Mariner's Mirror, vol.x (April 1924), pp.133–146.

449. FROUDE, *Professor* James Anthony.
English seamen in the sixteenth century. Lectures
delivered at Oxford, Easter terms, 1893–4.
London; Longmans Green; 1895. [vi], 241pp. 8vo.
*Copies of the 1908 and 1917 editions are also in the
Library.*

450. GLASGOW, Tom.
Revision in List of English Men-of-war, 1509–164.
The Mariner's Mirror, vol.lii (November 1966),
pp.390–392.

451. GOLDINGHAM, Cecil S.
The personnel of the Tudor Navy and the internal
economy of the ships.
US Magazine, vol.clxvii (March 1918), pp.427–451.

452. GOLDINGHAM . . .
Development of tactics in the Tudor Navy.
US Magazine, vol.clxxviii (June 1918), pp.207–215.

453. HALE, *Professor* J.R.
Armies, navies and the art of war.
Chapter vii in: *The New Cambridge Modern History.
volume iii. The Counter-Reformation and price
revolution, 1559–1610.* (1968).
pp.171–208. 8vo.

454. JURIEN DE LA GRAVIÈRE, *Amiral* Jean
Edmond. (1812–1892).
Les Marins du XV et du XVI siècles.
Paris; Plon; 1879. 2 vols. 8vo.

455. KINGSFORD, C.L.
The beginnings of English maritime enterprise.
History, vol.xiii (1928), pp.97–106 & 193–203.

456. LANDAUER, Ignacio Bauer.
La Marina Española en el siglo XVI – Don
Francisco de Benavides cuatralso de las galeras de
España.
Madrid; Jesús Lopez; 1921. 479 [+6]pp. 4to.

457. LA RONCIÈRE, Charles de.
Histoire de la Marine Française. vol.iii: Les guerres
d'Italie; Liberté de mers.
Paris; Plon-Nourrit; 1906. [vi], 612pp.; pls. 8vo.

458. LAUGHTON, Leonard G. Carr. (*d.*1955).
Early Tudor ship guns.
Edited by Michael Lewis.
The Mariner's Mirror, vol.xlvi (November 1960),
pp.242–285.

459. MARX, Robert F.
The Treasure fleets of the Spanish Main.
Cleveland & New York; World Publishing; 1968.
128pp.; illustr. large 8vo.

460. MORTON, R.G.
Naval activity on Lough Neagh, 1558–1603.
Irish Sword, vol.vii (1967–68), pp.288–293.

461. OAKESHOTT, Walter.
Founded upon the seas. A narrative of some English
maritime and overseas enterprises, during the period
1550 to 1616.
Cambridge; University Press; 1942. xii, 200pp.;
frontis. (port.); pls.; map. 8vo.

462. OMAN, *Sir* Charles.
The art of war in the sixteenth century.
London; Muller; 1937. xvi, 784pp.; pls.; maps. 8vo.

463. OPPENHEIM, Michael M.
Royal and merchant shipping under Elizabeth.
English Historical Review, vol.vi (July 1891), pp.465–
494.

464. OPPENHEIM, Michael M.
A history of the administration of the Royal Navy
and of merchant shipping in relation to the Navy.
From MDIX to MDCLX with an introduction treating
of the preceding period.
London & New York; John Lane; 1896. xiv,
411pp.; cold. frontis.; pls.; illustr.; tables. 8vo.
    A masterly study.

465. RICHMOND, *Admiral Sir* Herbert William,
(1871–1946).
The Navy as an instrument of policy, 1558–1727.
Edited by E.A.Hughes.
Cambridge; University Press; 1953. [viii], 404pp.
8vo.

466. ROUND, J.H., & OPPENHEIM, Michael M.
The Royal Navy under Elizabeth.
English Historical Review, vol.ix (1894), pp.709–715.

467. ROWSE, Alfred Leslie.
The expansion of Elizabethan England.
London; Macmillan; 1955. xiv, 450pp. pls. 8vo.

468. ROWSE...
Tudor Cornwall.
London; Macmillan; 1969. 482pp.; pls.; maps. 8vo.
    *Chapter xv is concerned with defence and war, 1569–
1603.*

469. TENISON, E.M.
Elizabethan England: being the history of this
country 'In relation to all foreign princes.' From
original manuscripts, many hitherto unpublished,
co-ordinated with XVIth century printed matter
ranging from royal proclamations to broadside
ballads.
Leamington Spa; privately printed; 1933–61. 14
vols. + portfolio. 4to.

470. WILLIAMSON, *Professor* James Alexander.
Maritime enterprise, 1485–1558.
Oxford; Clarendon Press; 1913. 416pp. 8vo.

471. WOODROOFFE, *Cmdr.* Thomas, B.R., RN.
The Enterprise of England. An account of her
emergence as an oceanic power.
London; Faber & Faber; 1958. 301pp.; pls.; maps.
8vo.

PART THREE

The Seventeenth Century

I. The Early Decades, 1603–1625

i. The Navy under James I

472. ANDERSON, *Dr.* R.C.
The *Prince Royal* and other ships of James I.
The Mariner's Mirror, vol.iii (September–November 1913), pp.272–5; 305–7; & 341–2.

473. ANDERSON . . .
The *Prince Royal* of 1610.
The Mariner's Mirror, vol.vi (December 1920), pp.365–8; 5 pls.

474. ANDREWS, K.R.
Sir Robert Cecil and Mediterranean plunder, 1603.
English Historical Review, vol.lxxxvii (July 1972), pp.513–532.

475. BRAND, John.
The names of His Majesty's Ships, with the number of men and furniture requisite for the setting forth of them, etc. Extracted from a manuscript of the beginning of James I.
Archaeologia, vol.xv (1806).

476. [BUCKINGHAM, *First Duke of* (1592–1628)].
Instructions to all officers of the Navy, 1623.
In: Historical Manuscripts Commission Reports, vol.vi – Leconfield MSS. Letters, &c., relating to the Navy, 1618–28.
In: Historical Manuscripts Commission Reports – Appendix, vol.xii, part 1. (1888).
For further material on the Duke of Buckingham and the Navy, including the expedition to La Rochelle, see part ii, ff. See also entry no.485 in this section.

477. CLAYTON, N.
Naval administration under James I.
University of Leeds MA thesis. (1948).

478. CLOWES, *Sir* William Laird, *et alia*.
The Royal Navy. A History from the earliest times to the present.
London; Sampson Low, Marston; 1897–1903. 7 vols. 4to.
Vol.ii (1898) contains – chapter xvii: Civil History of the Royal Navy, 1603–1649 (pp.1–28) & xviii: Military History of the Royal Navy, 1603–1649 (pp.29–81). The latter, written by L.Carr Laughton, includes material on Buckingham and the Navy; Sir Robert Mansell and the expedition to Algiers, 1621, and the Amboyna massacre.

479. CORBETT, *Sir* Julian S.
England in the Mediterranean. A study of the rise and influence of British power within the Straits, 1603–1713.
London; Longmans; 1904. 2 vols. 342; 351pp., 1 map, 1 pl. 8vo.
A major work of scholarship. For this period, there are important chapters in vol.i:– The Mediterranean at the beginning of the seventeenth century; Ward and the Barbary pirates; The Duke of Osuña; Sir Walter Ralegh and Genoa; England and the Venice conspiracy; The Navy under James I; The Navy and the Palatinate; Mansell in the Mediterranean; Richelieu's invitation and the naval results of James's reign.

480. HISTORICAL MANUSCRIPTS COMMISSION.
Buccleuch MSS – vol.i (1899).
Contains many references to the Admiralty, naval operations and ships of the period, 1601–1667.

481. [JAMES I].
Calendar of State Papers – Domestic: James I. 1618 (pp.100–101). : Report of the Special Commissioners to inquire into the State of the Navy, 1618.

482. [MAINWARING, *Sir* Henry (*d.*1653)].
The life and works of Sir Henry Mainwaring.
Edited by G.E.Manwaring & W.G.Perrin.
London; Navy Records Society series, vols.liv & lvi; 1920–2. 2 vols. 8vo.
Has much Jacobean material.

483. MANSELL, *Admiral Sir* Robert (1573–1653).
Journal of the Algiers expedition [1621].
In: Calendar of State Papers – Domestic: James I. vol.cxxii, p.106, ff.

484. MARSDEN, R.G.
English ships in the reign of James I.
RHS Trans., n.s., vol.xix (1905).
Lists over one thousand ships, royal and mercantile.

485. McGOWAN, *Dr.* A.P.
The administration of the Navy under the First Duke of Buckingham, Lord High Admiral of England, 1618–1628.
University of London Ph.D thesis; 1967.
Précis in IHRBull., vol.xl (November 1967), pp.225–7.

486. McGOWAN . . .
The Jacobean Commissions of Enquiry, 1608 and 1618.
London; Navy Records Society series, vol.cxvi; 1971. 319pp. frontis. 8vo.

487. [MONSON, *Sir* William. (*d.*1643)].
The Naval Tracts of Sir William Monson.
London; Navy Records Society series, vols.xxii–
xxiii; xliii; xlv; xlvii; 1902–1914.
Edited by Michael Oppenheim. 6 books in 5 vols.
8vo.

488. [NOTTINGHAM, Heneage Finch, *First Earl
of, et alia*].
A Report for contracting the charge of His Majesty's
Navy, keeping the coast of England and Ireland
safely guarded, &c.
By the Earl of Nottingham, Sir R.Mansell, and
principal officers of the Navy. *Repr. in*
CHARNOCK: *Naval Architecture*, vol.ii (1801),
pp.184–196; 211–270.

489. OPPENHEIM, Michael.
The Royal Navy under James I.
English Historical Review, vol.vii (1892), pp.471–496.

490. PARKES, Oscar.
Three Jacobean warships – *Anne Royal, Red Lion* and
Repulse. [*ca.*1613].
The Mariner's Mirror, vol.xxxvii (April 1951),
pp.99–103.

491. PENN, C.D.
The Navy under the Early Stuarts and its influence
on English history.
Leighton Buzzard & Manchester; The Faith Press;
1913. 302 + [15]pp. pls. 8vo.
    *A second (London & Portsmouth) edition was
published in 1920.*

492. PRATT, Margaret.
Naval construction during the reign of James I.
University of Leeds MA thesis; 1948.

493. ROBERTS, George.
The diary of Walter Yonge, 1604–1628.
Camden Society series, vol.xli (1848).
    *Includes much information on the decadence of the
early Stuart Navy.*

494. WOODWARD, Donald.
Sir Thomas Button, the *Phoenix* and the defence of
the Irish coast, 1614–1622.
The Mariner's Mirror, vol.lix (August 1973), pp.
343–4.

495. [Anonymous].
Algiers voyage in a Iournall or briefe Reportary of
all occurrents hapning in thi fleet of ships sent out
by the King . . . as well against the Pirates of
Algiers, as others: the whole body of the Fleete
consisting of 18 Sayle . . . Under the command of

Sir Robert Mansel Knight, Vice-Admirall of
England, and Admirall of that Fleet . . .
London; 1621. title; [42]pp. Small 8vo.

ii. Events and operations elsewhere

496. ANDERSON, *Dr.* R.C.
The Thirty Years' War in the Mediterranean.
The Mariner's Mirror, vols.lv (November 1969),
pp.435–451, & lvi (February 1970). pp.41–57.

497. BATTISTELLA, Antonio.
Una campagna navale Veneto-Spagnuola in
Adriatico poco conosciuta.
Venice, 1922. 141pp. 8vo.
    *About the campaign between Spanish and Venetian
squadrons in the Adriatic in 1617.*

498. BOXER, *Professor* C.R.
Nuno Álvares Bothelho e a sua armada de alta-
bordo (1624–1625).
Oporto; Imprensa Portuguesa; 1928. 30pp. 8vo.

499. BOXER . . .
Le combat naval de Mozambique (23–25 Juillet,
1622).
Armaïs do Club Militar e Naval (May/June 1930),
pp.4–20.

500. BOXER . . . [*editor*].
Ataque dos Holandeses a Macau en 1622. Relação
inédita di Fr. Álvaro de Rosário.
Lisbon; [*n.d.*]. 16pp., 8vo. wrappers.

501. DURO, Cesáreo Fernandez.
El Gran Duque de Osuña y su marina. Jornados
contra Turcos y Venecianos, 1602–1624.
Madrid; Rivadeneyra; 1885. 458pp. 8vo.

502. EDMONDSON, Sybil.
The fight of the *Dolphin*.
The Mariner's Mirror, vol.lii (August 1966), pp.280–1.
    *Against six Turkish men-of-war off Cagliari, Sardinia,
on 12 January 1616.*

503. GUISBERT, Julien.
La bataille d'Oliva (28 Novembre 1627).
Revue Maritime, vol.cxxxv (March 1931), pp.450–
456.

504. HANNAY, David.
The great carrack.
Blackwood's Magazine, vol.ccxii (1922), pp.395–407.
    An encounter with the Portuguese in 1616.

505. [MARINSTABEN = Historical Dept. of the Swedish Naval Staff].
Sveriges Sjökrig, 1611–1632.
Stockholm; Victor Pettersen; 1937. 324pp., pls. 4to.

Sweden's naval wars during the period, including accounts of: the struggle with Denmark; the Kalmar War of 1611–13; the war against Poland and blockade of her ports, 1617–29; Gustavus Adolphus & the operations against Stralsund and Wismar, 1628–9.

506. PENROSE, Boies. [editor].
Sea Fights in the East Indies in the years 1602–1639.
Cambridge, Mass.; Harvard University Press; 1931. 295pp., 8vo.

Comprising a collection of contemporary accounts, including:
[a]. 'A true and perfect relation concerning the fight of Five Dutch ships against the Portugal fleet, 1602' (*London; 1603*). [b]. *Thomas Best's:* 'The Fights off Swally Road, 1612'. (*from Purchas . . . book.iv.*) [c]. *Captain Nicholas Downton's:* 'The Repulse of the Portugalls, 1615'. (*from Purchas . . . book.iv.*) [d]. *Captain Martin Pring's:* 'Report of the Fights between the Dutch & Sir Thomas Dale'. (*from Purchas . . . book.v.*) [e]. 'The true Relation of the Fight with Four Portingals, 1620 . . . with the lamentable death of Captain Andrew Shilling.' (*London; 1622*). [f]. *John Taylor's:* 'A famous Fight where four English and four Dutch ships fought three days neere Ormus eight Portugall gallions and three Friggots.' (*London; [1627].*) [g]. 'A Terrible Sea-fight: . . . concerning the great fight between nine East India ships of the Hollanders, and three great Gallions, which happened about Goas Bare in the East Indies, the 20.30 of September, 1639.' (*London; 1640*).

507. SOUSA, *Vice-Admiral* Botelho de.
Subsídios para a Historia Militar Marítima da India (1585–1669) – volume iii. – 1618–1635.
Lisbon; Imprensa da Armada; 1953. 311pp., 8vo.

'. . . The principal naval events recorded in the present volume are the siege and capture of Ormuz by an Anglo–Persian force in 1622; the valiant efforts of Rui Freire de Andrade and Nuno Alvares Botelho to stem the tide of adversity and defeat; the operations of the Anglo–Dutch "fleets of defence", including the hard-fought actions in the Persian Gulf, 1625; the siege of Malacca by the Achinese and its relief by Botelho in 1629, which was the last great Portuguese naval victory in Asia; and the increasingly effective blockade of the Straits of Malacca by the Dutch, culminating in the fall of that key-fortress six years later.'
(from Professor Boxer's review in The Mariner's Mirror, vol.xli (February 1955), pp.87–88).

508. TYLER, Victor Morris.
A Spanish expedition to Chesapeake Bay in 1609.
American Neptune, vol.xvii (1957), pp.181–194.

509. WEBER, *Dr.* R.E.J.
De beveiliging van de zee tegen Europeesche en Barbarijsche Zeeroovers, 1609–1621.
Amsterdam; 1936. 233pp., 1pl. 8vo.

II. The Navy under Charles I, 1625–1649 and The English Civil War

i. The Navy under Charles I

510. ANDERSON, *Dr.* R.C.
The *Royal Sovereign* of 1637.
The Mariner's Mirror, vol.iii (April–July 1913),
pp.109–112; 168–170; 208–211; pls.

511. [ARGALL, *Sir* Samuel. (*d.*1626)].
Journal of the *Swiftsure* . . . [Cadiz: 1 October–5
December, 1625].
In: Calendar of State Papers. Domestic: Charles 1 –
vol.i, p.22.ff.

512. CALENDAR OF STATE PAPERS –
DOMESTIC: Charles I.
vols.i (1625–6) – xviii (1641–3).
London; HMSO; 1858–1887. 8vo.
   *Contain a wealth of naval documents and relevant
material, including references to:*
*In: vol.i. (1625–6).: Letters of the Duke of
Buckingham, Lord High Admiral; Special Commissioners on the State of the Navy; administration &
shipbuilding; the Cadiz expedition; operations against
Dunkirk privateers.*
*vol.ii. (1627–8).: Commissioners' Enquiry; impeach-
ment of Villiers; the Île de Rhé expedition; conversion of
Portsmouth into a naval station; survey of the Navy
(1627).*
*vol.iii. (1628–9).: La Rochelle expedition & assassina-
tion of Villiers; Admiralty correspondence & naval
estimates; increase in tonnage of Navy since the reign of
Henry VIII.*
vol.iv. (1629–31).: Naval administration.
*vol.v. (1631–3).: Many references to Admiralty &
Admiralty Court, including correspondence, orders &
warrants. Secretary Nicholas's minutes of Admiralty
business.*
*vol.vi. (1633–4).: Particularly large collection of
Admiralty papers; introduction of Ship Money: continuation of Nicholas's minutes;* DREADNOUGHT *sent to
Scotland in connection with the King's visit.*
*vol.vii. (1634–5).: Many references to Ship Money.
And Nathaniel Knott's:* 'Advice of a Seaman touching
the expedition intended against the Turkish pirates'.
1634. (pp.401–2).
vol.viii. (1635).: Ship Money; assembly of the Ship

*Money Fleet in the Downs, May 1635 and letters from
Lord Lindsey, in command; naval disputes with the
French and Dutch.*
*vol.ix. (1635–6).: Ship Money; letters on Sir John
Pennington's cruise in the Channel, 1635;
Northumberland's operations with the Ship Money
Fleet, 1636.*
*vol.x. (1636–7).: Ship Money; the end of
Northumberland's cruise, 1636; Rainborough's expedi-
tion against the Sallee corsairs; naval administration.*
*vol.xi. (1637).: Ship Money; Pennington in the Downs,
April–June 1637; Northumberland's convoy of Prince
Rupert to Holland and his cruise in the West with the
Ship Money Fleet; launch of the* SOVEREIGN OF THE
SEAS, *September 1637; fishing disputes with the Dutch.*
*vol.xii. (1637–8).: Ship Money & activities of the Ship
Money Fleet; Duke of York made nominal Lord High
Admiral, 1638; Nicholas's correspondence.*
vol.xiii. (1638–9).: Ship Money.
*vol.xiv. (1639).: Ship Money; Marquis Hamilton's
fleet in the Firth of Forth and the English Fleet sent north
against the Scots; papers of Algernon Percy, 10th Earl of
Northumberland, as Lord Admiral; ships impressed for
King's service and vessels convoyed by the King's ships.*
*vol.xv. (1639–40).: Ship Money; letters narrating the
battle of the Downs [q.v.] – October 1639; naval preparations for the invasion of Scotland.*
vol.xvi. (1640).: Ship Money & naval administration.
*vol.xvii. (1640–1).: The Royal Navy off the Scottish
coast; naval administration.*
*vol.xviii. (1641–3).: House of Commons declare Ship
Money illegal, 1641; naval administration.*
   ☞ *For the subsequent volumes in this series – see the
next section [English Civil War].*

513. CLOWES, *Sir* William, *et alia*.
The Royal Navy. A History from the earliest
times . . .
*vol.ii (London; Sampson Low; 1898) contains chapters
xvii–xviii: Civil and Military History of the Royal
Navy, 1603–1649. (pp.1–81).*

514. CORBETT, *Sir* Julian S.
England in the Mediterranean . . . 1603–1713.
London; Longmans; 1904. 2 vols. 342; 351pp.; 1
map, 1 pl. 8vo.
   *There is an important chapter in vol.i.: 'Naval
Strategy under Charles I' [pp.143–163].*

515. DUCKETT, *Sir* G.
Charles I's warrant to Admiral Pennington to
deliver the fleet under his command to the French
(28 July, 1625).
Archaeologia, vol.xviii (1814).

516. DYER, Florence E.
The Ship Money Fleet.
The Mariner's Mirror, vol.xxiii (April 1937), pp.198–209.

517. EAMES, A.
The King's pinnace – the *Swan*, 1642–5.
The Mariner's Mirror, vol.xlvii (February 1961), pp.49–55.

518. FAYLE, Charles Ernest.
The Ship Money fleets.
Edinburgh Review, vol.ccxxxiv (October 1921), pp.375–389.

519. GARDINER, S.R.
The Expedition to Cadiz, 1625 and to Rhé, 1627.
In his: History of England . . . vol.vi (1886).

520. [GLANVILL, John].
The Voyage to Cadiz in 1625. Being a journal written by John Glanvill, Secretary to the Lord Admiral of the Fleet . . .
Edited by the Reverend Alexander B.Grosart.
Camden Society Miscellany, n.s., vol.xxxii (1883).

521. GORDON, *Miss* M.D.
The collection of ship-money in the reign of Charles I.
RHS Trans., third series, vol.iv (1910).

522. GRAHAM, Richard.
Journal kept during the expedition to Rhé. (24 June–21 July, 1627).
In: Calendar of State Papers: Domestic – Charles I.: vol.ii (1627–8), pp.lxxi; 65.

523. [GRENVILLE *or* GRANVILLE, *Sir* Richard (1600–1658)].
Two original Journals of Sir Richard Granville, viz.,
I. Of the expedition to Cadiz anno 1625.
II. Of the expedition to the Isle of Rhee . . . anno 1627.
London; John Clarke; 1724. 2 parts; xiv; 56; 25pp. small 8vo.

524. HERBERT of CHERBURY, *Lord.*
The expedition to the Isle of Rhé. [1627].
London: Whittingham & Wilkins; 1860. 287pp. 8vo.
   A Latin edition of the original narrative was published at Oxford in 1656.

525. HISTORICAL MANUSCRIPTS COMMISSION:
(i) Documents and papers relating to the Cadiz expedition of 1625. (ii) Documents and papers relating to the La Rochelle expedition of 1628.
In. HMC *Reports*, vol.xii, part i. [Coke MSS]; 1888.

(iii) Lists of ships, burdens, men, &c. 1628. (iv) Journal of the expedition to Sallee, 1638. (v) Survey of the Navy, 1638, 1639 & 1641.
In. HMC *Reports*, vol.vi. [Leconfield MSS].

(vi) Many references to Naval Commissioners, administration, state of the Navy, stores & victualling, especially for the period 1619–32.
In. HMC *Reports* [Cowper MSS]; 3 vols., 1888–9.

(vii) Details about the Navy's activities, 1625–8, including the La Rochelle expedition.
In. HMC *Reports*, [Skrine MSS – Salvetti correspondence]; 1887.

(viii) Extracts from the logs of Admiral Sir John Pennington, 1631–6.
In. HMC *Reports*. [Westmorland MSS. Lord Muncaster's papers]; 1885.

526. HOLLOND, John.
Two Discourses of the Navy, 1638 and 1659 . . .
Edited by J.R.Tanner.
London; Navy Records Society series, vol.vii.; 1896. lxxxiii; 419pp. 8vo.

527. INGRAM, Bruce S. [*editor*].
Three Sea Journals of Stuart times. Being . . . the diary of Dawtrey Cooper, captain of the *Pelican* . . . kept during the expedition under the Earl of Lindsey to relieve La Rochelle . . . in 1628.
Secondly, the journals of Jeremy Roch, captain of the King's Navy . . . . . . Thirdly, the diary of Francis Rogers, London merchant . . .
London; Constable; [1936]. 244pp.; pls. 8vo.

528. KEPLER, J.S.
The value of ships gained and lost by the English shipping industry during the Wars with Spain and France, 1624–1630.
The Mariner's Mirror, vol.lix (May 1973), pp.218–220.

529. LINDSEY, Robert, *1st Earl of, Lord High Admiral.*
Instructions for the Ship Money Fleet, 1635.
In: Monson's 'Naval Tracts . . .' book iii. (Navy Records Society series; vols.xxix and xliii; (1905–13).

530. NORTHUMBERLAND, Algernon Percy, *10th Earl of.* (1602–1668).
Journal. (As Admiral of the Second and Third Ship

530. NORTHUMBERLAND, *continued*
Money Fleets: 15 May–9 October 1636; 7 June–10
September, 1637).
In: Calendar of State Papers – Domestic: Charles I.
vols.ix & x.

531. OPPENHEIM, Michael.
The Royal Navy under Charles I.
English Historical Review, vols.viii (1893), pp.467–499
and ix (1894), pp.92–116; 473–492.
An important study.

532. PETT, Phineas, *Commissioner of the Navy*
[*d.*1638].
The autobiography of Phineas Pett.
Edited by W.G.Perrin.
London; Navy Records Society series, vol.li.; 1918.
civ; 244pp.; 1pl. 8vo.

533. ROTHWELL, J.S.
The Rochelle expedition of 1627.
United Service Magazine, n.s., vol.vi (1892–3).

534. [Anonymous].
A Iournall, and relation of the action, which by his
Majestie's commandment, Edward Lord Cecyl,
Baron of Putney, and Viscount of Wimbledon,
Admirall, and Lieutenant Generall of his Maiestyes
forces, did undertake upon the Coast of Spaine,
1625.
[London]; 1626. pamphlet. 33pp. 8vo.
  First edition; a second (30pp.) appeared in London the
following year.

535. [Anonymous].
A Manifestation or remonstrance of the most
Honourable the Duke of Buckingham . . .
[London]; 1627. pamphlet. 14pp. 8vo.

536. [Anonymous].
Articles of Agreement made betweene the French
King and those of Rochell . . . 1628.
[London]; 1628. pamphlet. 13pp. 8vo.

ii. The English Civil War

537. ANDERSON, *Dr.* R.C.
The Royalists at sea in 1648.
The Mariner's Mirror, vol.ix (February 1923), pp.34–
46.

538. ANDERSON . . .
The *Constant Warwick* and early frigates. [*ca.*1645].
The Mariner's Mirror, vol.x (July 1924), p.304.

539. ANDERSON . . .
The Royalists at sea in 1649.
The Mariner's Mirror, vol.xiv (October 1928).
pp.320–338.
  For Dr. Anderson's later articles on this theme, see
entries nos. 602 & 604 in the Commonwealth section.

540. ANDERSON . . .
Popham in the Tagus (document).
The Mariner's Mirror, vol.xx (January 1934), pp.106–
111.

541. ANDRIETTE, E.A.
Devon and Exeter in the Civil War.
Newton Abbot; David & Charles; 1971. 211pp.
8vo.

542. BAUMBER, M.L.
The Navy and the Civil War in Ireland, 1641–3.
The Mariner's Mirror, vol.lvii (February 1971).
pp.385–397.

543. BAUMBER . . .
The Navy during the Civil Wars and the Common-
wealth, 1642–1651.
University of Manchester MA thesis; 1967.

544. CALENDAR OF STATE PAPERS –
DOMESTIC: Charles I.
vols.xviii (1641–3) – xxiii (1649).
London; HMSO; 1888–1897. 8vo.
  Contains a wealth of relevant material, including
references to:
In: vol.xviii. (1641–3): Naval administration;
Commons declare Ship Money illegal, 1641; the out-
break of hostilities.
vol.xix. (January–September 1644): Henrietta Maria
conveyed to France despite efforts of Earl of Warwick to
intercept her, July 1644; correspondence of Warwick and
Parliamentary Commissioners of the Navy; fleet
movements.
vol.xx. (October 1644–June 1645): Activities &
administration of Royal and Parliament Navies;
Warwick's naval correspondence, 1644–5.
vol.xxi. (1645–7): Ibid; & Admiralty letters, 1645–7.
vol.xxii. (1648–9): Many references to the activities of
the Parliament Navy and the revolted ships; Navy's
attitude during the War & letters and papers relating to
the Navy, 1648–9.
vol.xxiii. (Addenda: 1625–1649): Includes scattered
references to the Navy, 1625–1649.

545. JOHNS, A.W.
The *Constant Warwick*. [1645].
The Mariner's Mirror, vol.xviii (July 1932). pp.254–
266.

546. KENNEDY, D.E.
Parliament and the Navy, 1642–1648; a political history of the Navy during the Civil War.
University of Cambridge Ph.D. thesis; 1959.

547. KENNEDY . . .
The English naval revolt of 1648.
EHR, vol.lxxvii (April 1962), pp.247–256.

548. KENNEDY . . .
The establishment and settlement of Parliament's Admiralty, 1642–8.
The Mariner's Mirror, vol.xlviii (November 1962). pp.276–291.

549. [PHILIPS, John].
Exceeding joyful Newes from the Narrow Seas, Dover, and the Irish Seas. Being, a true and exact Relation of the Victorious Proceedings and Renowned Exploits, performed by . . . Robert, Earl of Warwicke, Lord Admirall of His Majestie's Navie Royall in this Expedition, MDCXLII . . . Likewise a true description of the manner of his scouring the Seas, and all the Ports thereabouts, the charlish waves seeming proud to bear his famous vessels. With the names of every particular ship belonging to the Navie, and the names of the ships appointed for the Irish Seas . . . Sent from his Majesties Royall Ship called the Rainbow, May the 9. by Master Iohn Philips, to his brother in Thames Street.
London; John Webb; May. 12. 1642. title; engr. portr; [6] pp. small 8vo.

550. POWELL, *Reverend* J.R.
The Parliamentary squadron at the siege of Duncannon in 1645 and Penn's attempt to relieve Youghal.
Irish Sword, vol.ii (1954–6). pp.83–87.

551. POWELL . . .
Blake and the defence of Lyme Regis. [April 1644].
The Mariner's Mirror, vol.xx (October 1934), pp.448–474.

552. POWELL . . .
The Navy in the English Civil War.
London; Archon; 1962. 240pp.; maps & pls., 8vo.
An important book, which in earlier form won the Julian Corbett naval prize in 1956. Ship Lists in the appendix include details of the Summer and Winter Guards, 1642–8 and ships captured by the Parliament Fleet. Introduction by C.V. Wedgwood.

553. POWELL . . . *and* TIMINGS, E.K. [*editors*].
Documents relating to the Civil War, 1642–1648.
London; Navy Records Society series, vol.cv; 1963. 462pp. 8vo.
With valuable original source-material of the period and introduction by the joint editors.

554. POWELL . . .
Penn's expedition to Bonratty in 1646.
The Mariner's Mirror, vol.xl (February 1954), pp.4–20; 1 map.

555. POWELL . . .
The siege of the Downs castles in 1648.
The Mariner's Mirror, vol.li (May 1965), pp.155–171; pls.
See further in the Commonwealth section, for the Rev. Powell's studies and articles on Blake.

Here follows a series of the numerous contemporary pamphlets, letters and broadsheets concerning the Navy, published by the opposing forces during and after the First Civil War. They are arranged approximately according to date of publication:-

556. [WARWICK, *Earl of*].
A Letter sent from the Rt. Hon. Robert, Earl of Warwick, Admirall of the Sea, to M. John Pym, Esq., and presented to both Houses of Parliament, July 6, 1642 . . .
From aboard His Majesties Ship the *James*, on the Downs, this 4 of July, 1642.
London; Ios. Hunscott & Io. Wright; [July 1642]. title; [7]pp. small 8vo.
Warwick's notification to Parliament of his being relieved of the command of the Fleet by the King and of his agreement after a Council of War with his commanders to obey '. . . the ordinance of Parliament, sent from the Houses for me to continue my charge'. Initially, five of his commanders – the Rear Admiral and Captains Fogge, Barley, Slingsby and Wake refused to comply ['The Revolted Ships'], but ultimately did so without bloodshed.

557. [WARWICK . . .].
The Earl of Warwick's letter from aboard His Majesties Ship called the *James*, in the Downs . . . dated July 4, 1642. Concerning his calling a Councell of War, and how his Rear-Admirall, and four other Captains refused to obey his Lordships Summons . . .
London; Luke Norton & Iohn Field; July 7, 1642. 7pp. 8vo.

558. [CHARLES I, *King*].
The Kings Maiesties Resolution concerning Robert Earl of Warwicke, Lord Admirall of His Majesties

558. [CHARLES I, *King*], *continued*
Navie Royall, wherein is declared the Kings full
resolution and intention concerning his Navie, now
lying upon the Downs . . .
[London]; J.Smith; July 12, 1642. [6]pp. 8vo.

559. [Anonymous].
True Newes from our Navie, now at Sea; shewing
the most remarkable passages there since . . . the
Earl of Warwicks departure thence, including these
particulars. Namely, the taking of a ship neere to
Silley, laden with Ammunition from Saint Maloes,
and bound for Sir Ralph Hopton in Cornwall . . .
the taking of two Turks men of warre, being Argier
Pirates, neere unto our Coast . . .
London; Francis Wright; 1642. title; 8pp. small
8vo.

560. [Anon].
A most true Relation of the great and bloody Battell
fought upon Monday last neer the Coast of England,
by three of the Earl of Warwicks ships; namely, the
James, *George*, and *Grey-hound*, against Col. Goring
with 7 ships, who was coming to assist his Majesty
against the Parl. Declaring also the Wonderfull
Victory which they hath obtained against the said
Col. Goring, smiting three of his ships, and making
all the rest to fly . . .
London; L.Wright; December 8, 1642. title; [6]pp.
small 8vo.

561. [Anon].
An Ordinance of the Lords and Commons . . . for
the speedy setting forth of certaine ships (in all points
furnished for War) to prevent the bringing over of
Souldiers, Money, Ordnance, and other Ammunition from beyond the Sea, to assist the King, against
the Parliament in England.
London; John Wright; December 12, 1642. 7pp.
8vo.

562. [SMITH, *Captain* William].
Several letters of great importance, and good
successe. Lately obtained against the Fellowship of
Bristoll, by Captain William Smith, Captain of His
Majesties Ship called the *Swallow*, now in service for
the King and Parliament. And likewise the Lord
Admiralls design upon Bristoll, and the Navy
making ready there under the Command of Sir Iohn
Pennington.
London; Laurence Blaiklock; 1643. title; 7pp. small
8vo.

563. [Anon].
Good Newes from the Sea, being A True Relation
of the late Sea-Fight, between Captain William

Thomas, Captain of the 8th Whelp, now imployed
for the service of the King and Parliament, against
Captain Polhill, Captaine of the ship call'd the
Mayflower, Admirall of Falmouth, with the taking
of the said ship . . .
London; Laurence Blaiklock; June 26, 1643. title;
5pp. small 8vo.

564. [BATTEN, *Sir* William].
A True Relation of very good service done by the
Antilope and some other ships, under the Earle of
Warwick's command, at Barwicke, Newcastle, and
the Holy Island, the latter end of May, and
beginning of Iune last 1643.
Faithfully expressed in a letter from a Gentleman of
Quality, who was in the Service, to a friend of his
in London.
London; Elizabeth Purslow; July 4, 1643. [6]pp.;
black-letter text. 8vo.
   *The authorship of this pamphlet has been attributed to
Sir William Batten.*

565. [Anon].
A true relation of some notable passages faithfully
performed on the Coasts of England and Ireland, by
some of the ships under the command of the . . .
Earle of Warwick for the service of King and
Parliament. As it was certified by two Letters sent to
the Honourable Committee for the Navy.
London; Francis Leach; July 8, 1643. 6pp. 12mo.

566. [Anon].
A true Narration of the most observable passages, in
and at the late Seige of Plymouth, from the fifteenth
day of September 1643, untill the twenty fift [*sic*]
of December following . . .
London; John White; 1644. 20pp., fold. plate
depicting Plymouth during the siege. 8vo.

567. [Anon].
The true Relation of the Queenes departure from
Falmouth into the Brest in the West of France.
After whom our Lord Admirall sent all his Ships to
overtake her, who made above a hundred shot at the
Ship . . . but she having a Galley of Sixteen Oares,
it is thought that all the Ships in the World could
not overtake her . . .
London; Mathew Walbancke; July 22, 1644. title;
[6]pp. small 8vo.

568. [SMITH, *Captain* William].
A true and exact relation of the proceedings and
victorious successe of the ships in the Service of the
King and Parliament, which were sent for the
Reliefe of Ireland, under the command of Captaine
Swanley, Admirall: in the taking divers ships in
Milford Haven . . .

568. [SMITH, *Captain* William], *continued*
Written by Captain William Smith, Vice-Admirall
in the same voyage.
London; Richard Cotes; 1644. [12]pp. 8vo.

569. [WARWICK, *Earl of*].
The Earl of Warwick's surrender of the Ordinance
and Authoritie formerly granted by both Houses of
Parliament, for his being Lord High Admirall of
England, &c. Presented in the House of Peeres 10.
April 1645 . . .
London; Richard Best; 1645. title; 5pp. small 8vo.

570. [Anon].
A Letter sent to the Earl of Warwick, from the
captain, officers, and company of His Majesties Ship
called the *Lyon*, declaring their resolution for the
service of the Parliament, with the Earl of
Warwick's answer thereunto. 7 Julii 1648.
London; Edward Husband; July 8, 1648. title; 8pp.
small 8vo.

571. [BATTEN, *Sir* William].
A Declaration of Sir William Batten Late Vice-
Admirall for the Parliament, concerning his
departure from London, to His Highnesse the Prince
of Wales. For satisfaction of all honest sea-men, and
others whom it may concerne.
London; 1648. title: 5pp. small 8vo.

572. [Anon].
The humble Petition and Desires of the Com-
manders, Masters, Mariners, Younger Brothers and
Seamen of the shipping belonging to the River of
Thames . . . presented to . . . Parliament on Thurs-
day the 29 of June, 1648 . . . and their undertaking
for the timely reducing of the revolted ships, &c. . . .
London; Geo. Lindsey; 1648. title; 16pp. small 8vo.

573. [Anon].
A Declaration of the Lords and Commons assembled
in Parliament concerning the reducing of the late
Revolted Ships to the obedience of Parliament . . .
London; John Wright; 1648. 5pp. 8vo.

574. [Anon].
Vindiciae Carolinae. Being a true relation of His
Highnesse the Prince of Wales, His Voyage at Sea,
since he parted from Calais in France, July 20, until
this very day, 1648.
[1648]. 8pp. small 8vo.

575. [WARWICK, *Earl of*].
A Letter from . . . Robert Earl of Warwicke Lord
High Admirall of England, fully relating the condi-

tion of the Affaires at Sea. With a list of the number
of the Parliaments Ships, and the names of the
several commanders in them, now riding in the
Downes . . .
London; John Wright; 1648. title; 6pp. small 8vo.

576. [WARWICK, *Earl of*].
A Declaration of His Excellency Robert Earle of
Warwick, Lord High Admirall of England, concerning the uniting of the two Navies, and restoring
of the King's Majesty, the Prince of Wales, the Duke
of York . . . to their just rights and priviledges . . .
London; 1648. title; 6pp. small 8vo.

577. [CHARLES, *Prince of Wales; later King*
Charles II].
His Highnesse the Prince of Wales. His Answer to
the Earl of Warwicks Summons . . . also the Princes
coming to his Navy with 10000.L. for the Sea-men;
and the Hollanders joyning with the Prince.
[*n.p.*]; 1648. title; 6pp. small 8vo.

578. [CHARLES . . .]
The Declaration of his Highnesse Prince Charles . . .
concerning the grounds and ends of His present
Engagement upon the Fleet in the Downes . . .
[*n.p.*]; 1648. title; 6pp. small 8vo.

579. [WARWICK, *Earl of*].
Prince Charles. His Summons sent to the Lord
Admiral, to take down his Standard, and come
under his Highnesse Obedience. And the Earl of
Warwicks Answer, and resolution to bear it still for
the Parliament, against all opposition whatsoever . . .
London; R.Smithurst; 1648. title; 6pp. 8vo.

580. [WARWICK . . .].
A Declaration of the Earle of Warwick . . . in
answer of a scandalous Pamphlet, falsely reflecting
upon His Lordships Honour and Proceedings . . .
London; John Wright; 1648. title; 5pp. small 8vo.

581. [WARWICK . . .].
The Earl of Warwick's letter to the . . . Committee
of Lords and Commons at Derby-House, containing
a Narrative of his proceedings in pursuit of the
Revolted Ships, and their declining the Engagement:
and of the Conjunction of the Portsmouth Fleet
with the Lord Admirals . . .
London; Edward Husband; September 6, 1648.
title; 8pp. small 8vo.

582. [WARWICK . . .].
A perfect Remonstrance and Narrative of all the
proceedings of . . . Earl of Warwick, Lord High

582. [WARWICK . . .], *continued*
Admirall of England, in his late expedition with the
Parliament Navy, in order to the reducing of the
Revolted Ships, commanded by His Highnesse,
Charles Prince of Wales . . . An exact Journall . . .
from the 29 of August, to the 25 of December,
1648.
London; Henry Crisp; [1649]. title; [8]pp. small
8vo.

583. [Anon].
A Letter from the Navy with the Earl of Warwick,
Lord Admirall: From Hellevoyt Sluice, November.
24. 1648. Being a Narrative of his Proceedings, in
reducing the Revolted Ships with the Prince . . .
London; Lawrence Blaiklock; 1648. title; 8pp.
small 8vo.

584. [RUPERT, *Prince*].
The Declaration of His Highnesse Prince Rupert,
Lord High Admirall of all the Navy Royall . . .
likewise His Highnesses resolution and intention;
together with the rest of the officers of the Navy
Royall. Touching the Death of the late King, the
illegall pretended Power of Parliament. And their
indeavours to Inthrone the now King Charles the
Second . . . Signed by the Princes owne hand aboard
the Navy Royall, now Riding an Anchor upon the
Downes, the 19th of March, 1649.
'n.p.]; 1649. title; 8pp. small 8vo.

585. [Anon].
Joyfull Newes from the Princes Fleet at Sea; con-
taining a Narrative of the Several Fights and
Ingagements, between the two Navies, the Bristoll
Men of War, and the London and Yarmouth
Marchants, since the first of Aprill 1649 . . .
London; R.Williamson; April 12, 1649. title; 6pp.,
small 8vo.

iii. Events and operations elsewhere, 1625–1649

586. BARNBY, Henry.
The Algerian attack on Baltimore, 1631.
The Mariner's Mirror, vol.lvi (February 1970),
pp.27–31.

587. BOER, *Dr.* Michael G.de.
De Armada van 1639.
Groningen; P.Noordhoff; 1911. 76pp., pls. 8vo.
   *An important study of the Spanish Armada of 1639
and the events leading up to its destruction by the Dutch*

*Fleet under Tromp in the Battle of the Downs, 21
October 1639. The folding frontispiece comprises a
reproduction of A. Verwer's fine panoramic engraving of
the action: 'Zeeschlach in Duyns door Marten Harperts.
Tromp den 21 October Anno 1639.'*
   See also entries nos. 588, 596, 599, 601.

588. BOXER, *Professor* C.R. [*translator & editor*].
The Journal of Maarten Harpertszoon Tromp anno
1639.
Cambridge; University Press; 1930. xviii; 237pp.
8vo.
*The scholarly introduction describes: the sources for the
study of the campaign of 1639; the preparation of
Oquendo's Armada in La Coruña; Tromp's cruise in the
Narrow Seas; the actions of September 16 & 18 and
Oquendo's final destruction in The Downs three days
later.*

589. BOXER . . .
The surprisal of Goa's Bar.
The Mariner's Mirror, vol.xvi (January 1930), pp.5–
17; illustr.
   *An action between Dutch & Portuguese squadrons off
Goa, 30 September 1639.*

590. BOXER . . .
The action between Pater and Oquendo, 12
September 1631.
The Mariner's Mirror, vol.xlv (August 1959), pp.179–
199.
   *Between Spanish and Dutch fleets off Pernambuco,
Brazil.*

591. BRUUN, Christian.
Slaget paa Kolberger Heide den 1 Juli 1644 og de
derefter følgende begiven-heider. . . .
Copenhagen; F.Hegel; 1879. 239pp., 1 chart. 8vo.
   *About the indecisive battle fought in Kiel Bay during
the Swedish–Danish War of 1643–5, in the course of
which King Christian IV of Denmark lost an eye.*

592. FOSTER, William.
The Anglo-Dutch attack on Bombay in 1626.
Indian Antiquary, vol.xxxii (1903), pp.47–8.

593. HANNAY, David.
Digby and Scanderoon.
Blackwood's Magazine, vol.ccxxii (1927), pp.535–549.
   *In 1628, Sir Kenelm Digby led a privateering
expedition into the Eastern Mediterranean, which
culminated in the defeat of a Franco–Venetian squadron
in Scanderoon (the modern Iskenderun or Alexandretta)
harbour.*

594. LIND, H.D.
Om King Christian den Fjerdes Orlogsflaaden.
Offprint, repr. from *Tidsskrift for Søvaesen* (1890),
pp.315–336; 409–452. charts. 8vo.
   *This is about the Danish Fleet under King Christian V
(1628–1643).*

595. NABER, S.P.L'Honoré. [*editor*].
Het Journaal van den Lieutenant-Admiraal . . .
Tromp, gehouden aan boord van's landschip *Amelia*
in den jare 1639 . . .
Utrecht; Kennink & Zoon; 1931. 320pp., charts &
fleet lists. 8vo.

596. [PENNINGTON, *Admiral Sir* John (1568–
1646), *et alia.*]
Relation by Pennington and others of the fight in
the Downs, 1639.
In: *Calendar of State Papers: Domestic – Charles I.*
vol.cxxx, p.74.

597. PIREY, B.de.
La bataille de galères de Gênes, 1er Septembre 1638.
La Revue Maritime, vol.xcix (March 1928), pp.285–
318.

598. STRACHAN, Michael.
Sampson's fight with Maltese galleys, 1628.
The Mariner's Mirror, vol.lv (August 1969), pp.281–9.
   Off Valletta on 8 August.

599. WARNSINCK, J.C.M.
Tromp en de slaag op de reede van Duins, September
1639.
Marineblad (1939), pp.1177–1202.

600. WARNSINCK . . .
Een mislukte aanslag op Nederlandsch Brazilie,
1639–40.
De Gids (February 1940), pp.1–33.
   '*An account of the failure of a combined Hispano–
Portuguese armada of 77 sail to take the Dutch stronghold
of Recife de Pernambuco and its decisive defeat in a four-
days battle off the eastern point of Brazil by a greatly
inferior Dutch force, 15–18 January 1640*'.

601. [WHITE, Peter].
A memorable Sea-Fight penned and preserved by
Peter White. One of the IIII Masters of Attend in
Englands Navie . . . or, a Narrative of all the
Principall Passages which were Trans-acted in the
Downes, in the Year, 1639. Between Antonio de
Oquendo, Admirall of the Spanish Armado, and
Martin van Tromp, Admirall for the States of
Holland . . .
London; T.Forcet; September 1649. 53pp., title in
black & red. 8vo.

III. The Commonwealth, 1649–1660, including the First Dutch War

602. ANDERSON, *Dr.* R.C.
The operations of the English Fleet, 1648–1652.
English Historical Review, vol.xxxi (1916), pp.406–
428.
   *There is an appendix containing a list of ships taken
during the period.*

603. ANDERSON . . .
Naval operations in the Mediterranean during the
Anglo-Dutch War of 1652–4.
RUSIJ. (May 1917).

604. ANDERSON . . .
The Royalists at Sea in 1650. *The Mariner's Mirror*,
vol.xvii (April 1931), pp.135–168.
The Royalists at Sea in 1651–3. *The Mariner's Mirror*,
vol.xxi (January 1935), pp.61–90.

605. ANDERSON . . .
English fleet-lists in the First Dutch War.
The Mariner's Mirror, vol.xxiv (October 1938),
pp.429–450.

606. ANDERSON . . .
The unfortunate voyage of the *San Carlo*.
The Mariner's Mirror, vol.xxxii (January 1946),
pp.50–54.
   The SAN CARLO *was a Venetian first-rate, commanded
by Admiral Angelo Emo, which was wrecked off the
Burlings in November 1658.*

607. ANDERSON . . .
The English Fleet at the Battle of Portland [18–20
February, 1652].
The Mariner's Mirror, vol.xxxix (August 1953),
pp.171–177.

608. ANDERSON . . .
The ships of the three Dutch Wars.
The Mariner's Mirror, vol.xli (February 1955),
pp.67–68.

609. ANDERSON . . .
The First Dutch War in the Mediterranean.
The Mariner's Mirror, vol.xlix (November 1963),
pp.241–265.

610. ANDERSON . . .
Denmark and the First Anglo–Dutch War.
The Mariner's Mirror, vol.liii (February 1967),
pp.55–62.

611. BALLHAUSEN, *Dr.* P.Carl.
Der Erste Englisch-Holländische Seekrieg, 1652–
1654, sowie der Schwedisch-Holländische Seekrieg,
1658–1659.
The Hague; Martinus Nijhoff; 1923. 804pp., 23
charts; 4 plans. 8vo.
*A key work. Includes chapters on: [a]. Dutch strategy,
ordnance and personnel; Martin Tromp's summer cruise,
1652; the battles of Kentish Knock, Dungeness, Portland, The Gabbard & Scheveningen; de Witt's cruise
and the concluding operations at sea. [b]. The battle of
Øresund (29 October 1658); the blockade of Landskrona
and the arrival of the English fleet.*

612. BARRINGTON, Francis.
Letters relating to the Jamaica expedition, 1655.
In: HISTORICAL MANUSCRIPTS
COMMISSION Reports, vol.vii (1879).

613. [BLAKE, *Admiral* Robert (1599–1657).].
The Letters of Robert Blake, together with
supplementary documents. Edited by the Reverend
J.R.Powell.
London; Navy Records Society series, vol.lxxvi;
1937. 501pp. frontis. 8vo.

614. BOXER, *Professor* C.R.
Naval actions between the Portuguese and Dutch in
India, 1654.
The Mariner's Mirror, vol.xiv (July 1928), pp.242–
258; 1 map.
   See also Professor Boxer's recent study: The Dutch
Seaborne Empire (Hutchinson; 1965).

615. BOXER . . .
Blake and the Brazil fleets in 1650.
The Mariner's Mirror, vol.xxxvi (July 1950), pp.212–
228.

616. BOXER . . .
The Tromps and the Anglo–Dutch Wars, 1652–
1674.
History Today, vol.iii (1953), pp.836–845.

**617. CALENDAR OF STATE PAPERS,
DOMESTIC – COMMONWEALTH.**
13 volumes, covering the period February 1649–
May 1660.
London; HMSO; 1875–1886. [*repr.* 1965].

*Contain many naval references, of which the following
is only a selection:*
*In: vol.i. [February 1649–February 1650]. Letters to the
Commissioners of the Fleet & Navy Commissioners;
Admiralty and Navy Committee; Dutch and Spanish
ships taken by the Parliamentary Fleet; Prince Rupert's
fleet in the Mediterranean; prizes; Cromwell's con-
sultations with the Navy Commissioners on the readiness
of the Fleet.*

*vol.ii. [February–December 1650.]. Orders of the Navy
Committee; correspondence of Admirals and Generals-at-
Sea; Edward Popham, Robert Blake, Richard Deane;
naval administration.*

*vol.iii. [1651]. Orders of the Navy Committee; papers
relating to Ayscue, Popham, Deane & Blake; ships
adhering to Charles II; naval administration.*

*vol.iv. [1651–2]. Opening of the First Dutch War; the
engagement between Blake and Tromp, 19 May, 1652;
seizure of Dutch vessels in English ports; impressment;
survey of ships fit for service; operations of Blake and
Tromp in the Channel; Badiley's action against the
Dutch off Leghorn.*

*vol.v. [1652–3]. Naval battles of 1652/3, including The
Downs, Dover, Three Days' Battle (Portland); the death
of Deane; many references to Admiralty correspondence
& orders; letters & papers relating to the Navy.*

*vol.vi. [1653–4]. Continuation of the War; Blake and
Monk versus Tromp, 29/31 July, 1653; Royalist
privateers; seamen's grievances; Admiral Bourne; letters
& papers relating to the Navy.*

*vol.vii. [March–December 1654]. Conclusion of the
Dutch War; Admiralty & Navy Commissioners;
coastal protection and convoys for troops; Admiralty
Court; papers of Admirals Blake, Penn, Lawson,
Badiley, Dakins, Goodson and Desborough.*

*vol.viii. [1655]. Penn in the West Indies and the
capture of Jamaica; Blake's operations against
Mediterranean pirates; naval precautions against Royalist
conspiracies.*

*vol.ix. [1655–6]. Discontent in Commonwealth Fleet;
naval dispute with Spain and outbreak of war; Navy
accounts & letters and papers relating to the Navy.*

vol.x. [1656–7]. Letters and papers relating to the Navy.

*vol.xi. [1657–8]. Naval expenses; relations with the
Dutch; the Anglo–French capture of Mardike; death of
Admiral Blake, August 1657; letters and papers relating
to the Navy.*

*vol.xii. [1658–9]. Cases examined before Admiralty
Commissioners; movements of the Fleet; letters and
papers relating to the Navy.*

*vol.xiii. [July 1659–May 1660]. Admiralty and Navy
Commissioners; Rear-Admiral John Bourne and
Commissioner Nehemiah Bourne.*

618. CLARENDON STATE PAPERS.
vols.ii [February 1649–December 1654] – iv [1657–60].
Oxford; Clarendon Press; 1869–1932. 8vo.
Contain a vast amount of material on naval affairs.
The following short extract from the contents of volume
ii illustrates its nature:
'. . . *page 178. Dutch close ports to Rupert, February*
1653. p.180. Dutch destroy 24 Parliament ships,
March. pp.184–5. Rupert in the Loire; Tromp on the
recent battle; English men of war at Leghorn; state of the
Fleet. p.191. Dutch capture Newcastle colliers. . . .'

619. CLARK, *Professor* G.N.
The Navigation Act of 1651.
History, vol.vii (1923).

620. CLOWES, *Sir* William Laird, *et alia.*
The Royal Navy. A History from the earliest times
to the present. . . .
Volume ii.
London; Sampson Low, Marston; 1898. 593pp.,
pls. & tables. 4to.
Chapters xx and xxi (The Civil & Military History
of the Navy, 1649–1660), pp.94–218, are relevant.

621. COLENBRANDER, *Dr.* H.T.
Bescheiden uit vreemde archiven omtrent de Groote
Nederlandsche Zeeoorlogen, 1652–1676.
The Hague; Nijhoff; 1919. 2 volumes. 618; 439pp.;
battle-plans. 4to.
The standard Dutch authority on the Anglo–Dutch Wars,
which reproduces much original source-material.

622. CORBETT, *Professor* Julian S.
England in the Mediterranean. A study of the rise
and influence of British power within the Straits,
1603–1713.
London; Longmans; 1904. 2 vols. 342; 351pp.;
maps. 8vo.
For this period, there are important chapters in
volume i.: 'xii. The New Navy; xiii. The campaign
against Rupert; xiv. The first Mediterranean Squadron.
xv. The Dutch War within the Straits. xvi. Cromwell
and the Mediterranean. xvii. Blake and the Turkish Sea
power. xviii. Cromwell's War with Spain.'

623. CURTIS, C.D.
The presence of Tromp during Blake's reduction of
the Scilly Isles in 1651.
The Mariner's Mirror, vol.xx (January 1934), pp.50–66.

624. CURTIS . . .
Blake and Vendôme.
The Mariner's Mirror, vol.xxi (January 1935), pp.56–60.

Being an account of Blake's attack on the French
squadron under Vendôme off Calais, 7 September 1652.

625. DALTON, Charles.
The Navy under Cromwell; its strength and cost.
RUSIJ, vol.xliv (1900), p.1181, ff.

626. DEWAR, *Captain* A.C.
Blake's last campaign, 1656–7.
United Service Magazine, vol.clxiv (1911), pp.117–128.

627. DEWAR . . .
The naval administration of the Interregnum.
The Mariner's Mirror, vol.xii (October 1926), pp.406–430.

628. ELIAS, Johan E.
Het voorspel van den Eersten Engelschen Oorlog.
The Hague; Martinus Nijhoff; 1920. 2 vols. in one:
185; 235pp., charts, 8vo.
Examines the Anglo–Dutch conflict: (a) in Europe; (b)
overseas (the colonial struggles in the East and West
Indies, Brazil and West Africa).

629. FIRTH, *Professor* Charles H.
Blake and the battle of Santa Cruz. [20 April 1657].
English Historical Review, vol.xx (April 1905),
pp.228–250.
See also volume I of the author's: Last years of the
Protectorate. (1909).

630. FIRTH . . .
The *Hampshire* frigate. [1653].
The Mariner's Mirror, vol.xii (April 1926), pp.342–5.

631. FIRTH . . .
Sailors of the Civil War, the Commonwealth and
the Protectorate.
The Mariner's Mirror, vol.xii (July 1926), pp.237–259.

632. FORTESCUE, J.W.
The expedition to the West Indies, 1655.
Macmillans Magazine, vol.lxix (1893–4).

633. FOSTER, William.
The acquisition of St Helena. [1658–9].
English Historical Review, vol.xxxiv (1919), pp.281–9.

634. GARDINER, Samuel Rawson.
History of the Commonwealth and Protectorate,
1649–1660.
London; Longmans; 1894–1901. 3 vols. 8vo.
With much detailed information, although the whole
work was not completed, stopping at the year 1656. Only

634. GARDINER, *continued*
the first chapter of the projected volume iv was ready for
publication at the time of the author's death.
　　Relevant chapters in vols.i–iii include: The seapower
of the Commonwealth, 1650–1; The first months of the
Dutch War; the command of the Channel; the struggle
for the North Sea (April 1652–October 1653);
Hispaniola and Jamaica (the expedition of Penn and
Venables, 1654–5); and the breach with Spain (Blake in
the Mediterranean, 1654–5).

635. GARDINER . . . *and* ATKINSON, C.T.
[*editors*].
Letters and papers relating to the First Dutch War.
Edited by S.R.Gardiner and C.T.Atkinson.
London; Navy Records Society series, vols.xiii,
xvii, xxx, xxxvii, xli & lxvi; 1898–1930. 6 vols. 8vo.
　　A fundamental source for the study of the First Dutch
War. Gardiner edited the first two volumes and part of
the third; Atkinson the remainder.

636. GARDINER . . .
Alleged fighting in line in the First Dutch War.
English Historical Review, vol.xiii (1898), p.533,ff.

637. GARDINER . . .
Blake at Leghorn [4 March 1653].
English Historical Review, vol.xiv (1899), pp.109–111.

638. GRAEFE, Friedrich.
Betrachtungen über den ersten Englisch–Holländis-
chen Kriegen (1652 bis 1654).
Marine Rundschau, vol.xxii (1911), pp.439–451;
569–581.
and:
Zur strategie des erstes Englisch–Holländischen
Krieges.
Marine Rundschau, vol.xli (1936), pp.421–9.

639. HISTORICAL MANUSCRIPTS
COMMISSION:
[a]. LEYBOURNE-POPHAM MANUSCRIPTS.
London; HMSO; 1899.
　　Pp.9–101 contain correspondence of Colonel Edward
Popham, General-at-Sea for the Commonwealth, 1648–
1651.
[b]. PORTLAND MANUSCRIPTS.
London; HMSO; 1891–2.
　　Vols.i and ii contain a number of naval references for
the period – including the journals of Sir William Penn,
1650–2; letters from Cromwell to Penn, 1653–5; and
other Penn documents.

640. [HOLLAND, John.[*fl.* 1638–1659].]
Two Discourses of the Navy, 1638 and 1659, by
John Holland . . .

Edited by J.R.Tanner.
London; Navy Records Society series, vol.vii.; 1896.
lxxxiii; 419pp. 8vo.

641. JAMES, G.F.
Soldiers and sea service; military elements among
the crews during the Anglo–Dutch War, 1652–4.
Soc. Army Hist. Res. Journal, vol.xiv (1935), pp.238–
240.

642. LIND, H.D.
Kong Kristian den Tredjes Sømagt. Det Danske-
Norske Søvaernshistorie, 1648–1670.
Odense; Milo'ske Boghandel; 1896. 324pp.; 8vo.

643. OPPENHEIM, Michael.
The Navy of the Commonwealth, 1649–1660.
English Historical Review, vol.xi (1896), pp.20–81.
　　An important study.

644. PEYSTER, J.Watts de.
The Battle of the Sound or Baltic; fought October
30th (o.s.), between the victorious Hollanders under
. . . Opdam and the Swedes commanded by . . .
Wrangel.
Poughkeepsie; Platt & Schram; 1858. 86pp. 8vo.

645. POWELL, *Reverend* John Rowland.
Blake's reduction of the Scilly Isles in 1651.
The Mariner's Mirror, vol.xvii (July 1931), pp.205–
222; 1 map.

646. POWELL . . .
Blake's arrival at Lisbon [30 March, 1649].
The Mariner's Mirror, vol.xvii. (October 1931),
pp.399–400.

647. POWELL . . .
Blake's reduction of Jersey in 1651.
The Mariner's Mirror, vol.xviii (January 1932),
pp.64–80; 1 map.

648. POWELL . . . [*editor*].
The Letters of Robert Blake . . .
Edited by J.R.Powell.
London; Navy Records Society series, vol.lxxvi;
1937. 501pp. 8vo.
　　See also the author's important recent biography:
'*Robert Blake, General at Sea.*' (Collins; 1973).

649. POWELL . . . [*editor*].
The Journal of John Weale, 1654–1656.
Edited by the Rev. J.R.Powell.
In: *The Naval Miscellany*, vol.iv.
London; Navy Records Society series, vol.xcii;
1952. 8vo.

650. POWELL . . .
Blake's capture of the French fleet before Calais, on 4 September 1652.
The Mariner's Mirror, vol.xlviii (May 1962), pp.192–207.

651. POWELL . . .
The expedition of Blake and Mountagu in 1655.
The Mariner's Mirror, vol.lii (November 1966), pp.341–369; figs.

652. POWELL . . .
Talbot and the divisions of the Fleet in 1666.
The Mariner's Mirror, vol.liii (May 1967), p.136.

653. POWELL . . .
Sir George Ayscue's capture of Barbados in 1651.
The Mariner's Mirror, vol.lix (August 1973), pp.281–280; 1 sketch.

654. ROBERTS, Michael.
Cromwell and the Baltic.
English Historical Review, vol.lxxvi (1961), pp.402–446.

655. ROBINSON, Gregory.
Wounded sailors and soldiers in London during the First Dutch War.
History Today, vol.xvi (1966), pp.38–44; illustr.

656. ROWBOTHAM, *Commander* W.B.
Blake and de Ruyter.
RUSIJ, vol.cii (November 1957), p.571.

657. SCHELVEN, A.A.van.
Het begin van den slag bij Dover, 29 Mai 1652.
Bijdr. Mededelingen. Hist. Gen. [Utrecht], vol.xlvii (1926), pp.235–248.
   An account of the opening engagement of the First Dutch War, between squadrons under Tromp and Blake, with Bourne in support.

658. [STAYNER, *Sir* Richard, *d.*1662].
A narrative of the battle of Santa Cruz [20 April 1657], written by Sir Richard Stayner, rear-admiral of the fleet.
Edited by C.H.Firth.
In: *The Naval Miscellany*, vol.ii, pp.[123]–136.
London; Navy Records Society; 1912. 8vo.

659. TANNER, *Dr.* J.R.
The Navy of the Commonwealth and the First Dutch War (1652–4).
In: *Cambridge Modern History* (Cambridge; 1906),

vol.4: 'The Thirty Years War', chapter xvi, pp.459–485.
   Invaluable introduction to the subject, with comments on: the administration of the Navy; Rupert at Kinsale and Lisbon and the final destruction of his fleet; Blake & Tromp in the North Sea and the sea-battles of the First Dutch War; Blake in the Mediterranean and at Santa Cruz; the Navy prior to the Restoration.

660. [THURLOE, John. (1616–1668)].
A Collection of the State Papers of John Thurloe, Esq., Secretary to the Council of State and the two Protectors Oliver and Richard Cromwell: to which is prefixed the life of Mr Thurloe . . .
London; 1742. 7 volumes. folio.

661. [VENABLES, Robert. (1612?–1687).]
Narrative; with appendix of papers relative to the expedition to the West Indies and the conquest of Jamaica, 1654–5.
Edited by Professor C.H.Firth.
Camden Society Misc., n.s., vol.lx. (1900).

662. WARD, M.F.B.
The strategy of the Anglo–Dutch Wars of the seventeenth century.
Naval Review, vol.xviii (1930), pp.289. & 431.

663. WARNER, Oliver.
Elsinore and the Danish Sound dues.
History Today, vol.xvii (1967), pp.619–625.

664. WARNSINCK, J.C.M.
Een Nederlandsche geschiedenis van den Eersten Engelschen Oorlog.
Gids, vol.xcv (1931), pp.259–271.

665. WARNSINCK . . .
Vlootroogden en Zeeslagen.
Amsterdam; Van Kampen & Zoon; 1940–4. 311pp. 8vo.
   Includes two essays relevant to the period: a. De laatste tocht van Wassenaer van Obdam. [= *the Battle of Lowestoft, June 1665.*]. *b. Een Nederlander Eskader in de Middelandsche Zee, 1651–3.* [= *operations in the Mediterranean under the Dutch Admirals Cornelis Tromp, van Galen, de Boer and Joris van Cats.*].

666. WRIGHT, Irene A. [*editor & translator*].
An account of what happened in the island of Jamaica from May 20 of the year 1655, when the English laid siege to it, up to July 3 of the year 1656, by Capitan Julian de Castilla.
Translated and edited by Irene A.Wright.
Camden Miscellany, vol.xii (1923).

667. WRIGHT . . .
The English conquest of Jamaica, 1655–6.
Camden Miscellany, vol.xiii (1924).

668. WRIGHT . . .
Spanish narratives of the English attack on San
Domingo, 1655.
Camden Miscellany, vol.xiv (1926).

669. WRIGHT . . .
The Spanish resistance to the English occupation of
Jamaica, 1655–1660.
RHS Trans., 4th series, vol.xiii (1930).

670. [Anonymous].
Prince Ruperts Declaration to the King of Portugall
. . . with a Relation of what passed between the two
Fleets on the River of Lisburne. Sent up in a letter
from Captain Thorowgood Captain of the Admirall.
London; Geo. Whittington; 1650. Pamphlet. title;
14pp. small 8vo.

671. [Anonymous].
Newes from Sea, concerning Prince Rupert, Capt.
Pluncket, Capt. Munckel, and others: with some
Transactions betwixt the King of Portingal, and
them. Together with the taking of certain Ships . . .
London; 'Printed for J.C. . . .'; 1650. Pamphlet.
title; 6pp. small 8vo.

672. [Anonymous].
The Answer of the Parliament of the Common-
wealth of England . . . As also a Narrative of the
late Engagement between the English Fleet under
the command of General Blake; and the Holland
Fleet under the command of Lieutenant Admiral
Trump . . .
London; John Field; 1652. Pamphlet. 39pp. 8vo.
The narrative is of the action off Dover, 29 May 1652.

673. [Anonymous].
Waarachtigschrijvens . . . aan-gaande den Zee-slag,
tusschen den Hollandschen Vice-Admiraal Cornelisz.
de Wit: ende den Engelschen Admiral Blake, den 8.
en 9. October 1652.
Rotterdam; Pieter Volbergen; 1652. [10]pp.; black-
letter text. 8vo.
    This is about the Battle of Kentish Knock [28/29
September, 8/9 October, 1652], in which Blake
defeated de Witt.

674. [Anonymous].
The Common-Wealths Great Ship commonly called
the Soveraigne of the Seas, built in the yeare 1637.
With a true and exact dimension of her bulk and
burden . . .

. . . With all the fights wee have had with the
Hollander, since the engagement of Lieutenant-
Admirall Tromp neare Dover against . . . Generall
Blake . . .
London; Thos. Jenner; 1653. 32pp., fold. engr. pls.;
small 4to.

675. [Anonymous].
A true and sad relation of the burning, sinking and
blowing up of the English ships in the River of
Thames, on Thursday and Fryday last . . . likewise
the discovery of a desperate and dangerous
Conspiracie upon the River; and the apprehending
of a gentleman on Fryday night last, with divers
Grenadoes and Fire-Works.
London; G.Horton; 1654. Pamphlet. title; 8pp.,
small 8vo.

676. [Anonymous].
Britain's Triumphs, or, a Brief History of the
Warres and other State-Affairs of Great Britain.
From the death of the late King, to the third year of
the government of the Lord Protector.
London; Edward Farnham; 1656. 184pp. 12mo.

677. [Anonymous].
De Beroerde Oceann, of twee-jaarige Zee-daaden
der Vereenigde Nederlanders en Engelsche . . .
Amsterdam; G.J.Valckenier; 1656. engr. & printed
titles; 243pp.; engr. pls. 12mo.
    An important contemporary Dutch source for the naval
events of the First Dutch War.

678. [Anonymous].
A Further Narrative of the passage of these times in
the Common-Wealth of England . . . of publick
thanksgiving . . . to this Nation in the island of
Teneriffe under Generall Blake, and giving them
great success against the Ships of the King of Spain,
16 foundered and not one of ours lost . . . . . .
[London]; Thos. Jenner; [1657]. 62pp.; engr. pls.
8vo.
    Pages 25–28, with an accompanying plate, describe
Blake's victory at Santa Cruz on 20 April, 1657.

679. [Anonymous].
A Great and Bloudy Fight at Sea: Between five Men
of War belonging to the Parliament of England and
a squadron of the Princes Fleet; wherein is con-
tained, the full particulars, and manner of the said
Fight; the number of ships that were sunk and taken,
together with divers prisoners, great store of Match
and Bullet, and 40 pieces of Ordnance, and the rest
of the Fleet quite dispersed and scattered . . .
[Bristol]; Theodore Jennings; 9 February 1659.
Pamphlet. [10]pp. small 8vo.

679. [Anonymous], *continued*
  The action took place in the Irish Sea off Dublin on 7 February – when a Commonwealth squadron under Captain Peacock, while searching for pirates, sighted by chance the Royalist warships.

680. [Anonymous].
A List of All the Ships and Frigots of England, with their number of men, guns, and of what rates. Also, the names of all the Commanders in their expedition in May 1653. against the Dutch . . . at that memorable fight on the 2d and 3d of June, 1653 . . .
London; M.Simmons; 1660. Pamphlet. [10]pp., 8vo.
  The battle referred to was that of The Gabbard or North Foreland.

681. [Anonymous].
Slaget i Öresund, 1658.
repr. from: Tidskrift i Sjöväsendet. (1900), pp.115–127.
  An account of the Battle of The Sound (29 October, 1658), between the Dutch and the Swedes, which includes lists of the opposing fleets.

IV. From the Restoration to the Revolution, 1660–1688

i. Charles II and the Pepysian Navy

682. [ALLIN, *Admiral Sir* Thomas (1612–1685)].
The Journals of Sir Thomas Allin, 1660–1678.
Edited by R.C.Anderson.
London; Navy Records Society series, vols.lxxix & lxxx; 1939–1940. 2 vols. 8vo.
  Volume i covers the period 1660–1666; ii, 1667–1678.

683. CALENDAR OF STATE PAPERS, DOMESTIC – Charles II.
vols.i (1660–1661) – xxvii (1684–1685) *and* xxviii (Addenda).
London; HMSO; 1860–1939. 28 vols. 4to.
  Invaluable sources for material about naval administration and events of the period. Inter alia, the main topics described include the following:

  vols.i–ii.: 1660–1662. Navy Commissioners' correspondence; Pepys' correspondence; English occupation of Dunkirk; Sir John Lawson.

  vol.iii.: 1663–4. Pett family; Pepys' & Navy Commissioners' correspondence; Fleet attending the King home.

  vol.iv.: 1664–5. Dispositions of the Fleet; Pepys' & Commissioners' correspondence.

  vol.v.: 1665–6. Correspondence as above; Dutch Fleet on the coast and the engagements of the Fleet including the Four Days' Battle.

  vol.vi.: 1666–7. Correspondence as above; the attack on the Vlie & Schelling.

  vol.vii.: 1667. Correspondence as above; the Naval War with the Dutch.

  vol.viii.: November 1667–September 1668. King's visit to the Downs & Portsmouth, June 1668; shipbuilding; the problem of ships sunk in the Medway; complaints against naval officers.

  vol.ix.: October 1668–December 1669. Wrecks in the Medway (contd.); correspondence as above; dockyards, especially Deptford.

  vol.x.: 1670. Navy Board; Pepys; Admiralty petitions; dockyards.

  vol.xi.: January–November 1671. King's visit to Chatham & Sheerness, May 1671; Naval finance; Sprague's victory in Bugia Bay, May 1671; shipbuilding; timber for the Navy; dispute with Holland over saluting the flag.

683. STATE PAPERS, DOMESTIC, *continued*
vol.xii.: December 1671–May 1672. The Third Dutch War (many references); Commissioners' enquiry into Pett's conduct at Chatham; operations against the Algerines.

vol.xiii.: May–September 1672. Third Dutch War; Pepys' & Navy Commissioners' correspondence.

vol.xiv.: October 1672–February 1673. Third Dutch War; administration; Navy Office burnt down.

vol.xv.: March–October 1673. Third Dutch War, incl. letters from Prince Rupert with the Fleet on the Summer campaign; capture and recovery of St Helena (January–May); resignation of Duke of York as Lord High Admiral; Scottish privateers.

vol.xvi.: November 1673–February 1675. Correspondence of Admiralty and Navy Commissioners; Lists of Ships in the Downs; Dover harbour; Captain Morgan in Jamaica.

vol.xvii.: March 1675–February 1676. Royal yachts & the King's visit to Portsmouth to see the ROYAL JAMES; *privateering; flag salute disputes; operations against Algerines; John Flamsteed and Greenwich Observatory.*

vol.xviii.: March 1676–February 1677. French & Dutch outrages on English shipping; Narbrough at Tripoli; the Franco–Dutch action off Augusta (22 April) & the death of de Ruyter.

vol.xix.: March 1677–February 1678. King's visits to Sheerness, Dover, Portsmouth and Plymouth; operations against the Algerines; Danes' defeat of the Swedish fleet at Kjöge Bight (1 July).

vol.xx.: March–December 1678. French and Dutch fleets in the Mediterranean; d'Estrées in the West Indies; relations with Algiers.

vol.xxi.: January 1679–August 1680. Portsmouth and the Admiralty; imprisonment of Sir Anthony Deane and Pepys.

vol.xxii.: September 1680–December 1681. Admiralty correspondence; King's visit to Lord Berkeley's ship the TIGER *at Woolwich.; Duquesne's operations against Tripoli.*

vol.xxiii.: 1682. Admiralty Commissioners; Act for regulating the Navy.

vol.xxiv.: January–June 1683. Admiralty Commissioners; report on supply of clothes to the Navy.

vol.xxv.: July–September 1683. Royal yachts; Greenwich Hospital.

vol.xxvi.: October 1683–April 1684. Admiralty correspondence; Lord Vaughan succeeds Brouncker as Commissioner of Admiralty.

vol.xxvii.: May 1684–February 1685. Pepys as Secretary of the Admiralty; Newfoundland convoys; Captain Greenvile Collins' coastal surveys.

vol.xxviii.: Addenda-1660–1685. Navy Board papers (1660–1673); prize commissioners (1664–6); the defences of the Medway; privateering; instructions to Sir Thomas Allin, in command of the Straits Fleet, 1668.

684. CLARENDON STATE PAPERS.
Edited by F.J.Routledge.
Volume v: 1 May 1660–March 1726.
Oxford; Clarendon Press; 1970. 8vo.
Contains many references to this period.

685. DIGGES, Thomas.
Englands Defence. A treatise concerning Invasion: or, a brief discourse on what orders were best for repulsing of Foreign Forces, if at any time they should invade us by Sea in Kent, or elsewhere . . . By Thomas Digges, Esq.; Muster-Master General of all His Majesty's Forces in the Low-Countries . . . London; F.Haley; 1680. 16pp. 4to.

686. [G., T.P.].
The Royal Navy of 1660.
Naval Review, vol.xxxix (1950), pp.297-9.

687. HANSEN, Harold A.[*editor*].
His Majestie's Present Fleet, 1672.
The Mariner's Mirror, vol.xxxiv (April 1948), pp. 129-131.
Being the postscript to a letter of 29 March 1672, written by Markus Gjøe, the Danish envoy in London, to King Christian IV of Denmark.

688. [MOUNTAGU, Edward, *1st Earl of Sandwich (1625–1672).*]
The Journal of Edward Mountagu, 1st Earl of Sandwich, admiral and general-at-sea, 1659–1665.
Edited by R.C.Anderson.
London; Navy Records Society series, vol.lxiv.; 1929. 329pp. 8vo.

689. OLLARD, Richard L.
Man of War: Sir Robert Holmes and the Restoration Navy.
London; Hodder & Stoughton; 1969. 240pp.; pls. 8vo.
See also the author's recent biography: Pepys. (Hodder; 1974).

690. PENN, Granville.
Memorials of the professional life and times of Sir William Penn, Knt., Admiral and General of the Fleet during the Interregnum; Admiral and Commissioner of the Admiralty and Navy after the Restoration. From 1644 to 1670.
London; James Duncan; 1833. 2 vols. 580; 619pp.; pls. 8vo.

691. PEPYS, Samuel. (1633–1703).
Memoires relating to the State of the Royal Navy
of England, for ten years, determin'd December
1688.
London; [1690]. [ii]; 214 + 18pp.; engr. frontis.,
fold. table. 8vo.
  Includes a ' . . . General list of all His Majesty's ships
and vessels in sea service, with their rates, commanders,
lieutenants, men and stations, 1688.'
  Another edition of this work, also in the Library, was
published in 1690, ' . . . printed for Ben. [jamin]
Griffin . . .'.

692. [PEPYS . . .].
Pepys' Memoires of the Royal Navy, 1679–1688.
Edited by J.R.Tanner . . .
[Oxford]; Clarendon Press; 1906. xviii; 131pp.,
fold. table. 8vo.

693. [PEPYS . . .].
Samuel Pepys's Naval Minutes.
Edited by J.R.Tanner.
London; Navy Records Society series, vol.lx; 1926.
xx; 513pp. 8vo.
  See also the entries under Tanner, J.R.
  ☞ For further material on Pepys – see volume ii of the
Library Catalogue: Biography, part i. – the Pepys
Section, 1134–1226, on pp.363–389.

694. [PETT, Phineas].
The autobiography of Phineas Pett.
Edited by W.G.Perrin.
London; Navy Records Society series, vol.li; 1918.
civ; 244pp., 1 pl. 8vo.
  With much on the naval history of the period.

695. POOL, Bernard.
Samuel Pepys and Navy contracts.
History Today, vol.xiii (1963), pp.633–641.

696. POOL . . .
Pepys and the Thirty Ships, 1677.
History Today, vol.xx (1970), pp.489–495.

697. ROBINSON, Gregory.
Admiralty and Naval affairs – May 1660 to March
1674.
The Mariner's Mirror, vol.xxxvi (January 1950),
pp.12–40.

698. [SLINGSBY, Sir Robert].
A Discourse upon the past and present state of His
Majesty's Navy . . . 1660.
In: Holland's: Two Discourses of the Navy . . . edited
by J.R.Tanner.
London; Navy Records Society series, vol.vii; 1896.
8vo.

699. TANNER, Professor J.R.
Pepys and the Popish Plot.
English Historical Review, vol.vii (1892), pp.281–290.

700. TANNER . . .
The administration of the Navy from the Restoration to the Revolution.
English Historical Review, vols.xii (1897) pp.17–66;
679–710; & xiii (1898), pp.26–54; & xiv (1899),
pp.47–70.
  An important series of articles.

701. TANNER . . .
A Descriptive Catalogue of the Naval Manuscripts
in the Pepysian Library at Magdalene College,
Cambridge.
London; Navy Records Society series, vols.xxvi,
xxvii, xxxvi, lvii; 1903–1923. 4 vols. 8vo.
  Essential source-material for the period. Volume i.
contains a preface history of naval administration, 1660–
1688, based on the Pepysian manuscripts; the Register of
Ships, 1660–1686 and the Register of Sea Officers in full.
  The subsequent volumes include a précis of Admiralty
letters, June 1673–May 1677.

702. TANNER . . .
Naval administration under Charles II and James II.
In: Cambridge Modern History, vol.v (1908) – with
bibliography.

703. TANNER . . .
Notes on Pepys's Admiralty Journal of 1674–9.
The Mariner's Mirror, vol.ix (April 1923), pp.110–
114.

704. TANNER . . .
Samuel Pepys and the Trinity House.
English Historical Review, vol.xliv (October 1929),
pp.573–587.

705. TAYLOR, Rear-Admiral A.H.
Pepys and his thirty ships of the line.
Naval Review, vol.xliii (1955), pp.55–60.

706. TEDDER, Arthur W.
The Navy of the Restoration. From the death of
Cromwell to the Treaty of Breda; its work, growth
and influence.
Cambridge; University Press; 1916. 234pp., maps.
8vo.
  Includes a valuable bibliography – 'The Sources of
English naval history, September 1658 to July 1667'.

707. TURNBULL, A.
The administration of the Navy under James, Duke
of York, 1660–1673.
University of Hull Ph.D. thesis; 1972.

708. VALE, V.
The dating of the Duke of York's Supplementary
Orders, 1672.
The Mariner's Mirror, vol.xxxviii (July 1952),
pp.223–4.

709. VALE . . .
Clarendon, Coventry and the sale of Navy offices,
1660–8.
Cambridge Historical Journal, vol.xii, no.2 (1956),
pp.107–125.

710. WILCOX, L.A.
Mr Pepys' Navy.
London; George Bell; 1966. 189pp., pls. 8vo.

711. [YORK, James, *Duke of; later King James II*
(1633–1701)].
Memoirs of the English affairs, chiefly Naval, from
the year 1660, to 1673. Written by His Royal
Highness James Duke of York, under his administration of Lord High Admiral, &c.
Published from his original letters and other royal
authorities.
London; 1729. 280pp. small 8vo.

ii. The Second and Third Dutch Wars, 1665–7; 1672–4

712. ANDERSON, *Dr.* R.C.
Naval operations in the latter part of 1666.
In: *The Naval Miscellany,* vol.iii (1928), pp.3–47.
London; Navy Records Society series, vol.lxiii;
1928. 8vo.

713. ANDERSON . . . [*editor*].
Journals and narratives of the Third Dutch War . . .
Edited by R.C.Anderson.
London; Navy Records Society series, vol.lxxxvi;
1946. 447pp. 8vo.

714. ANDERSON . . .
The loss of the *Salamander.*
The Mariner's Mirror, vol.l (November 1964), p.296.
    *In an Anglo–Dutch engagement off Gibraltar, May
1665.*

715. ATKINSON, C.T.
The Dutch Wars (1664–74).
In: *Cambridge Modern History,* vol.v, chapter 7: *The
Anglo–Dutch Wars,* pp.178–197.

716. BELL, A.Colquhoun.
The Third Dutch War, 1672–4.
Corbett Prize Essay, 1929. Summarised in: *IHR
Bull.* vol.ix, (November 1931), pp.109–112.

717. BOSSCHER, *Lieut.* P.M., R. NETHS. N.
The Four Days' Battle – some remarks and
reflections.
RUSIJ, (February 1967), p.56. ff.
    *This article also appeared in: La Revue Maritime,
vol.ccxli (March 1967), pp.313–320.*

718. BOXER, *Professor* C.R.
The Third Dutch War in the East, 1672–4.
The Mariner's Mirror, vol.xvi (October 1930), pp.
343–386.

719. BOXER . . .
The Tromps and the Anglo–Dutch Wars, 1652–74.
History Today, vol.iii (1953), pp.836–845.

720. BOXER . . .
Public opinion and the Second Dutch War, 1664–7.
History Today, vol.xvi (1966), pp.618–626.

721. BOXER . . .
Some second thoughts on the Third Anglo–Dutch
War, 1672–1674.
RHS Trans., 5th series, vol.xix (1969), pp.67–94.

722. BROWNING, Andrew. [*editor*].
Dutch account of the attack on the Thames, 1667.
In: English Historical Documents, vol.viii: 1660–1714.,
pp.835–6.
    Reprinted from the narrative in Calendar of State
Papers Domestic – Charles II, *pp.xxi–xxiii.:* 'Short
and reliable account of all that has happened in the river
of London and in the haven of Chatham, Sheppey, &c.,
9–13 June, 1667.'

723. BRUHIER, P.J.
La jonction des flottes française et anglaise en 1672 . . .
Assoc. des Amis Musée de la Marine Bull., vol.i, no.15
(1934), pp.202–7.

724. CALENDAR OF STATE PAPERS,
DOMESTIC – Charles II.
vols.iv (1664–1665) – vii (1667) and xii (December
1671–May 1672) – xvi, (November 1673 – February
1675).
London; HMSO; 1863–1904.
    *Each of these volumes contains valuable material on the
Second and Third Dutch Wars. See also the analysis of
these papers in the previous section.*

725. [CASTLEMAINE, *Earl* of].
A short and true account of the material passages in the First War between the English and Dutch since His Majestie's Restauration . . .
Savoy (London); Thos. Price; 1671. 103pp., frontis.; 12mo.

726. CLOWES, *Sir* William Laird, *et alia*.
The Royal Navy. A History from the earliest times . . . Vol.ii.
London; Sampson Low, Marston; 1898. 593pp. 4to.
   Pp.252–322 describe the period of the Second and Third Dutch Wars. See also entry no.621.

727. CORBETT, *Sir* Julian S. [editor].
Views of the battles of the Third Dutch War.
Portfolio containing ten coloured plates, with a note on the drawings in the possession of the Earl of Dartmouth, illustrating the Battle of Solebay, 1672 and the Battle of the Texel, 1673.
London; Navy Records Society series, vol.xxxiv.; 1908. folio.

728. CROFTON, *Commander* D.A.
The Dutch in the Medway, June 9–13, 1667.
RUSIJ, vol.xxix (1885–6), p.935,ff.

729. DYER, Florence.
Captain John Narbrough and the Battle of Solebay [28 May, 1672].
The Mariner's Mirror, vol.xv (July 1929), pp.222–232.

730. FARRÈRE, Claude.
Abraham Du Quesne à la bataille de Solebay.
La Revue Maritime, vol.clxxiii (April 1934), pp.577–584.

731. FOREEST, H.A.van, BOXER, *Professor* C.R., *et alia*.
De Vierdaagse Zeeslag, 11–14 Juni, 1666.
The Hague; 'Onze Vloot'; 1966. 63pp., pls. & charts. 8vo.
   A collection of essays by English and Dutch authorities and published in 1966 to mark the tercentenary of the Four Days' Battle.

732. GRAEFE, Friedrich.
Beiträge zur geschichte des 2 u. 3. Englisch-Holländische Seekrieges.
Marine Rundschau, vol.xxviii (1923), pp.107–113.

733. [GREGORY, Edward].
The Dutch invasion of the Thames, 1667. Edward Gregory's report.
Southend Antiq. Soc. Trans., vol.ii, no.4 (1934), pp.240–259.

734. HISTORICAL MANUSCRIPTS COMMISSION:
[a]. 10th Report: appendix, part vi (1887) – Braye Mss.
   Pp.104–252 contain material on Navy lists; lists of naval ordnance, 1644, and Dutch and French warships, 1665–6.
[b]. 15th Report: appendices, (3 vols. 1887–96) – Dartmouth Mss.
   Vol.iii, in particular, reprints important contemporary accounts, viz: (pp.5–13): extracts from the journals of Admiral Sir Edward Spragge, including accounts of the battles of Solebay and Bugia Bay. (pp.13–23): narrative of Solebay by Admirals Narbrough, Haddock, Spragge, Jordan, &c. (pp.33–54): George Legge's Tangier expedition, 1672.
[c]. 16th Report: appendix ii (1897) – Hodgkin Mss.
   Including accounts by both Rupert and Monk of some of the naval battles of 1665–7.

735. HANSEN, H.A.
The opening phase of the Third Dutch War.
JMH, vol.xxi (June 1949), pp.97–108.
   As described by the Danish envoy in London, March–June 1672.

736. HOSTE, Paul.
L'Art des Armées Navales . . .
Lyons; 1727. 2 vols. 4to.
[English translation & adaptation by Lieutenant C.O'Bryen. London; 1762].
   A standard work on naval tactics, which includes valuable accounts (with many engraved illustrations) of the battles of the Second Dutch War.

737. HOUSEHOLD, H.W.
The Four Day's Battle of 1666.
Chambers' Journal, ser.7, vol.ix (1919), pp.241–5.

738. [L'ESTRANGE, Roger.]
A Second Narrative of the signal victory . . . of His Majestie's Navy, under the command of His Royal Highness the Duke of York, against the States-Fleet of the United Neatherlands, on the Third of June 1665.
London; 1665. Pamphlet. 16pp. 8vo.
   The battle of Lowestoft, in which the Dutch were defeated and their commander-in-chief, Obdam van Wassenaer, killed.

739. MEIRAT, Jean.
Autour de Solebay, 1672.
Neptunia, vol.lxiii (April 1962), pp.7–10.

740. MUDDIMAN, Joseph G.
The Dutch at Chatham in 1667.
Notes & Queries, vol.clxx (1936), pp.254–8; 277–81.

741. NOVÉ-JOSSERAND, *Capitaine* H.
La bataille du Texel.
La Revue Maritime, vol.xx (August 1921), pp.160–181; plans.

742. PEPYS, Samuel (1633–1703).
☞ *See the entries in the earlier part of this section; also those on Pepys in Vol. ii of the Library Catalogue – Biography.*

743. POWELL, *Reverend* J.R. & TIMINGS, K.R. [editors].
The Rupert and Monck Letterbook, 1666.
London; Navy Records Society series, vol.cxii; 1970. 193pp. 8vo.

744. PRIOR, William.
The naval war with the Dutch, 1665–7. Diary of a Danish sailor [Hans Svendsen], who served under Tromp and de Ruyter.
United Service Magazine, n.s. vol.xliii (1911).

745. ROGERS, P.G.
The Dutch in the Medway. [June 1667].
Oxford; University Press; 1970. 192pp., 12 pls. 8vo.

746. [RUPERT, *Prince*. (1619–1682)].
Report to the House of Commons on: 'What miscarriages I have observed in the management of the said War & a particular account concerning the Division of the Fleet in 1666'.
In: Historical Manuscripts Commission Reports, vol.xv, part ii (1897).
See also his: 'Additional Instructions for fighting, 1666', in Navy Records Society volume xxix, (1905).

747. [SANDWICH, *First Earl of*. (1625–1672).].
Orders to the Fleet, 1665.
In: Navy Records Society vol.xxix, (1905).

748. SHAW, J.J.S.
The Commission of Sick and Wounded and Prisoners, 1664–7.
The Mariner's Mirror, vol.xxv (July 1939), pp.306–327.

749. SHELLEY, Roland J.A.
The division of the English fleet in 1666.
The Mariner's Mirror, vol.xxv (April 1939), pp.178–196.

750. TAYLOR, *Rear-Admiral* A.H.
The Four Days' Battle and St. James's Day Fight.
Naval Review, vol.xli (1953), pp.287–302.

751. TAYLOR . . .
The Battle of Solebay, 1672.
Naval Review, vol.xli (1953), pp.404–415.

752. TAYLOR . . .
Prince Rupert and de Ruyter, 1673.
Naval Review, vol.xlii (1954), pp.287–299.

753. WARNSINCK, J.C.M.
De laatste tocht van Wassenaer van Obdam, 24 Mai – 13 Juni 1665.
repr. from: Marineblad (1921), pp.424–60; 564–91.
This is about the Battle of Lowestoft (3/13 June 1665), at the height of which the Dutch flagship EENDRACHT *blew up, killing Obdam, the commander-in-chief, and over 400 of her crew.*

754. WARNSINCK . . .
Admiraal de Ruyter en de zeeslag op Schooneveld, Juni 1673.
The Hague; Martinus Nijhoff; 1930. xii; 178pp.; pls. 8vo.

755. [Anonymous].
Journael ofte Zee-Advysen, verhalende al het gene dat gepasseert en . . . de schrickelijcke, bloedighe, en noyt . . . ghehoorde Zee-Slagh . . . voor-gevallen omtrent Nieuwpoort, op den 11, 12, 13, en 14 Juny, Anno. 1666.
[Amsterdam; 1666]. 52pp.; black-letter text. oblong 8vo.
An important Dutch account of the Four Days' Battle.

756. [Anonymous].
Pertinente afbeeldinge van de victorieuse Vierdaegsche Zeeslagh bevochten door de Nederlantsche Vloot tegens de Engelsche op den 11/12/13 en 14 Junij 1666.
Amsterdam; Pieter Arentsz; 1666. Single sheet, with title & black-letter text. Folio.
About the Four Days' Battle.

757. [Anonymous].
Verhael van 't passende in de Zee-Slach, tusschen de Vlooten van Enghelandt ende van de Vereenigde Nederlanden . . . in date den 24 Junii 1666 . . .
The Hague; Hillebrandt van Wouw; 1666. title; [10]pp., small 8vo.
There is another copy of this pamphlet in the Library – same publisher, text and date, but with a slightly different title, which begins: 'Oprecht Verhael van 't ge-passeerde in de Zee-Slagh . . .'

758. [Anonymous].
Journael van de lesten nyltocht, Zee-slagh . . . tusschen de Vlooten van den Koninck van Engelant

758. [Anonymous], *continued*
ende de Vereenighde Nederlanden geschiet den 4
Augusti 1666 . . .
Amsterdam; Ter Goes; 1666. 42pp.; black-letter
text. oblong 8vo.
Describes the Battle of St James's Day.

759. [Anonymous].
(i) Pertinent Verhael van 't geene voorgevallen . . .
(ii) Derde en naerder Missive van de Heer Cournelis
de Witt . . .
The Hague; 1667. 7pp.; 8pp. 8vo.
Both these pamphlets describe the Dutch attack on the
Medway, led by de Ruyter and Cornelis de Witt, June
1667.

760. [Anonymous].
Kort en bondigh verhael van 't geene in den Oorlogh,
tusschen den Koningh van Engelant & de H.M.
Heeren Staten der vrye Vereenigde Nederlanden . . .
Beginnende in den Jare 1664. en eyndigende . . .
in 't Jaer 1667 . . .
Amsterdam; Marcus Doorwick; 1667. engr. title,
256pp. black-letter text, engr. pls. 8vo.
An important contemporary narrative of the Second
Dutch War.

761. [Anonymous].
Description exacte de tout ce qui s'est passé dans les
guerres entre le Roy d'Angleterre, le Roy de France,
les Estats des Provinces-Unies du Pays-Bas . . .
commencant de l'an 1664. & finissant . . . en l'an
1667 . . .
Amsterdam; Jacques Benjamin; 1668. 241pp., engr.
pls. oblong 8vo.
This is the French edition of the foregoing.

762. [Anonymous].
A true Relation of the engagement of His Majestie's
Fleet under the command of His Royal Highness
with the Dutch Fleet, May 28. 1672. . . .
London (In the Savoy); Thos. Newcomb; 1672.
pamphlet. 7pp. 4to.
That is, the Battle of Solebay (or Southwold Bay),
fought between the fleets commanded by the Duke of
York and de Ruyter.

763. [Anonymous].
A Relation of the Engagement of His Majesty's
Fleet with the Enemies, on the 11th of August, 1673.
As it has been represented by letters from the several
Squadrons . . .
London (in the Savoy); Thos. Newcomb; 1673.
pamphlet. 12pp. 4to.
Concerning the final, bitterly-fought battle of the Third
Dutch War – off the Texel.

764. [Anonymous].
An exact relation of the several engagements and
actions of His Majestie's Fleet under the command of
His Highnesse Prince Rupert. And of all Circumstances concerning this Somers expedition, Anno
1673.
Written by a Person in Command in the Fleet.
London; J.B.; 1673. pamphlet; title; 21pp. small
8vo.

iii. James II and the Glorious Revolution

765. CALENDAR OF STATE PAPERS –
DOMESTIC : JAMES II.
London; HMSO; 1960–1972. 3 vols. 8vo.
vol.i.: February–December 1685.
Includes references to Samuel Pepys, the Navy and
Admiralty, and several individual warships by name.
vol.ii.: January 1686–May 1687.
As above and material on the Bristol, Dartmouth,
Garland, Isabella, Oxford and Pearl.
vol.iii.: June 1687–February 1689.
Includes references to the activities of the British Fleet
in Home Waters, named H.M. ships, and Admiralty
courts and jurisdiction.

766. HISTORICAL MANUSCRIPTS
COMMISSION:
11th Report – Appendix, part 5.: The Dartmouth
Mss.
London; HMC; 1887–1896. 3 vols. 4to.
These are the papers of Admiral George Legge, First
Baron Dartmouth. The most important extracts relevant
to this period are:
vol.i. pp.139–252: Pepys' letters and instructions to
Lord Dartmouth (1688–90).
vol.iii. pp.59–71; 120–142: Papers of Lord Dart-
mouth as Admiral of the Fleet, 1688.

767. LAUGHTON, L.G.Carr.
The *Royal Sovereign*, 1685.
The Mariner's Mirror, vol.xviii (April 1932), pp.138–
150.

768. MAY, *Commander* W.E.
The Navy and the rebellion of the Earl of Argyle.
[1685].
The Mariner's Mirror, vol.lvii (February 1971),
pp.17–23.

769. POWLEY, Edward P.
The English Navy in the Revolution of 1688.
Cambridge; University Press; 1928. 188pp., 1 chart.
8vo.

770. ROSE, *Professor* John Holland.
The influence of James II on the Navy.
Fighting Forces, vol.i. (1924), pp.211–221.

771. SYDENHAM, M.J.
The anxieties of an admiral: Lord Dartmouth and
the Revolution of 1688.
History Today, vol.xii (1962), pp.714–720.

772. TANNER, *Dr.* J.R.
The naval preparations of James II in 1688.
English Historical Review, vol.viii (1893), pp.272–283.

773. TANNER . . .
The administration of the Navy from the
Restoration to the Revolution.
English Historical Review, vols.xii (1897), pp.17–66;
679–710, & xiii (1898), pp.26–54; & xiv (1899),
pp.47–70.

774. TANNER . . .
Naval administration under Charles II and James II.
In: Cambridge Modern History, vol.v (1908), with
bibliography.

iv. Events and operations elsewhere, 1660–1688

775. ANDERSON, *Dr.* R.C.
The Sicilian War of 1674–8.
The Mariner's Mirror, vol.lvii (August 1971), pp.239–
265.
   *With an account of the operations of the French,
Dutch and Spanish squadrons and the battles of
Stromboli (or Alicudi), Augusta and Palermo.*

776. BUISSERET, David.
The loss of HMS *Norwich* off Port Royal in June
1682.
The Mariner's Mirror, vol.liv (November 1968),
pp.403–7; pls. & map.

777. CALENDAR OF STATE PAPERS –
COLONIAL.
vols.v–xii: AMERICA and the WEST INDIES,
1660–1688.
London; HMSO; 1880–1899. 8 vols. 4to.
   *Reproduce many valuable documents relative to a
study of the period. For example, in vol.v [1660–1668],
there is material on: Dutch fleet under Crynsens seizing
fort at Surinam; recaptured by British Squadron under
Sir John Harrison (October 1667). Naval defence of the
West Indies and the French landing on Antigua (1666).
Willoughby's recapture of Antigua and Montserrat and*

*Captain Berry's relief of Nevis (January 1667). Jamaican
privateers take Tobago (1665); Navy's attempts to
control Caribbean piracy. The naval defence of Barbados.
Anglo–French naval battle in Nevis roads (10 May 1667).
Letters to Navy Commissioners.*

778. [CASTLEMAINE, *Earl of*].
An account of the present war between the
Venetians and Turks, with the state of Candie.: (In
a letter to the King, from Venice). . . .
London; H.Herringman; 1666. 39pp. 8vo.

779. [DARTMOUTH, *Admiral* George Legge,
First Baron].
An account of the Tangier expedition. August 1683
– March 1684.
and:
Papers relating to the Tangier expedition.
In: Historical Manuscripts Commission Reports, vols.xi
(1887) & xv (1896).

780. DELORT, *Lieutenant* Théodore.
La première escadre de la France dans les Indes . . .
rivalité de la France et de la Hollande, 1670–5.
Revue Maritime et Coloniale, vol.xlvii (1875), pp.29–
63; 443–471; & 841–866.

781. DYER, Florence.
Captain Christopher Myngs in the West Indies,
1657–1662.
The Mariner's Mirror, vol.xviii (April 1932), pp.168–
187.
   See also entries:– 783, 789.

782. FIELDING, Xan.
A seventeenth century Atlantic outpost: the British
occupation of Tangier.
History Today, vol.v. (July 1955), pp.463–472.

783. FIRTH, *Sir* Charles H.
The capture of Santiago in Cuba by Captain
Myngs, 1662.
English Historical Review, vol.xiv (1899), pp.536–540.

784. JAMIESON, A.
The occupation of Tangier and its relation to
English naval strategy in the Mediterranean, 1661–
1684.
University of Durham; MA thesis; 1962.

785. JENSEN, N.P.
Den Skaanske Krig, 1675–1679.
Copenhagen; Nordiske Forlag; 1900. 496pp. 4to.
   *This is an account of the five-year struggle between
Denmark and Sweden, known as the Scanian War.
There were two important naval battles – Oland (1 June
1676) and Kjöge Bight (1 July 1677).*

786. KAUFMAN, Helen Andrews. [editor.]
Tangier at high tide: the journal of John Luke,
1670–1673.
Paris & Geneva; 1958. 252pp., pls. 8vo.
'. . . three centuries ago it was the British under
Cromwell who first grasped the importance of Tangier. . . .
It was England who . . . received the city as part of the
dowry of Catherine of Braganza on her marriage to
Charles II in 1661. It was Charles, who after twenty-
two years of stormy possession abandoned the city to the
Moors . . . and surrendered "the brightest jewel in our
Crown." ' [from the introduction.]

787. KITCHING, G.C.
The loss and recapture of St Helena, 1673.
The Mariner's Mirror, vol.xxxvi (January 1950),
pp.58–68.

788. LEENT, Dr. F. J. van.
Étude sur la guerre des Hollandais contre l'Empire
d'Atjéh.
Revue Maritime et Coloniale, vol.xlv (1875), pp.483–
503; 824–831, & xlvi (1876), 75–86.

789. [MYNGS, Vice-Admiral Sir Christopher.
(1625?–1666.)].
Account of the taking of St Iago upon Cuba,
October 1662.
In: Historical Mss Commission Reports, (Heathcote
Mss).
London; HMC; 1899.

790. NEESER, Robert Wilden.
The British naval operations in the West Indies,
1650–1700; a study in naval administration.
USNIP, vol.xl (1914), pp.1599–1625.

791. [PEPYS, Samuel (1633–1703)].
The Tangier Papers of Samuel Pepys.
Edited by Edwin Chappell.
London; Navy Records Society series, vol.lxxiii;
1935. 376 pp. 8vo.
See elsewhere in this section for further Pepys
material and the chapter devoted to him in the Biography
volume of the Library Catalogue.

792. PETER, Dr. H.
Die Anfänge der Brandenburgischen Marine, 1675–
1681.
Berlin; C.H.Müller; 1877. 32pp. 4to.

793. REUSSNER, A.
L'Intendant Général Desclouzeaux et l'expédition de
Sicilie, (1675–6).
La Revue Maritime, vol.cxxxix (July 1931), pp.1–22.

794. ROBINSON, C.N.
The fight of the Mary Rose.
The Mariner's Mirror, vol.xii (January 1926), pp.97–
100; 2pls.
Captain John Kempthorne against seven Algerine
corsairs, 29 December 1669.

795. ROUTH, Enid M.G.
The English occupation of Tangier, 1661–1683.
RHS Trans., n.s., vol.xix (1905).

796. ROUTH . . .
Tangier. England's lost Atlantic outpost, 1661–1684.
London; John Murray; 1912. 388pp., pls. & index
of ships. 8vo.
Includes narrative on the part played by Samuel
Pepys in the Tangier events.

797. ROWBOTHAM, Commander W.B.
The Algerine War in the time of Charles II.
RUSIJ (May–November 1964), pp.160; 253; & 350.

798. SCHOOLCRAFT, Professor H.L.
The capture of New Amsterdam.
English Historical Review, vol.xxiii (1908), pp.674–
693.
By the English from the Dutch in August 1664.

799. SEARLES, P.J.
The Battle of Perico.
USNIP, vol.lxvii (October 1941), pp.1411–1414.
Between Spanish and English privateers in the Bay of
Panama, 1680.

800. [SVENDSEN, Hans.]
Til Orlogs under de Ruyter. Dagbogsoptegnelser af
Hans Svendsen en Dansk Somand i Hollandsk
tjeneste fra 1665 til 1667 . . .
Copenhagen; E.Groves; 1909. 179pp.; pls. 8vo.

801. WAARD, C.de.
De Zeeuwsche expeditie naar de West onder
Cornelis Evertsen den Jonge, 1672–4.
The Hague; Martinus Nijhoff; 1928. 273pp., pls. &
charts. 8vo.

802. WARNSINCK, J.C.M.
Abraham Crijnssen; de verovering van Suriname en
zijn aanstag op Virginie en 1667.
Amsterdam; 1936. 183pp., pls. 8vo.

803. WILSON, Charles H.
Who captured New Amsterdam?
English Historical Review, vol.lxxii (July 1957),
pp.469-474.
See also entry no.798.

804. [Anonymous].
A relation of the Siege of Candia. From the first
expedition of the French forces under . . . M. de la
Fueillade, Duke of Roannez, to its surrender, the
27th of September, 1669. Written in French by a
gentleman who was a Voluntier in that service, and
faithfully Englished.
London; T.Williams & I.Starkey; 1670. 118pp.
12mo.

805. [Anonymous].
Historisch Journael van den tocht op de Barbare
Turcken; door . . . Vice-Admirael Michiel Adriaen
de Ruyter, naer d'Expeditie van dien van Thunis . . .
op den 13 Marty tot den 14 May 1662 . . .
Amsterdam; Ambrosius Turckschaep; 5 June 1662.
Pamphlet. title; 19pp. black-letter text. small 8vo.

806. [Anonymous].
Journael . . . van 't gene gepassaert . . . de Vloot der
Vereenighde Nederlanden, soo in de Middellantsche
Zee, als op de kusten van Africa en America.
Onder 't belaydt van . . . Michiel de Ruyter, als
Admirael, . . . in den Jare 1664 en 1665.
Amsterdam; Jacob Venckel; 1665. engr. & printed
titles; 82 + [2]pp., incl. fleet list. 8vo.

V. William III, Louis XIV and the War of the English Succession, 1689–1697

807. Anderson, *Dr.* R.C.
The *Royal Louis* of 1692.
The Mariner's Mirror, vol.xxviii (July 1942), p.246;
2pls.

808. [ASHBY, *Admiral Sir* John (*d.*1693) and
ROOKE, *Admiral of the Fleet Sir* George (1650–
1703).]
An account given by Sir John Ashby Vice-Admiral,
and Reere-Admiral Rooke to the Lords Commissioners, of the engagement at sea, between the
English, Dutch, and French fleets. June the 30th.
1690.
With a journal of the fleet since their departure from
St Hellens, to their return to the Buoy-in-the-Nore,
and other material passages relating to the said
engagement.
London; Randal Taylor; 1691. [iv], 32pp. Pamphlet.
8vo.
    The engagement is that of Beachy Head, in which
Torrington and the Anglo–Dutch fleet were defeated by
the French under Tourville. Both Ashby and Rooke
were in the Allied centre squadron, wearing their flags in
the SANDWICH, *90, and* DUCHESS, *90, respectively.*

809. [B., N.].
The action between the *Chester* and the *Loire*.
The Mariner's Mirror, vol.xxx (July 1944), pp.162–4.
Off Martinique on 19 January, 1693/4.

810. BASSETT, W.G.
English naval policy in the Caribbean, 1698–1703.
IHR Bulletin, vol.xi (November 1933), pp.122–5.

811. BLANE, *Capitaine* L.
Les officers de la Marine de Louis XIV d'après
l'ordonnance du 15 avril 1689.
Revue Maritime, nos.xxviii (July 1921), pp.1–18 &
xxxvii (January 1923), pp.1–19.

812. BOULTER, W.C.
A contemporary account of the Battle of La Hogue.
English Historical Review, vol.xii (1892).

813. BURCHETT, Josiah. (1666?–1745).
Memoirs of Transactions at Sea during the War
with France, beginning in 1688 and ending in 1697 . . .

813. BURCHETT, *continued*
By J.B. Esq., Secretary to the Admiralty . . .
London; John Nutt; 1703. 408pp. small 8vo.
Invaluable for the naval aspects of the War of the English Succession. Burchett was Secretary to the Admiralty for fifty years, between 1692 and 1742.

814. [BURCHETT . . .].
Mr Burchett's Justification of his Naval Memoirs. In answer to reflections made by Col. Lillingston, on that part which relates to Cape Francois and Port de Paix. With some short observations on our West-India expeditions.
London (in the Savoy); Edward Jones; 1704. 166pp. 8vo.
Particularly in relation to Captain Wilmot's expedition to the West Indies in 1694/5 and the subsequent quarrels between him and Colonel Lillingston, who commanded the military force. Burchett here defends the account he gave of the expedition in his 'Memoirs of Transactions at Sea . . .', to which Colonel Lillingston took strong exception.

815. CALENDAR OF STATE PAPERS –
DOMESTIC: William III.
London; HMSO; 1895–1937. 11 volumes. 4to.
As with the earlier volumes of this series, full of references to naval aspects of the period. Some examples are given below, under each volume:

vol.i.: February 1689–April 1690. The siege of Londonderry; the Navy in general; Admiral Arthur Herbert (Lord Torrington).

vol.ii.: May 1690–October 1691. The naval disaster at Beachy Head; Russell; Torrington and his trial; Clowdisley Shovell.

vol.iii.: November 1691–December 1692. The battle of La Hogue; preparations for the invasion of France; Russell & Shovell; Wheler's expedition to the West Indies; the Navy in general; Navy Office & Navy Board.

vol.iv.: 1693. Proposed invasion of France; Rooke in general and with the Fleet in the Mediterranean; Benbow and the expedition to St Malo; the Navy.

vol.v.: 1694–June 1695. Plans for war at sea; Wheler's Turkey convoy meets with disaster, February 1694; the attack on Brest, May–June 1694 and later operations against the French coast; Fleet lists; Russell at Cadiz; the Navy and the Navy Board.

vol.vi.: July–December 1695. Lord Berkeley's attack on St Malo, Dunkirk and Calais; correspondence of Admirals Russell and Rooke; Sir Clowdisley Shovell; the Fleet and Navy Commissioners.

vol.vii.: 1696. Victualling; Anglo–Dutch naval affairs; Shovell; the Fleet and the Navy.

vol.viii.: 1697. Captain Mees in the West Indies; the Mediterranean squadron; prizes; Shovell; naval actions.

vol.ix.: 1698. The size of the Navy; the Mediterranean squadron.

vol. x.: January 1699–March 1700. Parliamentary Committee on Affairs of Admiralty (January 1699); Committee of Ways and Means on the Strength of the Navy (February 1699); manning of the fleet; Darien settlement; Russell & Rooke.

vol.xi.: April 1700–March 1702. (with Appendix, 1689–1702.) Naval engagements; naval stores; British & French squadrons in the Mediterranean; Shovell.

816. CALENDAR OF STATE PAPERS –
COLONIAL: America and the West Indies.
London; HMSO; 1901–1908. 5 volumes. 4to.
Again, a rich source of contemporary material. Examples of only some of the subjects are given under each volume.

vol.xiii.: 1689–1692. Naval expedition against Acadia & Quebec, April 1690; Codrington's recapture of St Kitts, 1690 and later operations in the West Indies.

vol. xiv.: January 1693–May 1696. Wheler's expedition to the West Indies and failures against the French at Martinique and Newfoundland; the defence of Jamaica, 1694 and Wilmot's expedition to Hispaniola, 1695.

vol.xv.: May 1696–October 1697. French attacks on Hudson's Bay and Newfoundland and the English expedition to retake the latter, April 1697; Admiral Nevill's squadron sent out to defend Jamaica, 1696; convoys to the West Indies; impressment; West Indies squadron; naval stores and Admiralty correspondence.

vol.xvi.: October 1697–December 1698. Admiral Nevill's expedition to the Caribbean; Commodore Norris in Newfoundland; piracy in the West Indies and off New York; Newfoundland fisheries; convoys; & Admiralty correspondence.

vol.xvii.: 1699. (and Addenda, 1621–1698). The Darien Expedition; Captain Kidd; piracy and the efforts to suppress it; inadequacy of the West Indies squadron; Admiralty correspondence.

817. CARMARTHEN, *Marquess of.*
A Journal of the Brest Expedition, by the Lord Marquiss of Caermarthen.
London; Randal Taylor; 1694. 46pp., 1 fold. chart. 8vo.
That is to Camaret Bay, Brest, 29 May–15 June, 1694. The text includes the line-of-battle of the Anglo–Dutch squadron, commanded by Admirals Russell and Allemonde.

818. CLARK, *Sir* George Norman.
Trading with the enemy and the Corunna packets, 1689–97.
English Historical Review, vol.xxxvi (1921), pp.521–539.

819. CLARK . . .
The Dutch Alliance and the War against French Trade, 1688–1697.
Manchester; University Press; 1923. xi; 160pp. 8vo.

820. CLOSE, C.C.S.
An early attempt at combined operations.
United Services Magazine, vol. cxi (May 1954).
   An article on Admiral Benbow's abortive operations against Dunkirk in 1694.

821. COHEN, K.H.S.
Naval operations of the War of 1689–97.
Naval Review, vol.xiv (1926), pp.431 & 633.

822. CORBETT, *Professor* Julian S.
England in the Mediterranean. A study of the rise and influence of British power within the Straits, 1603–1713.
London; Longmans, Green; 1904. 2 vols. 8vo.
   In volume 2, there are important chapters for this period, viz.:- 'xxvi. The naval strategy of William' (pp.143–160); 'xxvii. The main fleet in the Mediterranean.' (161–186). and 'xxviii. The Spanish Succession.' (187–202).

823. CRISENOY, J.de.
La campagne maritime de 1692.
Revue Maritime et Coloniale, vol.xiv (1865), pp.433–473.

824. CROUSE, Nellis M.
The French struggle for the West Indies, 1665–1713.
Columbia; University Press; 1943. 324pp. 8vo.
   Includes chapters on the Anglo–French conflict in the West Indies, 1689–1702, and the capture of Cartagena by de Pointis and Ducasse in 1697.

825. DAWSON, Charles.
A description of the Battle of Beachy Head.
Lewes & Folkestone; Farncombe; [1895]. 16pp. 8vo.

826. DELARBRE, J.
Tourville et la Marine de son temps. Notes, lettres et documents (1642–1701).
Paris; L.Baudouin; 1889. 463pp., pls. 8vo.
The author also wrote an article on the same subject in:
La Revue Maritime et Coloniale, *vol.xcix (1888), pp.577 ff.*

827. [DESBOROUGH, *Captain* Charles].
Papers relating to the Newfoundland expedition, 1697.
In: Historical Manuscripts Commission, House of Lords Mss., vol.iii (1905).

828. DYER, Florence.
An Anglo–Danish incident in 1694.
The Mariner's Mirror, vol.xiv (April & July 1928), pp.175–6; 278–81.
   About Admiral Shovell and the 'Gyldenlöve'.

829. EHRMAN, John P.W.
The official papers transferred by Samual Pepys to the Admiralty, 12 July 1689.
The Mariner's Mirror, vol.xxxiv (October 1948), pp.255–270; lists.

830. EHRMAN . . .
Pepys's organization and the naval mobilization of 1688.
The Mariner's Mirror, vol.xxxv (July 1949), pp.203–239.

831. EHRMAN . . .
William III and the emergence of a Mediterranean naval policy, 1692–4.
Cambridge Historical Journal, vol.ix (1949), pp.269–292.

832. EHRMAN . . .
The Navy in the War of William III, 1689–1697. Its state and direction.
Cambridge; University Press; 1953. 710pp.; plates; appendices. 4to.
   The standard modern authority on the subject. Includes comprehensive bibliography and appendices; (e.g.: tabular details on the English Fleet in December 1688; naval construction, 1691–8).

833. ЕЛАГИНА, С. [ELAGENA, S.]
ИСТОРІЯ РУССКАГО ФЛОТА. ПЕРІОДЪ АЗОВСКІЙ.
St Petersburg; 1864. 3 volumes: 319; 519; 513pp.; pls., charts & plans. 4to.
   This is a detailed history of the Imperial Russian Navy during the Azov period (i.e. 1696–1712).

834. [ESTRÉES, Victor Marie *Duc d'*. (1660–1737)].
Compte-rendu authentique de la reprise de Cayenne par l'Amiral d'Estrées.
La Revue Maritime, vol.cxliv (December 1931), pp.746–757.

835. EVERETT, George.
The Path-way to peace and profit: or, truth in its plain dress. Wherein is methodically set forth a sure

835. EVERETT, *continued*
and certain Way for the more speedy and effectual
building and repairing Their Majesties Royal Navy . . .
By George Everett, Ship-wright.
London; Randal Taylor; 1694. 23pp. Pamphlet. 8vo.
For the Navy Board's rejoinder to this pamphlet, see
the article on the Sergison Collection in the Naval
Miscellany *(Navy Records Society series), vol.ii, p.483.*

836. EVERETT . . .
Encouragement for seamen and mariners. In two
parts. Being a proposed method for the more speedy
and effectual furnishing Their Majesties Royal Navy
with able seamen and mariners. And for saving those
immense sums of money, yearly exhausted in
attending the Sea-press . . .
By George Everett, Ship-wright.
London; 1695. Pamphlet. title; [iii]–vi; 24pp. 8vo.

837. GRANT, James. [*editor*].
The Old Scots Navy, 1689–1710.
London; Navy Records Society series, vol.xliv;
1914. 448pp.; pls. 8vo.

838. GUTTRIDGE, George Herbert.
The colonial policy of William III in America and
the West Indies.
Cambridge; University Press; 1922. 190pp.; 1 map.
8vo.
With two chapters on the naval aspects: 'The War
with France in the West Indies, 1689–1697'; 'The West
Indies, 1697–1702.'

(839. [HADDOCK, *Admiral Sir* Richard (1629–
1715)].
Correspondence – including accounts of the Battles
of Barfleur and La Hogue.
In: Camden Society Miscellany, vol.viii. (1883).

840. HISTORICAL MANUSCRIPTS
COMMISSION:
[a.] BATH Mss. vol.iii (1908).
Includes: letters about the Admiralty and Fleet move-
ments, 1694–1700.
[b.] FINCH Mss. vols.ii (1922), iii (1957) *and* iv
(1965).
Being the papers of Daniel Finch, second Earl of
Nottingham. Contains almost complete collection of
letters to him from admirals and captains, whilst he held
the offices of First Lord of the Admiralty (1680–4) and
Secretary of State (1688–93). Also a valuable account of
the Battle of Beachy Head.
[c.] HOUSE OF LORDS Mss. 13th and 14th
Reports and Appendices (1892–4) and new series,
vol.i (1900).
With many references to the Admiralty and the Navy,
1690–1695.

[d.] PORTLAND Mss. vol.viii (1907).
With many documents relating to the Navy under
William III, including: De Schey's account of
Torrington's court-martial, 1690; privateering and
piracy, 1693–1704; an eye-witness account of the
Camaret Bay action, 1694; press-gang activities; and a
defence of Admiral Rooke's conduct in the Channel, 1696.
[e.] SHREWSBURY Mss. vol.ii (1903).
Includes numerous references to the Admiralty and
Navy Board, 1694–1704; letters of Admirals Russell,
Rooke and Shovell; ship lists, 1695–6; the naval
attempts on Brest and Dunkirk, 1694–6; and the naval
disputes with Denmark, 1694–5.

841. HODGES, William.
An humble representation of the seamens misery in
the loss and abuse of them in their payment, and
their being oftentimes extorted out of the one half of
it by some, and cheated of it all by others . . .
humbly represented to His Majesty, and the two
most honourable Houses, the Lords and Commons
of England . . .
London; Hodges; 1694. Pamphlet. 12pp. folio.

842. HODGES . . .
Humble Proposals for the relief, encouragement,
security and happiness of the loyal, couragious seamen of England . . . By a faithful subject of His
Majesty . . . To which is added, a dialogue concerning the Art of Ticket-buying . . .
London; Hodges; 1695. 63pp. 8vo.

843. JOHNSTON, J.A.
Parliament and the protection of trade, 1689–1694.
The Mariner's Mirror, vol.lvii (November 1971),
pp.399–413.

844. LAUGHTON, J.K. [*editor*].
Extracts from a Commissioner's Notebook, 1691–4.
In: The Naval Miscellany, vol.ii (Navy Records
Society series, vol.xl.; 1912).
Includes the Earl of Nottingham's account of the
Battle of Barfleur.

845. LAWSON, J.A.
Naval strategy during the War of the League of
Augsburg, 1689–97.
University of Leeds MA thesis; 1952.

846. LESMARIES, A. *and* CHARLIAT, P.J.
Jean Bart en Norvège, 1691–6.
La Revue Maritime, vol.cx (February 1929), pp.152–185.

847. MARTIN, J.J.
The defence of British possessions in the West
Indies during the War of the English Succession,
1688–1697.
University of Liverpool MA thesis; 1946.

848. MAY, *Commander* W.E.
The loss of the *Pembroke*, 1694.
The Mariner's Mirror, vol.lviii (May 1972), pp.167–172.
　　The PEMBROKE, *32, was taken by the French frigate* LEWIS, *40, off Plymouth on 23 February, 1694.*

849. MEIRAT, Jean.
(a) De Bantry à Bévéziers (1689–1690).
Neptunia, vol.lxvi (February 1962), pp.11–16.
(b) La campagne du large de l'Amiral Russell (1691).
Neptunia, vol.lxix (January 1963), pp.21–27.
'Bévéziers' is the French name for Beachy Head.

850. MERRIMAN, *Commander* R.D., RIN.
'Gilbert Wardlaw's allegations'.
The Mariner's Mirror, vol.xxxviii (April 1952), pp.106–131.
　　This is about a dispute between the Admiralty and the Navy Board, 1699–1700.

851. [MEDOWS, *Sir* Philip].
Observations concerning the dominion and sovereignty of the Seas; being an Abstract of the Marine Affairs of England.
By Sir Philip Medows, Knight.
London (in the Savoy); Samuel Lowndes & Edward Jones; 1689. title; 47pp. 8vo.

852. MORGAN, William Thomas.
The British West Indies during King William's War (1689–97).
Journal of Modern History, vol.ii (1930), pp.378–409.

853. [NORRIS, *Admiral of the Fleet Sir* John. (1660?–1749)].
Instruction and papers relating to the expedition to Newfoundland under Admiral Norris, 1697.
In: Historical Manuscripts Commission – House of Lords Mss, vol.iii (1905).

854. NORTON, H.Moses.
The British Navy and the Caribbean, 1689–1697.
The Mariner's Mirror, vol.lii (February 1966), pp.13–40.

855. OGG, David.
England in the reigns of James II and William III.
Oxford; Clarendon Press; 1955. xii; 567pp., 8vo.
　　Includes two relevant chapters: xii. – The war at sea, 1689–92; xiii – The war on land and sea, 1692–5.

856. PERRY, *Lieutenant* John.
A Regulation for Seamen wherein a method is humbly proposed, whereby their Majesties Fleet may at all times be speedily and effectually mann'd . . .

By John Perry, late Captain of the *Signet* = Fireship, now a prisoner in the Marshalsea . . .
London; 1695. Pamphlet. 48pp. 8vo.

857. [POINTIS, Jean Bernard Desjeans, *Amiral* de (1645–1707)].
Relation de ce qui s'est fait à la prise de Cartagene sçituée aux Indes Espagnoles; par l'escadre commandée par Mr. de Pointis.
Brussels; Jean Fricx; 1698. 141pp.; 1 plan. 8vo.
　　An account of the successful French expedition against Carthagena in 1697, commanded by de Pointis and Ducasse. A second edition was published in Paris in 1699.

858. [POINTIS . . .].
An account of the taking of Carthagena by the French, in the year 1697. Containing all the particulars of that Expedition, from their first setting out, to their return into Brest. By Monsieur De Pointis, Commander in Chief.
London; Sam. Buckley; 1698. [vi]; [136]pp.; 1 fold. plan (of Carthagena and de Pointis' attack). 8vo.
　　This is the first English edition of the foregoing. Another was published in London in 1740 by Oliver Payne.

859. POWLEY, E.B.
The naval side of King William's War: the opening phase – February 1688 to December 1691.
University of Oxford D.Phil. thesis; 1962.

860. ROQUEBRUNE, Robert de.
Le siège de Québec en 1690 par l'Amiral Phipps et la victoire du Comte de Frontenac.
Neptunia, vol.lxv (January 1962), pp.8–12.

861. [RUSSELL, *Admiral* Edward, *Earl of Orford*. (1653–1727)].
Admiral Russell's Letter to the Earl of Nottingham: containing an exact and particular relation of the late happy victory and success against the French Fleet . . . Published by Authority.
London, in the Savoy; Edward Jones; 1692. [8]pp. 4to.
　　That is, Russell's great victory at La Hogue. The text is also reproduced in: The Harleian Miscellany, *vol.xii (1811), pp.42–46; and* English Historical Documents, *vol.viii – 1660–1714, pp.836–8.*

862. RYAN, Anthony N.
William III and the Brest Fleet in the Nine Years' War.
In: Essays on William III and Louis XIV, 1680–1720.
(Edited by R.Hatton and Professor J.S.Bromley; Liverpool University Press; 1968).

863. [SERGISON, Charles (1654–1732)].
The Sergison papers, 1688–1702. Selected and
edited by R.D.Merriman.
London; Navy Records Society series, vol.lxxxix;
1950. 382pp., pls. 8vo.
  *Fundamental for the naval history of the period, as
Sergison was a Commissioner of the Navy and Clerk of
the Acts to the Navy Board, which post he held for over
thirty years from 1689 to 1719.*

864. ST LO, *Captain* George.
England's Safety: or, a Bridle to the French King.
Proposing a sure method for encouraging Navigation, and raising qualified seamen for the well
manning Their Majesties Fleet . . . without
Impressing . . .
London; W.Miller; 1693. titles, engr. & printed;
48pp. small 8vo.
  *A famous pamphlet. There is also a copy of 'the
second edition with additions' (also published by Miller
in 1693), in the Library.*

865. ST LO . . .
England's Interest: or, a Discipline for Seamen:
wherein is proposed, a sure method for raising
qualified seamen, for the well manning Their
Majesties Fleet on all occasions . . .
London; Robert Clavell; 1694. title; 52pp.; small 8vo.

866. [STEPHENS, Edward. d.1706].
A Plain Relation of the late action at sea between
the English & Dutch and the French fleets from
June 22 to July 5 last . . .
London; John Harris; 1690. 56pp. 8vo.

867. [TORRINGTON, Arthur Herbert, *Earl of*.
(1647–1716)].
The Earl of Torrington's speech to the House of
Commons, in November 1690. Occasion'd by the
Ingagement at Sea on the 30th of June that year,
between the Confederate and French Fleets.
To which is prefix'd, A Draught of the Line of
Battel, curiously engraven on copper.
London; 1690. title; fold. engr. plate. 62pp. 8vo.
  *This account by the English commander-in-chief at the
battle of Beachy Head includes a fine panorama
engraving: 'A Prospect of the late Engagement between
the English and the French Fleets on Monday the
thirtieth of Iune 1690 . . .', upon which the names of the
participating warships are shewn. A second edition was
published in London in 1710.*

868. [TORRINGTON . . .].
Memoirs relating to the Lord Torrington.
Edited by J.K.Laughton for the Camden Society; 1889.
  *'A good sketch of naval operations between 1678 and
1705 . . .'*

869. TOUDOUZE, Georges G.
La Bataille de la Hougue, 29 Mai 1692.
Paris; 1899. 91pp. 8vo.

870. TOUDOUZE . . .
La Hougue: de la victoire mutilée à la légende
mensongère.
Neptunia, vol.xlvi (February 1957), pp.8–15.

871. WARNSINCK, J.C.M.
De Vloot van den Koning-Stadhouder, 1689–1690.
Amsterdam; 1934. 244pp.; pls. 8vo.

872. WOOD, K.W.
The naval administration of England at the close of
the seventeenth century.
University of Leeds MA thesis; 1955.

873. [Anonymous].
Gloria Britannica; or, the Boast of the British Seas.
Containing a true and full account of the Royal
Navy of England, showing, where each ship was
built, by whom, and when . . . together, with every
man's Pay, from a Captain to a Cabin-Boy . . .
Carefully collected and digested by a true lover of
the Seamen . . .
London; Thomas Hawkins; 1689. title; 16 +
[4]pp.; small 8vo.
  *There is also in the Library a copy of the 1696 edition
(London; Samuel Clark; 1696), which continues the
narrative '. . . to the present year of 1696'.*

874. [Anonymous].
A modest enquiry into the causes of the present
disasters in England. And who they are that brought
the French fleet into the English Channel, described.
London; Richard Baldwin; 1690. Pamphlet. [ii];
38pp. 8vo.

875. [Anonymous].
An Account of the late great Victory obtained at
sea, against the French: by Their Majesties Fleet,
commanded in Chief by Admiral Russel; and the
Dutch commanded by Admiral Allemond, near the
Cape of Barfleur in May, 1692 . . .
London & Edinburgh; Andrew Anderson; 1692.
20pp.; [incl. fleet lists]. 8vo.

876. [Anonymous].
An exact Journal of the victorious expedition of the
Confederate Fleet, the last year, under the command
of . . . Admiral Russel; giving an account of his
relieving Barcellona, and the taking of a great
number of Prizes from the French . . . To which is
added, a relation of the Engagement between Capt.
Killegrew, and the Two French Men of War that
were taken in the Fare of Messina.
London; J.Whitlock; 1695. 28pp. 8vo.

877. [Anonymous].
An Account of the sorts and numbers of Ships and
Vessels now building for His Majesty:
added to His Royal Navy ⎫
cleaned and refitted yearly ⎪ Since this War.
Rebuilt and repair'd   ⎬
Kept in Sea-Pay   ⎭
As the same was Presented to His Majesty by the
Officers of His Navy at His going over to Holland.
London; 1695. [4]pp.; tables & lists. 4to.

878. [Anonymous].
An Account of the Men of War (not including
privateers) taken from the French since the
beginning of the War (Declared the 7th of May,
1689) to the 1st of October, 1695.
[London; 1695]. [4]pp.; tables & lists. 4to.

879. [Anonymous].
An Account of what English Men of War have been
taken, or otherwise lost, during the present War . . .
London (Savoy); Edward Jones; 1695. 11pp. 8vo.

880. [Anonymous].
The Navy and the capture of Cork and Kinsale,
1690.
Naval Review, vol.xxi (1933), pp.753–8.

VI. General Works

881. ANDERSON, *Dr.* Roger Charles.
Naval wars in the Baltic during the sailing-ship
epoch, 1522–1850.
London; C.Gilbert-Wood; 1910. vi; 423pp.; plans.
8vo.

882. ANDERSON . . .
Naval wars in the Levant, 1559–1853.
Liverpool; University Press; 1952. ix, 619pp.; plates.
8vo.

883. ANDERSON . . . *et alia.*
Lists of men of war, 1650–1700.
Cambridge; University Press (for the Society for
Nautical Research); 1935–9. 8vo.
    *Issued in five parts:– i. English ships: by R.C.
Anderson. ii. French ships: by Pierre Le Conte. iii.
Swedish ships: by H.Borjeson; Danish–Norwegian
ships: by P.Holck; German ships: by W.Vogel &
H.Szymanski. iv. Ships of the United Netherlands: by
A.Vreugdenhil. v. Index.*

884. ANDERSON . . .
Lists of English men of war, 1509–1649.
Cambridge; University Press (for the Society for
Nautical Research); 1959. 8vo.

885. BACKSTRÖM, P.O.
Svenska Flottans Historia.
Stockholm; Norstedt; 1884. 513pp.; pls. 8vo.
    Includes numerous appendices and fleet-lists.

886. BERNARDY, Amy A.
Venezia e il Turco nella seconda metà del secolo
xvii . . .
Florence; G.Civelli; 1902. 143pp.; pls. 8vo.

887. BOOY, *Lieut-Commander* A.de, RNN.
Holland in the Mediterranean, (1607–1704).
The Mariner's Mirror, vol.xxv (October 1939),
pp.392–416.

888. BOTELER, Nicholas.
Colloquia Maritima: or, sea-dialogues . . .
London; William Fisher & Richard Mount; 1688.
[xii], 404pp.; engr. frontis. small 8vo.

889. BOTELER . . .
Six dialogues about sea-service . . .
London; Moses Pitt; 1685. [ii]; 404pp. 8vo.

890. BOXER, *Professor* C.R.
European rivalry in the Indian Seas, 1600–1700.
The Mariner's Mirror, vol.xiv (January 1928), pp.
13–25.
  *See also the author's: Dutch Seaborne Empire and
Portuguese Seaborne Empire (Hutchinson; 1966 and
1969), both of which have important chapters on the
17th century.*

891. CASTEX, *Lieutenant* Edmond.
The cooperation of arms at sea during the seventeenth century.
Translated by C.N.Watts.
Revue Militaire & Generale (1914), pp.211; 359.

892. CLARK, *Sir* George Norman.
The seventeenth century.
Oxford; Clarendon Press; 1929. 372pp.; maps. 8vo.
  With an important chapter on armies and navies.

893. CLOWES, William Laird, *et alia*.
The Royal Navy. A History from the earliest times
to the present. Vol.ii.
London; Sampson Low, Marston; 1898. 593pp.;
pls. & charts. 4to.
  Volume ii covers the period 1603–1714.

894. COLEMAN, D.C.
Naval dockyards under the later Stuarts.
English Historical Review, vol.vi (2nd series), (1953/4),
pp.134–155.

895. COLLIBER, Samuel.
Columna Rostrata: or, a critical history of the
English Sea-Affairs: wherein all the remarkable
actions of the English Nation at Sea are described,
and the most considerable events (especially in the
Account of the three Dutch Wars) are proved, . . .
By Samuel Colliber.
London; R.Robinson; 1727. 312 + [8]pp. 8vo.
  *A copy of the second edition (1739) is also in the
Library.*

896. CORBETT, *Professor* Julian S.
England in the Mediterranean. A study of the rise
and influence of British power within the Straits,
1603–1713.
London; Longmans, Green; 1904. 2 vols. 342;
351pp. pls & charts. 8vo.
  A major work of scholarship.

897. CRUMP, Helen J.
Colonial Admiralty jurisdiction in the seventeenth
century.
University of London Ph.D thesis; 1931.

898. DURO, Cesàreo Fernandez.
Armada Española desde la union de los Reinos de
Castilla y de Leon.
Madrid; Rivadeneyra; 1895–1903. 9 vols. *ca.*
4,000pp. 8vo.
  *A monumental work and still the main authority for
Spanish naval history. Vols.iii, iv and v. cover the
periods 1588–1621; 1621–1650; and 1650–1690,
respectively.*

899. EDMUNDSON, G.
Anglo–Dutch rivalry during the first half of the
seventeenth century.
Oxford; Clarendon Press; 1911. 176pp. 8vo.

900. ELIAS, *Dr.* Johan E.
Schetsen uit de geschiedenis van ons Zeewezen.
The Hague; Martinus Nijhoff; 1916–1930. 6 vols.
8vo.
  *With extensive coverage of the seventeenth century,
and especially the Dutch Wars.*

901. ELIAS . . .
De Vlootbouw in Nederland, 1596–1655.
Amsterdam; 1933. xi; 173pp.; 8vo.

902. GARDE, H.G.
Den Danske-Norske sømagts historie, 1535–1700.
Copenhagen; Muhle; 1861. 346pp. 8vo.

903. GARDINER, Samuel Rawson.
(a) History of England from the accession of James I
to the outbreak of the Civil War, 1603–1642.
London; Longmans; 1883–4. 10 vols. 8vo.
(b) History of the Great Civil War, 1642–9.
London; Longmans; 1886–91. 3 vols. 8vo.
(c) History of the Commonwealth & Protectorate,
1649–1660.
London; Longmans; 1894–1901. 3 vols. 8vo.

904. GRAEFE, F.
The Flanders coast during the wars of the seventeenth century.
Marine Rundschau (October 1921). pp.365–379.

905. GUGLIELMOTTI, P.Alberto.
Storia della Marina Pontificia . . .
vol.viii.: La squadra ausiliaria della Marina Romana
a Candia . . . 1644 al 1699.
Rome; Voghera Carlo; 1883. 529pp. 12mo.

906. GYLLENGRANAT, C.A.
Sveriges sjökrigs-historia.
Carlskrona; Georg Ameen; 1840. 2 vols. [vol.i: to
1718]. 353; 343pp. 8vo.

907. HINTON, R.W.K.
The English interest in the Baltic, 1622–1670.
University of Cambridge Ph.D. thesis; 1950.

908. HOFMEISTER, A.
Die maritimen und colonialen bestrebungen des
Grossen Kurfürsten, 1640 bis 1688.
Emden; W.Haynel; 1886. 64pp.; 8vo.

909. INNES, A.D.
The maritime and colonial expansion of England
under the Stuarts, (1603–1714).
London; Sampson Low; [1931]. 376pp.; pls. 8vo.

910. JAMES, G.F. & SHAW, J.J.S.
[a]. Admiralty administration and personnel, 1689–
1714.
IHR Bull., vols.xiv (June 1936), pp.10–24 & xv
(February 1937), pp.166–183.
[b]. Some further aspects of Admiralty administration, 1689–1714.
IHR Bull., vol.xvii (June 1939), pp.13–27.

911. JANE, Fred.T.
The Imperial Russian Navy. Its past, present and
future.
London; W.Thacker; 1899. 755pp.; pls. 4to.
   *Includes an important chapter on the birth of the
Russian Navy, 1645–1725.*

912. JONGE, J.C.de.
Geschiedenis van het Nederlandsche Zeewezen.
Haarlem; A.C.Kruseman; 1858–62. 5 vols. 8vo.

913. LISK, Jill.
The struggle for supremacy in the Baltic, 1600–1725.
London; University Press; 1967. 232pp.; 1 map.
8vo.

914. MAHAN, *Rear-Admiral* Alfred Thayer. (1840–
1914).
The Influence of Sea Power upon History. 1660–
1783.
London; Sampson Low; 1890. xxiv; 557pp.; maps
& plans. 8vo.

915. LACOUR-GAYET, G.
La Marine Militaire de la France sous les règnes de
Louis XIII et de Louis XIV.
Paris; Honoré Champion; 1911. 2 vols.: 268;
327pp.; pls. 8vo.
   *Together with the works of Roncière [q.v.],
indispensable for the study of French naval history.
Volume i. covers the period 1624–1661, under the rule of
Richelieu and Mazarin; ii. 1661–1715 – Louis XIV,
Colbert, Seignelay and Pontchartrain.*

916. MAÎTREJEAN, M.F.
La flotte sous Colbert et l'Ordonnance Maritime de
1681.
Bordeaux; Gonouilhon; 1869. 286pp. 8vo.

917. MALONE, Joseph J.
England and the Baltic naval stores trade in the
seventeenth and eighteenth centuries.
The Mariner's Mirror, vol.lviii (November 1972),
pp.375–396.

918. MAYDMAN, Henry.
Naval Speculations, and maritime politicks: being a
modest and brief discourse of the Royal Navy of
England . . . Also necessary measures in the present
war with France, &c. . . .
London; William Bonny; 1691. [xxx]; 349pp.;
engr. frontis. 8vo.

919. MUNTHE, *Kommandörkapten* Arnold.
Sjömaktens inflytande på Sveriges Historia . . .
Stockholm; Marinlitteraturföreningens Förlag;
1921. 280pp. 8vo.

920. NAVARRETE, Fernandez de.
Coleccion de documentos y manuscriptos
compilados por . . .
Madrid; Museo Naval; [1971]. 32 vols. + index vol.
8vo.
   *A vast store-house of source-material for the study of
Spanish naval and colonial history. The volumes of
particular interest for the 17th century are:-
iii. (Instructions, Orders); viii & ix (Records and
projects, 1553–1725); xi. (Despatches and instructions,
1625–1706); xii (Engagements, 1601–1670); xxi–xxiv.
(Fleet Orders and events); and xxx (Navies, 1522–
1727).*

921. NEESER, Robert Wilden.
The British naval operations in the West Indies,
1650–1700 – a study in naval administration.
USNIP, vol.xl (1914), pp.1599–1625.

922. NILSON, Charles.
Profit and Power; a study of England and the Dutch
Wars.
New York; Longmans; 1958. 169pp.; pls. 8vo.

923. POOL, Bernard.
Navy Board contracts, 1660–1832.
London; Longmans; 1966. 170pp.; 8vo.

924. POWELL, Isobel G.
Seventeenth century 'profiteering' in the Royal
Navy.
The Mariner's Mirror, vol.vii (August 1921), pp.243–
250.

925. RONCIÈRE, Charles de la.
Histoire de la Marine Française . . .
Paris; Plon; 1899–1932. 6 vols. 8vo.
   *Vols. 4, 5 and 6 are concerned with the 17th century,
being subtitled: 'En quête d'un Empire Colonial –
Richelieu'; 'La guerre de Trente Ans – Colbert'; 'Le
crépuscule du Grand Régne – l'apogée de la Guerre du
Course', respectively.*

926. ROSE, *Professor* J.Holland.
Seapower and expansion, 1660–1763.
In: Cambridge History of the British Empire, vol.i
(1929).

927. SCHAFFALITZKY de MUCKADELL, *Baron.*
Haandbog i Nordens Søkrigshistorie.
Copenhagen; 1911. 548pp.; many charts & plans.
8vo.
   *A comprehensive general survey of Scandinavian
naval history.*

928. STRAUSS, Victor von.
Die Kurfürstlich Brandenburgische und die
Kaiserlich Deutsche Kriegsflotte.
Berlin; R.Decker; 1875. 86pp.; 1 plan. 8vo.

929. [SVENSSON, S.Artur (*editor*)].
Svenska Flottans Historia . . .
Malmö; A.B.Alhems; 1942–5. 3 vols. large 4to.
   Volume i covers the period 1521–1679.

930. SZYMANSKI, Hans.
Brandenburg-Preussen zur see, 1605–1815. Ein
beitrag zur frühgeschichte der Deutschen Marine.
Leipzig; Koehler & Amelang; [1939]. 200pp.; pls.
8vo.

931. 'THYSIUS, Antonius'.
Historia Navalis, sive celeberrimorum praeliorum
quae Mari ab antiquissimis temporibus usque ad
Pacem Hispanicam Batavi, foederatiq. . . .
Lugdunum Batavorum [Leyden]; Joannis Maire;
1657. Latin text. 305 + [7]pp. vellum. 8vo.
   *A very early Dutch naval history, describing events up
to the Peace of Westphalia, 1648.*

932. TORNQVIST, *Lieut.* Carl Gustaf.
Utkast till Svenska Flottans Sjö-tåg . . .
Stockholm; A.J.Nordström; [1788]. 2 vols. in one:
175 + 107 + [13]pp.; plans. 8vo.
   *Chronological narrative of Swedish naval history for
the period 1522–1719.*

933. WÄTJEN, *Dr.* Hermann.
Die Nederlander im Mittelmeergebiet zur zeit ihrer
höchsten machtstellung. Berlin; Karl Curtius; 1909.
416pp.; 8vo.

934. WILLIAMSON, James A.
The English Channel. A History.
London; Collins; 1959. 381pp.; pls. & maps. 8vo.
   With three chapters on the seventeenth century.

935. [Anonymous].
СПИСОКЪ РУССКИХЪ ВОЕННЫХЪ СУ-
ДОВЪ СЪ 1668 ПО 1860 ГОДЪ.
[Lists and Registers of Russian warships and the
fleet, 1668 to 1860].
St Petersburg; 1872. 799pp.; incl. appendices and
statistical tables. 4to.

936. [Anonymous].
Geschichte der K.und K. Kriegsmarine . . .
Vienna; Ministry of War (Marine Section); 1882–
1906. 5 vols. 8vo.
   *Standard official history of the Austrian Navy. Vol.i
covers the period 1500–1797.*

937. [Anonymous].
Essai de chronologie d'histoire maritime . . .
Triton; vols.lv, lviii, lix, lx, lxi–lxii, lxiv–lxvii;
[1960–1963].
   *An important and detailed analysis of events in French
naval history, arranged year by year. The period covered
is from 1650–1700.*

The Eighteenth Century (to 1815)

THE EARLY DECADES

I. The War of the Spanish Succession, 1702–1713

[a] Home waters and the Mediterranean

938. AUSSEUR, *Capitaine* J.P.
Le mentor du Comte de Toulouse.
Triton, vol.xci (March 1968), pp.2–8.
  Includes an account of the battle of Velez Malaga, 13 August 1704, and the Franco–Spanish fleet commander, Comte de Toulouse.

939. BERTHE, Jacques.
La querelle de Duguay-Trouin et de Forbin à propos du combat du 21 Octobre, 1707.
Revue Maritime, no.ccxlii (April 1967), pp.452–470.

940. CALENDAR OF STATE PAPERS: Calendar of Treasury Books.
vols.xvi [October 1700–December 1701] – xxvii [January–December 1713].
London; HMSO; 1938–1955.
  Includes material on:
[*vol.xvi*]: *Admiral Shovell in the Mediterranean.*
[*vol.xvii*]: *Admiral Rooke's fleet; the Cadiz squadron.*
[*vol.xviii*]: *War supplies and Navy accounts; Rooke's expedition to Cadiz; ships at Vigo; Shovell in the Mediterranean and the Straits.*
[*vol.xix*]: *Rooke at Vigo; Shovell's squadron; the Fleet at Lisbon; letters from Rooke.*
[*vol.xx*]: *The Cadiz expedition under Rooke; Rooke takes Gibraltar; Leake's victory over de Pointis at Marbella; Shovell.*
[*vol.xxi*]: *French privateers in the Channel; Shovell; ships lost in the Great Storm of 26/27 November 1703.*
[*vol.xxii*]: *The destruction of Shovell's squadron, wrecked on the Scillys; the Channel Fleet.*
[*vol.xxiii*]: *Byng and Jennings at Lisbon; Sir John Norris in the Mediterranean.*
[*vol.xxiv*]: *Channel Fleet; Norris.*
[*vol.xxv*]: *Leake's fleet.*
[*vol.xxvi*]: *Despatch of a fleet to the Mediterranean; Navy accounts, 1711–12.*
[*vol.xxvii*]: *Ships in the Mediterranean; Navy accounts, 1713.*

941. COOKE, James Herbert.
The shipwreck of Sir Cloudesley Shovell on the Scilly Islands in 1707; from original and con-temporary documents hitherto unpublished . . .
Gloucester; J.Bellows; 1883. 15pp., frontis., foldg. table. 4to.
  In a celebrated catastrophe, Admiral Shovell with his flagship the ASSOCIATION, *96, and many of his squadron returning home from the Mediterranean, were lost in thick weather on the Scilly Islands' rocks during the night of 22 October, 1707.*

942. CORBETT, *Sir* Julian Stafford, (1854–1922).
England in the Mediterranean. A study of the rise and influence of British power within the Straits, 1603–1713.
London; Longmans; 1904. 2 vols. 342; 351pp., maps. 8vo.
  A masterly study. The last six chapters of vol.2, relate to the period:
chap.xxviii. The Spanish Succession. xxix. The campaign of 1702. xxx. Marlborough and the Navy. xxxi. Gibraltar and Malaga. xxxii. Gibraltar and Toulon. xxxiii. Minorca.

943. DICKINSON, H.T.
The capture of Minorca, 1708.
The Mariner's Mirror, vol.li (August 1956), pp.195–204; map.

944. FRANKS, *Lieut.* Robert Denys, RN.
Mediterranean policy in the War of the Spanish Succession.
Naval Review, vol.xxv (1937), pp.493–509.

945. HISTORICAL MANUSCRIPTS COMMISSION: Marquis of Bath Mss.
London; HMSO; 1904. 2 vols. 8vo.
  Vol.i contains references to the movements of the English Fleet, 1705–7; and the activities of Admiral Shovell in the Mediterranean, 1704–7.

946. KAMEN, H.
The destruction of the Spanish silver fleet at Vigo in 1702.
IHR Bull., vol.xxxix (November 1966), pp.165–173.
  On returning home from the Mediterranean, the Allied fleet commander Admiral Sir George Rooke learned that the Spanish treasure fleet from Havana had arrived in Vigo Bay on the west coast of Galicia. On 12 October the assault squadron, led by Vice-Admiral Hopsonn, penetrated the strong harbour-boom and made a brilliantly successful attack. By sunset most of the Spanish treasure ships and the escorting French squadron under Châteaurenault had been taken or sunk in Vigo Bay.

947. KEPLER, J.S.
Sir John Jennings and the preparations for the naval expedition to the Mediterranean of 1711–1713.
The Mariner's Mirror, vol.lix (February 1973), pp.13–33.

948. LAUGHTON, L.G.Carr.
The battle of Velez Malaga, 1704.
RUSIJ, vol.lxviii (1923).
  Velez Malaga, or Malaga – fought between Anglo–Dutch (Admiral Rooke) and Franco–Spanish (Comte de Toulouse) fleets on 13 August 1704 – was the major sea battle of the war. Although indecisive, it foiled the Franco–Spanish attempt to recapture Gibraltar, which had been taken by the Allies three weeks before.

949. [LEAKE, *Admiral of the Fleet Sir* John, (1656–1720).].
Orders, Instructions, &c., 1705–1710.
In: Historical Manuscripts Commission – House of Lords Mss, vol.viii (1923).
  Leake was commander-in-chief Mediterranean Fleet and the victor of the battle of Marbella, (10 March 1705).

950. LOZAC, H.J.
Les trésors des galions de Vigo.
Neptunia, vol.xl (April 1958), pp.7–11.

951. MARCUS, *Dr.* Geoffrey J.
Sir Clowdisley Shovell's last passage.
RUSIJ. vol.cii (November 1957), pp.540–548.

952. MAIR, R.J.B.
The capture of Gibraltar, 24 July 1704.
United Service Magazine, vol.xxix, n.s. (1904).

953. MARTULLE DE BERGERAC, Jean.
Memoirs d'un Protestant.
Translated from the original documents by Lady Fawcett.
The Mariner's Mirror, vol.xl (May 1954), pp.145–151.
  'A French galley slave's description of an engagement in the Thames estuary between a fleet of French galleys under the command of Captain M.de Langeron of the French Navy and a British convoy under the protection of HMS NIGHTINGALE *(36-gun frigate) on 5 September, 1708,' . . .[from the introduction].*

954. MAY, *Commander* William Edward, RN.
The last voyage of Sir Cloudesley Shovell.
Journal of the Institute of Navigation, vol.xiii (1960), pp.324–332.

955. MEIRAT, Jean.
Le siège de Toulon en 1707.
Neptunia, vol.lxxi (March 1963), pp.2–9.

956. MERRIMAN, *Commander* Reginald Dundas, RIN. (d.1960).
Action between HMS *Nightingale* and six French galleys.
The Mariner's Mirror, vol.xl (August 1954), pp.232–3.
  See entry no.953, above. The note is followed by a short comment from Dr.R.C.Anderson.

957. MOLLEMA, J.C.
De verovering van de Zilvervloot in de baai van Vigos, 23 October 1702.
In: Jaarverslag Scheepvaarts Museum [Amsterdam], 1943–45.

958. OWEN, *Commander* John Hely, RN.
War at sea under Queen Anne, 1702–1708.
Cambridge; University Press; 1938. 316pp., pls., charts. 8vo.
  An important study. Includes chapters on: The naval war in the Mediterranean – Cadiz, Port Mahon, Barcelona (1705), Toulon (1707); French attacks on trade in the Channel; Cruisers and convoys; & Dunkirk, 1708.

959. PIETERS, E.
Vigo, 1702.
Belgian Shiplover, vol.lii (1956), p.165.

960. POWELL, *Commander* J.W.Damer, DSC, RNR.
The wreck of Sir Cloudesley Shovell.
The Mariner's Mirror, vol.xliii (November 1957), pp.333–6.

961. [ROOKE, *Admiral of the Fleet Sir* George, (1650–1708)].
[a]. The Journal of Sir George Rooke. [*edited by* Oscar Browning].
In: Navy Records Society series, vol.ix (London; NRS; 1897).
[b]. Orders and papers relating to the expedition to Cadiz and operations at Vigo.
In: Historical Manuscripts Commission: House of Lords Mss, vols.ii (1903) *and* v. (1910), *and* Finch Mss, vol.ii (1922).
[c]. Admiralty Instructions to Rooke on the fleet for Cadiz, 1702.
In: CSP – Domestic: Anne, 1702–3 (London; HMSO; 1916), pp.108–110; 215–217.

962. [SHOVELL, *Admiral of the Fleet Sir* Clowdisley, (1650–1707)].
[a]. Inquiry into his expedition to the Mediterranean, 1703.
In: Historical Manuscripts Commission: House of Lords Mss, vol.ii (1903).
[b]. Admiralty Orders & Instructions.
In: Historical Manuscripts Commission: House of Lords Mss, vol.ii (1903) and Finch Mss, vol.ii (1922).
[c]. Documents relating to the Valencia expedition, 1706.
In: Historical Manuscripts Commission: Bath Mss, vol.i (1904).

963. SINCLAIR-STEVENSON, Christopher.
The Jacobite expedition of 1708.
History Today, vol.xxi (1971), pp.264–272.

964. TAUBMAN, *Reverend* Nathaniel (*d.*1720?).
Memoirs of the British fleets and squadrons in the
Mediterranean, anno 1708 and 1709.
Wherein an Account is given of the reduction of
Sardignia, Minorca, the late sieges of Port Maon,
Alicant and Denia . . .
By the Rev^d. Mr. Nathaniel Taubman, Chaplain of
the Royal Navy.
London; D.Leach; 1710. 194pp., map. 8vo.
   *There is also a copy of the second edition in the
Library (London; Arthur Collins; 1714) – in which the
title reads: '. . . By the . . . , Chaplain to the English
Fleet at Leghorn.' A third edition appeared in 1721.*

965. [TOULOUSE, *Comte de*].
Account of the Battle of Malaga, 1704.
In: Historical Manuscripts Commission – Portland
Mss, vol.viii (1907).
   *In French. De Toulouse was the admiral in command
of the combined Franco–Spanish fleet.*

966. [Anonymous].
An impartial account of all the material transactions
of the Grand Fleet and Land Forces from their first
setting out from Spithead, June the 29., till His
Grace the Duke of Ormond's arrival at Deal . . .
In which is included a particular relation of the
Expedition at Cadiz, and the glorious victory at
Vigo.
By an Officer that was present in those Actions.
London; R.Gibson & J.Nutt.; 1703. title., 32pp.,
tables. small 8vo.

967. [Anonymous].
A narrative of Sir George Rooke's late voyage to the
Mediterranean, where he commanded as Admiral of
the Confederate Fleet. With a description of
Gibraltar . . . which was attack'd and taken by the
said Fleet, and now remains in the possession of the
Allies.
An account also of the Naval Battel fought betwixt
the Confederate and French King's Fleet; with a
judgement of the event.
In a letter to a person of quality.
London; Benjamin Took; 1704. 29pp. small 8vo.

968. [Anonymous].
A review of the late Engagement at Sea, being a
collection of private letters, never before printed . . .
Containing the truest and most authentick accounts;
with some remarks on the conduct of our Admirals,
particularly Sir G . . . R . . .
London; John Nutt; 1704. 23pp. 8vo.
   *A contemporary pamphlet describing the Battle of
Malaga.*

969. [Anonymous].
Die zur zee gebrochene macht der Kron Frankreich.
Oder: erfreuliche nachricht von Engl. = und
Holländische Zee-Armada den 24 Augusti, anno
1704; unwelt Malaga im Mittelländischen Meer . . .
Leipzig; Johann T.Boetio; 1704. title; 40pp., foldg.
plate. 8vo.

970. [Anonymous].
Eigentliche vorstellung der grossen See-Victori
zwischen der Engl. Holländischen und Französichen
Flotten so den 24 Augusti Anno 1704 . . .
Augsburg; Stephan Maystadter; [*ca.*1705].
folio sheet, with large engr. plate shewing the action
and descriptive black-letter text below.

971. [Anonymous].
Liste des navires perdus à la bataille de Vigo en 1702.
La Revue Maritime, no.cclviii (October 1968),
p.1278.

[b] The West Indies and North America

972. BARNETT, John.
Benbow and his last fight.
Cornhill Magazine, n.s., vol.xxix (1910), pp.97–112.
   *On 20 August 1702, Admiral John Benbow with six
of the line met a smaller French squadron under M.
Ducasse off Santa Marta on the coast of the Spanish
Main. During the four days' running fight the Admiral
led his flagship the* BREDA *against the enemy with great
gallantry, but the conduct of most of his subordinates was
disgraceful. On the last day Benbow was severely
wounded but refused to quit the quarterdeck. After the
action, four of the ships' commanders were court-
martialled and two sentenced to death. Benbow himself
later died of his wounds.*

973. BASSETT, W.G.
English naval policy in the Caribbean, 1698–1703.
précis in: *IHR Bull.*, vol.xi (November 1933),
pp.122–125.

974. [BENBOW, *Admiral* John (1653–1702)].
Admiralty Instructions to Admiral Benbow,
commander-in-chief West Indies station.
In: Calendar of State Papers. Domestic – Anne (1702),
pp.345–6; 545–7.

975. BOURNE, Ruth M.
Queen Anne's Navy in the West Indies.
New Haven, Conn.; Yale; 1939. viii, 334pp., 1 map.
8vo.

976. BOURNE, Ruth M.
Queen Anne's Navy in the West Indies.
EHR, vol.liv (1939), p.754.

977. BOURNE, Ruth M.
The exchange of prisoners in the West Indies in
Queen Anne's War.
Proc. South Carolina Hist. Assoc. (1944), pp.3–20.

978. CALENDAR OF STATE PAPERS –
COLONIAL: America and the West Indies.
vols. xviii (1700) – xxvii (1712–14).
London; HMSO; 1910–1926. 8vo.
Includes material on:
*[vol.xviii – 1700]: Piracy in North America & the West
Indies; Spanish seizure of English ships; friction
between Admiral Benbow and the Governor of Jamaica.*

*[vol.xix – 1701]: Preparations for war; privateers; naval
defence of St. Kitts; Newfoundland fisheries.*

*[vol.xx – 1702]: Benbow's engagement with Ducasse off
Santa Marta and the court-martial of Benbow's officers.
List of Châteaurenault's fleet at Martinique, March
1702; privateering at Massachusetts; Kidd and piracy;
the taking of St. Augustine, October 1702; naval
defence of Barbados & the Leeward Islands.*

*[vol.xxi – 1703]: The War in the West Indies;
Franco–Spanish expedition to the Bahamas; convoys;
naval protection for New England & Barbados.*

*[vol.xxii – 1704–5]: Rear Admiral Whetstone in West
Indies; naval defence of Jamaica, Antigua & Barbados;
privateers and pirates; unsuccessful French attack on St.
John's, Newfoundland.*

*[vol.xxiii – 1706–June 1708]: Commodore Wager's
action at Cartagena, 28 May 1708; Admirals Whetstone
and Jennings in the West Indies; French privateers;
d'Iberville's raids on the Leeward Islands.*

*[vol.xxiv – June 1708–December 1709]: Proposed
expedition against Canada; Navy in the West Indies;
piracy & privateering off the Spanish Main; shortage of
sailors at Jamaica; impressment; French & Spanish
privateers in New England, Virginia, Bahamas &
Jamaica.*

*[vol.xxv – 1710–June 1711.]: Ducasse in the West
Indies; privateers from Port Royal; Nova Scotia as a
prospective source of naval stores; French attacks on the
Leeward Islands; privateer attack on Montserrat, 1710.*

*[vol.xxvi – July 1711–June 1712]: New England &
Newfoundland fisheries; Admiral Sir Hovenden
Walker's expedition to the St. Lawrence; friction
between the Navy and West Indian governors; defence of
St. Kitts and Nevis.*

*[vol.xxvii – July 1712–July 1714]: Defence of Virginia
coast; guardships at Barbados; Jamaican privateers;
hurricane at Jamaica, August 12 and list of ships*

*wrecked; French squadron under Cassart raids Antigua,
July 1712, & later Montserrat; Newfoundland
fisheries; Ducasse at Martinique.*

979. CALENDAR OF STATE PAPERS: Treasury
Books.
vols. xviii (1703) – xxvii (1713).
London; HMSO; 1936–1955. 8vo.
Includes material on:
*Admirals Benbow and Graydon in the West
Indies[xviii]; Whetstone in the West Indies [xix]
and [xxii]; The Fleet in the West Indies and Admiral
Baker to sail there [xxxiii]; The Walker expedition
to Canada [xxvi–xxvii]; warship stations at New
England [xxvii].*

980. CROUSE, Nellis Maynard.
The French struggle for the West Indies, 1665–1713.
New York; Columbia; 1943. 324pp., pls. 8vo.
In the English Historical Review, *vol.lx (1945),
p.275, there is an article by the author under the same
title.*

981. GRAHAM, *Professor* Gerald Sandford. [*editor*].
The Walker Expedition to Quebec, 1711.
Edited with an introduction by G.S.Graham.
London; Navy Record Society series, vol.xciv;
1953. 241pp. 8vo.
*Concerning the disastrous expedition commanded by
Admiral Sir Hovenden Walker. This edition contains an
historical introduction, a reprint of Walker's Journal,
1720, and a number of relevant documents.*

982. OWEN, *Commander* John Hely, RN.
War at sea under Queen Anne, 1702–8.
Cambridge; University Press; 1938. 316pp., pls.;
charts. 8vo.

983. PARES, *Professor* Richard.
The manning of the Navy in the West Indies, 1702–
63.
RHS Trans., 4th series, vol.xx (1937), pp.31–60.

984. WALKER, *Admiral Sir* Hovenden, (d.1728).
A Journal: or full account of the late Expedition to
Canada. With an appendix containing commissions,
orders, instructions, letters, memorials, courts-
martials, councils of war, etc., relating thereto.
By Sir Hovenden Walker, Kt.
London; D.Browne; 1720. 304pp., tables. 8vo.

985. [Anonymous].
An account of the arraignments and trials of Capt.
Richard Kirkby, Capt. John Constable, Capt.
Cooper Wade, Capt. Samuel Vincent, and Capt.
Christopher Fogg . . . at a court-martial held on
board the ship *Breda* in Port Royal harbour in

985. [Anonymous], *continued*
Jamaica . . . the 8th, 9th, 10th and 12th days of
October 1702. For cowardice, neglect of duty,
breach of orders, and other crimes, committed by
them in a fight at sea . . . between John Benbow
Esq., and Admiral Du Casse . . . For which Capt.
Kirkby and Capt. Wade were sentenc'd to be shot
to death.
Transmitted from two eminent merchants at Port
Royal . . .
London; John Gellibrand; 1703. [ii], 10pp. small
folio.

II. The War with Spain, 1718–1720

986. BERETTI-LANDI, *Marquis de.*
Relacion veridica, del combate quel et dia once de
Agosto de mil' setecientos y diez y ocho, huvo entre
la Armada de España y de Inglaterra en las costas
orientales de Sicilia, y en la canal de Malta.
Madrid; Juan de Ariztia; 1718. 117pp. 8vo.
    *A Spanish account of the decisive battle off Cape
Passaro, Sicily on 11 August 1718 – in which the British
Mediterranean fleet under Admiral Sir George Byng
(later Viscount Torrington) overwhelmed the Spaniards
commanded by Vice-Admiral Castañeta. By the end of the
day the Spaniards had lost 22 warships, taken, burnt or
sunk. See also the entries which follow.*

987. [BYNG, *Admiral Sir* George, *Viscount
Torrington,* (1663–1733)].
An Account of the expedition of the British Fleet to
Sicily, in the years 1718, 1719 and 1720. Under the
command of Sir George Byng, Bart., . . . Admiral
and Commander-in-Chief of H.M. Fleet . . .
. . . Collected from the Admiral's manuscripts, and
other original papers.
London; J. & R.Tonson; 1739. 96pp. 8vo.

988. [BYNG, *Admiral Sir* George, . . .].
A true account of the expedition of the British Fleet
to Sicily in the years 1718, 1719 and 1720. Under
the command of Sir George Byng, Bart., . . .
. . . Collected from Sir George's manuscripts and
other original papers.
London; R.West; 1740. 86pp., tables (with fleet
lists). 8vo.

989. [BYNG, Pattee, *2nd Viscount Torrington,* (1699–
1747)].
Pattee Byng's Journal, 1718–1720.
Edited by J.L.Cranmer-Byng.
London; Navy Records Society series, vol.lxxxviii,
1950. 311pp. 8vo.
    *Written by Admiral Sir George Byng's son and
important for its information on the Cape Passaro
campaign.*

990. CALENDAR OF STATE PAPERS:
COLONIAL.
[a]. vol.xxx. (*August 1717 – December 1718*).
London; HMSO; 1930. [repr.1964]. In two parts.
8vo.
    *Includes material on: Navy estimates (28 November
1717); Admiral Byng and the Mediterranean Squadron;
the fleet at Minorca; Byng's victory off Cape Passaro;
(11 August 1718); Spanish activities in the West Indies;*

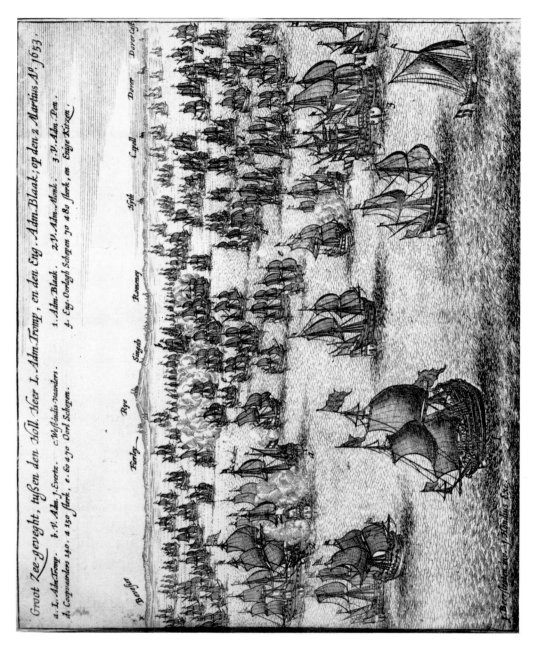

PLATE V: Jodocus Hondius' engraving of part of 'The Three Days Battle' between the fleets under Blake and Tromp, 28 February–2 March, 1653. From Arnoldus Montanus': *De Beroerde Oceaan, of twee-jaarige zee-daaden der Vereenigde Nederlanders en Engelsche . . .* Amsterdam; 1656

A GREAT AND
BLOVDY FIGHT
AT
SEA:

Between five Men of War belonging to the Parliament of *England*, and a Squadron of the Princes Fleet ; wherein is con-
tained, the full particulars, and manner of the said Fight ; the
number of ships that were sunk and taken, together with divers prisoners, great store of Match and Bullet, and 40 pieces
of Ordnance , and the rest of the Fleet quite dispersed and
scattered. Also, the Resolution of the *Welsh-men*, and the
Parliaments Declaration to the Kingdom.

Likewise, a *Proclamation* of the Kingdom of *Scotland*, touching
the crowning of the Prince of *VVales*.

    Imprimatur.   *Theodore* Jennings.

PLATE VI: Title-page of: *A Great and Bloudy Fight at Sea: Between five Men of War belonging to the
Parliament of England and a Squadron of the Princes Fleet* . . . [Bristol]; 1659

990. STATE PAPERS: COLONIAL, *continued*
piracy in the Caribbean; guardships for the Leeward Islands.
[*b*]. *vol.xxxi.(January 1719 – February 1720).*
London; HMSO; 1933. 8vo.
Includes material on: The War with Spain; expeditionary force assembling at Cadiz, 1719; Spanish seizure of Jamaican vessels and threat to the Bahamas; the English squadron at Jamaica; naval protection of Carolina; piracy in Bermuda and the Bahamas; the Admiralty Court, New England.
[*c*]. *vol.xxxii. (March 1720 – December 1721).*
London; HMSO; 1933. 8vo.
Includes material on: Spanish attack on the Bahamas, February 1720; the Havana fleet's threat to Carolina; piracy in the West Indies; Spanish privateers ignoring the conclusion of peace; Commodore Vernon's dispute with the Governor of Jamaica over searching merchant ships from Hispaniola; Navy guardships in the West Indies.

991. RICHMOND, *Admiral Sir* Herbert William. (1871–1946).
The expedition to Sicily, 1718, under Sir George Byng.
RUSIJ, vol.liii (1909), pp.1135–1152.

992. WARNER, Oliver.
Great Sea Battles.
London; Spring Books; 1966. 304pp., illustr. 4to.
Includes a chapter on Cape Passaro.

III. Events and operations elsewhere, 1714-1738

993. ANDERSON, *Dr.* Roger Charles.
Naval wars in the Baltic during the sailing ship epoch, 1522–1850.
London; C.Gilbert-Wood; 1910. 423pp., maps. pls. 8vo.
Includes chapters on the Baltic wars during the period and accounts (with plans) of the actions of Usedom (1 July 1715), Dynekilen (8 July 1716); the Danes' attack on Gothenborg (15 May 1717) and Stromstad (19 July 1717).

994. ANDERSON, . . .
Naval wars in the Levant, 1559–1853.
Liverpool; University Press; 1952. 619pp., pls., plans. 8vo.
There are accounts of the Corfu and Matapan operations, 1714–18 and the maritime struggle between Venice and the Ottoman Empire during the period.

995. ANDERSON, . . .
The two battles of Matapan, 1717 and 1718.
The Mariner's Mirror, vol.xxxi(January 1945), pp.33–42.

996. ANDERSON, . . .
Mediterranean galley-fleets in 1725.
The Mariner's Mirror, vol.xlii (August 1956), pp.179–187; figs.

997. BALLARD, *Admiral* George Alexander, (1862–1948).
The general situation in the Indian Ocean during the early Georgian period.
The Mariner's Mirror, vol.xii (October 1926), pp.375–395.

998. CALENDAR OF STATE PAPERS: COLONIAL.
[*a*]. *vol.xxxiii – 1722-1723.* (London; HMSO; 1934.) 8vo.
Includes material on: French and Indians' attack on shipping at Canso, June 1722; naval protection of St. Lucia and St. Vincent; Newfoundland fishery; piracy; transportation of convicts to Virginia; naval stores from the Plantations; the hurricane in Jamaica, 28 August 1722.
[*b*]. *vol.xxxiv – 1724-1725.* (London; HMSO; 1936.) 8vo.

998. STATE PAPERS: COLONIAL, *continued*
*Includes material on: fears of war with France;
Colonial Governors' disputes with the Navy; Jamaica
pirates.*
[*c*]. *vol.xxxv – 1726–1727.* (London; HMSO; 1936.)
8vo.
*Includes material on: depredations of Spanish 'guarda-
costas' on British shipping in the West Indies; outbreak of
war with Spain; Admiral Hosier off Cartagena and Porto
Bello; Vice-Admiralty Courts; Newfoundland fishery.*
[*d*]. *vol.xxxvi – 1728–1729.* (London; HMSO; 1937.)
8vo.
*Includes material on: War with Spain; Spanish
privateers in the Caribbean; the threat to Jamaica;
buccaneers at Campeachy.*
[*e*]. *vol.xxxvii – 1730.* (London; HMSO; 1937.) 8vo.
*Includes material on: Relations with Spain; the
logwood cutters of the Mosquito coast; H.M. ships on
Jamaica & Leeward Islands stations; colonial
privateering; the Newfoundland and Canso fisheries.*
[*f*]. *vol.xxxviii – 1731.* (London; HMSO; 1938.) 8vo.
*Includes material on: Depredations of Spanish 'guarda-
costas'; Havana fleet wrecked in the Windward
Passage, 1731; Newfoundland & Canso fisheries.*
[*g*]. *vol.xxxix – 1732.* (London; HMSO; 1939.) 8vo.
*Includes material on: Spanish seizure of British
shipping; French warships at Cape Breton Island, HMS
*SCARBOROUGH *involved; fisheries.*
[*h*]. *vol.xl – 1733.* (London; HMSO; 1939.) 8vo.
*Includes material on: Naval defence of the West
Indies; wreck of the Plate Fleet, July 1733; Campeachy
logwood dispute.*
[*i*]. *vol.xli – January 1734–June 1735.* (London;
HMSO; 1953.) 8vo.
*Includes material on: Danger to British commerce
from Danes in the West Indies; naval station at
Antigua; Admiralty instructions to Sir Chaloner Ogle;
Newfoundland fisheries.*
[*j*]. *vol.xlii – July 1735–December 1736.* (London;
HMSO; 1953.) 8vo.
*Includes material on: Reports on French threat to
Nova Scotia; Newfoundland fisheries; seizures by
Spanish 'guarda-costas'.*
[*k*]. *vol.xliii – 1737.* (London; HMSO; 1963.) 8vo.
*Includes material on: Naval preparations at Virginia,
New York and Carolina; further Spanish attacks on
British shipping.*
[*l*]. *vol.xliv – 1738.* (London; HMSO; 1969.) 8vo.
*Includes material on: British ships seized by Spaniards;
Naval officers' lists of shipping entering American and
West Indies' ports; Spanish naval preparations at Havana.*

999. CHANCE, James Frederick.
George I and the Northern War: a study of British–
Hanoverian policy in the north of Europe in the
years 1709 to 1721.
London; Smith, Elder; 1909. xviii, 516pp. 8vo.

1000. CHANCE, James Frederick.
The Baltic expedition and northern treaties of 1715.
English Historical Review, vol.xvii (1902), pp.443–
465.

1001. GWYN, Julian.
An incident on the Grain Coast, 1722.
The Mariner's Mirror, vol.lvi (August 1970), pp.315–
325.
When HMS GUERNSEY *was attacked by negroes at
Cape Mesurado, Liberia, on 10 December, 1722.*

1002. HARBON, H.W., TUXEN, A.P., WITH,
C.L. *and* HANSEN, A.L.
Den store Nordiske Krigs Historie.
Copenhagen; Ernst Bojesen; 1899–1920. 6 vols.
2, 678 pp. pls. & charts. 8vo.
*A comprehensive history of the Great Northern War.
The individual volumes are: i. Kong Frederik IV's
første Kamp om Sonderjylland Krigen, 1700. ii. Felttoget
i Skaane, 1709–1710. iii. Felttogene i Nordtyskland og
Baahuslen i Østersjøen og Kattegat, 1710–1712. iv. De
Nordiske Allieredes Kamp med Magnus Stenbock,
1712–1713. v. Kampen om Tønning, 1713–1714. vi.
Den Store Koalition mod Sverige af 1715.*

1003. HISTORICAL MANUSCRIPTS
COMMISSION.
See: Polworth Mss., vols.ii (London; HMSO; 1916)
for material on: Danish, Swedish and Russian naval
operations in the period, 1718–1720.
and iii (London; HMSO; 1931) for material on:
Baltic naval operations, 1720–1723.
See: 11th Report, appendix – part iv [Townshend
Mss, ff], (London; HMSO; 1887) for the:
Despatches of Admiral of the Fleet Sir John Norris,
relating to the Baltic Expedition, 1715.

1004. LESLIE, *Lieut.-Col.* J.H.
The siege of Gibraltar by the Spaniards, 1727.
Journ. Soc. Army Hist. Research, (July 1924).

1005. LOVENBRUCH, Pierre.
La flotte française à Copenhague en 1733.
Revue Maritime, vol.lxxx (August 1926), pp.156–171.

1006. MANFRONI, *Prof.* Camillo.
La Marina Pontificia durante la guerra di Corfù.
Rome, 1891. 61pp. 8vo.
That is, during the Turco–Venetian War, 1715–17.

1007. ROTHE, Casper Peter.
Forsög til naunkundige Danske Maends . . .
indeholdende den Danske söe-heldt og Vice-
Admiral Peder Tordenskjolds . . .
Copenhagen; 1747–1750. 401 + 332 + 300 +
64pp., black-letter text. charts & pls. oblong 4to.

1007. ROTHE, *continued*
*A contemporary narrative of the Danish–Swedish War
and Admiral Tordenskjolds' achievements at the battle of
Dynekilden, the blockade of Gothenburg and the attacks
on Strömstad and Mastrand, 1716–17.*

1008. WRANGEL, H.
Kriget i Östersjön, 1719–1721.
Stockholm; Wilhelmssons; 1906. 2 vols. in one:
466pp., appendix. 8vo.
*A narrative of the Baltic War, 1719–1721. Includes
accounts of the operations of the Russian and Swedish
fleets, 1719; the expedition to Danzig, 1719–20;
operations off Stockholm, 1720; Sparres' and Norris'
expedition, 1720; and the English and Russian fleets,
1721.*

1009. [Anonymous].
Relaçao do sucesso que teve a Armada de Veneza
onida com as esquadras auxiliares de Portugal . . . na
costa da Morea contra o Poder Othomano . . .
Messina; Vittorio Massei; 1717. 19pp. 8vo.
*Describes the victory of the Venetians – with
Portuguese galleys in support – over an Ottoman fleet off
the Morea on 19 July 1717.*
See also next entry.

1010. [Anonymous].
Relaçao do fortissimo combate que teve a Armada
Portugueza . . . contra todo o poder do Turco na
costa do Reyno de Moreya en 19 de Julho de 1717 . . .
Lisbon; Pedro Ferreira; 1757. 11pp. [verse text in
double columns]. small 8vo.

1011. [Anonymous].
Journal of the siege of Malta, 1727.
RUSIJ, vol.lxi (November 1916), pp.592–600.

1012. [Anonymous].
History of the Russian Fleet during the reign of
Peter the Great.
By a contemporary Englishman (1724).
Edited by Vice-Admiral Cyprian A.G.Bridge.
London; Navy Records Society series, vol.xv; 1899.
xxvi, 161pp. 8vo.

IV. General works, including administration

1013. ANDERSON, *Dr.* Roger Charles.
Second-hand men of war in 1712–14.
The Mariner's Mirror, vol.xvii (October 1931),
pp.321–6.

1014. ANDERSON, Olive.
The establishment of British supremacy at sea and
the exchange of naval prisoners of war, 1689–1783.
EHR, vol.lxxv (1960), pp.77–89.

1015. ATKINSON, C.T.
The War of the Spanish Succession – campaigns and
negotiations.
In: Cambridge Modern History, vol.v, chap.xiv,
pp.401–436.

1016. BROMLEY, *Professor* J.S.
Privateering and the prize system in the War of the
Spanish Succession.
University of Oxford; D.Phil. thesis; 1936.
Précis in *IHR Bull., theses supplement*, no.4. (June
1936).

1017. BURCHETT, Josiah. (1666?–1745).
A complete history of the most remarkable
Transactions at Sea, from the earliest accounts of
time to the conclusion of the last war with France.
Wherein is given an account of the most considerable
naval-expeditions, sea-fights, stratagems,
discoveries . . .
In Five Books.
London; J.Walthoe; 1720. 800pp., engr. pls.; charts.
folio.
*Invaluable for the naval aspects of the wars of
William and Anne. Burchett was a clerk to Samuel
Pepys and then for nearly fifty years Secretary to the
Admiralty, (1698–1742).*

1018. CHOMEL, *Capitaine* —.
La stratégie anglaise et française pendant la Guerre
de Succession d'Espagne.
Revue Maritime, no.ccxviii (February 1938), pp.145–
180.

1019. CLARK, *Sir* George N.
War trade and trade war, 1701–1713.
EHR, vol.i (1927–8), pp.262–280.

1020. CLOWES, *Sir* William Laird, (1856–1908),
et alia.
The Royal Navy. A history from the earliest times
to the death of Queen Victoria . . .
London; Sampson Low; 1897–1903. 7 vols. 4to.

1020. CLOWES, *continued*
volume ii contains sections: 'Civil history of the Royal
Navy, 1660–1714.' 'Military history of the Royal
Navy, 1660–1714: Major operations.' 'Military history
of the Royal Navy, 1660–1714: Minor operations.' and
appendices with warship losses.

1021. EVANS, R.J.Mordan.
Recruitment of British personnel for the Russian
service, 1734–8.
The Mariner's Mirror, vol.xlvii (May 1961), pp.126–
137.

1022. GRANT, James. [editor].
The Old Scots Navy, 1689–1710.
London; Navy Records Society series, vol.xliv;
1914. 508pp. 8vo.

1023. HINCHLIFFE, G.
Impressment of seamen during the War of the
Spanish Succession.
The Mariner's Mirror, vol.liii (May 1967), pp.137–142.

1024. JAMES, G.F. *and* SHAW, J.J.S.
Admiralty administration and personnel, 1619–1714.
IHR Bulls., vols.xiv (June 1936), pp.10–24 & xvi
(February 1937), pp.166–183.

1025. JAMES, G.F.
Some further aspects of Admiralty administration,
1689–1714.
IHR Bull., vol.xvii (June 1937), pp.13–27.

1026. LACOUR-GAYET, Georges.
La Marine Militaire de France sous les règnes de
Louis XIII et de Louis XIV.
Paris; Honoré Champion; 1911. 2 vols. 8vo.
   The second volume narrates the history of the French
navy, 1661–1715 and the administrations of Colbert,
Seignelay and Ponchartrain.

1027. MERRIMAN, *Commander* Reginald Dundas,
RIN. (d.1960).
Queen Anne's Navy.
London; Navy Records Society series, vol.ciii; 1961.
372 pp., 4pls. 8vo.

1028. RICHMOND, *Admiral Sir* Herbert William.
(1871–1946).
The Navy as an instrument of policy, 1558–1727.
Cambridge; University Press; 1953. [viii]; 404pp.
8vo.
   There are four comprehensive chapters (xii–xv) on
The War of the Spanish Succession; and chapter xvi
discusses: The Northern War and the Spanish Wars of
1718 and 1725. The work was edited by E.A.Hughes,
following Admiral Richmond's death.

1029. SCHOMBERG, *Captain* Isaac, RN (1753–
1813).
Naval Chronology; or, an historical summary of
naval and maritime events . . . to the Treaty of
Peace, 1802.
London; T.Egerton; 1802. 5 vols. 8vo.

1030. WATSON, Paula K.
The commission for victualling the Navy, the
commission for sick and wounded seamen and
prisoners of war and the commission for transport,
1702–1714.
University of London Ph.D thesis; 1965.
   Précis in IHRBull.: theses supplement no.xxvii,
(May 1966).

1031. WELCH, P.J.
The maritime powers and the evolution of the war
aims of the Grand Alliance, 1701–4.
University of London MA thesis; 1940.
   Précis in IHRBull.: theses supplement no.xviii,
(November 1941).

1032. [Anonymous].
The old and true way of manning the fleet: or, how
to retrieve the glory of the English arms by sea . . .
and to have seamen always in readiness, without
pressing. In a letter from an old Parliament sea-
commander, to a member of the present House of
Commons, desiring his advice on that subject.
London; 1707. 31pp. small 4to.

1033. [Anonymous].
The three establishments concerning pay of the sea-
officers. To which is prefixed, an introduction, for
the better understanding by what occasions they
came to be produced . . . To which is added, Queen
Anne's establishment in 1704.
London; John Danby; 1714. second edition. xxviii,
56pp., foldg. table. small 4to.

1034. [Anonymous].
Naval expeditions and engagements of the English
nation . . . from the year 1693 to the year 1735.
Collected from Lediard, Burchett, and other
authentick authorities.
London; 1736. 484pp. small folio.

1035. [Anonymous].
Historical Manuscripts Commission: House of
Lords Manuscripts, n.s.
vols.v (1702–4), vi (1704–6) & vii (1706–8).
London; HMSO; 1910–1921. 8vo.
   Plentiful references to the Navy and Admiralty during
the period. Vol.vii, for instance, contains the Report of
the House of Lords Committee on Convoys and Cruisers,
1707.

THE WAR OF 1739–1748
and related events

I. Jenkins' Ear, Admiral Vernon and the Anglo-Spanish War in the Caribbean, 1739-1744

1036. BIZEMONT, *Lieutenant* H. de.
Historique des évènements maritimes pendant le blocus de Carthagène.
La Revue Maritime et Coloniale, vol.xliv (1875), pp.139–156.

1037. DOUGHTY, Katharine Frances.
The attack on Carthagena, 1741.
United Service Magazine, vol.clxxix (October 1919), pp.40–52.

1038. HART, Francis Russell.
The attack upon the Spanish Main by Admiral Vernon.
New Haven, Conn.; 1908. 24pp., illustr. 8vo.
Reprinted in: *Journal of American History*, vol.ii (1908), pp.315–338.
  The operations of the British squadron under Vice-Admiral Vernon against the Spaniards in the West Indies, 1739–40 – culminating in the attack on Porto Bello and the bombardment of Chagres – aroused great public enthusiasm in England. The later operations, in conjunction with Rear-Admiral Chaloner Ogle's reinforcement squadron, were less successful.

1039. KING, James Ferguson.
Admiral Vernon at Portobello, 1739.
Hispanic–American Historical Review, vol.xxiii (May 1943), pp.258–282.

1040. [KNOWLES, *Admiral Sir* Charles. (*d*.1777)].
An account of the expedition to Carthagena . . .
with explanatory notes and observations by [Sir Charles Knowles].
London; M.Cooper; 1743. 58pp. 8vo.

1041. LAUGHTON, *Sir* John Knox. (1830–1915).
Jenkins' Ear.
English Historical Review, vol.iv (1889), pp.741–749.

1042. LEWIS, Frank R.
John Morris and the Carthagena expedition, 1739–40.
The Mariner's Mirror, vol.xxvi (July 1940), pp.257–269.

1043. OGELSBY, J.C.M.
The British attacks on the Caracas coast, 1743.
The Mariner's Mirror, vol.lviii (February 1972), pp.27–40; maps.

1044. OWEN, *Sir* Douglas.
Vernon and Porto Bello.
United Service Magazine, vol.xxxv (1907), pp.262–266.

1045. PARES, *Professor* Richard.
War and Trade in the West Indies, 1739–1763.
Oxford; Clarendon Press; 1936. 631pp., 1 map. 8vo.
  A brilliant study of the subject.

1046. PARES, *Professor* Richard.
The manning of the Navy in the West Indies, 1702–1763.
RHS Trans., 4th series, vol.xx (1937), pp.31–60.

1047. PARES, *Professor* Richard.
Colonial blockade and neutral rights, 1739–1763.
Oxford; Clarendon Press; 1938. 323pp. 8vo.

1048. PEREZ DE LA RIVA, Juan.
Inglaterra y Cuba en la primera mitad del siglo xviii: expedición de Vernon contra Santiago de Cuba en 1741.
Rev. Bimenstra Cubana, vol.xxxvi (1935), pp.50–66.

1049. RICHMOND, *Admiral Sir* Herbert William. (1871–1946).
The Navy in the War of 1739–1748.
Cambridge; University Press; 1920. 3 vols. 282; 279; 284pp., pls. & charts. 8vo.
  Detailed and comprehensive; the standard work on the Royal Navy's operations during the period. On the war in the Caribbean, there are these chapters:
In: vol.i. Operations in the West Indies, 1739–1744, including the expeditions to Cartagena, Santiago and Panama.

vol.ii. The War in the West Indies and North America, 1744–5.

vol.iii. Concluding operations in the West Indies. Each volume has detailed appendices.

1050. ROBERTSON, James Alexander.
The English attack on Cartagena in 1744; and plans for an attack on Panama.
Hispanic–American Historical Review, vol.ii (1919), pp.62–71.

1051. RODGERS, *Vice-Admiral* William Ledyard, USN. (1860–1944).
A study of attacks upon fortified harbours.
USNIP, vol.xxx (1904), pp.533–566.
  Includes a survey of Vernon's assault on Cartagena, 1741.

1052. SHERMAN, Forrest.
The British occupation of Guantanamo Bay. [1741].
United Service Magazine, vol.cliii (1906), pp.274–9.

1053. SPEED, Samuel.
Letters from the West Indies, 1740–1741.
Historical Manuscripts Commission: Buccleuch Mss,
vol.i. (1899).

1054. SPENCE, Lewis.
The Cartagena expedition. Evacuation two
centuries ago.
Scots Magazine, vol.xxxv (July 1941), pp.246–257.

1055. TEMPERLEY, *Professor* Harold V.
The causes of the War of Jenkins' Ear, 1739.
RHS Trans. 3rd series, vol.iii (1909), pp.197–236.

1056. VERNON, *Admiral* Edward. (1684–1757).
Original papers relating to the expedition to
Carthagena ...
London; M.Cooper; 1744. 154pp. 8vo.
   *See also the relevant entries in vol.2 of the Catalogue
of the National Maritime Museum Library: Biography.*

1057. [VERNON, *Admiral* Edward. (1684–1757).]
Additional Instructions ... 1740.
In: Fighting Instructions (London; Navy Records
Society series, vol.xxix; 1905).

1058. [VERNON, *Admiral* Edward. (1684–1757).]
The Vernon Papers.
Edited by Professor B.McLl.Ranft.
London; Navy Records Society series, vol.xcix;
1958. xii; 600pp., pls. & map. 8vo.
   '*The aim of this volume is to print the bulk of the
manuscripts relating to Admiral Edward Vernon deposited
in the National Maritime Museum, Greenwich ....*'.
[*from the preface*].

1059. [WENTWORTH, *General* Thomas].
A Journal of the Expedition to Carthagena, with
notes. In answer to a late pamphlet; entitled, An
account of the expedition to Carthagena.
London; J.Roberts; 1744. ii; 59pp. 8vo.
   *See entry no.1040 for the pamphlet which occasioned
this reply.*

II. The Anglo-French War, 1744–1748: Toulon and the Mediterranean

1060. ALLEN, Joseph. (1810–1864).
Admirals Mathews and Lestock.
United Service Journal, no.clxiv (July 1842), pp.321–
334.

1061. CHABANNES LA PALICE, E.de.
La défense de la rade de Toulon en été 1744.
La Revue Maritime, vol.cxxxvi (April 1931), pp.634–
662.

1062. LAUGHTON, *Sir* John Knox. [*editor*].
(1830–1915).
The Journal of M.de Lage de Cueilly, captain in the
Spanish Navy during the campaign of 1744.
In: The Naval Miscellany, vol.2. pp.207–288.
London; Navy Records Society series, vol.xl; 1912.
   *The author of the journal was on board the Spanish
flagship* REAL FELIPA, *114, during the Battle of Toulon,
11 February 1744.*

1063. LEGG, L.G.Wickham.
Newcastle and the counterorders to Admiral
Haddock.
English Historical Review (April 1931) pp.272–274.

1064. RICHMOND, *Admiral Sir* Herbert William.
(1871–1946).
The Navy in the War of 1739–1748.
Cambridge; University Press; 1920. 3 vols. 282;
279; 284pp., pls & charts. 8vo.
   *An important work. There are chapters on: the
Mediterranean command (in vol.i); the Battle of Toulon
(vol.ii); & concluding operations in the Mediterranean
(vol.iii).*

TOULON and the MATHEWS-LESTOCK
controversy.
   *The following entries, which form a group, are con-
cerned with the indecisive and unsatisfactory action fought
between the English and Franco–Spanish fleets off
Toulon on 11 February, 1744. They are also concerned
with the court-martial and bitter controversy, which
subsequently arose between the British commander-in-
chief, Admiral Thomas Mathews, his deputy, Vice-
Admiral Richard Lestock and their subordinates. The
dispute gave rise to a remarkable series of pamphlets.*

1065. [Anonymous].
A Narrative of the proceedings of His Majesty's
Fleet in the Mediterranean, and the combined

1065. [Anonymous], *continued*
Fleets of France and Spain, from the year 1741, to
March 1744. Including an accurate account of the
late Fight near Toulon, and the causes of our
miscarriage:
The lines of Battle on both sides . . . the French
Admiral's Journal in French and English, from the
time he left Toulon, until he anchored with his
fleet in Alicant Road . . .
By a Sea-Officer.
London; J.Millan; 1744. 112 + [8]pp. charts; battle-
plans. 8vo.
    A second edition was also published in 1744.

1066. [Anonymous].
The History of the Mediterranean Fleet from 1741
to 1744, with the original letters, etc, that passed
between the Admirals Mathews and Lestock. Also
all the other Tracts on that important affair.
London; J.Millan; 1745. 112pp. maps & 1 plan. 8vo.

1067. [Anonymous].
Admiral Mathews' charge against Vice-Admiral
Lestock dissected and confuted by a King's letterman.
London; J.Millan; 1745. 56pp. 8vo.

1068. [Anonymous].
Vice-Ad . . . . l Le . . st . . . k's Account of the late
engagement near Toulon.
London; 1745. 56pp. 8vo.

1069. [Anonymous].
Ad . . . l M . . . . ws's conduct in the late engagement
vindicated. Wherein the whole affair is com-
pendiously stated. The several pieces published by
Mr. L . . . k examined with candor . . .
By a Gentleman of the Royal Navy.
London; M.Cooper; 1745. [ii], 47pp. small 4to.

1070. [Anonymous].
The charge of Thomas Mathews, Esq.,; also the
defence of Admiral Mathews, to the said charge, etc.
London; E.Cooper; [*n.d.*]. [ii], 53pp. small 4to.

1071. [Anonymous].
Minutes taken at a court-martial, assembled on
board His Majesty's Ship *Torbay*. Began the 28th of
January 1744[/45] and ended the 5th of February
following . . . Being an enquiry into the conduct of
Captain Richard Norris, in the engagement between
the English fleet under the command of Admiral
Mathews, and the United Fleet of French and
Spaniards in the Mediterranean, on the 11th of
February 1744.
London; W.Webb; 1745. 92pp. small 4to.

1072. [Anonymous].
An appendix to the minutes taken at a court-martial,
appointed to enquire into the conduct of Captain
Richard Norris; containing the result of the said
court-martial, . . . together with letters to and from
Admiral Rowley, Captain Norris, and other
officers, which proceedings were voted by the Hon.
House of Commons to be partial, arbitrary and
illegal.
London; W.Webb; 1745. 48pp. small 4to.

1073. [LESTOCK, *Admiral* Richard (1679?–1746).].
Vice-Admiral Lestock's recapitulation, as spoke by
him at the bar of the Honble House of Commons, on
Tuesday the 9th of April 1745. Containing his
remarks on the evidence that have been examined,
relating to the late miscarriage of His Majesty's
fleet off Toulon . . . Wherein he points out the true
cause of the miscarriage; supporting the whole by
quoting Admiral Mathew's account.

1074. [Anonymous].
The sentence pronounc'd by the court-martial,
sitting on board His Majesty's Ship the *Prince of
Orange* at Deptford on Tuesday, the 3rd of June
1746, on Vice-Admiral Lestock.
London; H.Cooper; 1746. 23pp. small 4to.

1075. [Anonymous].
Remarks on the sentence of the C . . . t M . . . l.,
and Admiral L . . . k's defence.
London; W.Webb; 1746. [ii]; 52pp., foldg. map.
small 4to.

1076. [MATHEWS, *Admiral* Thomas. (1676–1751)].
Admiral Mathews' remarks on the evidence given
and the proceedings had, on his trial, and relative
thereto.
London; 1746. 72pp. small 4to.

1077. [Anonymous].
Some notes on Mathews' action off Toulon, 11
February 1744.
United Service Magazine, vol.cliii (1906), pp.274–279.

III. The Anglo-French War, 1744-1748: Home Waters and the Forty-Five

1078. BRINDLEY, Harold Hulme.
The action between *HMS Lyon* and the *Elisabeth*, July 1745.
In: The Naval Miscellany, vol.iii, pp.85–122.
London; Navy Records Society series, vol.lxiii; 1928.

1079. BRINDLEY, Harold Hulme.
The Hinchingbrooke drawings of the action between the *Lyon* and the *Elisabeth*.
The Mariner's Mirror, vol.xvii (July 1931), pp.270–278; 3 pls.

1080. DIVERRES, Paul.
L'attaque de Lorient par les anglais, (1746).
Rennes; Oberthur; 1931. 188pp. 8vo.
In September 1746, a combined expeditionary force under the overall command of Admiral Richard Lestock attempted a landing in Brittany and to seize Lorient. But the operation was ill-managed and ended in dismal failure.

1081. FORTESCUE, *Sir* John William. (1859–1933).
A sideshow of the eighteenth century. [Lorient, 1746].
Blackwoods Magazine, vol.ccxxxiii (1933), pp.330–345.

1082. GIBSON, John S.
Ships of the '45. The rescue of the Young Pretender.
London; Hutchinson; 1967. 172pp., pls., & maps. 8vo.
A valuable account; selective bibliography in the appendix.

1083. IRELAND, J.de Courcy.
The seamen of the '45.
Irish Sword, vol.ii (1945–6), pp.149–153 & 286–8.

1084. MAY, *Commander* William Edward, RN.
The *Shark* and the Forty Five.
The Mariner's Mirror, vol.liii (August 1967), pp.281–5.

1085. RICHMOND, *Admiral Sir* Herbert William. (1871–1946).
The Navy in the War of 1739–1748.
Cambridge; University Press; 1920. 3 vols. 8vo.

*There are chapters (in vol.ii): 'Operations in Home Waters and the French attack, 1744'; 'Operations in Home Waters and the Jacobite rising, 1745.'
(in vol.iii): 'Lorient and the Western Squadron, 1746–7'; 'Concluding operations of the War in Home Waters and the negotiations for peace.'*

1086. VERNON, *Admiral* Edward. (1684–1757).
A Specimen of naked truth, from a British sailor, a sincere well-wisher to the honour and prosperity of the present Royal Family and his Country . . .
London; W.Webb; 1746. 30pp. 8vo.
Relates largely to French preparations for the invasion of England and Vernon's anxiety over the general state of unreadiness at home.

1087. [Anonymous].
Correspondence between the Duke of Newcastle and Admiral Lestock and General St. Clair, relating to the expedition against L'Orient in 1746 . . .
Bull. New York Public Library, vol.x (1906), pp.303–328.

1088. [Anonymous].
The attempted invasion of 1745.
Naval Review, vol.iii (1915), p.75.

IV. North America and operations elsewhere, 1739-1748

1089. BAKER, Henry Moore.
The first siege of Louisbourg, 1745.
Concord, New Hampshire; 1909. 17pp. 8vo.

1090. BALLARD, *Admiral* George Alexander.
(1862–1948).
The general situation in the Indian Ocean during the early Georgian period.
The Mariner's Mirror, vol.xii (October 1926), pp.375–395.

1091. BALLARD, *Admiral* George Alexander.
(1862–1948).
The first and second Anglo–French conflicts in the Indian Ocean.
The Mariner's Mirror, vol.xiii (January 1927), pp.14–37; 1 pl.

1092. BUFFINGTON, Arthur H.
The Canada expedition of 1746; its relation to British politics.
American Historical Review, vol.xlv (1939–40), pp.552–580.
   Especially during its early stages – that is when the destination of the combined force under Admiral Lestock and Lt.-Gen. St. Clair was altered from Quebec to Lorient, in Brittany.

1093. CHAPIN, Howard Millar.
New England vessels in the expedition against Louisbourg, 1745.
North Eastern Hist. Register, vol.lxxvii (1923), pp.59–71; 95–110.

1094. FOREST, G.W.
The siege of Madras, 1746 and the action of La Bourdonnais.
RHS Trans., vol.ii (1908).
   Includes an account of the Anglo–French action off Fort St. David on 25 June 1746 – between squadrons under La Bourdonnais and Commodore Peyton.

1095. GRAHAM, *Professor* Gerald Sandford.
The naval defence of British North America, 1739–1763.
RHS Trans., vol.xxx (1948), pp.95–110.

1096. MAY, *Commander* William Edward, RN.
The mutiny of the *Chesterfield*.
The Mariner's Mirror, vol.xlvii (August 1961), pp.178–187.
   The mutiny on board this 44-gun frigate took place off Cape Coast Castle, West Africa on 8 October, 1748.

1097. RICHMOND, *Admiral Sir* Herbert William.
(1871–1946).
The influence of seapower on the struggle with France in North America and India.
National Review, vol.lxxv (1920), pp.397–411.
   See also entry no.1064 for this author's: 'The Navy in the War of 1739–1748 . . .', which includes: (in vol. ii) – chapters on the War in North America, (1744–5) and the capture of Louisbourg; (in vol.iii) Cape Breton and concluding operations overseas.

1098. TYLER, Willard Curtis.
The siege and capture of Louisbourg.
USNIP, vol.lviii (1932), pp.81–87; illustr.

1099. WOOD, W.H.W.
The great fortress; a chronicle of Louisbourg, 1720–1760.
Toronto; University Press; 1915. xi; 144pp., pls. 8vo.

1100. WOOD, Anthony.
Sveaborg and the defence of Finland in 1748.
History Today, vol.vi (1956), pp.536–545.

1101. [Anonymous].
Benjamin Cleave's journal of the expedition to Louisbourg, 1745.
New England Hist. Reg., vol.lxvi (1912), pp.113–124.

1102. [Anonymous].
Journal kept by Lt. Daniel Giddings of Ipswich, during the expedition against Cape Breton in 1744–45.
Essex Instit. Hist. Coll., vol.xlviii (1912), pp.293–304.

V. General works, including administration

1103. BAUGH, *Dr.* Daniel A.
British naval administration in the age of Walpole.
Oxford; University Press; 1966. 576pp., pls. &
tables. 8vo.
   *A detailed and valuable study. Originally a Cambridge
University doctoral thesis (1961) entitled: 'British naval
administration in the War of 1739–1748'. (précis in
IHR Bulletin – May 1962).*

1104. BROCK, *Lieut.* (now *Rear-Admiral*) P.W.
Anson and his importance as a naval reformer.
Naval Review, vol.xvii (1929), p.247.

1105. CHEVALIER, Édouard.
Histoire de la Marine Française depuis les débuts de
la monarchie, jusqu'au traité de paix de 1763.
Paris; 1902. ix; 405pp. 8vo.

1106. CLOWES, *Sir* William Laird (1856–1905),
et alia.
The Royal Navy. A history from the earliest times
to the present day . . .
London; Sampson Low; 1897–1903. 7 vols. 4to.
*volume iii (609pp.) contains long chapters: – Civil
history of the Royal Navy, 1714–1762. – Military
history of the Royal Navy, 1714–1762: major
operations. – Military history of the Royal Navy, 1714–
1762: minor operations. Also tabulated warship losses,
arranged by country, in the appendices.*

1107. COSTET, *Capitaine* E.
La stratégie britannique de 1739 à 1748.
La Revue Maritime, no.clxxviii (October 1934),
pp.433–464.

1108. EKINS, *Admiral Sir* Charles. (1768–1855).
Naval battles from 1744 to the peace in 1814,
critically reviewed and illustrated . . .
London; Baldwin, Cradock & Jay; 1824. xxix;
425pp.; pls. & diagrs. 4to.

1109. FAYLE, Charles Ernest.
Economic pressure in the war of 1739–48.
RUSIJ, vol.lxviii (1923), pp.434–446.

1110. LACOUR-GAYET, Georges.
La Marine militaire de la France sous la règne de
Louis XV . . .
Paris; Honoré Champion; 1902. 571pp., pls. &
tables. 8vo.

1111. MAHAN, *Rear-Admiral* Alfred Thayer, usn.
(1840–1914).
The influence of sea power upon history. 1660–1783.
London; Sampson Low; [1893]. 8th edition. 557pp.,
maps. 8vo.
   See the chapters relevant to the period.

1112. RANFT, *Professor* B.McLeod.
Labour relations in the royal dockyards in 1739.
The Mariner's Mirror, vol.xlvii (November 1961),
pp.281–291.

1113. RICHMOND, *Admiral Sir* Herbert William.
(1871–1946).
English strategy in the War of the Austrian
Succession.
RUSIJ, vol.lxiv (1919), pp.246–254.
   *On the same subject, see also the author's: 'National
policy and naval strength and other essays', pp.144–160.*

1114. RICHMOND, *Admiral Sir* Herbert William.
(1871–1946).
The Navy in the War of 1739–1748.
Cambridge; University Press; 1920. 3 vols. 282;
279; 284pp., pls. & charts. 8vo.
   *Comprehensive and still the key on the operations of
the Royal Navy during the period. The more important
chapters are analysed in the appropriate sections
previously.*

THE SEVEN YEARS' WAR, 1756–1763
and related events

I. The struggle for Canada

☞ *See also entry no.1218.: CORBETT, Sir Julian S.: England in The Seven Years' War . . .*

1115. CARON, Ivanhoe.
La capitulation de Québec, (18 Septembre 1759).
Proc. & Trans. Royal Society of Canada, ser.3., vol.xviii (1924), pp.15–32.

1116. DIONNE, Narcisse E.
Le siège de Québec en 1759.
Revue Canadienne, vol.xliv (1903), pp.5–14.

1117. FRÉGAULT, Guy.
Canada: The war of the conquest. Translated by Margaret M.Cameron.
Toronto; University Press; 1955. xviii, 427pp., maps. 8vo.
    First published in 1955 as 'La Guerre de la conquête'.

1118. FYERS, *Major* E.W.H.
The loss and recapture of Newfoundland in 1762.
Army Historical Society Review (July 1932).

1119. GRAHAM, *Professor* Gerald Sanford.
The naval defence of British North America, 1739–1763.
RHS Trans. (4th series), vol.xxx (1948), pp.95–110.

1120. GRAHAM, *Professor* Gerald Sanford.
Empire of the North Atlantic: the maritime struggle for North America.
Toronto; University Press; 1950. xvii, 338pp. 8vo.
    A comprehensive strategic study, covering the period 1689–1815.

1121. HISTORICAL MANUSCRIPTS COMMISSION.
Ninth Report (1883), part iii – Stopford Sackville Mss.
    Includes letters & despatches relating to the war in Canada, 1758–60.
Eleventh Report (1887), part iv – Townshend Mss.
    Includes papers relating to Saunders, Wolfe and the capture of Quebec, 1759.

1122. HITSMAN, J.M. *and* BOND C.C.J.
The assault landing at Louisbourg, 1758.
Canadian Historical Review (December 1954), 17pp.

1123. LITTLE, *Instructor-Commander* Charles Herbert, RCN.
(a) The influence of seapower on the Conquest of Canada. *Maritime Museum of Canada*: Occasional Papers no.i. 16pp.
(b) Despatches of Rear-Admiral Sir Charles Hardy and Vice-Admiral Francis Holburn, 1757–8. Occasional Papers, no.ii. 52pp.
(c) Despatches of Vice-Admiral Charles Saunders, 1759–60. Occasional Papers, no.iii. 52pp.
(d) Despatches of Rear-Admiral Philip Durell and Rear-Admiral Lord Colville, 1758–9. Occasional Papers, no.iv. 28pp.
(e) The recapture of St. John's, Newfoundland, 1761–2. Occasional Papers, no.vi. 38pp.
(f) The Battle of the Restigouche, 1760. Occasional Papers, no.x. 24pp.

1124. LLOYD, *Professor* Christopher C.
The capture of Quebec.
London; Batsford; 1959. [British Battles series]. 175pp., pls. & map. 8vo.

1125. LOTURE, *Lieutenant* R. de.
Un episode de La Guerre de Sept. Ans: le siège de Louisbourg en 1758.
Revue Maritime, no.175 (June 1934), pp.52–70.

1126. LYDEKKER, John Wolfe.
The Navy at Quebec.
Blue Peter, vol.xix (September 1934), pp.396–403.

1127. MAHON, Reginald Henry.
The mystery of the Anseau Foulon.
Blackwood's Magazine, vol.cci (1917), pp.367–378.
    The Anseau Foulon was the landing place chosen by Wolfe and Saunders for the attack on Quebec in September 1759.

1128. MAY, Richard Middleton.
A naval reinforcement for North America, Summer 1787.
IHRBull., vol.xlii (May 1969), pp.58–72.

1129. PALSITS, Victor Hugo. [*editor*].
The almanacs of Roger Sherman, 1750–1761.
Proc. American Antiq. Soc. [n.s.], vol.xviii (1907), pp.213–238.
    Includes extracts on the capture of Quebec.

1130. RIDDELL, William Renwick.
The pilots of Wolfe's expedition, 1759.
Proc. & Trans. Royal Society of Canada, series 3., vol.xxi (1927), pp.81–2.

1131. ROBJOHNS, Sydney.
The siege of Quebec.
RHS Trans., vol.v (1877), pp.144–172.

1132. [SAUNDERS, *Admiral Sir* Charles, (1713?–
1775)].
Sailing orders, instructions and signals, 1759.
In: J.Knox: Journal (1769), vol.i, pp.260–7.

1133. SHAFROTH, John Franklin.
(a). The capture of Louisbourg in 1758; a joint
military and naval operation.
USNIP, vol.lxiv (January 1938), pp.78–96.
(b). The capture of Quebec in 1759.
USNIP, vol.lxiv (February 1938), pp.187–201.

1134. SMILLIE, Eleanor Arma.
The achievement of Durell in 1759.
Proc. & Trans. Royal Society of Canada, series 3.,
vol.xix (1925), pp.131–5.
   *About Admiral Philip Durell and the St. Lawrence
expedition.*

1135. STACEY, Charles Perry.
Quebec 1759. The siege and the battle.
Toronto; Macmillan; 1959. 210pp., pls. & map.
8vo.

1136. TURNER, F.C.
The taking of Quebec.
RUSIJ, vol.xxxviii (1909), pp.335–344.

1137. WHITEHOUSE, Archibald.
Amphibious operations.
London; Muller; 1964. 351pp., pls., maps. 8vo.
   *Chapter ii, (pp.39–58), is concerned with Louisbourg
and Quebec.*

1138. WOOD, William Charles Henry.
The Fight for Canada. A naval and military sketch
from the history of the great imperial war.
London; Constable; 1904. xxi, 363pp. 8vo.
   A revised and illustrated edition was published in 1906.

1139. WOOD, William Charles Henry.
The Logs of the conquest of Canada. (Louisbourg,
1758; Quebec, 1759; Montreal, 1760).
Toronto; Champlain Society, (vol.iv); 1909. xxvi;
335pp., charts & plan. 8vo.

1140. WYLLIE, Robert E.
The Quebec campaign of 1759: a strategical study of
a joint operation.
Journal U.S. Mil. Service Instit., vol.lxi (1917),
pp.25–42; 166–181; 303–323; map.

1141. [Anonymous].
The siege of Quebec.
Edinburgh Review, vol.cxcviii (1903), pp.234–155.

1142. [Anonymous].
Documents relating to the engagement between
English and French ships in the Baie des Chaleurs,
1760.
Toronto; Champlain Society, (vol.x); 1916. pp.353–4.

1143. [Anonymous].
Les noms des vaisseaux et frègates construits au
Canada pour la France jusqu'au 1758, et dates de
mise sur cale et de lancement.
Revue Maritime, no.266 (June 1969), p.832.

II. Operations in the West Indies

☞ *See also entry no.1218.: CORBETT, Sir Julian S.: 'England in the Seven Year's War . . . '.*

1144. BALDRY, W.Y.
The expedition against Martinique, 1762.
Army Historical Society Review, vol.i, no.6. (1922).

1144a. BURTON, Robert.
The siege and capture of Havana in 1762.
Maryland Historical Magazine, vol.iv (1909), pp.321–335.

1145. CHAWNER, W. Hampden.
The capture of Havannah.
United Service Magazine, vol.cl (1904), pp.87–91; plan.

1146. FORTESCUE, Sir John William. (1859–1933).
Guadeloupe, 1759.
Blackwood's Magazine, vol.ccxxxiv (1933), pp.552–566.

1147. GARDINER, Captain Richard.
An Account of the expedition to the West Indies, against Martinico, with the reduction of Guadelupe and the other Leeward Islands subject to the French King, 1759. By Captain Gardiner of the King's Royal Musqueteers, late Captain of Marines on board His Majesty's Ship *Rippon*, employed on this expedition.
Birmingham; John Baskerville; 1762. 91pp., 4 engr. plts. oblong 4to.
This is a copy of the third edition; the first and second were published in 1759 and 1760, in London.
The plates comprise: i. 'Island of Martinico'. [shewing Commodore Moore's squadron bombarding]. ii. 'View of the town and bay of Fort Royal . . . Martinique'. iii. 'View of the burning of the town of Basse-Terre . . . Guadelupe, Jany 23, 1759'. iv. 'View of the squadron and convoy at sea, on their passage to England'.

1148. GUITERAS, P.J.
Historia de la conquista de la Habana por los Ingleses . . .
Havana; 1932. xxvi, 280pp. 8vo.

1149. HART, Francis Russell.
The siege of Havana, 1762.
Boston; 1931. 54pp., illustr., map. 8vo.

1150. HART, Francis Russell.
Spanish documents relating to the siege of Havana, 1762.
Proc. Massachusetts Hist. Soc., vol.lxiv (1932), pp.435–9.

1151. LLAVERÍAS, Joaquín.
Papeles sobre la toma de la Habana por los Ingleses en 1762.
Havana; 1948. 208pp., pls. 8vo.
Based on documents in the Cuban national archives preserved at Havana.

1152. PARES, Professor Richard.
War and Trade in the West Indies, 1739–1763.
Oxford; Clarendon Press; 1936. ix; 631pp., 1 map. 8vo.
A masterly study, as were all the publications [qqv.] of this distinguished historian.

1153. PARES, Professor Richard.
The manning of the Navy in the West Indies, 1702–1763.
RHS Trans., vol.xx (1937), pp.31–60.

1154. PARES, Professor Richard.
Colonial blockade and neutral rights, 1739–1763.
Oxford; Clarendon Press; 1938. vii; 323pp. 8vo.

1155. POCOCK, Tom.
The capture of Havana, 1762.
History Today, vol.xii (1962), pp.580–6.

1156. SMELSER, Marshall.
The insular campaign of 1759 – Martinique.
American Neptune, vols.vi (1946), pp.290–300 & vii (1947), pp.21–34.

1157. SMELSER, Marshall.
The campaign for the Sugar Islands, 1759. A study of amphibious warfare.
Chapel Hill; North Carolina University Press; 1955. 212pp., maps. 8vo.
With emphasis on the Anglo–French struggles for possession of Guadeloupe and Martinique.

1158. SYRETT, Dr. David.
The British landing at Havana: an example of an 18th century combined operation.
The Mariner's Mirror, vol.lv (August 1969), pp.325–331; pls.

1159. SYRETT, Dr. David.
The siege and capture of Havana, 1762.
London; Navy Records Society, vol.cxiv; 1970. 355pp.; 9 illustr., & 2 maps. 8vo.
An important study, which makes full use of contemporary documents and sources.

A Prospect of the late Engagement at Sea between the English and the
the wind from NNE to the ENE with an exact List of ye English Dutch & French

A List of the
FRENCH Fleet

The Royall Sun	The Splendor	The Belliqu.	The Henry	The Shining	The Proud	The
The Royall Dolphin	The Conqueror	The Crown	The Serious	The Unicable	The Fierce	The
The Great	The Holy Ghost	Lintrpede	The Content	The Vermandois	The Marquis	The
The Soveraigne	St Phillip	The Harry hen	The Courtier	The Lovely	The Strong	The
	The Thunderer	The Splendor	The Bourbon	The Perfect	The Undertaker	The
	The Haughty	The Brightness	The Eager	The Amiable	The Brave	The
	The Terrible	The Illustre	The Firme	The Excellent	The Ambitious	The
	The Conqueror	The Pomp	The Touquex	The Prince	The Unparallelld	The

A List of the English
and Dutch Fleet

Ships names	Capt names								
		4 Vice Admirall	Ashby	12 Soveraign Adm^ll of ye Red Torrington	20 Hope	Bings	28 Coronation	Vi
								Blew Do
1 Plimouth	Carter	5 Expedition	Clements	13 Windsor Castle	Churchill	21 Restauration	Betham	29 Katherine	
2 Deptford	Kerr	6 Waspite	Fairborne	14 Lenox	Greenhill	22 Anne	Tirrell	30 Cambridge	
3 Elizabeth	Mitchell	7 Woolwich	Gother	15 Sterling Castle	Haistings	23 Bonadventure	Hubbard	31 Berwick	
		8 Lyon	Torpley	16 York	Hobson	24 Edgar	Tenefor	32 Swallow	
		9 Rupert	Dunvoy	17 Suffolk	Cornwall	25 Exeter	Mies	33 Defiance	
		10 Albemarle	Wheeler S^r	18 Hampton Court	Layton	26 Bredah	Tennant	34 Capitaine	
		11 Grafton	Grafton Duke	19 Dutchess	Rear Admirall Rook	27 St Andrew	Dorrell		

PLATE VII: Detail of: *A Prospect of the late Engagement at Sea between the English and the French Fleets on Monday the thirtieth of June 1690*. From: *The Earl of Torrington's Speech to the House of Commons, in November, 1690 . . .* London; 1710

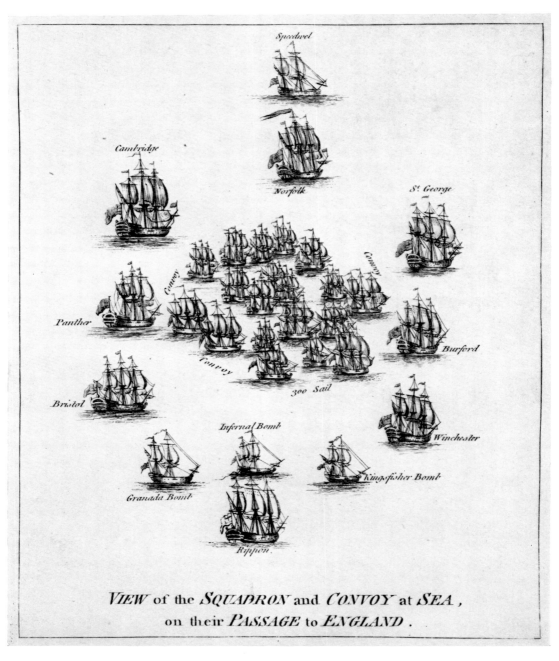

VIEW of the *SQUADRON* and *CONVOY* at *SEA*, on their *PASSAGE* to *ENGLAND*.

PLATE VIII: View of the Squadron and Convoy at sea, on their passage to England. From Captain Richard Gardiner's: *An Account of the expedition to the West Indies, against Martinico and Guadelupe . . . 1759.* Birmingham; 1762

1160. TRAMOND, J.
Saint-Dominigue en 1756–1757.
Revue d'Histoire Coloniale Française, vol.iv (1927),
pp.509–542.

III. European Waters and the Mediterranean

☞ *See also entry no.1218.: CORBETT, Sir Julian
S.: 'England in the Seven Years' War . . .'.*

1161. AMAN, Jacques.
La fin du *Soleil Royal* et du *Héros*.
Neptunia, vol.xlii (February 1956), pp.6–9.
   *The fate of de Conflans' flagship and another French
ship of the line at the Battle of Quiberon Bay, 20
November 1759.*

1162. BARRAULT, *Capitaine* E.P.
Épaves des Cardinaux.
Neptunia, vol.xlii (February 1956), pp.10–13.
   *The dangerous shoals which played an important part
in the Battle of Quiberon Bay.*

1163. BERESFORD, Marcus.
François Thurot and the French attack at Carrickfergus, 1759–60.
Irish Sword, vol.x no.41, (winter 1972), pp.250–274.,
map.

1164. BINET, *Commandant* E.
La préparation de l'expedition particulière en
Bretagne.
Bulletin Géographique, vol.xlix (1935), pp.89–132.
   *This is about Choiseul's proposed expedition against
England in 1759.*

1165. [BOSCAWEN, *Admiral* Edward. (1711–
1761)].
Additional Instructions, 1759.
In: Fighting Instructions, 1530–1816. [London; Navy
Records Society, vol.xxix; 1905], pp.219–225.
   *Of importance in its relation to his action against a
French squadron under de la Clue, off Lagos Bay on 18
August 1759.*

1166. BRUCE, R.Stuart.
Thurot in Shetland.
The Mariner's Mirror, vol.v. (November 1919),
p.155.
   *A note on the activities of the French privateer in those
waters in 1757.*

1167. [BYNG, *Admiral* John. (1704–1757)].
An appeal to the people: containing the genuine and
entire letter of Admiral Byng to the Secretary of the
Admiralty . . .
London; J.Morgan; 1756. [ii]., 76pp. small 4to.

1168. [BYNG, *Admiral* John (1704–1757)].
The trial of the Honourable Admiral John Byng at a
court martial as taken by Mr. Charles Fearne, judge-
advocate of His Majesty's Fleet.
Published by order of . . . the Lords Commissioners
of the Admiralty . . .
London; R.Manby; 1757. 130 + [19]pp. 4to.

1169. [BYNG, *Admiral* John (1704–1757)].
An extract of a remarkable letter from Admiral
Byng to the Right Hon. W – P – , Esq., dated
March 12 1757, two days before his execution.
London; J.Reason; 1757. [ii]., 22pp. small 4to.

1170. [BYNG, *Admiral* John (1704–1757)].
Testament politique de l'Amiral Byng.
Traduit de l'Anglais.
Paris; 1759. 259pp. 12mo.
☞ *See also entries nos.1167–9; 1172; 1174; 1185;*
1189–90; 1196.

1171. COURSON DE LA VILLENEUVE,
A.G.M.J.
La descente des Anglais à Saint-Cast en 1758.
Vannes; 1903. 124pp., maps. 8vo.
    Part of the abortive British expedition against
Brittany in 1758; equally unsuccessful landings were
made at St. Malo and Cherbourg.

1172. FRENCH, *Lieutenant-Colonel* Edward
Gerald. (*d.*1970).
The martyrdom of Admiral Byng.
Glasgow; MacLellan; 1961. 108pp., pls., map. 8vo.

1173. [HOLBROOKE, *Lieutenant* Bernard].
The siege of Belle Isle, 1761.
RUSIJ, vol.xliii (February 1899), p.77.
    Extracts from his contemporary diary.

1174. HUNT, Livingston.
The tragedy of Admiral Byng.
USNIP, vol.liv (1928), pp.361–371.

1175. KENNEDY, David.
Thurot's landing at Carrickfergus, [1760].
Irish Sword, vol.vi (1964), pp.149–153.
    See also entry no.1163.

1176. LACOUR-GAYET, Georges.
La bataille de M.de Conflans.
Revue d'Histoire, vol.lxxvi (1901), pp.26–47.
    That is – Quiberon Bay, 20 November 1759.

1177. LAUGHTON, *Sir* John Knox, (1830–1915).
[*editor*].
Glorious England. A translation of 'Inglaterra

Gloriosa' – a Portuguese account of the Battle of
Quiberon Bay.
In: The Naval Miscellany, vol.i. (1902).
London; Navy Record Society series, vol.xx; 1902.

1178. LEVOT, P.
La descente des Anglais à Camaret.
Revue Maritime et Coloniale, vol.xxxiii (1873),
pp.27–57.

1179. LLOYD, *Professor* Christopher C.
Hearts of Oak. The battle of Quiberon Bay, 20th
November 1759.
History Today, vol.ix (1959), pp.744–751.

1180. LOYER, P.
La défense des côtes de Bretagne pendant La Guerre
de Sept Ans: la bataille de Saint-Cast.
Revue Maritime, vol.clvi (December 1932), pp.721–
739, & clvii (January 1933), pp.75–98.

1181. MACALLESTER, Oliver.
A series of letters discovering the scheme projected
by France in 1759 for an intended invasion upon
England with flat-bottom'd boats . . .
London; 1767. 2 vols. in one. 4to.

1182. MARCUS, Geoffrey J.
Hawke's blockade of Brest.
RUSIJ, vol.civ (November 1959), p.475.

1183. MARCUS, Geoffrey J.
Quiberon Bay. The campaign in Home Waters,
1759.
London; Hollis & Carter; 1960. 212pp., pls. &
maps. 8vo.
    An important modern account of Hawke's great
victory and the events leading up to it. The appendices
include a list of the opposing fleets and a note on the loss
of the RESOLUTION.

1184. McGUFFIE, T.H.
The defence of Minorca, 1756.
History Today, vol.i (1951), pp.59–66 *and RUSIJ*
(May 1951), p.281.

1185. POPE, Dudley.
At 12 Mr Byng was shot . . .
London; Weidenfeld & Nicolson; 1962. 338pp.,
pls. 8vo.

1186. [POTTER, Thomas].
The expedition against Rochefort fully stated and
considered . . . . . . by a Country Gentleman.
London & Dublin; 1758. 67pp. 8vo.

1187. RICHMOND, *Admiral Sir* Herbert William, (1871–1946). [*editor*].
Papers relating to the loss of Minorca in 1756.
London; Navy Records Society series, vol.xlii; 1911. 351pp. 8vo.

1188. TOUDOUZE, Georges G.
La descente à Saint-Cast – 11 Septembre 1758.
Neptunia, vol.lii (April 1958), pp.2–9.
   About the abortive English landing in Brittany; see also entries nos.1171; 1178; 1180; 1191; 1194; 1197.

1189. TUNSTALL, Brian. [*editor*].
Admiral Byng and the loss of Minorca.
London; P.Allan; 1928. x, 294pp., frontis., pls., diagrs. 8vo.

1190. TUNSTALL, Brian. [*editor*].
The Byng Papers. Selected from the letters and papers of Admiral Sir George Byng, First Viscount Torrington and of his son Admiral the Hon. John Byng . . .
London; Navy Records Society series, vols.lxvii, lxviii & lxx; 1930–1, 1933. 3 vols. 8vo.

1191. VANEL, Gabriel.
Étude sur la prise de Cherbourg par les Anglais en 1758.
Mémoires Académiennes Caen. (1906), pp.31–47.

1192. WARNER, Oliver.
Strike!
National Review, vol.cxviii (June 1942), pp.545–8.
   This is a short article on the Battle of Quiberon Bay.

1193. [Anonymous].
The secret expedition impartially disclos'd: or an authentick, faithful narrative of all occurrences that happened to the fleet and army commanded by Sir E . . . H . . . and Sir J . . . M . . . , from its first sailing to its return to England . . . By a commissioned officer on board the fleet . . .
London; [1757]. pamphlet. [8]pp. 8vo.
   On the abortive expedition against Rochefort in September 1757, in which the naval and military forces were commanded by Admiral Sir Edward Hawke and Lieutenant-General Sir John Mordaunt respectively.

1194. [Anonymous].
An authentic account of our last attempt upon the Coast of France. By an Officer, who miraculously escaped being cut to pieces, by swimming to a Boat at a considerable distance from the Shore. In a letter to a friend.
London; P.Griffiths; 1758.
   This is about the unsuccessful St. Malo expedition in September 1758.

1195. [Anonymous].
A letter from an officer on board the *Royal George* . . . dated the 23rd of November 1759, to his uncle . . . containing a genuine and circumstantial account of the battle fought between the English and the French fleets on the coast of France, November 20th 1759.
London; 1759. Pamphlet. [6]pp., 8vo.

1196. [Anonymous].
Traits of Admiral Byng.
From the journal of an officer engaged in the action off Minorca in 1756.
United Service Journal, no.xiii (January 1830), pp.19–23.

1197. [Anonymous].
British minor expeditions, 1746 to 1814.
London; HMSO; 1884. 91pp., maps & plans. 8vo.
   Although chiefly a military survey, there is important naval material on the expeditions described. In this period they include: St. Malo, Cherbourg & St. Cast, 1758; the siege and capture of Belleisle, 1761.

IV. Events and operations overseas

1198. BALLARD, *Admiral* George Alexander. (1862–1948).
The first and second Anglo–French conflicts in the Indian Ocean.
The Mariner's Mirror, vol.xiii (January 1927), pp.14–37; 1 pl.
 The second part of this article discusses the operations in the Indian Ocean during the Seven Years' War, including the squadron actions between Pocock and D'Aché.

1199. CALKINS, Carlos Gilman.
British conquests in the Philippines.
USNIP, vol.xxvii (1901), pp.79–114; plan.
 Especially the capture of Manila on 6 October, 1762.

1200. CAMBRIDGE, Richard Owen. (1717–1802).
An account of the War in India, between the English and French on the coast of Coromandel, from 1750 to the year 1760 . . . with the operations of the Fleet.
London; T.Jefferys; 1767. 176pp. 8vo.

1201. CHAPMAN, *Capt.* William C., USN.
Prelude to Chesme.
The Mariner's Mirror, vol.lii (February 1966), pp.61–76.
 Describes the Russo–Turkish naval struggle in the Black Sea, up to the decisive Battle of Chesme (or Tchesme), 26 June 1770.

1202. COLGATE, H.A.
Trincomalee and the East Indies squadron, 1746–1844.
University of London MA thesis; 1959.
Summary in: IHRBull., vol.xxxiii (November 1960), pp.238–241.

1203. CUSHNER, Nicholas.
Documents illustrating the British conquest of Manila, 1762–1763.
London; Royal Historical Society; 1971. ix; 222pp. 8vo.
 This work is vol.viii in the Camden Society publications, 4th series.

1204. FLETCHER, W.J.
A naval chapter in Indian history.
Macmillan's Magazine, vol.lxxxiii (1901), pp.204–211.
 A short account of the Pocock/d'Aché engagements, 1758–9.

1205. LEEBRICK, K.C.
The English expedition to Manila in 1762 and the government of the Philippines by the East India Company.
California; University of Berkeley Ph.D thesis; 1917.

1206. MARSH, A.J.
The taking of Gorée in 1758.
The Mariner's Mirror, vol.li (May 1965), pp.117–130; figs.
 In December 1758 a naval expeditionary force under Commodore Keppel captured the French settlement on Gorée Island, Senegal in West Africa. This followed an earlier attempt, which had been repulsed in May that year.

1207. ROSE, *Professor* John Holland. (1855–1942).
The influence of seapower on Indian History, 1746–1802.
In: Journal of Indian History; (Allahabad; 1924).

1208. TRACY, J.Nicholas.
Admiral Cornish and the operations in Far Eastern waters during the Seven Years' War.
University of Southampton M.Phil. thesis; 1967.
précis in: IHR Bull., no.xxix (May 1968).

1209. TRACY, J.Nicholas.
The capture of Manila, 1762.
The Mariner's Mirror, vol.lv (August 1969), pp.311–323; figs.

1210. [Anonymous].
The capture of Manila in 1762.
RUSIJ, vol.lxi (May 1916), p.412.

1211. [Anonymous].
The place of India in naval strategy, 1744–1783.
Naval Review, vol.xviii (1930), p.461.

V. General works, including administration and studies of the whole period

1212. ABEL, Francis.
Prisoners of war in Britain, 1756 to 1815. A record of their lives, their romances and their sufferings.
Oxford; University Press; 1914. viii; 464pp., pls. 8vo.

1213. BEATSON, Robert. (1742–1818).
Naval and military memoirs of Great Britain from 1727 to 1783.
London; Longmans; 1804. 6 vols. 8vo.
Detailed; includes appendices in vols.iii & vi – with numerous fleet and ship lists, station commands, relevant to the period.
There is also a copy of the earlier and shorter edition of this work (London; Strachan; 1790) in the Library.

1214. BECKFORD, William.
The Royal Navy – men's advocate. Wherein, from a collection of several original tracts, are fully set forth the corrupt practices of victualling the Royal Navy. To which is prefix'd . . . some proposals for a better future conduct.
London; H.Slater; 1757. ii; 59pp. small 4to.

1215. BROCK, *Lieutenant* (now *Rear Admiral*) P.W.
Anson and his importance as a naval reformer.
Naval Review, vol.xvii (1929), p.497.

1216. CHEVALIER, *Capitaine* Edouard.
Histoire de la Marine Française . . .
Paris; Hachette; 1877–1902. 5 vols. in 3. 8vo.
Volume i: 'Histoire de la Marine Française depuis les débuts de la monarchie jusqu'au traité de paix en 1763.'

1217. CLOWES, *Sir* William Laird (1856–1905), *et alia*.
The Royal Navy. A history from the earliest times to the present . . . 7 vols. 4to.
London; Sampson Low, Marston & Co.; 1897–1903.
vol.iii (609pp.,), contains the sections relevant to the period: (a). Civil History of the Royal Navy, 1714–1762. (b). Military History of the Royal Navy, 1714–1762 – major operations. (c). Military History of the Royal Navy, 1714–1762 – minor operations. And in the appendices there are detailed lists of warship losses in the British, French and Spanish navies, 1714–1763.

1218. CORBETT, *Sir* Julian Stafford. (1854–1922).
England in the Seven Years' War. A study in combined strategy.

London; Longmans; 1907. 2 vols. 476; 407 pp.,; maps & plans. 8vo.
Still the standard authority and a brilliant strategic study. Chapters include: – (vol.i): 'The French opening – Minorca; the first containing attack – Rochefort; Fleet and coastal operations, 1758 – St. Malo, Cherbourg, St. Cas; Louisbourg, 1758; Commerce protection, East and West Indies; The French Antilles and Quebec operations, 1759; Home Waters, 1759 – Quiberon.' (vol.ii): 'Montreal, 1760; The resumption of coastal pressure – Belleisle; Completion of the West Indian attack – Martinique; The intervention of Spain; The attack on Spain – Havana and Manila; Lessons of the war.'

1219. CROWHURST, R.P.
British oceanic convoys in The Seven Years' War, 1756–63.
University of London Ph.D thesis; 1970.
précis in: IHR Bull., vol.xxxii (May 1971).

1220. CROWHURST, R.P.
The Admiralty and the convoy system in The Seven Years' War.
The Mariner's Mirror, vol.lvii (May 1971), pp.163–173.

1221. DOBSON,[John].
Chronological Annals of the War . . . in two parts.
Part i from April 2, 1755 to end of 1760. Part ii from the beginning of 1761 to the signing of the Peace . . . by Mr. Dobson.
Oxford; Clarendon Press; 1763. 327pp. 8vo.
With valuable contemporary naval material.

1222. DONEAUD DU PLAN, *Professeur*. —.
L'Académie de Marine de 1752 à 1765.
La Revue Maritime et Coloniale, vols.lviii–lx (1877), pp.476–509; 300–313; & 389–409, respectively.

1223. DURO, Césareo Fernández.
Armada Española desde la unión de los Reinos de Castilla y de Leon.
Madrid; Rivadeneyra; 1895–1903. 9 vols. 8vo.
The standard work on the history of the Spanish Navy, with a wealth of detail and original source material. Volume vii covers the period 1750–1788 and includes sections on: the war in the West Indies; the loss of Havana and Manila, 1762.

1224. EKINS, *Admiral Sir* Charles. (1768–1855).
Naval Battles, from 1744 to the Peace in 1814 . . . critically reviewed and illustrated . . .
London; Baldwin, Craddock & Jay; 1824. 425pp., num. plates & battle plans. 4to.

1225. ENTICK, *Reverend* John. (1703?–1773).
The General History of the late War [i.e.1756–63]:
containing its rise, progress, and event, in Europe,
Asia, Africa and America . . .
London; Edward & Charles Dilly; 1765. 5 vols. 8vo.
   This is a copy of the second edition corrected; the first
was published in 1763-4.

1226. ENTICK, *Reverend* John. (1703?–1773).
A New Naval History: or, compleat view of the
British Marine . . .
London; R.Manby; 1757. lxii; 887pp.; frontis. &
map. folio.
   On pp.863-5 is an analysis: 'The exact state of the
British Navy as it stood, September 1755 . . .'.

1227. JAMES, G.J.
Select documents: the Admiralty establishment,
1759.
IHR Bull., vol.xvi (June 1938), pp.24–27.

1228. LACOUR-GAYET, Georges.
La Marine Militaire de la France sous la règne de
Louis XV.
Paris; Honoré Champion; 1902. 571pp., pls. &
tables. 8vo.
   The appendices include valuable lists of the composition
of French naval squadrons and expeditionary forces
during the period – for example: 'Escadres de L'Etanduère
& de la Galissonnière; Annements pour Louisbourg en
1758; Escadre de la Clue; Escadre de Conflans en 1759;
Expedition de Terre Neuve en 1762; & Escadre de
D'Aché au combat du Septembre, 1759'.

1229. McCALL, J.H.
A Kempenfelt letter [dated 23 July, 1758].
Naval Review, vol.xxvii (1939), pp.294–300.
   A first-hand account of Pocock's action with D'Aché
off Cuddalore, 29 April 1758.

1230. MIDDLETON, Richard.
Pitt, Anson and the Admiralty, 1759–1761.
History, vol.lv (1970), pp.189–198.

1231. ROSE, *Professor* John Holland. (1855–1942).
A French memoir on Pitt's naval operations of
1757–8.
EHR, vol.xxviii (1913), pp.748–751.

1232. SCHOMBERG, *Captain* Isaac, RN. (1753–
1813).
Naval Chronology, or an historical summary of
naval and maritime events . . . to the Treaty of
Peace, 1802.
London; T.Egerton; 1802. 5 vols. 8vo.
   With detailed & comprehensive statistical appendices

in vols.iv and v; including, for this period: List of the
Royal Navy 1755; and 1760; State of the Royal Navy,
1763.

1233. SENIOR, William.
The Battle of New Brighton.
The Mariner's Mirror, vol.i (1911), pp.148–151.
   The account of a skirmish between the Royal Navy
and merchantmen over impressment in 1755.

1234. SYRETT, *Dr.* David.
The methodology of British amphibious operations
during the Seven Years' and American Wars.
The Mariner's Mirror, vol.lviii (August 1972),
pp.269–277.

1235. [Anonymous].
Britannia Triumphant; or, an account of the sea-
fights and victories of the English Nation . . . to the
conclusion of the late war [i.e. 1763] . . .
London; R.James; 1766. The second edition. 224pp.,
pls. 8vo.
   There is also a copy of the third edition (R.James;
1777) in the Library.

1236. [Anonymous].
Additional Fighting Instructions, 1756–1762.
In: Fighting Instructions, 1530–1816. [edited by Julian
S.Corbett].
London; Navy Records Society series, vol.xxix;
1905., pp.217–224.
   Being the instructions of Sir Edward Hawke in 1756
and Admiral Boscawen in 1759.

THE AMERICAN WAR OF INDEPENDENCE, 1775–1783
and contemporary events elsewhere

I. Events and operations in North America

1237. ABBOT, Willis John.
Blue Jackets of '76. A history of the naval battles of the American Revolution.
New York; Dodd Mead; [1888]. 311pp. 8vo.

1238. ALLEN, Gardner Weld.
A naval history of the American Revolution.
Boston & New York; Houghton Mifflin; 1913. 2 vols. 8vo.

1239. ANDERSON, Troyer S.
The command of the Howe brothers during the American Revolution.
Oxford; University Press; 1936. 368pp., pls. & maps. 8vo.

1240. [ARBUTHNOT, *Admiral* Marriot. (1711–1794)].
Letters and papers during the American War, 1779–81.
In: Historical Manuscripts Commission: Stopford-Sackville Mss, vol.ii. London; 1910.

1241. BARRINGTON, *Admiral the Hon.* Samuel. (1729–1800).
The Barrington Papers.
Selected . . . and edited by D.Bonner-Smith.
London; Navy Records Society; 1937–41. 2 vols. 8vo.
    Includes much on Barrington's part in the North American operations.

1242. BARTON, John A.
The Battle of Valcour Island.
History Today, vol.ix (1959), pp.791–799.
    In the autumn of 1776, General Carleton established a lake fleet of 29 vessels mounting 87 guns at the northern end of Lake Champlain. Meanwhile Colonel Benedict Arnold hurriedly assembled an American fleet of 16 vessels carrying 83 guns. On October 11, Carleton met Arnold off Valcour Island and in a seven-hour battle the American flotilla was severely crippled. Arnold escaped but Carleton pursued the next day and at Split Rock the Americans were forced to abandon their ships and retreat overland.

1243. BEATTIE, Donald W. *and* COLLINS, *Dr.* J.Richard.
Washington's New England Fleet: Beverly's role in its origins, 1775–6.
Salem, Mass.,; Newcomb & Ganns; 1969. 69pp. 8vo.

1244. 'BEAVER'. [*i.e.* BROCK, *Rear-Admiral* P.W.]
An order and letter book of the American Revolutionary War.
Naval Review, vol.xxvii (1939), pp.679–693.
    This belonged to Captain (later Admiral) J.T. Duckworth.

1245. BERKELEY, Edmund.
The Naval Office in Virginia.
American Neptune, vol.xxxiii (1973), pp.20–23.

1246. BOLTON, Reginald Pelham.
The bombardment of New York and the fight for independence . . . against the seapower of Great Britain in the year 1776.
New York; 1915. 75pp., illustr. 8vo.

1247. BONNER-SMITH, David. (1890–1950).
The capture of the *Washington.*
The Mariner's Mirror, vol.xx (October 1934), pp. 420–425.
    On 15 December, 1775 off Cape Ann, Boston.

1248. BRADFORD, Gershom.
Nelson in Boston Bay.
The American Neptune, vol.xi (1951), pp.239–244.
    In the summer of 1782, a British convoy crossed the Atlantic and arrived safely in the St. Lawrence River. Among her escort was HMS ALBERMARLE, 28 guns, with the twenty-three year old Horatio Nelson in command. After the convoy had dispersed, the ALBERMARLE cruised off the New England coast, seeking prizes among the shipping of the American colonies.

1249. BREEN, K.C.
The Navy and the Yorktown campaign, 1781.
University of London M.Phil thesis; 1971.

1250. BREWINGTON, Marion Vernon.
The battle of Delaware Bay, 1782.
USNIP, vol.lxv (1939), pp.231–237.

1251. CALENDAR OF HOME OFFICE PAPERS – George III.
vol.iv.: 1773–1775.
London; 1899.
    : Rear-Admiral Montagu's reports on the Boston Tea Party, 1774. p.iv; 474, &c.: Naval preparations against the colonists and the French threat. p.517; nos.141, &c.: Admiral Graves at Boston. pp.vii–xi; nos.323, &c.: Admiral Graves' report on the progress of the war in America. pp.xvii–xix; nos.373.: HMS SCARBOROUGH at Boston. pp.x–xi; nos.374, &c.: HMS ROSE at Rhode Island, 1774–5. pp.vii–xii; nos.325, &c.: HMS ASIA at New York. pp.xiii–xv; nos.358, &c.: Dutch arms for America intercepted. pp.v–vi; nos.717, &c.

1252. CHADWICK, French Ensor. [*editor*].
The Graves papers and other documents relating to
the naval operations of the Yorktown campaign,
July to October 1781.
New York; Naval History Society; 1916. lxxviii;
268pp. 8vo.

1253. CLARK, William Bell.
George Washington's Navy. Being an account of
his Excellency's fleet in New England waters.
Baton Rouge, Louisiana; State University Press;
1960. xi; 276pp., plates. 8vo.

1254. CLARK, William Bell *and* MORGAN,
William James. [*editors*].
Naval Documents of the American Revolution.
vol.i.: December 1774–September 1775.
vol.ii.: September–December 1775.
vol.iii.: December 1775–February 1776.
vol.iv.: February–May 1776.
vol.v.: May–July 1776.
Washington; US Navy Department; 1964 – (*in
progress*).
1,451; 1,463; 1,486; 1,580; 1,486pp., num.illustr. &
plans. 8vo.
    *An exhaustive and valuable coverage of every aspect of
the subject, which is still in series. There is much on the
creation of the Continental Navy and the British war
effort.*

1255. DAVIS, W.
The Continental Navy of the USA, 1775–1785.
Belgian Shiplover, vol.xciv (1963), p.285.

1256. FROTHINGHAM, *Captain* Thomas
Goddard, USN.
The sequence that led to Yorktown.
USNIP, vol.lvii (1931), pp.1327–1330.
    Includes mention of naval aspects.

1257. GOODRICH, Cooper Frederick.
Howe and D'Estaing: a study in coast defence.
USNIP, vol.xxii (1896), pp.577–586.

1258. GOULD, Edward Kalloch.
British and Tory marauders on the Penobscot.
Rockland, Maine; 1932. 46pp., illustr. 8vo.

1259. GRAVES, W.
Two letters from W.Graves, Esq.; respecting the
conduct of Rear Admiral Thomas Graves in North
America during his accidental command there for
four months in 1781.
London; November 1782. 48 + [19]pp., chart. 4to.
    *An important contemporary source during the critical
period 1781/2 for British naval operations in North*

*American waters, including the Chesapeake Bay action.
Letters written at the time by Admirals Rodney, Thomas
Graves, Affleck and Samuel Hood are included, with
important fleet lists and a fine folding chart of the
Chesapeake Bay action: 'A Representation of the sea
fight on the 5th of Sepr 1781, between Admiral Graves
and the Count De Grasse'.*

1260. GUIOT, Pierre.
Notes de campagne du Comte Rigaud de Vaudreuil,
1781–1782.
Neptunia, vols.xlv (January 1957), pp.33–40; xlvi
(February), pp.34–42; xlvii (March) pp.33–40; xlviii
(April), pp.32–41; xlix (May), pp.34–41; l (June),
pp.29–35.; li (July), pp.34–41; & lii (August 1957),
pp.31–40.

1261. HIGGINSON, Francis J.
Naval operations during the Revolutionary War.
Proc. New York State History Association, vol.xxi
(1923), pp.65–77.
    *Especially about the Battle of Valcour Island, 11
October 1776. See the entry under Barton, John A.*

1262. HISTORICAL MANUSCRIPTS
COMMISSION.
: 11th Report, part v. : Dartmouth Mss – vol.2.
London; 1895.
    *With several references to the British squadron in
America, 1774–6.*
: Stopford-Sackville Mss. – vol.2.
London; 1910.
    *With papers relating to the American War, including
despatches to the Secretary of State for the Colonies from
Rodney (1779–82), Arbuthnot and Sir George Collier.
The appendix to part iii of the H.M.C. 9th Report
(1883) also prints material from the Stopford-Sackville
Mss (on pp.1–184), in which there are letters and
despatches relating to the American War.*
: American Mss – vols.1–4.
London; 1904–9.
    *With many official papers relating to the American
War.*

1263. [HOWE, *Admiral of the Fleet* Richard, Earl
Howe (1726–1799)].
Instructions regarding the order of battle, &c, 1782.
In: Fighting Instructions, 1530–1816. (London; Navy
Records Society, vol.xxix; 1905).
Orders and battle instructions, 1776–7.
In: Signals and Instructions, 1776–94. (London; Navy
Records Society, vol.xxxv; 1908).
Letters and Instructions during the American War.
In: H.M.C. Stopford-Sackville Mss, vol.ii (London
1910).

1264. HUNT, Richard Caulter.
Alexander Hamilton and the regular naval
establishment.
USNIP, vol.lxxxiii (1957), pp.806–7.

1265. JAMES, *Admiral Sir* William Milburne.
(1881–1973).
The British Navy in adversity. A study of the War
of American Independence.
London; Longmans; 1926. 459pp., maps, diagrs.,
appendices.
  *Includes many chapters on the North American
operations. Within the appendices are lists of: the
British and American Fleets on Lake Champlain,
1776; Sir Peter Parker's squadron at Charleston, 1776;
Howe's fleet at New York, July 1776; the opposing
fleets in North America in October 1778; Byron's
squadron, 1778; Chevalier de Ternay's squadron at
Rhode Island, 1780; the rival fleets at the actions of
Cape Henry, 16 March, 1781 and the Chesapeake, 5
September, 1781.*

1266. JENKINS, C.W.
Combined operations in the Revolutionary War –
Yorktown.
Coast Artillery Journal, vol.lxxii (1930), pp.315–333,
maps.

1267. KANI, C.Henry.
Military and naval operations on the Delaware
River in 1777.
Philadelphia Historical Society publications, no.i (1910),
pp.177–203.

1268. KNOX, *Captain* Dudley Wright, USN.
The naval genius of George Washington.
Boston; Houghton Mifflin; 1932. [vi]; 137pp.; pls.
8vo.

1269. KNOX, *Captain* Dudley Wright, USN.
D'Estaing's fleet revealed.
USNIP, vol.lxi (1935), pp.161–168.

1270. KNOX, *Captain* Dudley Wright, USN.
Yorktown: September–October 1781.
USNIP, vol.lxxi (1945), p.952.

1271. KNOX, *Captain* Dudley Wright, USN.
Early naval use of rocket weapons.
USNIP, vol.lxxii (1946), pp.257–261.

1272. KOKE, Richard J.
Forcing the Hudson River passage, October 9, 1776.
New York Hist. Soc. Quarterly, (October 1952), 8pp.
  *Describes the action of the British frigates in
penetrating the American defences above New York.*

1273. KOKE, Richard J.
The struggle for the Hudson: the British naval
expedition under Captain Hyde Parker and Captain
James Wallace, July 12–August 18, 1776.
New York Hist. Soc. Quarterly, (April 1956).

1274. LABAREE, Benjamin Woods.
The Boston Tea Party.
Oxford; University Press; 1964. 347pp., pls. 8vo.

1275. LANDERS, H.L.
The Virginia campaign and the blockade and siege
of Yorktown, 1781.
Washington; 1931. vii, 219pp.; illustr. 8vo.

1276. LANGLE, *Capitaine* Fleuriot de.
Contribution de la marine française à la victoire de
Yorktown.
La Revue Maritime, vol.cclxxiii (February 1970),
pp.177–183.

1277. LARRABEE, Harold A.
Decision at the Chesapeake.
New York; Potter; 1964. 317pp. 8vo.
  *A modern narrative of the decisive action of 5
September, 1781.*

1278. LAWRENCE, Alexander A.
Storm over Savannah. The story of Count d'Estaing
and the siege of the town in 1779.
Athens, Ga.; University of Georgia Press; [1951].
x; 220pp.; pls. 8vo.

1279. LEIBY, A.C.
The Revolutionary War in the Hackensack Valley:
the Jersey Dutch and the neutral ground, 1775–1783.
New Jersey; 1962. 311pp., 8vo.
  Includes accounts of minor boat raids.

1280. LEWIS, Charles Lee.
Admiral de Grasse and American independence.
Annapolis, Md.; US Naval Institute; 1945. 403pp.
8vo.

1281. MALONE, J.J.
The New England trade in naval stores in the
eighteenth century.
University of London Ph.D thesis; July 1953.

1282. McCLAY, Edgar Stanton.
A sea view of our Revolution.
USNIP, vol.xxxvii (1911), pp.219–237.

1283. McCLAY, Edgar Stanton.
New details of the *Randolph–Yarmouth* naval battle.
USNIP, vol.xliii (1917), pp.1445–8.

1284. McCLELLAN, Edwin North.
American marines in the Revolution.
USNIP, vol.xlix (1923), pp.957–963.

1285. McMASTER, Gilbert Totten.
Original codes used by our Revolutionary commanders for the convoy of merchantmen.
USNIP, vol.xxxviii (1912), pp.1041–5.

1286. MELVILLE, Phillips.
Lexington: brigantine of war, 1776–1777.
USNIP, vol.lxxxvi (1960), pp.51–59.

1287. MILES, Alfred Hart.
Sea power and the Yorktown campaign.
USNIP, vol.liii (1927), pp.1169–1184; plans.

1288. MILES, Alfred Hart.
Naval views of the Yorktown campaign.
USNIP, vol.lvii (1931), pp.1305–1312; illustr.

1289. MILLER, Samuel Davis.
The capture of His Majesty's ship *Syren*.
Rhode Island Hist. Soc. Coll., vol.xvii (1924), pp.24–8.
   The sloop SYREN, 20, (Capt. Tobias Furneaux) was wrecked off Rhode Island on 10 November, 1777.*

1290. MORGAN, William James.
Captains to the northward. The New England captains in the Continental Navy.
Barre, Mass.,; 1959. 260pp., pls. 8vo.

1291. MORSE, Sidney G.
'The Fleet'.
The American Neptune, vol.v (1945), pp.177–193.
   Describes the creation of the US naval squadron in 1777.

1292. NEESER, Robert Wilden. [*editor*].
The despatches of Molyneux Shuldham, Vice-Admiral of the Blue, commander-in-chief of His Britannic Majesty's ships in North America, January–July 1776.
New York; Navy History Society; 1913. xxxvii, 330pp. 8vo.

1293. NEESER...
Letters and papers relating to the cruises of Gustavus Conyngham, a captain of the Continental Navy, 1777–1779.
New York; Naval History Society; 1915. liii; 240pp.; pls. 8vo.
   There is also in the Library a facsimile reprint of this work, published by the Kennikat Press in 1970.

1294. OWEN, *Commander* John Hely, RN.
The Navy and the surrender at Yorktown, 1781.
Naval Review, vol.xiv (1926), pp.18; 223.

1295. OWEN, *Commander* John Hely, RN.
Howe and d'Estaing in North America.
Naval Review, vol.xv (1927), p.257.

1296. PAULLIN, Charles Oscar.
(a). Classes of operations of the Continental Navy of the American Revolution.
USNIP, vol.xxxi (1905), pp.153–164.
(b). The administration of the Continental Navy of the American Revolution.
USNIP, vol.xxxi (1905), pp.625–675.
(c). The administration of the Massachusetts and Virginia navies of the American Revolution.
USNIP, vol.xxxii (1906), pp.131–164.

1297. PAULLIN, Charles Oscar.
The Navy of the American Revolution; its administration, its policy and its achievements.
Cleveland; Burrows; 1906. 549pp. 8vo.

1298. PAVEY, Frank D.
The Battle of Chesapeake Bay.
Franco–American Review, (Spring 1938).

1299. PERRY, James H.
Disaster on the Delaware. [1775].
USNIP, vol.lxxxviii (1962), pp.84–92, illustr.

1300. PRATT, Julius W.
The British blockade and American precedent.
USNIP, vol.xlvi (1920), pp.1789–1802.

1301. RATHBUN, Frank H.
Rathbun's raid on Nassau [1778].
USNIP, vol.xcvi (1970), pp.40–47.

1302. RAWSON, *Lieutenant-Commander* Geoffrey, RIM.
The case of *HMS Vulture*.
The Mariner's Mirror, vol.xxxv (January 1949), pp.47–50.
   On 22 September 1780, the sloop VULTURE *(Lt. Andrew Sutherland) was surprised in the Hudson River by a rebel battery mounted on Teller's Point.*

1303. RODDIS, Louis H.
The New York prison ships in the American Revolution.
USNIP, vol.lxi (1935), pp.331–336.

1304. RUSSELL, *Captain* Peter.
The siege of Charleston; journal, 25 December 1779 – 2 May 1780.
American Historical Review, vol.iv (1898–9).

1305. RUTHERFORD, G.
Admiral de Ternay and an 'English convoy'.
The Mariner's Mirror, vol.xxvi (April 1940), pp.158–162.
    Describes an encounter off Chesapeake Bay on 4 July 1780, between a large French squadron under de Ternay and a much smaller English force, which had been despatched to Virginia by Admiral Arbuthnot at New York.

1306. SHAFROTH, John Franklin.
The strategy of the Yorktown campaign, 1781.
USNIP, vol.lvii (1931), pp.721–736, map.

1307. STEWART, Robert Armistead.
The history of Virginia's navy of the Revolution.
Richmond, Va.,; 1933. 279pp. 8vo.

1308. STOUT, Neil R.
Manning the Royal Navy in America, 1763–1775.
The American Neptune, vol.xxiii (1963), pp.174–185.

1309. SUTHERLAND, Robert Theodore.
The blockade of Boston.
USNIP, vol.lxiii (1937), pp.195–8.

1310. SYRETT, David.
The disruption of *HMS Flora's* convoy, 1776.
The Mariner's Mirror, vol.lvi (November 1970), pp.423–7.
    A disaster off the New England coast, in which the Americans captured six military transports out of a convoy of 33 ships which had sailed from the Clyde.

1311. WATSON, W.C.
Naval operations in Lake Champlain in 1776.
American Historical Record, vol.iii (1874).

1312. WEED, Richmond.
The battle of the Virginia Capes, 1781.
USNIP, vol.lxvi (1940), pp.524–532.

1313. WILLCOX, W.B.
Rhode Island in British strategy, 1780–1781.
Journal of Modern History, vol.xvii (December 1945), pp.304–331.

1314. WILLCOX, W.B.
British strategy in America, 1778.
American Historical Review, vol.lii (1947), p.33.

1315. [Anonymous].
The action between American and British barges in Chesapeake Bay, November 1782.
Maryland Historical Magazine, vol.iv (1909), pp.115–133; 381–2.

1316. [Anonymous].
The Battle of Valcour Island.
Bull. Fort Ticonderoga Museum, vol.ix (1930–2), pp.163–8.
    See also entry no.1242.

II. Operations in the West Indies

1317. BARRINGTON, *Admiral the Hon.* Samuel, (1729–1800).
The Barrington Papers. Selected from the letters and papers of Admiral the Hon. Samuel Barrington and edited by D.Bonner-Smith.
London; Navy Records Society; 1937–41. 2 vols. 8vo.
Includes much about Barrington's operations in the West Indies.

1318. BARROW, *Sir* John, (1764–1848).
Rodney's Battle of the 12th April.
The Quarterly Review, vol.xliii (1830).
An account of his decisive victory against de Grasse at The Saints, 12 April 1782.

1319. BONNER-SMITH, David, (1890–1950).
Byron in the Leeward Islands, 1779.
The Mariner's Mirror, vol.xxx (January 1944), pp.38–48; 81–92.

1320. BRITTON, C.J. (d.1946).
Nelson and the River San Juan.
The Mariner's Mirror, vol.xxviii (1942), pp.213–221.
*Describes Nelson's abortive expedition against the forts of San Juan, Nicaragua, March–September 1780.
See also entry no.1345.*

1321. CALENDAR OF HOME OFFICE PAPERS: George III.
vol.iii: 1770–1772.
London; 1881.
*Includes the following material:
Fire in Grenada, 1771; Rear-Admiral Man's failure to assist. p.x. &c. Spaniards detain HM Schooner SIR EDWARD HAWKE, at Carthagena, 1771. p.xvii, &c.*
vol.iv: 1773–1775.
London; 1899.
HM Ships at Carthagena; HMS WINCHELSEA entered port without permission of the Spanish Government, 1775. p.519, &c.

1322. CASTEX, Raoul Victor Patrice.
L'envers de la guerre de course; la verité sur l'enlèvement du convoi de St. Eustache par Lamotte – Picquet (Avril–Mai 1781).
Paris; 1912. 55pp., map. 8vo.
About the seizure of an important St. Eustatius convoy by a French privateering squadron under Lamotte-Picquet, in the spring of 1781.

1323. CLASEN, W. [*editor*].
La Bataille des Saintes, racontée par un officier de marine suèdois au service de la France.
La Revue Maritime (March 1936), pp.331–349.

1324. CONTENSON, Ludovic de.
La prise de Saint-Christophe en 1782.
La Revue Historique Antilles, vol.ii (1929), pp.17–41.

1325. DE GRASSE, François Joseph Paul, *Comte* (1732–1788).
Mémoire du Comte De Grasse, sur le combat naval du 12 Avril 1782, avec les plans des positions principales des Armées respectives.
[Paris; 1783]. 28pp., 8 foldg. battle plans; tables; pls. oblong 4to.
The Battle of the Saints (or les Saintes) from the French point of view. The plans comprise: the position at dawn; 7 a.m.; 8 a.m.; 8.15 a.m.; 10 a.m.; 11.30 a.m.; 3.30 p.m.; and 7 p.m. There is also an important table shewing the French line of battle, the ships engaged and their commanders.

1326. DUSIEUX, Joseph.
Conquête de l'Île Saint-Christophe en 1782.
Carnet Sabretache, vol.vii (1924), pp.407–419.

1327. FORTESCUE, *Sir* John William, (1859–1933).
St. Lucia, 1778.
Macmillan's Magazine, vol.lxxxv (1902), pp.419–427.

1328. FRASER, Edward.
Famous fighters of the Fleet.
London; Macmillan; 1904. 323pp., pls. 8vo.
Includes a vivid account of Rodney at the Battle of the Saints, 12 April 1782.

1329. HEWITT, M.J.
The West Indies in the American Revolution.
University of Oxford D.Phil thesis; 1938.

1330. HISTORICAL MANUSCRIPTS COMMISSION.
: 12th Report, part iv: Rutland Mss. – vol.3.
London; 1894.
With a number of naval documents 1775–86, including: Papers of Lord Robert Manners, 1777–82, with accounts of the actions at St. Kitts and Dominica, 1782; Sir Samuel Hood's criticisms of Rodney's conduct, 1782.
: 11th Report, part v.: Dartmouth Mss. – vol.2.
London; 1895.
With several references to the Admiralty and operations in the West Indies, 1768–75.
: Stopford-Sackville Mss. – vol.2.
London; 1910.

1330. HISTORICAL MANUSCRIPTS
COMMISSION, *continued*
 *With papers on events in the Caribbean 1777–80,
including Rodney's actions off Dominica, April/May
1780.*

1331. [HOOD, *Admiral* Samuel, *Viscount Hood,*
(1724–1816)].
Letters written by Sir Samuel Hood (Viscount Hood)
in 1781–2–3. Edited by David Hannay; illustrated
with extracts from logs and public records.
London; Navy Records Society; 1895. frontis.,; 170
+ [2]pp. 8vo.
*With much on Hood's part in the operations against
the French in the Caribbean.*

1332. [HOOD, *Admiral* Samuel, *Viscount Hood,*
(1724–1816)].
Letters from Sir Samuel Hood, 1780–1782.
Edited by Lt-Cmdr. J.H.Owen.
The Mariner's Mirror, vol.xix (January 1933), pp.75–
87.
 *A series of nine letters, including one on the capture of
St. Eustatius in February 1781 and four on Hood's
action off Martinique, the loss of Tobago and St. Kitts
and the battle of The Saints.*

1333. HOPE, *Reverend* L.P.
A unique relic of Rodney and the Battle of the
Saints.
Proc. Soc. of Antiquaries of Scotland, vol.lxiii (1929),
pp.98–101.

1334. KEMP, *Lieutenant* N.H.
Letters from the Leeward Islands, 1781.
Naval Review, vol.xxiii (1935), pp.127–137.
 These are taken from the Bridport collection.

1335. MACLAY, Edgar Stanton.
A forgotten seafight of the Revolution.
Magazine of History, vol.xvii (New York, 1913),
pp.36–8.
 On 12 December 1782, the Mediator, *44, sighted five
French and American storeships off Florida bound for the
West Indies. Three were taken by her without loss. The
Captain of the* ALEXANDRE *attempted to foment a
mutiny, while a prisoner aboard the* MEDIATOR *and was
clapped in irons.*

1336. MACLAY, Edgar Stanton.
New details of the *Randolph–Yarmouth* naval battle.
USNIP, vol.xliii (1917), pp.1445–8.
 On 7 March 1778, the YARMOUTH, *64, met some
American ships cruising off Barbados. After a running
fight, the 32-gun frigate* RANDOLPH *blew up and only
four of her entire crew of 315 survived.*

1337. MARIE, *Lieutenant* René.
D'Estaing aux Antilles.
La Revue Maritime, vol.xxiii (December 1921),
pp.735–758.

1338. [MATTHEWS, John].
Twenty-one Plans, with explanations, of different
actions in the West-Indies, during the late War:
By an Officer of the Royal Navy, who was present.
Chester; J.Fletcher; 1784. 24pp., 21 foldg. plans.
oblong 8vo.
 *This is an important contemporary source for events in
the Caribbean theatre during the war, including fleet lists
& the following plans of the actions:*
*i–v.: Plans of the action off Grenada on 6 July 1779.
[Byron v d'Estaing] – positions at 5 a.m.; 7.15 a.m.;
8 a.m.; 10.30 a.m.; & 3 p.m.*
*vi.: Plan of the situation of the British fleet at anchor off
Basseterre on the 2nd July, 1779.*
*vii–ix.: Plans of the action off Martinique, 29 April
1781. [Hood v de Grasse].*
*x–xii.: Plans of the actions in and off Basseterre Road,
St. Kitts, 25/26 January 1782. [Hood v de Grasse].
– position at noon; 3.30 p.m. on 25 January; situation on
26 January.*
*xiii–xxi.: Plans of the actions off Dominica and the
Saints, 9 & 12 April 1782. [Rodney v de Grasse]. –
(Dominica) positions at 6 a.m.; 9.45 a.m.; noon. – (The
Saints) positions at 6 a.m.; 7.45 a.m.; 10 a.m.; noon;
3 p.m.; sunset.*

1339. McLARTY, R.N.
The expedition of Major-General John Vaughan to
the Lesser Antilles, 1779–1781.
University of Michigan Ph.D thesis; 1951.

1340. MORAN, Charles.
Saint Eustatius, the island that was different.
USNIP, vol.lxviii (January 1942), pp.73–77.
 *The important Dutch possession & privateer stronghold
in the Leeward Islands, which was seized by Rodney in
1781.*

1341. OWEN, *Commander* John Hely, RN.
The Navy and the capture of St. Lucia, 1778.
Fighting Forces, vol.ii (1925), pp.42–54; 1 map.

1342. OWEN, *Commander* John Hely, RN.
Rodney and de Guichen.
Naval Review, vol.xiii (1925), pp.195; 433.

1343. OWEN, *Commander* John Hely, RN.
The Battle of Grenada, 6 July 1779.
Naval Review, vol.xiv (1926), p.458.

1344. OWEN, *Commander* John Hely, RN.
Rodney and de Grasse.
Naval Review, vol.xvi, (1928), pp.148; 213; 436.

1345. ROBINSON, *Commander* Charles Napier.
Nelson at Nicaragua.
The Mariner's Mirror, vol.x (1924), pp.78–9; plate.
See also entry no.1320.

1346. ROWBOTHAM, *Commander* W.B.
The West Indies hurricanes of October 1780.
RUSIJ, vol.cvi (November 1961), p.573.
A series of terrible hurricanes swept the Caribbean in October 1780, especially on the 10th/11th of that month. Widespread damage and loss of life occurred on the islands. No fewer than thirteen warships of the Royal Navy were wrecked or sunk – including the THUNDERER, *74,* STIRLING CASTLE, *64 &* PHOENIX, *44 – and many more were damaged. There were corresponding losses among the Spanish and French squadrons.*

1347. SPINNEY, J.David.
The *Amazon* in the 1780 hurricane.
The Mariner's Mirror, vol.xlix (November 1963), p.305.
See the previous entry.

1348. SPINNEY, J.David.
Sir Samuel Hood at St. Kitt's: a reassessment.
The Mariner's Mirror, vol.lviii (May 1972), pp.179–181.

1349. WHITE, *Captain* Thomas.
Naval Researches; or a candid inquiry into the conduct of Admirals Byron, Graves, Hood and Rodney, in the actions off Grenada, Chesapeake, St. Christopher's and of the ninth and twelfth of April 1782 . . . illustrated with plans of the battles.
London; Whittaker, Treacher & Arnott; 1830.
136pp., 10 battle plans. 8vo.
White was a midshipman in Hood's flagship, the BARFLEUR, *in several of these battles.*

1350. [Anonymous].
Relation authentique des trois combats sur mer, entre l'Escadre Française, commandée par . . . Comte de Guichen . . . & l'Amiral Rodney . . . donnée le 17 Avril, 15 & 17 Mai 1780 . . .
Marseilles; Jean Mossy; 28 July 1780. 1 sheet. 4to.
This is based on the official account in 'La Gazette de France' (11 July, 1780) of the three indecisive squadron actions fought between Rodney and de Guichen off Martinique in April and May 1780.

1351. [Anonymous].
A short account of the Naval Actions of the last war, in order to prove that the French nation never gave such slender proofs of maritime greatness as during that period . . .
By an Officer.
London; John Murray; 1788. 148pp. 8vo.
Includes narratives of Rodney's actions versus de Guichan and d'Estaing; Hood against de Grasse at St. Kitts; and the Battle of the Saints.

1352. [Anonymous].
The battle of the 12th April 1782 between the British and French fleets off Guadeloupe.
The Naval Chronicle, vol.xxxvi (1816), pp.464–8; & xxxvii (1817), p.409.

1353. [Anonymous].
Breaking the line on 12th April 1782.
Naval Review, vol.xiv (1926), p.249.
Letters showing that this was mainly due to Sir Charles Douglas, Rodney's Captain of the Fleet.

1354. [Anonymous].
Hood at Saint Christopher's, 1782.
Naval Review, vol.xv (1927), p.496.

1355. [Anonymous].
April 12, 1782: The Battle of the Saints.
History Today, vol.v (1955), p.272.

III. Events and operations in Home Waters

1356. ADAMS, *Captain* Scarritt.
The loss of the *Royal George*.
History Today, vol.ix (1959), pp.837–840.
This is a statement based on one person's recollections, not supported by the facts which came out at the Court Martial.

1357. BARNES, John Sanford.
The logs of the *Serapis*, *Alliance* and *Ariel* . . . 1779–80.
New York; Naval History Society; 1911.
Including an account of the historic action between John Paul Jones' BONHOMME RICHARD *and HMS* SERAPIS *off Flamborough Head, 23 September 1779.*

1358. BEATSON, Robert, (1742–1818).
A new and distinct view of the memorable action of the 17th July 1778. In which the whole of the aspersions cast on the characters of the flag-officers are shown to be totally unfounded; and the miscarriage traced to its true cause.
London; J.Strahan; 1791. viii; 38pp. 8vo.
About the Battle of Ushant and the notorious Keppel-Palliser dispute which followed [qqv.].

1359. BOLANCHEV, Louis H.
The log of the *Ranger*.
USNIP, vol.lxii (1936), pp.201–211.
During her cruise in 1778 in British waters, while under the command of John Paul Jones.

1360. BONNER-SMITH, David, (1890–1950).
The case of the *Sartine*.
The Mariner's Mirror, vol.xxi (July 1935), pp.305–322.
On 1 May 1780, the cartel ship SARTINE, *carrying French officers and soldiers who had surrendered at Pondicherry, was sighted off Cape St. Vincent and fired upon by the* ROMNEY, 50 (*Capt. Roddam Home*). As she flew both a French flag and a cartel flag, the French complained strongly of the* ROMNEY's *conduct.*

1361. BROOMFIELD, J.H.
The Keppel-Palliser affair, 1778–1779.
The Mariner's Mirror, vol.xlvii (August 1961), pp. 195–207.
See also the entries under Admirals Keppel and Palliser.

1362. BRUCE, R.Stuart.
Shetland and the Dutch War, 1781.
The Mariner's Mirror, vol.xxxvii (October 1951), pp.282–292.

1363. CALENDAR OF HOME OFFICE PAPERS: George III.
vol.iii: 1770–1772.
London; 1881.
Fire at Portsmouth dockyard, 1770. pp.liv–lvi; 300; &c.

1364. CALLENDER, *Sir* Geoffrey A.R. (1875–1946).
With the Grand Fleet in 1780.
The Mariner's Mirror, vol.ix (September/October 1923), pp.258–270; 290–304.
*'There are few passages in our naval history more depressing than the story of the Channel Fleet during the War of American Independence (1778–83). Between the time when Keppel struck his flag in order to undergo trial by Court Martial at the instance of Sir Hugh Palliser, his second-in-command, until the time when Lord Howe marshalled the force that was to relieve Gibraltar, a dark pall of gloom and obscurity seemed to settle down upon the main fleet and deprive it of all chance of distinction. . . .' [from the opening paragraph].
The article contains extracts from the Geary papers.*

1365. CHENEVIX TRENCH, R.B.
An eighteenth century invasion alarm.
History Today, vol.vi (1956), pp.457–465.
A short account of the Franco–Spanish expeditionary threat against England in the Summer of 1779.

1366. GRAEME, Alan.
Threat from the sea. An east coast bombardment of yesterday.
Scots Magazine, vol.xxxiii (August 1940), pp.345–352.
Describes the French attack on Arbroath in 1781.

1367. GUIOT, Pierre.
Les sequelles du combat d'Ouessant.
Neptunia, vol.xlv (January 1947), pp.14–19.
An assessment of the consequences of the Battle of Ushant (27 July 1778), from the French point of view.

1368. HARDY, *Admiral Sir* Charles, (1716?–1780).
Orders to the Grand Fleet, 1779.
In: *Signals and Instructions, 1776–94.* (Navy Records Society, vol.xxxv), *edited by* Julian S.Corbett.
London; Navy Records Society; 1908.

1369. HENDERSON, *Admiral Sir* William Hannom.
The Loss of the *Royal George*, 1782.
Naval Review, vol.xiii (1925), pp.456; 779.
Shows that the popular accounts of the loss of the ROYAL GEORGE *were based on the recollection of one witness 57 years later and were completely at variance with the finding of the court martial held immediately afterwards.*

1370. HISTORICAL MANUSCRIPTS
COMMISSION.
12th Report, part iv: Rutland Mss. – vol.3.
London; 1894.
*With a number of naval documents, 1775–86,
including:*
*'An eye-witness account of John Paul Jones' action off
Flamborough Head, 23 September 1779.'*

1371. JOHNSON, *Brigadier* R.F.
The *Royal George*.
London; Charles Knight; 1971. xviii, 200pp.;
plates; diagrs. 8vo.

1372. [KEPPEL, *Admiral* Augustus, *1st Viscount
Keppel*, (1725–1786)].
An address to the Lords Commissioners of the
Admiralty on their conduct towards Admiral Keppel.
London; J.Almon; 1778. 46pp. small 4to.

1373. [KEPPEL, *Admiral* Augustus, *1st Viscount
Keppel*, (1725–1786)].
An authentic and impartial copy of the trial of the
Hon. Augustus Keppel, Admiral of the Blue, held at
Portsmouth on the 7th of January 1779 and con-
tinued ... to the 11th day of February, 1779 ...
Portsmouth; 1779. 415pp., frontis. 8vo.

1374. [KEPPEL, *Admiral* Augustus, *1st Viscount
Keppel*, (1725–1786)].
Minutes of the proceedings at a court-martial,
assembled for the trial of the Honourable Augustus
Keppel as a charge exhibited against him by Vice-
Admiral Sir Hugh Palliser ... (as taken by George
Jackson Esq., judge-advocate of His Majesty's
Fleet ...
London; Strachan & Cadell; 1779. 182pp. folio.

1375. [KEPPEL, *Admiral* Augustus, *1st Viscount
Keppel*, (1725–1786)].
The proceedings ... of the court-martial on the
trial of the Honourable Augustus Keppel ... held on
board His Majesty's ship the *Britannia* ... January
7th 1779 ... till February 11th, when the Admiral
was honourably acquitted ...
Dublin; 1779. 588pp., 8vo.

1376. [KEPPEL, *Admiral* Augustus, *1st Viscount
Keppel* (1725–1786)].
An address to the Hon. Admiral Augustus Keppel.
Containing candid remarks on his defence before the
court-martial; the second edition, with considerable
observations on the late trial and acquittal of Vice-
Admiral Sir Hugh Palliser ...
By a seaman[John Stevenson].
London; W.Nicoll; [n.d.]. viii; 120pp. 8vo.
See also under Admiral Palliser.

1377. [KEPPEL, *Admiral* Augustus, *1st Viscount
Keppel*, (1725–1786)].
*Other reports of his court-martial, 1779, and the
Keppel-Palliser dispute generally are in: Campbell's
Naval History, vol.v (1818). P. Burke: 'The trial of
Keppel', in his: Naval & Military Trials (1876).*

1378. KLEBER, Louis C.
Jones raids Britain.
History Today, vol.xix (1969), pp.277–282.
*About John Paul Jones' landing at Whitehaven,
April 1778.*

1379. LACOUR-GAYET, Georges.
La campagne navale de la Manche en 1775.
La Revue Maritime, vol.cl (1901), pp.1629–1673.

1380. LAUGHTON, L.G.Carr.
The loss of the *Royal George*.
Naval Review, vol.xiii (1925), p.456.
*Summarises the findings of the court-martial, which
held that the ship had not overset. Her loss in fact was
due to decay, which caused some material part of her
frame to give way.*

1381. LOSTANGES, *M.de.*
Relation du combat de la frégate française *La
Surveillante* contre la frégate anglaise *La Quebec*.
Paris; 1817. 44pp. 8vo.
*The story of a memorable and desperate frigate action
fought off Ushant on 6 October 1779.*

1382. MACLAY, Edgar Stanton.
A sea fight long forgot.
New York Magazine of History, vol.xi (1910),
pp.150–154.
*An engagement off Nantes, 9 September 1778,
between a British convoy and French privateers.*

1383. MACLAY, Edgar Stanton.
Another seafight of the Revolution discovered.
USNIP, vol.xxxix (1913), pp.1461–8; illustr.
Fought off Ferrol, on 12 December 1782.

1384. MARS, James.
The battle of Ushant – and after.
USNIP, vol.xc (1964), pp.80–87.

1385. MARSHALL, M.A.N.
The armed ships of Dover, [*ca.*1780].
The Mariner's Mirror, vol.xlii (February 1956),
pp.73–77.

1386. MEIRAT, Jean.
Les turpitudes du Duc de Chartres à la bataille
d'Ouessant.

1386. MEIRAT, *continued*
Neptunia, vol.lxxxiv (March 1966), pp.24–31.
    A criticism of the French commander-in-chief's conduct at the Battle of Ushant, 27 July 1778.

1387. OWEN, *Commander* John Hely, RN.
Western cruisers in 1777.
Naval Review, vol.xix (1931), p.41.

1388. OWEN, . . .
Operations of the Western Squadron, 1781–2.
Naval Review, vol.xv (1927), p.33.

1389. [PALLISER, *Admiral Sir* Hugh, (1723–1796)].
Minutes of the proceedings at a court martial, assembled for the trial of Vice-Admiral Sir Hugh Palliser, Bart.
As taken by George Jackson, Esq; judge-advocate of His Majesty's Fleet . . .
London; Strachan & Cadell; 1779. 95pp. Folio.

1390. [PALLISER . . .].
The defence of Vice Admiral Sir Hugh Palliser Bart., at the court martial lately held upon him, with the court's sentence.
London; T.Cadell; 1779. [iv], 71pp. 8vo.

1391. [PALLISER, . . .].
The speech of Sir Hugh Palliser, Bart., in a committee of the House of Commons on Monday the 4th of December, 1780.
[London; 1780]. [ii], 34pp. 8vo.

1392. PATTERSON, *Professor* A.Temple.
The Other Armada. The Franco–Spanish attempts to invade Britain in 1779.
Manchester; University Press; 1960. 247pp., pls. & maps. 8vo.
    An important study of a neglected episode. 'It is true that the Armada of 1779 did not penetrate far into the Channel and that the army which lay encamped on the French coast was not commanded by a Napoleon. Yet . . . the country made a hair's breadth escape.' [from the preface].

1393. PEMBERTON, W.Baring.
The Keppel–Palliser affair.
Naval Review, vol.xxvii (1939), pp.286–293.

1394. PERRIN, Walter Gordon, (1874–1931).
[editor].
The Channel Fleet in 1779. Letters of Benjamin Thompson to Lord George Germain.
In: The Naval Miscellany, vol.iii., pp.123–156. 8vo.
London; Navy Records Society; 1928.

1395. PERROT, Maurice.
La Surprise de Jersey en 1781 . . .
Paris; Berger-Larrault; 1929. 418pp. 8vo.

1396. RENAUT, F.P.
Le crépuscule d'une puissance navale. La marine hollandaise de 1776 à 1783.
Paris; Graouli; 1932. 266pp. 8vo.

1397. RUTHERFORD, G.
The capture of the *Ardent*.
The Mariner's Mirror, vol.xxvii (April 1941), pp.106–131.
    In a humiliating action – off Plymouth on 17 August 1779 – the ARDENT, *64 guns, struck to four French frigates, which were in the van of D'Orvilliers' fleet.*

1398. SYDENHAM, J.J.
Firing His Majesty's dockyard. Jack the Painter and the American mission to France, 1776–1777.
History Today, vol.xvi (1966), pp.324–331.

1399. TAYLOR, *Rear-Admiral* A.H.
The French fleet in the Channel, 1778–1779.
The Mariner's Mirror, vol.xxiv (July 1938), pp.275–288.

1400. THERROZ, G.
Iconographie du combat de *La Surveillante* et du *Quebec*.
Neptunia, vol.xlv (January 1957), pp.20–26.
    This action took place off Ushant on 6 October, 1779.

1401. TRAMOND, J.
L'affaire Keppel–Palliser.
La Revue Maritime, vol.xxi (September/October 1921), pp.361–379; 504–521.
    See also the entries under Admirals Keppel and Palliser.

1402. WARNER, Oliver.
Paul Jones in battle.
History Today, vol.xv (1965), pp.613–618.
    A general article on John Paul Jones' career, but includes an account of his famous action off Flamborough Head on 23 September 1779.

1403. WILLCOX, William B.
Admiral Rodney warns of invasion, 1776–1777.
American Neptune, vol.iv (July 1944), pp.193–8.
    About Rodney's memoranda to Lord Shelburne concerning the danger of a French attack.

1404. [Anonymous].
Dreadful catastrophe of the *Royal George*, at Spithead, August 29, 1782, Captain Waghorne,

1404. [Anonymous], *continued*
Commander, by which the *Lark* sloop, victualler, was lost, and near nine hundred persons perished, among whom was the brave and much lamented Rear Admiral Kempenfeldt . . .
London; Thomas Tegg; [*n.d.*]. 28pp., frontis; 8vo.

1405. [Anonymous].
A narrative of the loss of *HMS Royal George* of 108 guns, sunk at Spithead, August 29th, 1782; with a concise account of Colonel Pasley's operations on the wreck in 1839 & 1840 . . .
Portsmouth; John Miller; 1840. 80pp., frontis.,; pls. 16mo.
At least nine further editions of this work, with altered titling – and some 'bound in the wood of the wreck' – were published at Portsea and Portsmouth between 1840 and 1845. The later ones include '. . . a statement of her sinking, written by her then flag-lieutenant, the late Admiral Sir P.C.H.Durham . . .' Copies of each of these are held in the Library.

1406. [Anonymous].
The conduct of the Channel Fleet in 1779 against superior force.
Naval Review, vol.xi (1923), p.17.

IV. Operations in the Mediterranean

1407. ANCELL, Samuel.
A Circumstantial Journal of the long and tedious blockade and siege of Gibraltar from the 12th of September, 1779, to the 23rd of February, 1783, . . .
Liverpool; Charles Wosencroft; 1784. 290pp.; pls. & charts. 8vo.
Five editions of this work were published between 1783 and 1802; this is a copy of the second.

1408. ANDREWS, Allen.
Proud Fortress. The fighting story of Gibraltar.
London; Evans; 1958. 220pp.; pls. 8vo.
Includes chapters on the siege of 1779–83.

1409. AYALA, Ignacio Lopez de.
Historia de Gibraltar.
Madrid; Antonio de Sancha; 1782. xlviii; 387pp., pls. & charts. 8vo.

1410. CALENDAR OF HOME OFFICE PAPERS: George III.
vol.iii: 1770–1772.
London; 1881.
British squadron in the Mediterranean. pp.x–xi, &c. French forces in the Mediterranean. pp.xi–xiii, &c. Spanish complaint of British blockade, 1770. pp.xiv–xv &c. HM Ships off the Barbary coast. pp.xvii–xviii, &c.

1411. CLARKE, C.P.R.
Gibraltar as a British possession to 1783.
University of Oxford B.Litt thesis; 1934.

1412. DODD, *Surgeon* J.S.
The ancient and modern history of Gibraltar, and the sieges and attacks it hath sustained, with an accurate journal of the siege of that fortress by the Spaniards, from February 13 to June 23, 1779.
By J.S.Dodd, late surgeon in the Royal Navy.
London; John Murray; 1781. 203pp.; 8vo.

1413. DRINKWATER, [*afterwards* BETHUNE], *Colonel* John.
A History of the late Siege of Gibraltar, with a description and account of that Garrison, from the earliest periods.
London; T.Spilsbury; 1790. xxiv; 356pp.; pls. & charts. large 8vo.
This is a copy of the fourth edition; the first was published in 1785. A copy of the new edition of 1905,

1413. DRINKWATER, *continued*
published by John Murray, is also in the Library.
   The author also wrote an important narrative of the
Battle of Cape St. Vincent, 14 February, 1797 [q.v.].

1414. FIELD, James A.
America and the Mediterranean World, 1776–1882.
Princeton, N.J.; 1969. xv, 485pp. 8vo.

1415. GIRARD, Albert.
Le grand siège de Gibraltar de 1782, vu par un
témoin.
Bulletin Hispanique, vol.xiv (1912), pp.140–173.

1416. GOWER, Richard Hall.
A description of the siege of Gibraltar. [1782].
The Naval Chronicle, vol.ix (1803), pp.271–5.

1417. [HERIOT, J.]
An historical sketch of Gibraltar, with an account of
the siege which that fortress stood against the com-
bined forces of France and Spain . . .
London; J.Edwards; 1792. viii; 148pp.; frontis.
Small 4to.

1418. HISTORICAL MANUSCRIPTS
COMMISSION.
: Stopford-Sackville Mss. – vol.1.
London; 1904.
Papers on the defence of Minorca, 1776–82, pp.370–3.

1419. KONETZKE, Richard.
Die grosse belagerung von Gibraltar in den jahren
1779 bis 1783.
Ibero-Amerikanisches Archiv, vol.xv (April 1941),
pp.20–26.

1420. McGUFFIE, T.H.
General Eliott and the defence of Gibraltar, 1779–
1783.
History Today, vol.xiv (1964), pp.782–790.

1421. McGUFFIE, T.H.
The siege of Gibraltar, 1779–1783.
London; Batsford; 1965. 208pp.; pls. & maps. 8vo.

1422. RUSSELL, Jack.
Gibraltar besieged, 1779–83.
London; Heinemann; 1965. 308pp., 8pls. 8vo.

1423. SPILSBURY, *Captain* John.
A Journal of the siege of Gibraltar 1779–1783.
By Captain Spilsbury, 12th Regiment. Edited by
B.H.T.Frere, Hon. Librarian of the Gibraltar
Garrison Library.
Gibraltar; 1908. 143pp.,; pls. 8vo.

1424. VENAULT, Raymond.
Une tentative contre Gibraltar: le siège de 1782.
Revue de France, vol.iii (May 1923), pp.271–4.

1425. WHITTON, Frederick Ernest.
The great siege of Gibraltar, 1779–83.
Blackwoods Magazine, vol.ccxlii (July 1937), pp.35–55.

1426. WYNDHAM, Horace.
The siege of 'The Rock'.
National Review, vol.cxv (December 1940), pp.699–
705.

V. Operations in the Indian Ocean

1427. ARCHIBALD, Edward H.H.
The maritime struggle for India, 1781–1783.
Historical notes to the series of paintings by Dominic Serres in the Town Hall, Ipswich.
Ipswich; 1973. 32pp., illustr. 8vo.

1428. BALLARD, *Admiral* George Alexander, (1862–1948).
The last battlefleet struggle in the Bay of Bengal.
The Mariner's Mirror, vol.xiii (April 1927), pp.125–144; 2 pls.
Being an account of the Hughes–Suffren campaigns, 1781–3.

1429. BALLARD, *Admiral* George Alexander, (1862–1948).
Hughes and Suffren.
The Mariner's Mirror, vol.xiii (October 1927), pp.348–356.
In the July 1927 issue of The Mariner's Mirror, *Admiral Richmond [q.v.] criticised Admiral Ballard's article on the Hughes–Suffren campaigns and this is his reply.*

1430. CAVALIERO, Roderick.
Admiral Suffren in the Indies.
History Today, vol.xx (1970), pp.472–480.

1431. COLGATE, H.A.
Trincomalee and the East Indies Squadron, 1746 to 1844.
University of London MA thesis; May 1960.

1432. DELFINI, P.Eustachio.
Ragguaglio della spedizione della flotta francese all' Indie Orientali seguita negli anni 1781, 1782, 1783 sotto la condotta del Generale de Suffren.
Turin; Ignazio Soffietti; 1785. xvi; 239pp. 8vo.

1433. HENNEQUIN, Joseph François Gabriel.
Essai historique sur la vie et les campagnes du Bailli de Suffren.
Paris; 1824. 37pp., 8vo.

1434. KANAPATHYPILLAI, V.
Dutch rule in maritime Ceylon, 1766–1796.
University of London Ph.D thesis; May 1970.

1435. MORIS, Henri. [*editor*].
Journal de bord du Bailli de Suffren dans d'Inde, 1781–1784.
Paris; Challamel; 1888. 349pp. 8vo.

1436. RENNEL, *Captain* James. (1742–1830).
Letters from Captain James Rennel, 1771–6.
Historical Manuscripts Commission: report on Palk Mss.
London; 1922.
Captain Rennel served in the Navy during the Seven Years' War and was a marine surveyor in the service of the East India Company, 1763–73.

1437. RICHMOND, *Admiral Sir* Herbert William, KCB. (1871–1946).
The Hughes–Suffren campaigns.
The Mariner's Mirror, vol.xiii (July 1927), pp.219–237.
A criticism of Admiral Ballard's article on the subject, in the April 1927 issue of the journal [q.v.].

1438. RICHMOND, *Admiral Sir* Herbert William, KCB. (1871–1946).
The Navy in India, 1762–1783.
London; Benn; 1931. 432pp., charts. pls. diagrs. 8vo.
With important chapters for the period 1775–83 on: the policy of the East Indies Squadron; the capture of Negapatam and Trincomalee; and the actions between Hughes and Suffren.

1439. ROSE, *Professor* John Holland. (1855–1942).
The influence of sea power on Indian history, 1745–1802.
Journal of Indian History, (Allahabad; 1924).

1440. TRUBLET, *Capitaine* —.
Histoire de la campagne de l'Inde, par l'escadre française sous les ordres de M.Le Bailli de Suffren, années 1781, 1782, 1783.
Rennes; 1802. 8vo.

1441. [Anonymous].
Relation détaillée de la campagne de M.le Commandeur de Suffren, dans l'Inde du Ier Juin 1782 au 29 Septembre Suivant.
Port Louis (Mauritius); 1783. 32pp. 12mo.

1442. [Anonymous].
The place of India in naval strategy, 1744–1783.
Naval Review, vol.xviii (1930), p.461.

1443. [Anonymous].
The maritime defences of India under the East India Company, 1763–83.
Naval Review, vol.xviii (1930), p.475.

1444. [Anonymous].
Détail des opérations dans l'Inde en 1782, 83, 84 et 85.
La Revue Maritime, vol.cxlv (January 1932), pp.32–66 & cxlvi (February 1932), pp.198–223.

VI. Events and operations elsewhere

1445. BOUQUET, Michael.
The Papal Navy and its English ships, 1755–1870.
Dublin Review, vol.cciii (July–September 1938),
pp.62–77.

1446. BREEN, K.
The foundering of the *Ramillies*.
The Mariner's Mirror, vol.lvi (May 1970), pp.187–
197.
   The RAMILLIES, *74, sank in the North Atlantic on 21
September 1782, after enduring a four-day gale.*

1447. BRUYNE, A.de.
Convoy protection in 1778.
Nautical Magazine, vol.cl (September 1943), pp.149–
151.

1448. CALENDAR OF HOME OFFICE PAPERS
– George III.
vol.iii: 1770–1772.
London; 1881.
– : Russo–Turkish war at sea. pp.xiii–xiv, 72–3, &c.
– : Rear-Admiral Elphinstone in Russian service . . .
pp.167, 190, &c.

1449. CASTEX, *Lieutenant* Edward.
La manoeuvre de la Praya (16 Avril 1781): étude
politique, stratégique et tactique . . .
Paris; Fournier; 1913. 416pp. 8vo.
   *A full account of Suffren's brilliant action of 16 April
1681, when he surprised Commodore Johnstone's
squadron (en route for the Cape) as it lay in Porto Praya
Roads, Cape Verde Islands and inflicted a sharp defeat.*

1450. HÄGG, *Rear-Admiral* J. R. SWED. NAVY.
Some peculiar Swedish coast-defence vessels of the
period 1762–1808.
The Mariner's Mirror, vol.iii (January–March 1913),
pp.46–49, 77–80; illustr.

1451. [JOHNSTONE, *Commodore* George, RN.
(1730–1787)].
Blake's remarks on Commodore Johnstone's account
of his engagement with a French squadron, under
the command of Mons. de Suffrein [*sic*], on April 16,
1781, in Port Praya Road, in the Island of St. Jago.
London; J.Debrett; 1782. 38pp. one chart [of
Praya Bay]. 8vo.

1452. [JOHNSTONE . . .].
Considerations on the question now in litigation
between Commodore Johnstone and Captain
Sutton . . .
[London; 1781]. Pamphlet. [12]pp. 8vo.

1453. KROTKOVA, A.
РУССКІЙ ФЛОТЪ ВЪ ЦАРСТВОВАНІЕ
ИМПЕРАТРИЦЫ ЕКАТЕРИНЫ II СЪ 1772
ГПО 1783 ГОДЪ.
St. Petersburg; 1889. Russian text.
341pp., 8vo.
   *A history of the Russian Navy in the reign of the
Empress Catherine II, 1772–1783.*

1454. MADARIAGA, Isabel de.
Britain, Russia, and the Armed Neutrality of 1780 . . .
London; Hollis & Carter; 1962. xiv, 496pp. 8vo.

1455. PERSEN, William.
The Russian occupation of Beirut, 1772–4.
Royal Central Asian Journal, (July 1955).

1456. RAMSHART, *Contreadmiral* P.
Den Danske Flaades Tjeneste . . . fra aar 1752 og til
den dag 1807 . . .
Copenhagen; E.V.H.Møller; 1808. 340 pp. 8vo.
   *This is a detailed analysis of the warships of the
Danish Fleet from 1752–1807, with their service
histories.*

1457. REA, Robert R.
John Blankett and the Russian Navy in 1774.
The Mariner's Mirror, vol.xli (August 1955), pp.245–9.

1458. SCHOPPEN, Werner.
Grossbritannien und die Ostsee, 1780 bis 1812.
Wissen und Wehr (1939), pp.713–720; 745–757.

1459. WILLCOX, W.B.
The Battle of Porto Praya, 1781.
The American Neptune, vol.v (1945), pp.64–78.

1460. [Anonymous].
An authentic narrative of the Russian Expedition
against the Turks by sea and land containing every
material circumstance of their proceedings from
their first sailing from Petersburg to the destruction
of the Turkish Fleet, in the Archipelago. Compiled
from several authentic journals by an officer on
board the Russian Fleet.
London; S.Hooper; 1772. 168 + [8]pp., 2 charts.
8vo.
   *Especially on the events leading to the Battle of
Tchesme, 7 July 1770, in which the Turkish fleet was
shattered.*

VII. General works, Administration and studies of the whole period

1461. ALBION, Robert Greenhalgh.
Forests and Sea Power. The timber problem of the Royal Navy, 1652–1862.
Cambridge, Mass.,; Harvard; 1926. xv, 485pp. 8vo.
Chapter 7 is entitled: 'Masts and American independence'.

1462. ALMON, John. [*editor*].
A Collection of papers relative to the dispute between Great Britain and America, 1764–1775.
New York; De Capo Press; 1971. [vi], 280 + 3(index)pp. 8vo.
Facsimile reprint of the 1777 London edition.

1463. ATKINSON, C.T.
The War of American Revolution, 1775–82.
In: Cambridge History of the British Empire, vol.i (1929).

1464. BARRITT, M.K.
The Navy and the Clyde in the American War, 1777–1783.
The Mariner's Mirror, vol.lv (February 1969), pp.33–42.

1465. BEATSON, Robert. (1742–1818).
Naval and military memoirs of Great Britain from 1727 to 1783.
London; Longmans; 1804. 6 vols. 8vo.
Includes detailed appendices in vols.iii & vi, with fleet-lists, ships in commission, station commands, &c.

1466. BOLTON, Reginald Pelham.
The British Navy in the Revolution.
New York Magazine of History, vol.ii (1905), pp.223–7; 311–4.

1467. BREWINGTON, Marion Vernon.
American naval guns, 1775–1785.
The American Neptune, vol.iii (1943), pp.11–18; 148–158.

1468. BROOMFIELD, J.H.
Lord Sandwich at the Admiralty Board. Politics and the British Navy, 1771–1778.
The Mariner's Mirror, vol.li (February 1965), pp.7–17.

1469. BROWN, G.S.
The Anglo–French naval crisis, 1778; a study of conflict in the North Cabinet.
William & Mary Quarterly (January 1956), 23pp.

1470. BUELL, Augustus C.
Paul Jones, founder of the American Navy: a history.
New York; Scribners; 1901. 2 vols. 328; 379pp., pls. 8vo.

1471. CALENDAR OF HOME OFFICE PAPERS: George III.
vol.ii: 1766–9. vol.iii. 1770–2. vol.iv: 1773–5.
London: 1879–1899.
With important naval material. Note that after vol.iv, which covered until the end of 1775, no further volumes in the series were published.

1472. CALKINS, Carlos Gilman.
The American Navy and the opinions of one of its founders John Adams, 1735–1826.
USNIP. vol.xxxvii (1911), pp.455–483.

1473. CASTEX, Raoul Victor Patrice.
Les idées militaires de la Marine du XVIIIᵐᵉ siècle.
De Ruyter à Suffren.
Paris; [1911]. 371pp., pls. 8vo.

1474. CHEVALIER, *Capitaine* Edmond.
Histoire de la Marine Française . . .
vol.ii. Histoire de la Marine Française pendant la Guerre de L'Indépendance Américaine.
Paris; Hachette; 1877. 517pp. 8vo.

1475. CLARKE, Thomas.
Naval history of the United States of America from the commencement of the Revolutionary War to the present time.
Philadelphia; M.Carey; 1814. 2 vols. 4to.
The first United States naval history to be written. As a contemporary of the events about which he wrote, the author relied heavily on personal communication with some of the major participants.

1476. CLOWES, *Sir* William Laird (1856–1905), *et alia*.
The Royal Navy. A History from the earliest times to the present . . .
London; Sampson Low; 1897–1903. 7 vols. 4to.
With long chapters: Military history of the Royal Navy, 1763–1792: major operations (in vol.iii); minor operations (in vol.iv) and appendix: naval losses of HM ships, 1775–83; of the US Navy, 1777–82; of the French Navy, 1778–83; of the Spanish Navy, 1779–82; and of the Dutch Navy, 1780–82 (in vol.iv).

1477. COONEY, *Lieutenant-Commander* David M., USN.
A chronology of the United States Navy, 1775–1965.
New York; Franklin Watts; 1965. vii; 471pp. 8vo.

1478. CRISPIN, Barbara.
Clyde shipping and the American War.
Scottish Historical Review, vol.xli (October 1962),
p.124.

1479. DAVIES, J.A.
An inquiry into faction among British naval officers
during the War of the American Revolution.
University of Liverpool MA thesis; May 1965.

1480. DOYLE, John A.
The War of Independence, 1775–1783.
In: *Cambridge Modern History*, vol.vii: The United
States, chap.vii. pp.209–234.

1481. EMMONS, George F.
The navy of the United States from the commencement 1775 to 1853, with a brief history of each
vessel's service and fate as appears on record . . .
Washington; Gideon; 1853. 208pp. 4to.

1482. FIELD, James A.
America and the Mediterranean World, 1776–1882.
Princeton, N.J.; University Press; 1969. 485pp. 8vo.

1483. GILBERT, William Roope.
A glimpse of the Fleet in 1781.
Naval Review, vol.xxv (1937), pp.513–5.

1484. GRAHAM, *Professor* Gerald Sandford.
British policy and Canada, 1774–1791. A study in
18th century trade policy . . .
London; Longmans; 1930. xi, 161pp. 8vo.
  *Originally a University of Cambridge Ph.D thesis,.
conferred in February 1930.*

1485. GRAHAM, *Professor* Gerald Sandford.
Considerations on the War of American
Independence.
IHR Bulletin, vol.xxii (May 1949), pp.22–34.
  *Based on a paper read at the Anglo–American
Conference, London, 10 July 1948.*

1486. GRAHAM, *Professor* Gerald Sandford.
Empire of the North Atlantic. The maritime
struggle for North America.
Toronto; University Press; 1956. xvii; 338pp. 8vo.

1487. HENDERSON, *Lieutenant* J.R., RN.
Rodney as a strategist and tactician.
Naval Review, vol.xv (1927), pp.467; 718.

1488. HIGGINBOTHAM, Don.
The War of American Independence. Military
attitudes, policies, and practice, 1763–1789.
New York; Macmillan; 1971. [xviii], 509pp.,
plates, maps. 8vo.

1489. HILL, Frederic Stanhope.
The romance of the American Navy. As embodied
in the stories of certain of our public and private
armed ships from 1775 . . .
New York; Putnams; 1910. xxxi; 394pp.,; pls. 8vo.

1490. HISTORICAL MANUSCRIPTS
COMMISSION.
: 10th Report, appendix part vi, (1887):
Abergavenny Mss.
  *Political correspondence of John Robinson (1770–99);
includes letters on the war with the American colonies;
strength of British & foreign naval forces; proposed
naval enquiry (1782); Rodney's dispositions (1782);
letters from Earl of Sandwich at the Admiralty.*
: American Mss. in the Royal Institution of Great
Britain, 21, Albemarle Street, London, W.1.
  *– 4 vols. (1904–9), covers the period 1774–1783.
Contains headquarters papers of British commanders-in-
chief in the War of Independence, with a large number of
references to HM and rebel ships, privateers, merchant
ships and naval operations.*
: Stopford–Sackville Mss, vol.ii (1910).
  With papers on the American War.
: Bathurst Mss. (1923).
  *Large number of references to naval ships and
privateers, 1778–97.*

1491. [HOOD, *Admiral* Samuel, *Viscount Hood*
(1724–1816)].
– *Letters of Sir Samuel Hood . . . 1781–3.* [London;
Navy Records Society; 1895].
edited by David Hannay.
– *extracts from his papers, 1778–98. In: The Naval
Miscellany*, vol.i [London; Navy Records Society;
1901].
edited by J.K.Laughton.

1492. JAMES, *Admiral Sir* William Milburne,
(1881–1973).
The British Navy in adversity. A study of the War
of American Independence.
London; Longmans; 1926. 459pp., maps & diagrs.
8vo.

1493. JOHNSON, Gerald W.
The First Captain. The story of John Paul Jones.
New York; Coward-McCann; 1947. viii; 312pp.
8vo.

1494. [JONES, John Paul (1747–1792)].
Memoirs of Rear-Admiral Paul Jones . . . now first
compiled from his original journals and corre-
spondence . . . prepared for publication by himself.
Edinburgh; Oliver & Boyd/London; Simkin &
Marshall; 1830. 2 vols. 331; 341pp. 16mo.

1495. [JONES, John Paul].
The life and correspondence of John Paul Jones ...
New York; A.Chandler; 1830. 555pp. 8vo.

1496. [JONES, John Paul].
The life and character of John Paul Jones, a captain in the United States Navy during the Revolutionary War.
By John Henry Sherburne.
Second edition.
New York; Adriance, Sherman; 1851. xvi; 408pp. 8vo.

1497. [JONES, John Paul].
Letters of John Paul Jones. Printed from ... the Bixby collection, with introductory remarks by Horace Porter and Franklin B.Sandborn.
Boston; Bibliophile Society; 1905. 123pp. 8vo.
.... *For further biographical works on John Paul Jones, see entries nos.727–744 inclusive, in the: Catalogue of the Library, vol. ii: Biography, part i.*

1498. JULLIEN, P.
L'Amiral d'Estaing et la Marine de son temps.
Neptunia, vol.lvi (April 1949), pp.10–15.

1499. KERGUELEN-TRÉMAREC, *Amiral* Yves Joseph de. (1734–1797).
Relation du combat et des évenements de la guerre maritime de 1778 entre la France et l'Angleterre.
[Paris]; 1796. 121pp. 4to.
A second edition was published in 1801.

1500. KEMP, *Lieutenant* W.H.
French naval strategy and tactics in the eighteenth century, as illustrated by the French war of 1778–83.
Naval Review, vol.xxii (1934), pp.720–746.

1501. KNIGHT, *Dr* Roger J.B.
Sandwich, Middleton and dockyard appointments.
The Mariner's Mirror, vol.lvii (May 1971), pp.175–193.

1502. KNIGHT, *Dr.* Roger J.B.
The royal dockyards in England at the time of the American War of Independence.
University of London Ph.D thesis; 1972.
A précis in IHR. Bulletin, vol.xlv (May 1973), pp.148–150. Won the Julian Corbett prize essay for 1970.

1503. LACOUR-GAYET, G.
La Marine Militaire de la France sous la règne de Louis XVI.
Paris; Honoré Champion; 1905. 719pp., pls., table. 8vo.

An important and detailed study of the French navy under Louis XVI (1774–1789). There are chapters on: Sartine, Secrétaire d'Etat de la Marine; the Battle of Ushant; Admiral d'Estaing's campaign in America and the West Indies; operations in the Channel, 1779; the siege of Gibraltar, 1779–83; Admiral de Grasse in America and the West Indies and Suffren's operations in the Indian Ocean. The appendices include important ship-lists and details of the squadrons of Guichen, 1775; du Chaffault, 1776; d'Orvilliers' in his expedition of 1778; d'Estaing, 1778 and the reinforcements sent to him the following year; de Fabry, 1778; de Guichen, 1780; de Grasse, 1781 and Suffren, 1781–3.

1504. LINCOLN, Charles Henry.
Calendar of naval records of the American Revolution, 1775–1788.
Washington; Library of Congress; 1906. 549pp. 8vo.

1505. MACKESY, *Professor* Piers.
The War for America, 1775–1783.
London; Longmans; 1964. xx, 565pp., pls. and maps. 8vo.

1506. MACLAY, Edgar Stanton.
A History of the United States Navy from 1755 to 1901 ...
New York; Appleton; 1901. 3 vols. 660; 559; 499pp., illustr. maps. 8vo.

1507. MAHAN, *Rear-Admiral* Alfred Thayer, USN. (1840–1914).
The Influence of sea power upon history, 1660–1783.
London; Sampson Low; 1890. xxiv, 557pp., maps & plans. 8vo.

1508. MAHAN, *Rear-Admiral* Alfred Thayer, USN. (1840–1914).
Major operations of the Royal Navy, 1762–83.
In: Laird Clowes: The Royal Navy. A History ... vol.iii (London; Sampson Low; 1898).

1509. MAHAN, *Rear-Admiral* Alfred Thayer, USN. (1840–1914).
The major operations of the Navies in the War of American Independence ...
London; Sampson Low; 1913. xxiii, 280pp., plans & maps. 8vo.

1510. [MATTHEWS, *Lieutenant* John, RN.]
The maritime campaign of 1778. A collection of all the papers relative to the operations of the English and French fleets. To which are added strictures upon the publications made in France, by order of the Ministry concerning the engagement on the

1510. [MATTHEWS, *Lieutenant* John, RN.], *continued*
27th of July; illustrated with charts and plans . . .
By J.M., a lieutenant in the fleet.
London; William Faden; 1779. [vi]; 24pp., engr.
plans & charts. folio.

1511. NEESER, Robert Wilden.
A statistical and chronological history of the United
States Navy, 1775–1907.
New York; Macmillan; 1909. 2 vols. 453; 487pp.
4to.

1512. PAULLIN, Charles Oscar. [*editor*].
The out-letters of the Continental Marine Com-
mittee and Board of Admiralty, August 1776 to
September 1780.
New York; Naval History Society; 1914. 2 vols.
8vo.

1513. PAULLIN, Charles Oscar.
Paullin's history of naval administration, 1775–1911.
A collection of articles from the United States Naval
Institute Proceedings.
Annapolis, Md.,; United States Naval Institute;
1968. 485pp. 8vo.

1514. PEARSON, Michael.
Those Damned Rebels. Britain's American Empire
in revolt.
London; Heinemann; 1972. 446pp., pls., maps. 8vo.

1515. PIGGOTT, *Sir* Francis Taylor *and* OMOND,
George William Thomson.
Documentary history of the Armed Neutralities,
1780 and 1800, together with selected documents
relating to the War of American Independence,
1776–1783 . . .
London; University Press; 1919. xxxviii; 541pp. 8vo.

1516. POOL, Bernard.
Navy contracts in the last years of the Navy Board,
1780–1832.
The Mariner's Mirror, vol.l (August 1964), pp.161–
176.

1517. RENAUT, François Paul.
Le secret service de l'Amirauté Britannique au
temps de la Guerre d'Amérique, 1776–1783.
Paris; Graouli; 1936. 117pp. 8vo.

1518. RESBECQ, H.de.
L'administration centrale de la Marine avant 1793.
Revue Maritime et Coloniale, vol.lxi (1877), pp.149–
154.

1519. RIDDICK, S.
Lord Barham and naval administration, 1778–1806.
University of Liverpool MA thesis; 1939.

1520. [RODNEY, *Admiral* George Brydges. (1719–
1792)].
Rodney's Fighting Instructions, 1780, and
Additional Instructions, 1782.
   See: Navy Records Society, vols.xxix (1905),
Fighting Instructions, 1530–1816. and xxxv (1908):
Signals and Instructions, 1776–94.

1521. [RODNEY, *Admiral* George Brydges. (1719–
1792)].
Letter-books and order book of George, Lord
Rodney, Admiral of the White Squadron, 1780–
1782.
New York; Naval History Society; 1932. 2 vols.
932pp., 8vo.
   *For further material on Rodney, see the West Indies
and North American sections in this group and also the
relevant entries in the Library Catalogue, vol.ii –
Biography.*

1522. ROWKARD, M.L.
Les répercussions de la Guerre Américaine
d'Independence sur le commerce et le pavillon belge.
Marine Academic Medelingen, book vii, (Antwerp,
1953), pp.51–90, illustr.

1523. SAINTE-CROIX, Alexandre Lambert de.
Essai sur l'histoire de l'administration de la marine
de France, 1689–1792.
Paris; Hachette; 1892. 457pp. 8vo.

1524. [SANDWICH, John Montagu, *Fourth Earl of.*
(1718–1792)].
The private papers of John Montagu, Earl of
Sandwich, First Lord of the Admiralty, 1771–1782.
Edited by G.R.Barnes and Commander J.H.Owen.
London; Navy Records Society; 1932–8. 4 vols.
nos.lxix, lxxi, lxxv & lxxviii. 8vo.
   *An insight into the part which Sandwich played in the
naval maladministration and war policy of the period.
The papers are presented chronologically: vol.i – August
1770 to March 1778; vol.ii – March 1778 to May 1779;
vol.iii – May 1779 to December 1780; vol.iv – 1781 to
1782.*

1525. SELEMENT, George.
Impressment and the American Merchant Marine,
1782–1812: an American view.
The Mariner's Mirror, vol.lix (November 1973),
pp.409–418.

1526. SNODGRASS, Gabriel.
Letters on the mode of improving the Navy and
evidence before the Committee of the House of
Commons, 1771, to consider how His Majesty's
Navy might be better supplied with timber.
Naval Chronicle, vol.v (1801) pp.129–156.
*A list of Royal Navy warships lost or foundered,
1775–84, is included.*

1527. SOARES, Joaquim Pedro Celestino.
Quadros Navaes, ou collecao dos folhetins maritimos
do patriota seguidos de huma epopeia naval
Portuguese . . .
Lisbon; Imprensa Nacional; 1861–9. 4 vols. 444;
557; 601; 421pp.; pls. 8vo.
*Includes many official naval gazettes and supplements
printed verbatim from the 1770's to 1810.*

1528. SPEARS, John R.
History of the United States Navy from its origin
to the present day, 1775–1897.
London; Bickers; 1898. 4 vols. 416; 425; 469;
607pp., illustr. & maps. 8vo.

1529. SPENCER, Frank.
Lord Sandwich, Russian masts and American
independence.
The Mariner's Mirror, vol.xliv (May 1958), pp.116–
127.

1530. SYRETT, David.
Lord George Germain and the Navy Board in
conflict: the *Adamant* and *Arwin* Galley dispute,
1777.
IHR Bulletin, vol.xxxviii (November 1965), pp.163–
171.

1531. SYRETT, David.
The Navy Board's administration of the maritime
logistics of the British forces during the American
War, 1775–83.
University of London Ph.D thesis; May 1967.

1532. SYRETT, David.
Living conditions on the Navy Board's transports
during the American War, 1775–1783.
The Mariner's Mirror, vol.lv (February 1969), pp.87–
94.

1533. SYRETT, David.
Shipping and the American War, 1775–1783. A
study of British transport organization.
London; Athlone Press; 1970. 274pp. 8vo.
Based on the author's earlier doctoral thesis [q.v.].

1534. SYRETT, David.
The methodology of British amphibious operations
during the Seven Years and American Wars.
The Mariner's Mirror, vol.lviii (August 1972),
pp.269–277.

1535. TRACY, J.N.
The Royal Navy as an instrument in British foreign
relations, 1763–1775.
University of Southampton Ph.D thesis; 1971.

1536. USHER, R.G.
The civil administration of the British Navy during
the American Revolution.
University of Michigan Ph.D thesis; 1943.

1537. WELBY, Alfred.
The Royal Navy, 1775.
Notes & Queries, vol.clxvi (6 January 1934), pp.3–6.

1538. WILSON, Herbert Wrigley, (1866–1940).
Minor operations of the Royal Navy, 1763–1802.
In: Laird Clowes: The Royal Navy. A History . . .
vol.iv (1899).

1539. WILSON, Herbert Wrigley, (1866–1940).
The armed neutrality, 1780–1801.
In: Cambridge Modern History, vol.ix (1906).

1540. YORKE, H.R. *and* STEVENSON, W.
British naval achievements; being an accurate
account of the lives and actions of British seamen
from 1780 to . . . 1816 . . .
London; C.J.Barrington; 1822. 2 vols. 552; 389pp.,
pls. 8vo.
*Another edition, published by Richardson, followed in
1823.*

1541. [Anonymous].
Substance of the charge of mismanagement in His
Majesty's naval affairs in the year 1781, compared
with authentic papers laid before the House on Mr.
Fox's motion in the month of February 1782 . . .
London; J.Stockdale; 1782. 113pp., 8vo.
*A Parliamentary attack on Sandwich's administration
of the Admiralty during the critical year 1781. Fox's
motion of censure accused the Admiralty of neglecting to
watch the port of Brest, prevent the junction of the
enemy fleets and their appearance in the English Channel.
Also, the capture of the St. Eustatius convoy was
condemned.
After a long and bitter debate, the motion was
narrowly defeated when the House divided 217 ayes
against 236 noes.*

1542. [Anonymous].
A short account of the Naval Actions of the last war,
in order to prove that the French nation never gave
such slender proofs of maritime greatness as during
that period . . .
By an Officer.
London; John Murray; 1788. 148pp., 8vo.

THE DECADE 1783–1792

I. The Baltic and the Russo-Swedish War, (1788–90)

1543. ANDERSON, Dr. Roger Charles.
Naval wars in the Baltic during the sailing ship epoch, 1522–1850.
London; C.Gilbert-Wood; 1910. 423pp., maps & plans. 8vo.
Contains a detailed account of the Russo–Swedish War, with sketch plans of the following engagements: Hogland (17 July 1788); Öland (26 July 1789); Svenskund I & II (24 August 1789 & 9 July 1790); Revel (13 May 1790); Styrsudden (3–4 June 1790); and Viborg Bay (6 June–2 July 1790).

1544. GOLOVACHEVA, B.
ДѢЙСТВІЯ РУССКАГО ФЛОТА ВЪ ВОЙНѢ СО ШВЕДАМИ ВЪ 1788—90 ГОДАХЪ.
[The operations of the Russian fleet in the War against Sweden, 1788–90].
St. Petersburg; 1871–3. Russian text. 2 vols., 268, 178pp., charts. 8vo.

1545. GYLLENGRANAT, C.A.
Sveriges Sjökrigs-Historia.
Carlskrona; Georg Ameen; 1840. 2 vols, 353, 343pp., plates. 8vo.
Volume ii covers the period 1718–90 and includes fleet-lists in the appendices and action plans of the naval battles of the Russo–Swedish War and of the Viborg/Björkösund operations, June–July 1790.

1546. HÄGG, *Rear-Admiral* J., R.SWED.N.
Some peculiar Swedish coast-defence vessels of the period, 1762–1808.
The Mariner's Mirror, vol.iii (February–March 1913), pp.46–49; 77–80; illustr.

1547. HOLM, Edward.
Danmarks politik under den Svensk-Russiske Krig fra 1788–1790.
Copenhagen; F.S.Muhle; 1868. 92pp., 4to.

1548. JANE, Fred T. (*d.*1916).
The Imperial Russian Navy. Its past, present and future.
London; W.Thacker; 1899. 755pp., numerous illustr., 2 charts. 4to.
There is a chapter on the Russian navy under Catherine II and, in the appendices, details of the battles of Kalkboden, Öland, Viborg ('Sweden's Aegospotami') and Revel.

1549. KROTKOVA, A.
РУССКІИ ФЛОТЪ ВЪ ЦАРСТВОВАНІЕ ИМПЕРАТРИЦЫ ЕКАТЕРИНЫ II...
[The Russian Navy in the reign of the Empress Catherine II . . .].
St. Petersburg; 1889. 341pp. Russian text. 8vo.

1550. JANSSON, E.Alfred.
Trå brev från Svensk sjøøficier som Klarade silt fartyg genom Viborgska gatloppet den 3 Juli 1790.
Forum Naval (Uppsala), no.16, (1960). pp.43–57, illustr.

1551. МАТЕРІАЛЫ ДЛЯ ИСТОРІИ РУССКАГО ФЛОТА.
[Materials for the History of the Russian Navy].
St. Petersburg; 1865–1904. 17 vols, *ca.* 12,000pp. Russian text. 4to.
Volumes xiii and xiv describe events and operations in the Baltic between 1783–96, including the Russo–Swedish War. Volume xv covers the Black Sea over the same period.

1552. MUNTHE, *Kommendörkapten* Arnold.
Flottan och Ryska Kriget, 1788–1790 . . .
Stockholm; P.A.Norstedt; 1914–1923. 6 vols. 8vo.
An exhaustive analysis of the operations by the Swedish fleet during the War with Russia, 1788–90. The individual volumes are:
i. Om fattande tiden från . . . Mars 1784 till och med slaget vid Hogland den 17 Juli 1788. 245pp.
ii. Slutet af första och början af andra krigsåret. 171pp.
iii. Örlogsflottornas operationer under andra Krigsåret intill Augusti 1789. 296pp.
iv. Senare delen af andra Krigsåret. Slaget vid Svensksund den 24 Augusti. 184pp.
v. Krigshändelserna till sjöss intill Svenska flottans indragende i Viborgska Viken i Början af Juin 1790. 290pp.
vi. Senare delen av tradje Krigsåret: Svenska flottornas blockering i och utbrytning ur Viborgska Viken. 376pp.

1553. MUNTHE, *Kommendörkapten* Arnold.
Henrik af Trolle, Frederik af Chapman, Gustaf III, politiken och flottan, 1772–1784.
Stockholm; P.A.Norstedt; 1911. 278pp. 8vo.

1554. RAMSHART, *Contreadmiral* P.
Den Danskes flaades tjeneste . . . fra aar 1752 ogtil . . . 1807.
Copenhagen; E.V.H.Moller; 1808. 340pp. 8vo.
A detailed analysis of the warships of the Danish fleet, presented alphabetically.

1555. SCHAFFALITZKY DE MUCKADELL, *Baron*.
Haandbog i Nordens Søkrigshistorie.
Copenhagen; 1911. 548pp., charts & plans. 8vo.
  A general history, which includes an account of the Russo–Swedish War, 1788–90 and a chart of the Russian fleet's bombardment of Revel, 13 May 1790.

1556. SCHOPPEN, Werner.
Grossbritannien und die Ostsee 1780 bis 1812.
Wissen und Wehr (1939). pp.713–720; 745–757.

1557. СКАЛОВСКАГО, Р.
ЖИЗНЬ АДМИРАЛА ѲЕДОРА ѲЕДОРО-
ВИЧА УШАКОВА.
St. Petersburg; 1856. Russian text. 444pp., charts & plans. 8vo.
  A biography of Admiral Ushakov.

1558. UNGER, *Kontre-amiral* Gunnar.
Några märkliga dokument från 1788–1790 års ryska krig.
Tidskrift i sjöväsundet (1906), pp.356–66; 425–9 *and* (1908), 83–98.
  Papers relating to the Russo–Swedish War, 1788–90.

1559. UNGER, *Kontre-amiral* Gunnar.
Gustav III vid Viborg och Svensksund.
Stockholm; P.A.Norstedt; 1932. 84pp., 5 charts. 8vo.
  A detailed account of the operations of the Swedish fleet in both battles, July 1790.

1560. UNGER, *Kontre-amiral* Gunnar.
Vem Var I Själva Venket Segerherren vid Svenskund 1790?
Skriften Utgivna av Sjöhistoriska Samfundet (Uppsala) No.6, (1945). pp.120–126.

1561. [Anonymous].
En månad på Amphion; minnen från sjötåget, 1790. Upptecknade af en deltagare.
Stockhom; Looström & Kompis; 1890. 108pp. 8vo.
  Recollections of an officer aboard the Swedish flagship AMPHION, *who took part in the operations against the Russian fleet in 1790.*

II. The Black Sea and the Mediterranean

1562. ANDERSON, M.S.
Russia in the Mediterranean, 1788–1791.
The Mariner's Mirror, vol.xlv (February 1959), pp.25–35.

1563. KING, Cecil.
The Russian armament.
The Mariner's Mirror, vol.xxiv (April 1938), pp.176–183.
  About the fleet assembled at Spithead in 1791, when the British Government became apprehensive about Russian aggression in the Black Sea, following the seizure of Oczakoff from the Turks.

III. Events elsewhere, especially the 'Bounty' mutiny

1564. ANTHONY, Irvin Whittington. [*editor*].
The saga of the 'Bounty'. Its strange history as
related by the participants themselves.
New York; Putnams; 1935. 358pp., plates. 8vo.
   A compilation from the narratives of Bligh, Fletcher
Christian and others.

1565. AYERBE, *Marqués de.*
Tres pechos memorables de la Marina Española en
el siglo xviii.
Madrid; 1907. 239pp. 8vo.
   Two of these essays comprise: 'The naval struggle
between Spain and Portugal in 1776'; 'An account of the
Anglo–Spanish crisis in the Nootka Sound incident,
1789.'

1566. BARROW, *Sir* John. (1764–1848).
The eventful history of the mutiny of *HMS Bounty*;
its cause and consequence.
London; John Murray; 1831. xi, 356pp., plates.
small 8vo.
   A copy of the 1847 edition (London; Murray & Tegg),
is also in the Library.

1567. [BARROW, *Sir* John. (1764–1848)].
The mutiny and piratical seizure of *HMS Bounty* . . .
With an introduction by Admiral Sir Cyprian
Bridge.
London; Humphrey Milford; 1914. [World's
Classics series]. xxiii, 376 pp. 16mo.
   A reissue of the second edition, (1835).

1568. BELCHER, *Lady* Diana.
The mutineers of the *Bounty* and their descendants
in Pitcairn and Norfolk Islands.
New York; Harper; [*ca.*1870]. 377pp., pls. 8vo.

1569. BLIGH, *Vice-Admiral* William. (1754–1817).
A narrative of the mutiny on board His Majesty's
Ship *Bounty* . . .
London; G.Nichol; 1790. iv, 88pp., diagr. & charts.
4to.

1570. BLIGH, *Vice-Admiral* William. (1754–1817).
Bligh and the *Bounty*. His narrative of the voyage
to Otaheite, with an account of the mutiny and of
his boat journey to Timor.
With illustrations and a preface by Laurence Irving.
London; Methuen; 1936. xxx, 284pp., plates. 8vo.
   See also volume 2 of the Library Catalogue for
biographies of Bligh.

1571. BURKE, Peter.
Celebrated naval and military trials.
London; W.H.Allen; 1866. vi, 399pp. 8vo.
   Includes the mutiny of the BOUNTY.

1572. CHRISTIAN, Fletcher.
Letters from Mr. Fletcher Christian, containing a
narrative of the transactions on board His Majesty's
Ship *Bounty*, before and after the mutiny, with his
subsequent voyages and travels in South America.
London; H.D.Symonds; 1796. [viii]; 188pp. 8vo.

1573. CRIMMIN, Patricia K.
Admiralty Administration, 1783–1806.
University of London M.Phil thesis (1967).

1574. DANIELSSON, Bengt.
What happened on the *Bounty*.
London; Allen & Unwin; 1962. 230pp., maps. 8vo.

1575. DARBY, Madge.
Who caused the mutiny on the *Bounty*?
Sydney; Angus & Robertson; 1965. [vi], 127pp. 8vo.

1576. KNIGHT, *Dr.* Roger J.B.
The administration of the Royal dockyards in
England, 1770–1790.
Julian Corbett Prize essay, 1970.
Summary in: *IHR Bulletin*, xlv, no.3 (May 1972).
148–150pp.

1577. MACKANESS, George. [*editor*].
A book of the *Bounty*.
London; Dent; 1938. [Everyman's Library]. xviii,
326pp. 8vo.
   Includes abridgements of Bligh's: 'A Narrative of the
Mutiny . . .' and 'A voyage to the South Sea . . .'
and the minutes of the court-martial of the mutineers,
compiled by Stephen Barney.

1578. McFARLAND, Alfred.
Mutiny on the *Bounty* and the story of the Pitcairn
Islanders.
Sydney; J.J.Moore; 1884. xx, 240pp. 8vo.

1579. [MORRISON, James].
The journal of James Morrison, boatswain's mate of
the *Bounty*, describing the mutiny and subsequent
misfortunes of the mutineers . . .
With an introduction by Owen Rutter.
London; Golden Cockerel Press; 1935. 243pp.,
illustr. 8vo.

1580. [RIOU, *Captain* Edward, RN. (1758–1801)].
The log of the *Guardian*, 1789–90; edited from the
journal of Captain Riou by Ludovic Kennedy.
In: The Naval Miscellany, vol.iv. (1952). [Navy
Records Society series, vol.xcii].

1581. ROSE, *Professor* J.Holland.
Sea power and the winning of British Columbia.
The Mariner's Mirror, vol.vii (March 1921), pp.74–79.
   *Includes material on the Anglo–Spanish dispute over
Nootka Sound in 1790.*

1582. RUTTER, Owen. [*editor*].
The court-martial of the *Bounty* mutineers.
Edinburgh & London; William Hodge; 1931. xii;
202pp.; plates. 8vo.

1583. SMITH, David Bonner. (1890–1950).
Some remarks about the mutiny of the *Bounty*.
The Mariner's Mirror, vol.xxii (April 1936), pp.200–
237.

1584. SMITH, David Bonner.
More light on Bligh and the *Bounty*.
The Mariner's Mirror, vol.xxiii (April 1937), pp.210–
228.

1585. WEBB, P.L.C.
The use of the navy as an instrument of British
diplomacy, 1783–93.
University of Cambridge Ph.D thesis; 1972.

1586. WILSON, Herbert Wrigley. (1866–1940).
The Armed Neutrality, 1780–1801.
In: the *Cambridge Modern History*, vol.ix, (1906).

1587. YOUNG, Rosalind Amelia.
The mutiny of the *Bounty* and the story of Pitcairn
Island, 1790–1894.
Wellington, New Zealand; David Nield; 1924.
303pp.; illustr. 8vo.

1588. [Anonymous].
The story of the mutiny of the good ship *Bounty*
and her mutineers . . .
Edinburgh; W.P.Nimmo; 1880. [iv]; 160pp. 16mo.

THE FRENCH REVOLUTIONARY WAR, 1793–1802
and contemporary events elsewhere

I. The Mediterranean

1589. ANDERSON, Aeneas.
A Journal of the forces, which sailed from the Downs in April 1800 . . . under the command of Lieutenant General Pigot, till their arrival in Minorca, and continued . . . to the surrender of Alexandria, with a particular account of Malta, during the time it was subject to the British Government . . .
London; J.Debrett; 1802. xxxvii, 532pp. 4to.

1590. AUZOUX, A.
Linois à Algéciras, Juillet 1801.
Revue Historique, vols.lxxxi (1907), pp.535–565 *and* lxxxii (1908), pp.57–78.
A French assessment of the hard-fought action of July 6, in which Rear-Admiral Sir James Saumarez' squadron attacked three French ships-of-the-line and a frigate anchored in Algéciras Bay. Admiral Linois ran his ships ashore but during the action the HANNIBAL, *74, went aground near the Spanish batteries and was forced to surrender. After repairing his ships with great energy at Gibraltar, Saumarez got his revenge in a second engagement six days later. On this occasion he defeated a Franco–Spanish squadron under Linois and Moreno (of twice his strength and three times his gunpower) in the Straits.*

1591. BARRITT, M.K.
Nelson's frigates, May to August 1798.
The Mariner's Mirror, vol.lviii (July 1972), pp.281–295.

1592. BARNBY, H.G.
The Prisoners of Algiers. An account of the forgotten American–Algerian War, 1785–1797.
Oxford; University Press; 1966. 343pp., pls. 8vo.

1593. BENNETT, *Captain* Geoffrey, RN.
Admiral Ushakov: Nelson's Russian ally.
History Today, vol.xxi (1971), pp.724–731.
Describes cooperation between the British and Russian fleets in the Mediterranean, 1798–1800.

1594. [BERRY, *Admiral Sir* Edward. (1768–1831)].
An authentic narrative of the proceedings of His Majesty's Squadron, under the command of Rear-Admiral Sir Horatio Nelson, from its sailing from Gibraltar to the conclusion of the glorious Battle of the Nile; drawn up from the minutes of An Officer of Rank in the Squadron.

London; T.Cadell; 1798. 56pp., 8vo.
Three editions of this work were published by Cadell in 1798.

1595. BRUN, Victor.
Guerres maritimes de la France: port de Toulon, ses armements, son administration depuis son origine jusqu'à nos jours.
Paris; Plon; 1861. 2 vols. 560; 684pp. 8vo.
Includes material on Hood at Toulon in 1793 and the development of the port as principal naval base and arsenal of the French Mediterranean fleets in the seventeenth and eighteenth centuries.

1596. BUNYON, C.S.
The invasion of Malta by the French under Napoleon Buonaparte in 1798. Abridged from the Italian of the Canon Panzacchia of Malta . . .
United Service Journal, vol.cclxvii (February 1851), pp.255–267.

1597. BURGOYNE, *Lieutenant-Colonel Sir* John H.
A short history of the naval and military operations in Egypt, 1798–1802.
London; Sampson Low; 1885. vii, 181pp. 8vo.

1598. CARRILLO, E.A.
The British occupation of Corsica, 1794–6; a study in Mediterranean politics.
Fordham Ph.D thesis; 1953.

1599. CHARRIER, *Capitaine*. —.
Charrier's contemporary account of the Battle of the Nile.
New Review, vol.ix (1893).

1600. CHURCHILL, *Lieutenant* P.N., RN.
Naval operations in the Mediterranean from 1793 to the English evacuation of the Mediterranean (1796), with special reference to their influence on the campaigns on land.
Naval Review, vol.xvi (1928), p.239.

1601. COTTIN, Paul.
Toulon et les Anglais en 1793 . . .
Paris; 1898. 455pp., plans. 8vo.

1602. DALY, Robert D.
Napoleon's first defeat.
USNIP, vol.lxv (1939), pp.1727–1736.
Narrative of the Siege of Acre, 1799.

1603. DOUIN, *Lieutenant* Georges.
La flotte de Bonaparte sur les côtes d'Egypte. Les prodromes d'Aboukir.
Paris; Champion; 1922. 8vo.

1604. DOUIN, *Lieutenant* Georges.
La campagne de Bruix dans la Méditerranée, (Mars–
Août, 1799).
Paris; Challamel; 1923. 230pp. 8vo.

1605. FIELD, James A.
America and the Mediterranean World, 1776–1882.
New Jersey; Princeton University Press; 1969. xv,
485pp. 8vo.
   Includes chapters on the Barbary Wars during the
period.

1606. [FOOTE, *Captain* —.].
Captain Foote's vindication of his conduct, when
Captain of His Majesty's ship *Sea-Horse*; and senior
officer in the Bay of Naples, in the summer of 1799.
London; T.Cadell & W.Davies, 1807. 171pp. 8vo.
   When Nelson brought the British fleet into the Bay of
Naples on 24 June 1799, he observed a flag of truce
flying on board the SEA-HORSE, *Captain Foote, and also*
on the castles of Uovo and Nuovo. He learned that
Captain Foote had signed an armistice with the local
insurgents. Nelson at once annulled the armistice, on the
grounds that it should not have been entered into without
the approval of the King of Sicily.
   A second edition of Foote's defence, published by
Hatchard in 1810, is also in the Library.

1607. GIAMPAOLI, Lorenzo.
Un episodio della guerra navale anglo–francese nel
Mediterraneo durante la prima coalizione. La fine
dell'*Illustrious*.
[La Spezia; 1795]. 17pp., 12mo.
   After Hotham's indecisive action with the French
fleet off Genoa, 13–14 March, 1799, he sailed for La
Spezia taking in tow his dismasted ships and the prizes.
During a gale on the night of 17 March, the damaged
ILLUSTRIOUS, 74, *lost her tow and the following evening*
ran ashore in Valence Bay and was wrecked.
   See also: Laird Clowes . . . vol.iv, p.273.

1608. GODFREY, *Admiral* J.H. [editor].
Corsica, 1794. Edited from the Nelson–Hood letters
by Admiral J.H.Godfrey.
In: The Naval Miscellany, vol.iv (London; Navy
Records Society series, vol.xcii; 1952).

1609. GRIEVE, *Lieutenant* J.S.Mackenzie.
Naval operations in the Mediterranean, 1793–1801.
RUSIJ, (August 1917), p.506.

1610. GUTTERIDGE, H.L. [editor].
Nelson and the Neapolitan Jacobins: documents
relating to the suppression of the Jacobin revolution
at Naples, June 1799.

London; Navy Records Society series, vol.xxv;
1903. 351pp., maps. 8vo.
   See also entry no.1635.

1611. HANNAY, David.
Napoleon and Nelson.
Cornhill Magazine (n.s.), vol.xix, (1905).

1612. HARDMAN, William.
A History of Malta during the period of the French
and British occupations, 1798–1815.
Edited with introduction and notes by J.Holland
Rose.
London; Longmans Green; 1909. 657pp.; pls. 4to.

1613. HERBERT, J.B.
Sir T.Foley's action at the Nile.
United Service Magazine (n.s.), vol.xv, 1897.
   Captain Thomas Foley commanded the GOLIATH, 74,
during the battle.

1614. HEROLD, J.Christopher.
Bonaparte in Egypt.
London; Hamish Hamilton; 1963. 424pp., pls. 8vo.
   Includes chapters on the Battle of the Nile; Admiral
Sir Sidney Smith & the siege of Acre.

1615. [HILL, *Lieutenant* John].
Log of *HMS Minotaur* at the Nile, kept by
Lieutenant John Hill . . . edited by Admiral Sir E.R.
Fremantle.
United Service Magazine (n.s.), vol.xxviii, 1903–4.

1616. HISTORICAL MANUSCRIPTS
COMMISSION.
13th Report, appendix part iii: Fortescue Mss.
London; 1905–8.
   vol.iv (1905) contains documents on Nelson's
Aboukir Bay campaign, 1798; vol.vi (1908): Nelson at
Malta and Naples, 1799–1800.

1617. [HOOD, *Admiral* Samuel, *Viscount Hood*.
(1724–1816)].
Toulon Papers . . . Lord Hood's transactions at
Toulon, 1793.
Naval Chronicle, vol.ii (1800), pp.102–119; 192–201;
183–304; foldg. diagr.

1618. HOWLAND, Felix.
Eaton's declaration of the blockade of Tripoli, 1801.
USNIP, vol.lviii (1932), pp.1186–90.

1619. INGLIS, *Commander* Charles, RN.
Operations on the coast of Egypt, 1801.
In: The Naval Miscellany, vol.ii. (London; The Navy
Records Society series, vol.xl, 1912). pp.333–350.

1620. JACKSON, *Admiral Sir* Thomas Sturges.
(1842–1934). [*editor*].
The Nile – 1798.
In: Logs of the Great Sea Fights, 1794–1805, vol.ii.
(London; The Navy Records series, vol.xviii; 1900),
pp.1–79.
   *An important primary source. Reproduces extracts
from the logs of the following British ships engaged in the
battle* – GOLIATH, ZEALOUS, AUDACIOUS, ORION,
THESEUS, VANGUARD, DEFENCE, BELLEROPHON,
MAJESTIC, ALEXANDER, SWIFTSURE, CULLODEN; *also a
battle-plan, fleet lists and signals exchanged.*

1621. KNOX, Dudley Wright. [*editor*].
Naval documents relating to the Quasi-War
between the United States and France. Naval
operations from February 1797 . . . December 1801.
Washington; US Govt. Printing Office; 1935–8.
7 vols. *ca*, 4,200pp. 8vo.

1622. KNOX, Dudley Wright.
Documents on the naval war with France.
USNIP, vol.lxi (1935), pp.535–8.

1623. LABROUSSE, *Capitaine* H.
La Mer Rouge et l'expedition de Bonaparte en
Egypte.
La Revue Maritime, vol.ccxliv (June 1967), pp.747–
755.

1624. LACOUR-GAYET, Georges.
Napoléon et l'empire de la mer. La traversée de
Mediterranée en 1798.
Revue Études Napoléoniennes, vol.xx (1923), pp.1–27.

1625. LA JONQUIÈRE, Clement Taffanel de.
L'expédition d'Égypte, 1798–1801.
Paris; Lavauzelle; [1889–1907]. 3 vols. pls., charts,
plans. 4to.
   *Naval material includes accounts of the expedition's
fleet; the voyage across the Mediterranean; the capture of
Malta and the battle of the Nile.*

1626. LANGARA, *Admiral Don* Juan de. (*d*.1800).
Manifiesto del Vice Almirante de la Esquadra
Española anclada en la rada de Tolon, a todo el
pueblo Frances en 27 de Septiembre, año primero
del reyno de Luis XVII.
Barcelona; Carlos Gilbert y Tuto; 1793. 113pp. 8vo.

1627. LATHAM, *Lieutenant* G.D., RN.
The Nile campaign.
Naval Review, vol.ix (1921), p.511.

1628. LAUGHTON, *Sir* John Knox. (1830–1915).
The Battle of the Nile.
Cornhill Magazine, (August 1896).

1629. LEHUERT, J.R.von. [*editor*].
Geschichte der K. und K.Kriegs Marine.
vol.ii, part 2: Die Österreichisch-Venetianische
Kriegs Marine vährzend der jahre 1797 bis 1802.
Vienna; Ministry of War (Marine Section); 1891.
464pp., 1 chart; 3 plans. 8vo.
   *This part of the 5-volume history of the Austrian Navy
(published between 1882–1906), deals with the activities
of the Austro-Venetian fleet between 1797 and 1802.*

1630. LEPOTIER, *Contre-Amiral* R.
Le grand dessein naval de Napoléon.
Neptunia, vol.xcii (April 1963), pp.2–9.

1631. LLOYD, *Professor* Christopher C.
The Nile Campaign. Nelson and Napoleon in
Egypt.
Newton Abbot; David & Charles; 1973. 120pp.,
illustr. 8vo.

1632. LOIR, Maurice Eugène.
La livraison de Toulon aux Anglais (1793). La
bataille d'Aboukir.
In: Études d'Histoire maritime. Paris; 1901. 8vo.

1633. LONGSDON, *Lieutenant* E.H., RN.
Naval operations in the Mediterranean, 1793–1801.
Naval Review, vol.x (1922), p.352.

1634. MAHAN, *Rear-Admiral* Alfred Thayer, USN.
(1840–1914).
Nelson in the Battle of the Nile.
Century Magazine (n.s.), vol.xxxi (1876–7).

1635. MAHAN, *Rear-Admiral* Alfred Thayer, USN.
(1840–1914).
Nelson at Naples.
English Historical Review, vol.xv (1900), pp.699–727.

1636. MALLESON, *Lieutenant-Commander* W.
Britain and France in the Eastern Mediterranean,
1798–1802.
Julian Corbett Naval Prize essay; 1954.

1637. MARCHESE, C.
L'ammiraglio Nelson alla Maddalena e la Marina
Sarda di quei tempi.
Revista Marittima, vol.xxxv (1902), pp.5–39; map.

1638. MIOT, Jacques François.
Mémoires pour servir à l'histoire des expéditions en
Égypte et en Syrie . . .
Paris; 1814. 8vo.
   This is a copy of the second edition.

1639. MIROT, Léon.
Deux représentations de la bataille d'Aboukir.
Rev. Hist. Coll. Franc., vol.iv (1916), pp.301–318;
illustr.

1640. MORDACQ, R.
L'expédition des Îles de la Maddalena.
Neptunia, vol.xliv (April 1956), pp.36–40.
   *Islands off the NE coast of Sardinia, occupied by the
French in February 1793.*

1641. MORRIS, William O'Connor.
The great campaigns of Nelson . . .
London; Blackie; 1892. 156pp., illustr. 8vo.
   Includes chapters on the Battle of the Nile.

1642. NASH, Howard P.
The Forgotten Wars. The role of the United States
Navy in the Quasi War with France and the
Barbary States, 1798–1805.
New York; A.S.Barnes; 1968.
308pp., pls., maps. 8vo.

1643. PAUL, Louis.
An artist's notes at the Battle of the Nile.
The Mariner's Mirror, vol.iv (August 1914), pp.266–
274, 2 pls.

1644. RODGER, A.B.
The War of the Second Coalition, 1798–1801: a
strategic commentary.
Oxford; Clarendon Press; 1964. 312pp., maps. 8vo.
   *An important study. Includes chapters on the
Egyptian expeditions of 1798 and 1801; the Battle of the
Nile; Bruix's cruise, 1799 and Ganteaume's cruise, 1801.*

1645. ROSE, *Professor* John Holland. (1855–1942).
The Egyptian expedition, 1798–1801.
In: Cambridge Modern History, vol.viii (1904), chap.
xix, pp.594–619.

1646. ROSE, *Professor* John Holland.
Lord Hood and the defence of Toulon.
Cambridge; University Press; 1922. 175pp., pls.,
charts. 8vo.
   *There are six valuable appendices – [a]. Admiralty
instructions to Hood: [b]. Hood's journal, May 25–
December 19, 1793; [c]. Extracts from the logs of the*
VICTORY, BRITANNIA, PRINCESS ROYAL, ST. GEORGE,
and WINDSOR CASTLE *during the period; [d]. Instructions
to the royal commissioners at Toulon, October 18,
[e]. Hood's correspondence, May–December; and
[f]. Confidential correspondence between Pitt, Dundas and
Lord Mulgrave, September 15–October 24.*

1647. SAP, *Amiral* F.
La leçon d'Aboukir.
Neptunia, vol.xcv (March 1969), pp.8–12.

1648. SAUZET, Armand.
La prise de Malte par Bonaparte.
Neptunia, vol.xxxvii (January 1955), pp.21–25.

1649. SAVAGEAU, David LePere.
The United States Navy and its 'Half-War'
prisoners, 1798–1801.
American Neptune, vol.xxxi (July 1971), pp.159–176,
map.

1650. SCICLUNA, Hannibal P., *Chevalier.*
Documents relating to the French occupation of
Malta in 1798–1800.
Valletta; 1923. 303pp., pls. 8vo.

1651. SPINNEY, J.David.
The *Albanaise* affair.
The Mariner's Mirror, vol.xliii (August 1957),
pp.194–202.
   The ALBANAISE *was a bomb-ketch captured from the
French and taken into the Navy in June 1800. While
under the command of Captain Francis Newcombe, the*
ALBANAISE*'s crew mutinied off the Spanish Mediter-
ranean coast during the night of 23/24 November, 1800.*

1652. TERRINONI, F.Giuseppe.
Memoire storiche della resa di Malta ai Francesi nel
1798 . . .
Rome; Tipografia delle Belle Arti; 1867.
[210]pp. 8vo.

1653. TRAMOND, Joannes.
L'enigme d'Aboukir.
La Revue Maritime, vol.xxxix (March 1923), pp.343–
350.

1654. VIGO, Pietro.
La battaglia d'Aboukir narrata in una lettera
contemporanea.
Archiva Storiche Italiana, ser.5, vol.xxix (1902),
pp.63–66.

1655. WARNER, Oliver.
The Battle of the Nile.
London; Batsford; 1960. ['British battles' series].
184pp., pls. 8vo.

1656. WARNER, Oliver.
Nelson's battles.
London; Batsford; 1965. ['British battles' series].
254pp., pls. 8vo.
  Includes an account of the Battle of the Nile.

1657. WILLYAMS, *Reverend* Cooper A.M.
A voyage up the Mediterranean in HM ship the
Swiftsure, one of the squadron under the command
of Sir Horatio Nelson, K.B. With a description of
the Battle of the Nile, 1st August, 1798.
London; T.Bentley; 1802. xxiii, 309pp., cold. pls.,
maps. 4to.
  *The author also wrote an important contemporary
narrative of the Grey–Jervis expedition to the West
Indies, 1793–4. [q.v.].*

1658. WILSON, Herbert Wrigley. (1866–1940).
The Nile campaign.
The Navy League Journal, (August 1899).

1659. WILSON, Herbert Wrigley. (1866–1940).
The struggle for the Mediterranean.
In: Cambridge Modern History, vol.viii (1904): The
French Revolution, chap.xx, pp.620–632.

1660. [Anonymous].
The British Navy triumphant! Being copies of the
London Gazettes Extraordinary; containing the
accounts of the glorious victories obtained . . .
. . . and again over the French Fleet by Rear-Admiral
Sir Horatio Nelson near the mouth of the Nile;
August 1 and 2, 1798.
Oxford; 1798. 28pp., 8vo.

1661. [Anonymous].
A Form of Prayer and thanksgiving to Almighty
God; to be used in all churches and chapels through-
out England, Wales and the town of Berwick upon
Tweed on Thursday the twenty-ninth day of
November 1798 . . . for the late glorious victory
obtained by His Majesty's ships of war under the
command of Rear-Admiral Lord Nelson of the Nile
over the French fleet . . .
London; 1798. [1] sheet. Pamphlet. 8vo.

1662. [Anonymous].
An authentic narrative of the proceedings of His
Majesty's Squadron, under the command of Rear-
Admiral Sir Horatio Nelson, from its sailing from
Gibraltar to the conclusion of the glorious Battle of
the Nile. Drawn up from the minutes of an Officer
of Rank in the Squadron.
Dublin; J.Milliken; 1799. 44pp., 1 chart. 8vo.
  *The same narrative was reproduced in: 'The Naval
Chronicle', vol.i.(January–June 1799), pp.43–66.*

1663. [Anonymous].
An account of the engagement off the Nile by a
French Officer.
The Naval Chronicle, vol.i. (January–June 1799),
pp.149–154.

1664. [Anonymous].
Toulon papers.
The Naval Chronicle, vol.ii (July–December 1799),
pp.102–119; 192–201; & 288–304.

1665. [Anonymous].
The French account of the capture of the *William
Tell*, 84.
The Naval Chronicle, vol.iv (July–December 1800),
pp.233–6; 317–19.
  LE GUILLAUME TELL, *84, the last survivor of the
Battle of the Nile, was taken on 29 March 1800 while
trying to escape from Malta. The only other survivor of
the Battle –* LE GÉNÉREUX, *74 – had been captured on 18
February.*

1666. [Anonymous].
The Battle of Algeçiras Bay, 1801: an authentic
narrative of the proceedings of His Majesty's
Squadron under the command of Rear-Admiral Sir
J.Saumarez . . . from the period of its sailing from
Plymouth to the conclusion of the action with the
combined fleets.
By an Officer of the Squadron.
London; Bunney & Gold; 1801. 32pp. 8vo.

1667. [Anonymous].
Particulars relating to the late action in Algeçiras
Bay, July 6, 1801.
The Naval Chronicle, vol.vi (July–December, 1801),
pp.194–198.

1668. [Anonymous].
Summary account of the proceedings of the fleet and
army employed at Toulon, in 1793, with observations
on the claim that has been made by Admiral Lord
Hood, for the remuneration of the Navy exclusively
for that service.
Brentford; P.Norbury; 1805. 17pp. 8vo.

1669. [Anonymous].
The British Flag triumphant! or, the Wooden Walls
of Old England: being copies of the *London
Gazettes*, containing the accounts of the great
victories and gallant exploits of the British Fleets,
during the last and present War . . .
London; F.C. & J.Rivington; 1806. 108pp. 8vo.
  Contains London Gazette *reports and supplements,
including, for events in the Mediterranean, those of: the
Nile; Sir Sidney Smith and the siege of Acre, 1799; and
Saumarez' action off Algeçiras, 6 July 1801.*

1670. [Anonymous].
Nelson at Bastia. By 'An Old Agamemnon'.
United Service Journal, no.147. (February 1841),
pp.212–18.

1671. [Anonymous].
Il blocco anglo–napoletano nel Mar di Toscana.
La Revista Marittima, (December 1905).

1672. [Anonymous].
A study in friction.
Naval Review, vol.x (1922), pp.172–180.
   *Describes the operations of Rear-Admiral Man in the
Mediterranean during 1796.*

II. Home Waters, the North Sea and the Baltic

1673. ALLEN, Joseph. (1810–1864).
The heroes of Camperdown.
United Service Journal, no.182 (January 1844),
pp.77–88.

1674. ANDERSON, *Dr*. Roger Charles.
Naval wars in the Baltic during the sailing ship
epoch, 1522–1850.
London; Gilbert-Wood; 1910. 423pp., pls. 8vo.
   *Includes an account of the Battle of Copenhagen, 2
April 1801.*

1675. BOM, G.D.
D'Vrijheid, 1781–1797. Geschiedenis van een
vlaggeschip.
Amsterdam & London; 1897. 300pp., pls. 8vo.
   *A study of the 74-gun flagship of the Dutch fleet and
her service career, notably when commanded by Admiral
de Winter at the Battle of Camperdown, 11 October
1797.*

1676. BONNER-SMITH, David, (1890–1950).
The naval mutinies of 1797.
The Mariner's Mirror, vols.xxi (October 1935),
pp.428–449 & xxii (January 1936), pp.65–86.

1677. BONNER-SMITH, David,
The mutiny at the Nore, 1797.
The Mariner's Mirror, vol.xxxiii (October 1947),
pp.199–203.

1678. BROCK, François van.
Dilemma at Killala.
Irish Sword, vol.viii (1967–8), pp.261–273; diagr.
   *This is an account of the action of the Mulhet, 28
October 1798, which followed Rear-Admiral Warren's
action with the French expeditionary squadron under
Bompart, off Donegal two weeks before.*

1679. BROOKS, Frederick William.
Naval recruiting in Lindsey, 1795–7.
English Historical Review, vol.xliii (April 1928),
pp.230–240.

1680. BRUNON, Jean *and* Raoul.
Au Texel le 23 janvier 1795; des Hussards
s'emparent d'une armée navale.
Neptunia, vol.lviii (February 1960), pp.19–27.
   *The famous episode, when French hussars galloped
across the frozen Zuyder Zee and captured the Dutch
fleet trapped in the ice.*

1681. BULLOCKE, *Professor* John Greville.
Sailors' rebellion: a century of naval mutinies.
London; Eyre & Spottiswoode; 1938. 318pp., pls.
8vo.

1682. BUNDESEN, *Lieutenant* P.C.
Mindeskrift i anledning af hundredaarsdagen for
Slaget paa Reden deu 2 April 1801.
Copenhagen; Vilhelm Tryde; 1901. 91pp., 1 foldg.
chart. 8vo.
    A Danish narrative of the Battle of Copenhagen, 1801.

1683. BURKE, Peter.
Celebrated naval and military trials.
London; W.H.Allen; 1866. vi, 399pp. 8vo.
    *Includes an account of the mutiny at the Nore and the
trial of the mutineers.*

1684. CLOWES, *Sir* William Laird. (1856–1905).
The French share in the mutiny at the Nore.
Cornhill Magazine, n.s., vol.xiii (1902), pp.38–52.

1685. COLOMB, *Vice-Admiral* Philip Howard.
(1831–1899).
Notes on attempted invasions of Ireland by the
French in 1796–8.
RUSIJ, vol.xxxvi (1892).

1686. COLPOYS, *Vice-Admiral Sir* Edward Griffith.
A letter to Vice-Admiral Sir Thomas Byam Martin
KCB, containing an account of the mutiny of the
fleet at Spithead in the year 1797 . . .
London; G.Woodfall; 1825. 47pp. 8vo.

1687. CONNENBURG, W.V.
De zeeslag bij Kamperduin, 11 October 1797.
In: Jaarverslag Scheepvaarts Museum (Amsterdam);
1946/7.
    *An account of the battle of Camperdown from the
Dutch side.*

1688. COOPER, Guy E.
Pellew and the departure of the Bantry expedition,
December 1796.
The Mariner's Mirror, vol.vi(June 1920), pp.178–183;
diagr.

1689. CRIMMIN, P.K.
Victualling the Russian fleet in 1795–6.
The Mariner's Mirror, vol.li (May 1965), p.172.

1690. CUNNINGHAM, *Rear-Admiral Sir* Charles.
(1755–1834).
A narrative of the occurrences that took place during
the mutiny of the Nore . . . 1797. With a few
observations upon the impressment of seamen . . .
Chatham; Burrill; 1829. xii; 141 pp. 8vo.

1691. DESBRIÈRE, Edouard.
Projets et tentatives de débarquement aux Îles
Britanniques, 1793–1805.
Paris; R.Chapelot; 1900–2. 5 vols. 8vo.
    *A classic study of French naval plans in the
Revolutionary and early Napoleonic periods, with
special reference to projects for the invasion of Britain.
Vol.i. has chapters on the Dunkirk flotilla and the first
French expedition to Ireland (Bantry Bay), 1796;
vol.ii; the second expedition to Ireland (Lough Swilly),
1798, and the Boulogne flotilla, 1801.*

1692. DOBSON, Jessie.
Mutiny at the Nore.
Annals of the Royal College of Surgeons; 1956.

1693. DONALD, T.F.
Britain's first line of defence and the mutiny of 1797.
Scottish Historical Review, vol.xii (1915), pp.311–17.

1694. [DUNCAN, *Admiral* Adam, *Viscount Duncan.*
(1731–1804)].
Letters relating to the Battle of Camperdown, 11
October 1797.
Navy Records Society, vol.xlviii (1914).

1695. [DUNCAN, *Admiral* Adam, *Viscount Duncan.*
(1731–1804)].
Admiral Duncan and naval defence.
Edinburgh Review, (1898), p.188.

1696. EVANS, G.E.
The French invasion of Pembrokeshire in 1797.
Trans. Carmarthenshire Antiq. Soc., vol.lv (1932).

1697. FIELD, *Colonel* Cyril, RMLI.
The mariner in the great naval mutinies, 1797–1802.
RUSIJ, vol.cviii (May 1963), pp.166–171.

1698. FREMANTLE, Anne.
The battle of Copenhagen, April 2nd 1801.
Blue Peter, vol.xv (April 1935), pp.165–7.

1699. GILL, Conrad.
The naval mutinies of 1797.
Manchester; University Press; 1913. xx; 412pp.,
maps. 8vo.

1700. GORE, John.
The last invasion of Britain.
Quarterly Review, vol.cclxiv (April 1935), pp.270–83.
    Being an account of the Fishguard invasion, 1797.

1701. GRIBAY, V.
The French invasion of Ireland in 1798.
New York; 1890. 211pp., 8vo.

1702. HARGREAVES, R.
A forgotten invasion.
Blackwoods Magazine, vol.ccxli (February 1949),
pp.249–57.
   *This is about the French landing in Bantry Bay in
1796.*

1703. HERBERT, David.
Great historical mutinies, comprising the story of
the *'Bounty'*, the mutiny at Spithead, the mutiny at
the Nore . . .
London & Edinburgh; W.P.Nimmo; 1876. 607pp.
8vo.

1704. [JACKSON, *Admiral Sir* Thomas Sturges.
(1842–1934).].
Logs of the great sea fights, 1794–1805.
London; Navy Records Society; 1899–1900. 2 vols.
[vols.xvi & xviii in the series].
   *Includes detailed narratives of the battles of
Camperdown and Copenhagen, including extracts from
the logs of the ships engaged.*

1705. JAMES, M.E.
The Fishguard invasion. Some passages taken from
the diary of the late Reverend Daniel Rowlands,
sometime Vicar of Llanfiangelpenybont.
London & Cardiff; Western Mail, Tudor Printing
Works; 1897. Centenary edition. frontis.,; 123pp.,;
pls. 8vo.

1706. JONES, *Commander* E.H.
Mutiny in Bantry Bay.
Irish Sword, vol.i (1949–53), pp.202–9.
   Which occurred on board L'INDOMPTABLE *during the
French landing in Ireland in 1796.*

1707. KJØLSEN, *Rear-Admiral* F.H., R.DAN.N.
Nelson and Copenhagen.
RUSIJ, vol.cviii (May 1963), pp.166–171.

1708. KOGAN, M.
Vesstanie Britanskoge voennogo flota v. 1797
godn . . .
Borussia Klassov, vol.x (1936), pp.51–59. Russian text.
   *A Russian account of the 1797 mutinies at Spithead
and the Nore.*

1709. LANGMAID, *Captain* Kenneth, RN.
The Blind eye.
London; Jarrolds; 1972. xx, 166pp., pls. 8vo.
   Includes a chapter on the battle of Copenhagen, 1801.

1710. LAWS, E.
The French landing at Fishguard.
Archaeologia Cambrensis, vol.xiv, series 4. (1883).

1711. LLOYD, *Professor* Christopher.
New light on the mutiny at the Nore.
The Mariner's Mirror, vol.xlvii (November 1961),
pp.286–295.

1712. LLOYD, *Professor* Christopher.
St. Vincent and Camperdown.
London; Batsford; 1963. [British Battles series].
184pp., pls., plans. 8vo.
   *As well as Camperdown, there is a chapter on the
French expedition to Bantry Bay, December 1796 –
January 1797.*

1713. MACKESY, *Professor* Piers.
Regulations in troopships: Home Popham and the
Russian expedition of 1799. A document.
The Mariner's Mirror, vol.lvi (May 1970), pp.229–
230.

1714. MAHAN, *Rear-Admiral* Alfred Thayer, USN.
(1840–1914).
The battle of Copenhagen.
Century Magazine, n.s., vol.xxxi (1876–7).

1715. MANWARING, George Ernest, (1882–1939),
and DOBRÉE, Bonamy.
The Floating Republic.
An account of the mutinies at Spithead and the
Nore in 1797.
London; Bles; 1935. xii, 299pp., pls. 8vo.

1716. MARCUS, Geoffrey J.
The Baltic campaign of 1801.
RUSIJ (November 1961), p.517.

1717. MEIRAT, Jean.
Les mutineries de la flotte anglaise, (1797).
Neptunia, vols.lxxiv (January 1964), pp.2–8, & lxxv,
pp.11–18, & lxxvi pp.19–23.

1718. [MOORE, *Admiral Sir* Graham (1764–1843).].
The Mutiny of the Fleet at Spithead, April 1797.
Being extracts from the journals of the late Admiral
Sir Graham Moore . . .
Naval Review, vol.xv (1927), pp.519–529.

1719. [MOORE, *Admiral Sir* Graham (1764–1843).].
The French landing in Ireland, August 1798 and the
subsequent defeat of the Brest squadron by Sir John
Warren, November 1798.
Naval Review, vol.xvi (1928), pp.58–76.
   Further extracts from Moore's journals.

1720. NEALE, William Johnson.
History of the mutiny at Spithead and the Nore
with an enquiry into its origin and treatment; and

1720. NEALE, *continued*
suggestions for the prevention of future discontent
in the Royal Navy.
London; Thomas Tegg; 1842. x; 415pp. small 8vo.

1721. OLIVARIUS, *Professeur.* —.
Description du combat naval qui a eu lieu le 2 Avril
1801 dans la rade de Copenhague.
Kiel; [*n.d.*]. 37pp. 8vo.

1722. PATTERSON, *Professor* A.Temple.
The Naval mutiny at Spithead, 1797.
Portsmouth; The Portsmouth Papers; 1968. 15pp.
8vo.

1723. PATTON, *Admiral* Philip, (1739–1815).
Account of the mutinies at Spithead and St. Helen's
in April and May 1797, written at the end of June
of the same year . . .
Edinburgh; [1797]. 32pp. small 4to.

1724. PIETERS, E.
Copenhagen, 1801.
Belgian Shiplover (1955), pp.1–66.

1725. PLOWMAN, Stephanie.
Earl Spencer and the naval mutinies of 1797.
The Mariner's Mirror, vol.xxxix (1953), pp.220–1.

1726. POPE, Dudley.
The Great Gamble; Nelson at Copenhagen.
London; Weidenfeld & Nicholson; 1972. 579pp.,
pls. 8vo.

1727. RICHMOND, *Professor* A.A.
Napoleon and the Armed Neutrality of 1800. A
diplomatic challenge to British Seapower.
RUSIJ. vol.civ (May 1959), p.186.

1728. ROBINSON, C.
A report of the judgment of the High Court of
Admiralty on the Swedish convoy; pronounced by
the Rt. Hon. Sir William Scott, June 11, 1799.
London; Strachan; 1799. 37pp., 8vo.
     *The case arose out of the treatment to be given by the
Royal Navy to merchant ships belonging to the Baltic
powers encountered at sea, in view of their embargo upon
trade with Britain. The judge took the view that the
right to rigorous stop and search – although they were
neutral vessels – was fully justified in the circumstances.*

1729. ROWLANDS, *Reverend* Daniel.
The Fishguard invasion by the French in 1797.
London; Unwin; 1892. 234pp. small 8vo.

1730. SALMON, David.
The French invasion of Pembrokeshire in 1797.
West Wales Historical Society, vol.xiv (January 1929).

1731. SALMON, David.
A sequel to the French invasion of Pembrokeshire.
Y Cymmroder, vol.xliii (July 1933).

1732. SALMON, David.
The French in Pembrokeshire, 1797.
Notes & Queries, vol.clxxviii (11 May 1940), pp.
332–4.

1733. SCHOPPEN, Werner.
Grossbritannien und die Ostsee, 1780 bis 1812.
Wissen und Wehr (1939), pp.713–720; 745–757.

1734. SPROULE, H.D.
James Burney's opinions on the Naval Mutinies of
1797.
The Mariner's Mirror, vol.xlvi (February 1961),
pp.61–2.

1735. STUART-JONES, *Commander* E.H., RN.
An Invasion that failed. The French expedition to
Ireland 1796.
Oxford; Basil Blackwell; 1950. 256pp., pls.; chart.
8vo.

1736. SYKES, W.S.
The threatened invasion by the French in 1798.
Milford-on-Sea Record Society Mag., vol.ii. (1912).

1737. TAYLOR, *Rear-Admiral* A.H.
The battle of Copenhagen, April 2nd 1801.
Naval Review, vol.xxxix (1950), pp.125–141.

1738. TIMINGS, E.K.
New light on the mutiny at the Nore: a postscript.
The Mariner's Mirror, vol.xlvii (February 1961),
pp.61–63.

1739. TURNER, Eunice H.
The Russian squadron with Admiral Duncan's
North Sea fleet, 1795–1800.
The Mariner's Mirror, vol.xlix (August 1963),
pp.212–222.

1740. WARNER, Oliver.
Nelson's Battles.
London; Batsford; 1965. [British Battles series].
254pp., pls. 8vo.
     Includes a narrative of the Battle of Copenhagen.

1741. WARNER, Oliver.
Elsinore and the Danish Sound dues.
History Today, vol.xvii (1967), pp.619–625.

1742. [WATSON, James].
The mutiny at the Nore: a letter from James
Watson to Admiral Robert Digby [1797].
In: The Naval Miscellany, vol.ii [Navy Records
Society, vol.xl, 1912].

1743. WILSON, Herbert Wrigley. (1866–1940).
The Armed Neutrality, 1780–1801.
Chapter in the *Cambridge Modern History*, vol.ix
(1906).

1744. [Anonymous].
An impartial account of the life of Richard Parker,
who was president of the delegates at the Nore;
tried for mutiny, and condemned by a court martial
held on board HM Ship *Neptune*, at Greenhithe . . .
London; J.Fairburn; 1797. 24pp. 8vo.

1745. [Anonymous].
Memoirs of Richard Parker, the mutineer; together
with an account at large of his trial by court martial,
defence, sentence and execution, and a narrative of
the mutiny at the Nore and Sheerness, from its
commencement to its termination.
London; G.Cawthorn; 1797. Fourth edition. 36pp.,
small 4to.

1746. [Anonymous].
Trial complete. The trial of Richard Parker, for
mutiny, on board of His Majesty's Ship the
Sandwich at the Nore in May 1797. Before a court
martial held on board the *Neptune* 98 guns, laying
off Greenhithe . . .
London; J.S.Jordan; [1797]. 35pp. 8vo.

1747. [Anonymous].
Proceedings on a court-martial . . . on Richard
Parker, late a supernumerary on board His Majesty's
Ship *Sandwich*, for mutiny, disobedience of orders
and contempt of his officers.
Accurately taken in short-hand by George Farquhar.
London; W.Wilson; [1797]. 42pp., small 4to.
*A similar pamphlet – a shorthand account of the trial,
taken by Job Sibley – is also in the Library.*

1748. [Anonymous].
The victory off Copenhagen.
Naval Chronicle, vols.v. pp.334–343 *and* vi, pp.117–
123.[July 1801].

1749. [Anonymous].
The trial of the mutineers, late of His Majesty's Ship
Temeraire held on board the *Gladiator* in Portsmouth
Harbour, January 6, 1802.
London; J.Lee; 1802. Second edition. 64pp. 8vo.
*J.Lee further published, also in 1802: 'A continuation
of the trial of the mutineers . . . January 14, 1802'
(22pp., 8vo), of which there is a copy in the Library.*

1750. [Anonymous].
Trial of the mutineers late of His Majesty's Ship
Temeraire held on board His Majesty's Ship
Gladiator, Portsmouth Harbour.
London; J.Davenport; [1802]. 8pp. 8vo.

1751. [Anonymous].
The trials of fourteen seamen for mutiny . . . late of
His Majesty's Ship *Temeraire* . . . with the sentence
of the court . . . to which is added an account of the
execution.
London; J.Fairburn; [1802] 32pp. small 4to.

1752. [Anonymous].
The French at Fishguard in 1797.
United Service Journal, vol.clxxi (February 1843),
pp.202–213.

1753. [Anonymous].
Copenhagen 1801.
Naval Review, vol.xv (1927), pp.283–4.
*Admiral Sir Hyde Parker's letter to the Admiralty,
requesting a Court of Enquiry to clear his name.*

1754. [Anonymous].
The mutiny in the Fleet at Spithead, April 1797.
Naval Review, vol.xv (1927), pp.519–529.
*Extracts from the journal of Admiral Sir Graham
Moore, GCB.*

1755. [Anonymous].
The French landing in Ireland, August 1798 and the
subsequent defeat of the Brest squadron by Sir John
Warren, November 1798.
Naval Review, vol.xvi (1928), pp.58–76.
*Further extracts from the diary of Admiral Sir
Graham Moore.*

1756. [Anonymous].
The invasion scare of February – March 1794.
Société Jersiaise Bulletin, vol.xii (1935), pp.525–8.

1757. [Anonymous].
The Mutinies of 1797.
Naval Review vol.lix (1971), pp.242–52; 322–31.

III. The Atlantic and coast of France

1758. ALLEN, Joseph. (1810–1864).
Lord Howe on the First of June.
United Service Journal (June 1843), pp.174–186.

1759. BULL, David.
The 'Glorious First of June.'
Lloyd's Log, vol.xl (June 1970), pp.14–18.

1760. CAGIGAS, Dionisio de las.
El ataque de Nelson a Tenerife . . .
Santander; 1936. 37pp., illustr. 8vo.

1761. CANO, Francisco Lanuza.
Ataque y derrota da Nelson en Santa Cruz de
Tenerife. Relato histórico con arraglo a documentos
oficiales de la época.
Madrid; 1955. 793pp., 71pls. 4to.

1762. CHAIR, *Lieutenant* H.C.D.de, RN.
Howe and the Battle of 1 June, 1794.
Naval Review, vol.xx (1932), pp.132–138.

1763. COOPER, *Lieutenant* Guy E.
The methods of blockade and observation employed
during the Revolutionary and Napoleonic Wars.
RUSIJ, vol.lxi (1916), pp.523–550, maps.

1764. CORDOBA Y RAMOS, *Don* Joseph de.
Defensa facultiva, que expone al Consejo Don Juan
Ruiz de Apodaca . . . justificacion de la conducta y
vindicacion del honor del Teniente General Don
Joseph de Cordoba y Ramos . . . y combate que
tuvo con la Inglesa del Vice-Almirante Jervis, en
las aguas del Cabo de S.Vicente, el dia de Febrero
año de 1797.
[Cadiz; Manuel Ximenez Carreno; 1797]. [77]pp.
8vo.
*An attempt by the commander of the Spanish Fleet at
the Battle of Cape St. Vincent, 14 February 1797, to
explain his shattering defeat at the hands of Jervis and
Nelson.*

1765. DRINKWATER-BETHUNE, *Colonel.*
A Narrative of the Battle of St. Vincent; with
anecdotes of Nelson, before and after that battle . . .
London; Saunders & Otley; 1840. xii, 97pp., 8
track charts. 8vo.
*One of the most important eye-witness accounts of the
battle, by a spectator rather than a participant.*

*This is a copy of the second edition; the first was
published in 1797. There is also a copy of the 1969
reprint edition (Conway Maritime Press) in the Library.*

1766. [DUCKWORTH, *Admiral Sir* John Thomas.
(1748–1817)].
Proceedings of *HMS Orion,* John Thomas Duckworth Esq., Commander, and his observations
during the actions of the 28th and 29th of May, and
1st of June 1794.
Naval Chronicle, vol.i (January 1799), pp.293–300.

1767. DU PLESSIS, G.
The armed boats of the Loire and Indre during the
Vendée Wars.
Bulletin de la Société Archivistes de Nantes . . . , vol.lxx
(1932).

1768. GRIEVE, J.S.Mackenzie.
The observation and blockade of the French fleets
during the Revolutionary and Napoleonic Wars,
(1793–1805).
United Service Magazine, (April–June 1916).

1769. HANNAY, David. (1853–1934).
Lord Howe's Victory (1 June 1794) & The blockade
of Brest.
In his: 'Ships and Men'. (London; 1910).

1770. [HOWE, *Admiral of the Fleet* Richard, *Earl
Howe* (1726–1799)].
Lord Howe's actions, 28/29 May and 1 June, 1794
(With logs of the ships engaged).
In: Logs of the Great Sea Fights, 1794–1805, vol.i.
[London; Navy Records Society; vol.xvi, 1899).

1771. [HOWE, *Admiral of the Fleet* Richard, *Earl
Howe* (1726–1799)].
The Glorious 1st of June 1794; letters written by
Admiral Howe on board the *Queen.*
In: W.H.Long: 'Naval Yarns' (London; 1899).

1772. [HOWE, *Admiral of the Fleet* Richard, *Earl
Howe* (1726–1799)].
Instructions for the conduct of the Fleet preparatory
to their engaging . . . 1794.
In: 'Fighting Instructions', 1530–1816. [London;
Navy Records Society, vol.xxix; 1905).

1773. HUTT, Maurice.
The British government's responsibility for the
divided command of the expedition to Quiberon,
1795.
English Historical Review, vol.lxxvi (1961), pp.479–
89.

1774. 'KIM'.
St. Vincent, February 1797.
United Service Magazine, vol.clxvi (1912), pp.471–496, pls.

1775. LACOUR-GAYET, Georges.
À propos du combat du *Vengeur* (1 Juni 1794).
Séances Travails Academie de Science, (1930), pp.433–441.
After a tremendous duel with the BRUNSWICK, *74, in the Glorious First of June battle,* LE VENGEUR DU PEUPLE, *74, struck and later foundered.*

1776. LLOYD, *Professor* Christopher.
St. Vincent and Camperdown.
London; Batsford; 1963. [British Battles series].
184pp., pls.; battle-plans. 8vo.
The appendices include lists of the opposing fleets in both actions.

1777. LOZACH, J.
Poussière navale au temps du Consulat: les flotilles 'à l'espagnole' devant Brest et Boulogne (1799–1801).
Neptunia, vol.lxxxix (April 1969), pp.6–14.

1778. MAHAN, *Rear-Admiral* Alfred Thayer, USN. (1840–1914).
Nelson at Cape St. Vincent.
Century Magazine, n.s., vol.xxix (1895–6).

1779. MANWARING, George Ernest. (1882–1939).
The expedition to Ostend, 1798.
RUSIJ, vol.lxiii (November 1918), pp.624–627.

1780. MANWARING, George Ernest Popham's expedition to Ostend in 1798.
The Mariner's Mirror, vol.vii (November 1921), pp.332–341.

1781. McPEAKE, B.Y.
With Nelson at Cape St. Vincent.
Blue Peter, vol.xiv (January 1934), pp.3–6.

1782. [MONEVERDE, *Lieutenant-Colonel Don José de*].
Relacion circunstanciada de la defensa que hizo la plaza de Santa Cruz de Tenerife, invalida por una esquadra inglesa, al mando del Contra-Almirante Horacio Nelson, la madsugada del 25 de Juilio de 1797.
Madrid; 1798. 60pp. 12mo.
A contemporary Spanish account of Nelson's attack on Santa Cruz, Teneriffe, at daybreak, on 25 July, 1797.

1783. MORRIS, William O'Connor.
The great campaigns of Nelson: St. Vincent, the Nile, Copenhagen, Trafalgar.
London; Blackie; [1892]. 156pp., illustr. 8vo.

1784. PERRIN, Walter Gordon. (1874–1931).
The Naval Miscellany, vol.iii.
London; Navy Records Society; 1928.
Part 4 contains documents relating to the engagement between HMS BRUNSWICK *and* LE VENGEUR *in the Glorious First of June action. See also the article by Lacour-Gayet in this section.*

1785. ROGER, Paul.
La révolte de la frégate anglaise 'La Danae', Mars 1800. Une page peu connue du blocus de Brest.
Neptunia, vol.lxiv (April 1961), pp.10–17.
See also the article by J.D.Spinney on this event.

1786. SAXBY, R.C.
The escape of Admiral Bruix from Brest. [April 1799].
The Mariner's Mirror, vol.xlvi (May 1960), pp.113–119.

1787. SPINNEY, J.David.
The *Danae* mutiny.
The Mariner's Mirror, vol.xlii (February 1956), pp.38–53.
On 14 March, 1800, the crew of HMS DANAE, *a 32-gun frigate, mutinied off Ushant and forced their commander to surrender his ship to the French.*

1788. SPINNEY, J.David.
Nelson at Santa Cruz.
The Mariner's Mirror, vol.xlv, (August 1959), pp.207–223; figs.
An account of the attack on Teneriffe, July 1797.

1789. SAINT-ANDRÉ, Jean Bon.
Rapport sur les mouvements qui ont en lieu sur l'escadre commandée par le Vice-Amiral Morard de Galles.
Brest; 1793. 81pp. 8vo.
Suspicious of the loyalty of their naval officers, the Jacobin government frequently installed their agents and informers on board squadron flagships in the early years of the Revolutionary War. This is a typical report by one of them.

1790. STEER, D.M.
The blockade of Brest by the Royal Navy in the late eighteenth century.
University of London MA thesis; May 1971.

1791. TAYLOR, *Rear-Admiral* A.H.
The Battle of Cape St. Vincent.
The Mariner's Mirror, vol.xl (August 1954), pp.228–230; *and Naval Review*, vol.xlii (1954), pp.68–77.

1792. UDEN, Grant.
John Wilkinson and the Glorious First of June.
The Mariner's Mirror, vol.xliii (November 1957), pp.323–5.

1793. USHERWOOD, Stephen.
The Siege of Toulon, 1793.
History Today, vol.xxii (January 1972), pp.79–84, illustr.

1794. VANEL, Gabriel.
Les anglais aux Îles Saint-Marcouf: l'expédition de 1798 . . .
Musée Acad. Caen (1909), pp.229–324.

1795. WARNER, Oliver.
The Glorious First of June.
London; Batsford; 1965. [British Battles series]. 254pp., pls. 8vo.
The appendices include a reprint of Howe's letter to the Admiralty from the QUEEN CHARLOTTE *at sea, 2 June 1794; and lists of the opposing fleets.*

1796. [WYKE, *Lieutenant* William Bryan, RN].
The Battle of Cape St. Vincent (from his journal), 14 February 1797: with Sir John Jervis' account of the action.
RUSIJ, vol.lix (1914).

1797. [Anonymous].
Official documents and interesting particulars of the glorious victory obtained over the French Fleet on Sunday, June 1, 1794, by the British Fleet under the command of Admiral Earl Howe: illustrated with an accurate engraving of the manoeuvring and line of battle . . .
London; J.Debrett; 1794. 36pp., engr. plates. 8vo.
Includes a battle-plan and fleet lists.

1798. [Anonymous].
A narrative of the proceedings of His Majesty's Fleet, under the command of Earl Howe, from the second of May to the second of June M.DCC.XCIV.
London; T.Burton; 1796. 118pp., one plan. 4to.
Particularly of the Glorious First of June action. Appendices include: (i) list of French ships taken; (ii) full casualties in the British fleet; (iii) Howe's despatch of 2 June to the Admiralty; (iv) full list of officers in each ship which took part; (v) the French line of battle; (vi) a reproduction of Jean Bon Saint-André's journal entry for 1 June on board LE MONTAGNE.

1799. [Anonymous].
A Narrative of the proceedings of the British Fleet commanded by Admiral Sir John Jervis, KB, in the late action with the Spanish Fleet, on the Fourteenth of February 1797, off Cape St. Vincent's . . .
London; J.Johnson; 1797. 27pp., 8 battle-plans; appendices. 4to.
See also under Colonel Drinkwater-Bethune (entry: 1765).
The three appendices comprise: return of killed & wounded on board the British ships; ships and commanders of both fleets.

1800. [Anonymous].
The British Navy Triumphant! Being copies of the London Gazettes Extraordinary; containing the accounts of the glorious victories obtained . . . over the French Fleet, by Admiral Lord Howe, on the 1st of June, 1794; the Spanish Fleet, by Admiral Sir J.Jervis, near Cape St.Vincent, February 14, 1797 . . .
Oxford; 1798. 28pp. 8vo.

1801. [Anonymous].
An account of the Glorious First of June action; 1794.
Naval Chronicle, vol.i. (January 1799), pp.25–28.

1802. [Anonymous].
The British Flag Triumphant! or, the Wooden Walls of Old England: being copies of the London Gazettes, containing the accounts of the great victories and gallant exploits of the British Fleets, during the last and present war . . .
London; F.C. & J.Rivington; 1806. 108pp. 8vo.
Includes the London Gazette reports and supplements of the Glorious First of June action; Cape St. Vincent; and Île de Groix, 23 June 1795 (Bridport's action). A copy of the second edition of this work – also published by Rivingtons in 1806 – is in the Library.

1803. [Anonymous].
Cape St. Vincent. A few particulars of the action off Cape St. Vincent on the 14th February 1797, extracted from a letter of an officer on board Nelson's ship, the *Captain*.
United Service Journal, no.118 (September 1838) pp.57–66.

1804. [Anonymous].
The Glorious First of June. From the log of an officer of the *Culloden*, 74, engaged in that memorable action.
United Service Journal, no.173 (April 1843), pp.518–524.

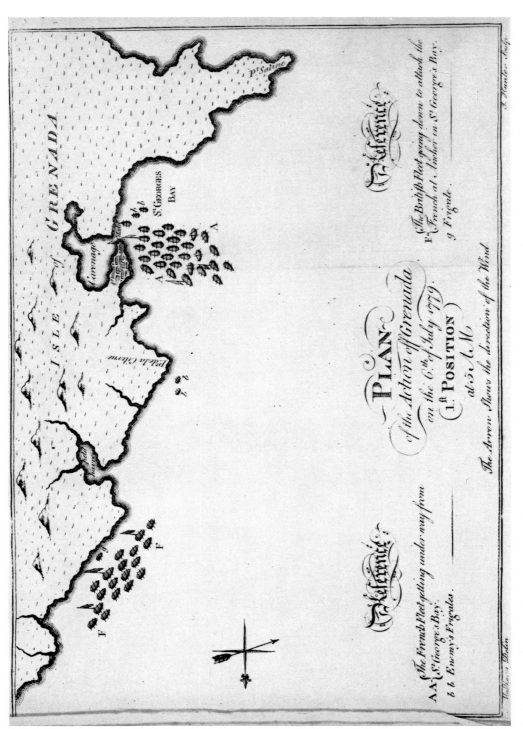

PLATE IX: Plan of the action off Grenada on the 6th of July 1779 . . . From John Matthews': *Twenty-one Plans of different actions in the West Indies, during the late War . . . By an officer of the Royal Navy, who was present.* Chester; 1784

PLATE X: The capture of L'Hercule, April 20th 1797: by Thomas Whitcombe. From James Jenkins': *The Naval Achievements of Great Britain, from the year 1793 to 1817.* London; [1817]

1805. [Anonymous].
Lord Howe on the First of June.
United Service Journal, no.176 (June 1843), pp.175–186.

1806. [Anonymous].
British minor expeditions, 1746 to 1814.
London; HMSO; 1884. 91pp., numerous maps & plans. 8vo.
Although chiefly a military survey, this work includes important naval material. In this period there are narratives of the expedition to Quiberon, 1795; Ostend, 1798; and the Helder, 1799.

1807. [Anonymous].
The Battles of Cape St. Vincent and The Nile. By one of the crew of the *Goliath*.
In: W.H.Long's 'Naval Yarns' (London; 1899).

1808. [Anonymous].
The blockade of Brest.
Edinburgh Review, vol.cxcvii (1903), pp.1–33.

1809. [Anonymous].
The battle of Cape St. Vincent.
RUSIJ (1914), p.321.

1810. [Anonymous].
Jervis and the Spanish Fleet.
Naval Review, vol.x (1922), p.511.

1811. [Anonymous].
Jervis' victory off Cape St. Vincent, 14 February 1797.
History Today, vol.v (1955), p.128.

IV. The West Indies and North America

1812. BONNEL, Ulane.
La France, les États-Unis et la guerre de course, (1797–1815).
Paris; Éditions Latines; 1961. 489pp., pls., charts. 8vo.
Especially on privateering in American waters during the period.

1813. BURDON, *Sir* John.
The battle of St. George's Cay.
United Empire, n.s., vol.xix (1928), pp.248–257.
In September 1798 a Spanish force of transports, schooners and sloops bent on attacking the British settlements in the Gulf of Honduras, was sharply defeated off Belize by a British flotilla under Commander Moss with the MERLIN, *16, armed gun-boats and schooners.*

1814. CAMPBELL, *Captain* John F.
The Havana incident.
The American Neptune, vol.xxii (1962), pp.264–276.
Occurred on 16 November 1798 when the USS BALTIMORE, *lying off Havana, was boarded by a junior officer from* HMS CARNATIC, *who impressed fifty-five seamen. President John Adams thought the incident serious enough to justify his personal intervention.*

1815. CARDEW, *Major* F.S.
The taking of Tobago, 1793.
RUSIJ, vol.lxx (August 1925), pp.411–415.

1816. GRAHAM, *Professor* Gerald Sandford.
Sea Power and British North America, 1783–1820.
A study in British Colonial policy.
Cambridge, Mass.; 1941. xii; 302pp., maps. 8vo.

1817. LESTER, M.
Anglo–American diplomatic problems arising from British naval operations in American Waters, 1793–1802.
University of Virginia Ph.D thesis; 1954.

1818. MAY, *Commander* W.E.
Mortality in the *Chichester*, 1802.
The Mariner's Mirror, vol.liv (August 1968), p.392(n).
The CHICHESTER *was a 44 stationed in the West Indies, when her crew was ravaged by yellow fever.*

1819. NASATIR, Abraham P.
Spanish war vessels on the Mississippi, 1792–1796.
New Haven, Conn.; Yale; 1968. viii, 359pp. 8vo.

1820. SANDERSON, *Dr.* Michael. W.B.
English naval strategy and maritime trade in the
Caribbean, 1793–1802.
University of London Ph.D thesis; 1969.

1821. SMITH, Thomas W.
Halifax and the capture of St. Pierre in 1793.
Nova Scotia Hist.Soc. Collection, vol.xiv (1910),
pp.80–105.

1822. STEWART, *Lieutenant-Commander* James,
RN.
The Leeward Islands command, 1795–1796.
The Mariner's Mirror, vol.xlvii (November 1961),
pp.270–280.
    *Discusses in particular the Laforey-Christian
command crisis.*

1823. TRISTRAM, J.
The frigate actions between the British *Blanche* and
the French *Pique* . . .
United Service Journal, vol.ccxlviii (July 1849),
pp.375–382.
    *A desperate night-action fought off Guadeloupe on
January 5/6, 1795. The French frigate was finally taken
but Captain Robert Faulknor – in command of the
BLANCHE and the hero of the attack on Fort Royal,
Martinique the previous March – was killed.*

1824. WILLYAMS, *Reverend* Cooper.
An account of the campaign in the West Indies in
the year 1794, under the command of . . .
Lieutenant General Sir Charles Grey, KB, and Vice
Admiral Sir John Jervis, KB, commander in chief in
the West Indies; with the reduction of the islands of
Martinique, St. Lucia, Guadaloupe, Marigalante,
Desiada . . . and the events that followed . . .
By . . . late chaplain of *HMS Boyne*.
London; G.Nichol, B.J.White & J.Robson; 1796.
152 + [62]pp., engr. pls. 4to.
    *A contemporary account of the very successful Grey–
Jervis expedition to the West Indies in 1794, which
temporarily wrested control of the theatre from the
French. A second edition of this book was published by
T.Bentley, also in 1796.*

1825. [Anonymous].
An account of the La Guaira expedition.
Naval Chronicle, vol.i (January 1799), pp.204–206.
    *Against the Spaniards in 1798 on the coast of
Venezuela.*

1826. [Anonymous].
The French expedition to San Domingo. [1802].
Naval Chronicle, vol.vii (July 1802), pp.258–267.

1827. [Anonymous].
American vessels captured by the British during the
Revolution and War of 1812; the record of the
Vice-Admiralty Court at Halifax, Nova Scotia.
Salem, Mass.,; 1911. 166pp., 8vo.

1828. [Anonymous].
Essex County [Massachusetts] vessels captured by
foreign powers, 1793–1813; compiled from
American state papers.
Essex Inst. Hist. Colln., vols.lviii (1922), pp.280–7,
and lix (1923), pp.25–32.

V. Events and operations elsewhere

1829. AUZOUX, A.
Une campagne sur les côtes de l'Inde au début de la Révolution, (1791–2).
La Revue Historique, vol.lxxxix (1911), pp.433–458.

1830. COLGATE, H.A.
The Royal Navy base at Trincomalee and the East Indies squadron, 1795–1802.
University of London MA thesis; 1959.

1831. DALY, Robert Walter.
Operations of the Russian Navy during the French Revolution and Empire, 1795–1801.
USNIP, vol.lxxii (1947), pp.555–561.

1832. PARKINSON, *Professor* C.Northcote.
Trade in the Eastern Seas, 1793–1813.
Cambridge; University Press; 1937. xii, 434pp.; 8 pls. 8vo.

1833. PARKINSON, *Professor* C.Northcote.
British operations in the Red Sea, 1799–1801.
Royal Central Asian Society Journal, vol.xxv (April 1938), pp.248–259.

1834. PARKINSON, *Professor* C.Northcote. [*editor*].
The Trade Winds. A study of British overseas trade during the French Wars, 1793–1815.
London; Allen & Unwin; 1948. 336pp., pls. 8vo.

1835. PARKINSON, *Professor* C.Northcote.
War in the Eastern Seas, 1793–1815.
London; Allen & Unwin; 1954. 477pp., pls. 8vo.

1836. PERRIN, Walter Gordon (1874–1931). [*editor*].
Account of Lord Keith's compelling a Dutch squadron directed at Cape Town to surrender in Saldanha Bay and the capture of the Cape of Good Hope, (1796).
In: Letters and papers of Admiral Viscount Keith, vol.i. [London; Navy Records Society series, vol.lxii; 1927], edited by W.G.Perrin.

1837. RAINBOW, S.G.
English expeditions to the Dutch East Indies during the Revolutionary and Napoleonic Wars.
University of London MA thesis; 1933.

1838. ROSE, *Professor* John Holland, (1855–1942).
The influence of seapower on Indian history, (1746–1802).
Journal of Indian History, vol.iii (Allahabad; 1925), pp.188–204.

1839. [Anonymous].
The intercepted letters taken on board the *Admiral Aplin,* East Indiaman, translated from the *Moniteur* of the 16 of September: to which is prefixed the French official account of the engagement of Linois' squadron with the East India Fleet.
London; John Ginger; 1804. 95pp. 8vo.

1840. [Anonymous].
Trade defence in Indian seas.
Naval Review, vol.xviii (1930), pp.62–72.
   Includes a memorandum by Admiral Sir Peter Rainier dated 1801, on the defence of trade in the Indian Ocean and a report by Vice-Admiral Sir Edward Pellew (later Admiral Lord Exmouth), on his return from the station in 1809.

THE NAPOLEONIC WARS, 1803–1815

I. The Trafalgar Campaign

1841. ANDERSON, *Dr.* Roger Charles.
Spanish propaganda after Trafalgar.
The Mariner's Mirror, vol.xliv (February 1958),
pp.69–72, (n).

1842. ANDERSON, *Dr.* Roger Charles.
The lee line at Trafalgar.
The Mariner's Mirror, vol.lvii (May 1971), pp.157–
161.

1843. BRIDGE, *Admiral Sir* Cyprian Arthur George,
(1839–1924).
Nelson; the centenary of Trafalgar.
Cornhill Magazine, vol.xix (September 1905),
pp.312–325; plans.
    There is also a reprint (14pp., wrappers) of this essay.

1844. BRIDGE, *Admiral Sir* Cyprian Arthur George,
(1839–1924).
Naval strategy and tactics at the time of Trafalgar.
In his: *Sea-Power, and other studies*, (London; 1910).

1845. BRITTON, C.J. (*d.*1946).
The first published plan of the Battle of Trafalgar.
The Mariner's Mirror, vol.xxxi (July 1945), pp.168–
9, (n).

1846. CLOWES, *Sir* William Laird. (1856–1905).
Trafalgar from the Spanish side.
Cornhill Magazine, n.s., vol.ii, (1896).

1847. CLOWES, *Sir* William Laird *and*
BURGOYNE, Alan H.
Trafalgar refought.
London; Nelson; 1905. 328pp., pls. & plans. 8vo.

1848. COBB, J.Wheatley.
The Nelson touch at Trafalgar.
RUSIJ, vol.lvi (September/October 1911),
pp.1156–80; 1265–92. pls.

1849. COLOMB, *Vice-Admiral* Philip Howard,
(1831–1899).
The battle of Trafalgar.
United Service Magazine (n.s.), vols.xix, (1899) and
xxxi, (1905).

1850. CORBETT, *Professor Sir* Julian Stafford,
(1854–1922).
The Trafalgar Memorandum. *and* 'Further
particulars of the Trafalgar fight'.

In: Fighting Instructions, 1530–1816. (Navy Records
Society series, vol.xxxix; 1905), pp.316–320 &
351–358.

1851. CORBETT, *Professor Sir* Julian Stafford,
(1854–1922).
The campaign of Trafalgar.
London; Longmans; 1910. 473pp., pls., charts &
diagrs. 8vo.
    *Still a most valuable study of the subject in all its
aspects.*

1852. CORBETT, *Professor Sir* Julian Stafford,
(1854–1922).
Napoleon and the British Navy after Trafalgar.
Quarterly Review, (April 1922).

1853. COUTO, *Don* José F.de.
Historia del combate naval de Trafalgar precedida
de la renaciemiento de la Marina Española durante
el siglo xviii.
Madrid; Ayguals de Ixco; 1851. 187pp. 8vo.

1854. DAY, Robert.
A memento of Trafalgar.
Journal of Cork History, vol.xviii (1911), pp.116–7.
    Being an engraved medal of the VICTORY.

1855. DESBRIÈRE, Édouard.
La campagne maritime de 1805: Trafalgar.
Paris; R.Chapelot; 1907. 620pp.; many plans &
facsimiles. 8vo.
    *The standard French authority and the sequel to the
author's:* 'Projets et tentatives de débarquement aux
Îles Britanniques, 1793–1805'., [q.v.].

1856. [DESBRIÈRE, Édouard].
The naval campaign of 1805: Trafalgar.
Translated & edited by Constance Eastwick.
Oxford; Clarendon Press; 1933. 2 vols.: i (text),
320pp., ii (appendix), 444pp. 8vo.
    The English translation of the above.

1857. DORMER, E.W.
Admiral Villeneuve and Berkshire.
Berks. Archaeological Journal, vol.xxiv, no.2. (April
1931).

1858. EARDLEY-WILMOT, *Rear-Admiral Sir*
Sydney. (1847–1929).
Sir Robert Calder's action, July 22, 1805.
United Service Magazine, vol.cxliv (1901), pp.335–342.

1859. EARDLEY-WILMOT, *Rear-Admiral Sir*
Sydney. (1847–1929).
Nelson's last campaign.
London; Stanford; 1905. 54pp., plans. 8vo.

1860. FESTING, E.G.
Contemporary Spanish reports on Trafalgar.
United Service Magazine, vol.cxvi, (1897–8).

1861. FITCHETT, William Henry, (1845–1928).
The picturesque side of Trafalgar.
Cornhill Magazine (n.s.), vol.xix, (1905).

1862. FRASER, Edward.
The enemy at Trafalgar.
An account of the battle from eye-witnesses'
narratives and letters and despatches from the French
and Spanish fleets.
London; Hodder & Stoughton; [1906]. 436pp., pls.,
charts. 8vo.
   *An excellent account of the battle from the opposing
viewpoint.*

1863. FREMANTLE, A.F.
Trafalgar.
London; Peter Davies; 1933. 168pp., pls., charts.
8vo.

1864. FREMANTLE, *Admiral Sir* Edward Robert,
(1856–1929).
Nelson's tactics at Trafalgar . . .
United Service Magazine, vol.cliii (1906), pp.38–51;
plans.

1865. FROST, *Commander* Holloway Halstead, USN.
(1889–1935).
Letters on naval strategy, based on the naval
campaign of 1805.
USNIP, vol.xliv (1918), pp.1241–66; 1465–93;
1763–99; 2025–62; 2297–2331; illustr.

1866. GLATZEL, R.
Trafalgar; das letzte wort darüber? *and* Ein
Englisches Blau-buch über die Trafalgar-taktik.
Marine Rundschau, vols.xxi (1910), pp.983–92 *and*
xxv (1914), pp.470–6.

1867. HOLLAND, *Captain* Lancelot Ernest, RN.
No.4 flag at Trafalgar.
The Mariner's Mirror, vol.xx (October 1934),
pp.415–9.

1868. HOUSEHOLD, H.W.
Our guardian fleets in 1805.
London; Macmillan; 1919. 226pp., pls. 8vo.

1869. HOWARTH, David.
Trafalgar; the Nelson touch.
London; Collins; 1969. 254pp., pls., charts. 8vo.

1870. HOWARTH, David.
The man who lost Trafalgar.
The Mariner's Mirror, vol.lvii (1971), pp.361–370.
   That is, Admiral Villeneuve.

1871. JACKSON, *Rear-Admiral* Thomas Sturges.
[editor].
Logs of the Great Sea Fights, 1794–1805.
London; 1900. 2 volumes. Navy Records Society
series, vol.xviii.
   *Part vi in vol.2, (pp.139–327), is concerned with
Trafalgar and contains extracts from the logs of the
following warships engaged:* EURYALUS; VICTORY;
BRITANNIA; PRINCE; DREADNOUGHT; TONNANT;
BELLEISLE; REVENGE; MARS; SPARTIATE; DEFIANCE;
CONQUEROR; DEFENCE; COLOSSUS; LEVIATHAN;
ACHILLE; BELLEROPHON; ORION; MINOTAUR; SWIFT-
SURE; AJAX; THUNDERER; POLYPHEMUS; AFRICA;
AGAMEMNON; NAIAD; PHOEBE; SIRIUS; PICKLE *and*
ENTREPRENANTE; *and also private journals and letters.*

1872. KERR, *Admiral* Mark Edward Frederick,
(1864–1944).
How Nelson's memorandum was carried out at
Trafalgar.
The Nineteenth Century, vol.lxx (October 1911),
pp.679–704; plans & diagrs.

1873. KOCH, Frederik.
Trafalgar, 1805.
Forum Naval, no.14 (Uppsala; 1957), pp.108–23.

1874. LACAVE, Augusto Conte.
En los dias de Trafalgar.
Cadiz; Escelicer; 1955. 280pp., pls. 8vo.

1875. LACHOUQUE, *Commandant* Henri.
L'affaire du *Bellerophon*.
Neptunia, vol.xlviii (April 1957), pp.9–18.

1876. LAUGHTON, *Sir* John Knox, (1830–1915).
The story of Trafalgar.
Portsmouth; Griffin; 1890. 40pp. 12mo.

1877. LAUGHTON, *Sir* John Knox, (1830–1915).
The Navy in 1805.
United Service Magazine, n.s., vol.xxxii (1905–6).

1878. LAUGHTON, L.G.Carr.
The attack at Trafalgar.
United Service Magazine, vol.cxliv (1901), pp.441–7.

1879. LAUGHTON, L.G.Carr.
Sir Richard Strachan's action.
United Service Magazine, vol.cxlv (1902), pp.459–63.
   *In which Strachan's squadron chased and captured off
Cape Ortegal on 4 November 1805, four French ships of*

1879. LAUGHTON, *continued*
the line under Rear-Admiral Dumanoir which had
survived Trafalgar – the FORMIDABLE, 80; DUGUAY-
TROUIN, 74; MONT BLANC, 74, *and* SCIPION, 74.

1880. LAUGHTON, L.G.Carr.
HMS *Victory*. Report . . . of a search among the
Admiralty records.
The Mariner's Mirror, vol.x (October 1924), pp.173–
211.

1881. LEGG, Stuart. [*editor*].
Trafalgar. An eye-witness account of a great battle.
London; Hart-Davis; 1966. 133pp., pls. 8vo.

1882. LEYLAND, John.
The campaign of Trafalgar.
In: The Naval Annual (Portsmouth; J.Griffin; 1905),
pp.215–29.

1883. LEYLAND, John.
The Trafalgar centenary and its literature.
In: The Naval Annual (Portsmouth; J.Griffin; 1906),
pp.192–203.

1884. LLOYD, *Professor* Christopher.
Trafalgar: October 21, 1805: the 150th anniversary.
History Today, vol.v (1955), pp.689–696.

1885. LOVELL, *Vice-Admiral* William Stanhope,
(1787–1859).
Letter when a midshipman in *HMS Neptune*,
describing the battle of Trafalgar.
English Historical Review, vol.5 (1890).

1886. MACKENZIE, *Colonel* Robert Holden.
The Trafalgar Roll, containing the names and
services of all officers of the Royal Navy and Royal
Marines who participated . . . together with a history
of the ships engaged in the Battle.
London; Geo.Allen; 1913. xii, 336pp., pls. 8vo.
    *A detailed and valuable analysis, covering every
British ship engaged from the flagship* HMS VICTORY *to
the cutter* HMS ENTREPRENANTE.

1887. MADAN, Falconer.
The Battle of Trafalgar.
Antiquary, vol.iii, (1881).
    Being an account by the purser's clerk of the NAIAD.
Includes a table of signals.

1888. MAHAN, *Rear-Admiral* Alfred Thayer, USN.
(1840–1914).
Nelson at Trafalgar.
The Century Magazine n.s., vol.xxxi (1876–7).

See also his: The Life of Nelson . . . (London; 1897),
in 2 volumes, in vol.ii of the Library Catalogue,
(Biography).

1889. MAINE, René.
Trafalgar. Napoleon's naval Waterloo.
Translated by R.Eldon and B.W.Robinson.
London; Thames & Hudson; 1957. viii, 261pp. 8vo.

1890. MALTZAHN, Curt von.
Theorie und praxis in die Schlacht von Trafalgar;
and: Nelson und die Schlacht von Trafalgar.
Marine Rundschau, vols.xv (1904), pp.887–903; *and*
xvii (1906), pp.259–273.

1891. MARLIANI, *Don* Manuel.
Combate de Trafalgar. Vindicacion de la Armada
Española.
Madrid; Impresa de Orden Superior; 1850. xxiv,
632pp. 8vo.

1892. MARSH, *Lieutenant* R.M., RN.
Spanish and French accounts of the battle of
Trafalgar.
United Service Journal, vol.cclxxvi (November 1851),
pp.337–352.

1893. MEAD, *Commander* Hilary Poland, RN.
Trafalgar signals.
London; Percival Marshall; 1936. 47pp.; illustr. 8vo.

1894. MOULLEC, R.
Quelques à côtés de Trafalgar du point de vue
espagnol.
La Revue Maritime, no.xcviii (February 1928),
pp.172–190.

1895. MORAN, Charles.
Trafalgar, the death knell of an alliance.
USNIP, vol.lxiii (1937), pp.1567–75.

1896. MORRIS, William O'Connor.
The great campaigns of Nelson. St. Vincent, The
Nile, Copenhagen, Trafalgar.
London; Blackie; [1892]. 156pp.; illustr. 8vo.

1897. [NELSON, *Vice-Admiral Lord* Horatio,
(1758–1805)].
Nelson's memorandum at Trafalgar.
    *Reproduced in: House of Commons Parlt. Paper.
Cmnd. 7120 (1913); Julian Corbett's:* 'The Trafalgar
Campagin'; & *vol.xxix of Navy Records Society
series (1905)* [q.q.v.].

1898. NEWBOLT, *Sir* Henry John, (1862–1938).
The year of Trafalgar. Being an account of the battle
and of the events which led up to it . . .
London; John Murray; 1905. 244pp. pls. 8vo.

1899. NEWBOLT, *Sir* Henry John, (1862–1938).
Trafalgar in theory and fact.
National Review, vol.xlvi. (1905–6).

1900. OLOW, Ned.
Fartygen vid Trafalgar.
Unda Maris, (Göteborg; Sjöfartsmuseet; 1971–2),
pp.95–109, illustr.

1901. PEREZ de GUZMAN y GALLO, Juan.
Documentos sobre el combate naval de Trafalgar.
Bulletin. Real. Acad. Hist., vol.xlix (1906), pp.391–406.

1902. PEREZ GALDÓS, Benito.
Trafalgar.
Edited with notes & introduction by F.A.
Kirkpatrick.
Cambridge; 1905. xv, 296pp. 8vo.

1903. POPE, Dudley.
England Expects.
London; Weidenfeld & Nicholson; 1959. 368pp.,
pls. & charts. 8vo.

1904. ROSE, *Professor* John Holland, (1855–1942).
The true significance of Trafalgar.
Independent Review, (November 1905).

1905. ROSE, *Professor* John Holland, (1855–1942).
Nelson's approach at Trafalgar.
Discovery, vol.i (1920), pp.327–330; plan.

1906. ROSE, *Professor* John Holland, (1855–1942).
The state of Nelson's fleet before Trafalgar.
The Mariner's Mirror, vol.viii (March 1922),
pp.75–81.

1907. ROSKRUGE, *Engineer-Commander* F.J., RN.
The *Victory* after Trafalgar.
The Mariner's Mirror, vol.vii (September 1921),
pp.267–271.

1908. SARGEAUNT, B.E.
Lord Nelson's signal.
RUSIJ, vol.lii (October 1908), pp.1403–1405.

1909. SENHOUSE, *Sir* Humphrey le Fleming.
Trafalgar.
Macmillan's Magazine (April 1900), pp.415–425.

1910. SMITH, *Dr.* David Baird.
The *Defiance* at Trafalgar.
Scottish Historical Review (1923), pp.116–121.

1911. STEEL, David.
Steel's Naval Chronologist of the late war . . .
including also a copious description of Lord Nelson's
victory off Cape Trafalgar in 1805.
London; Steel; 1806. xii, 122pp. oblong 12mo.
  The author also of 'Steel's Navy Lists . . .', *over the
same period.* [q.q.v. *in vol.ii of the Library Catalogue:
Biography, part i: Navy lists*].

1912. TAYLOR, *Rear-Admiral* Alfred Hugh.
Some new aspects of the battle of Trafalgar.
RUSIJ, vol.lxxxii (November 1937), pp.692–709.

1913. TAYLOR, *Rear-Admiral* Alfred Hugh.
The battle of Trafalgar.
The Mariner's Mirror, vol.xxxvi (October 1950),
pp.281–321, plans, figs., & appendices.

1914. TAYLOR, *Rear-Admiral* Alfred Hugh.
Trafalgar – 21st October 1805.
Naval Review, vol.xliii (1955), pp.386–395.

1915. THOMAZI, Auguste Antoine.
Trafalgar.
Paris; 1932. 202pp.; illustr., plans. 8vo.

1916. THURSFIELD, *Sir* James Richard, (1840–1923).
The tactics of Trafalgar.
In: The Naval Annual, (Portsmouth; J.Griffin; 1911),
pp.111–140.

1917. TIZARD, *Captain* Thomas Henry, RN (1839–1924).
Report on the track of the British Fleet, 19–21
October 1805.
*In: House of Commons, Parliamentary Paper, Cmnd.
7120. (1913)*.

1918. VILLIERS, Alan.
The Battle of Trafalgar. Lord Nelson sweeps the sea.
London; Macmillan; 1965. 96pp., pls. 8vo.

1919. WARNER, Oliver.
Trafalgar.
London; Batsford; 1959. ['British battles' series].
184pp., illustr. 8vo.

1920. WARNER, Oliver.
Nelson's Battles.
London; Batsford; 1965. ['British Battles' series].
254pp., pls. 8vo.

1921. WARNER, Oliver.
The court-martial of Sir Robert Calder, 1805.
History Today, vol.xix (1969), pp.863–8.

1921. WARNER, *continued*
    The unsatisfactory outcome of the action off Finisterre on 22 July 1805 – in which Calder met Villeneuve and the French fleet returning from the West Indies, but failed to achieve decisive results, notwithstanding the foggy weather – led to the admiral's court-martial.

1922. WESTALL, A.L.
Nelson and the Trafalgar centenary.
Monthly Review, vol.xx (1905).

1923. WILSON, Herbert Wrigley, (1866–1940).
Trafalgar and today.
National Review, vol.xxviii, (1896–7).

1924. [Anonymous].
The Monthly Mirror, (November 1805).
    Contains long accounts of the battle of Trafalgar; the Extraordinary Gazettes of 6, 11, 16 and 27 November 1805; Collingwood's despatches and Strachan's account of his action of 4 November 1805.

1925. [Anonymous].
The Naval Chronicle, vols.xiv, xv & xvi. (1806–7).
    Includes detailed contemporary accounts of the battle of Trafalgar, as addenda to the biographical memoir of Nelson.

1926. [Anonymous].
The British Flag triumphant! or, the Wooden Walls of Old England; being copies of the London Gazettes, containing the accounts of the great victories . . . of the British Fleets, during the last and present war . . .
London; Rivington; 1806. 108pp. 8vo.
    With accounts of Trafalgar and Strachan's action off Cape Ortegal, 4 November 1805.

1927. [Anonymous].
Facsimile of a letter from a French naval officer describing the battle of Trafalgar, with plan.
RUSIJ, vol.lii (1908), p.1321.

1928. [Anonymous].
Historical Manuscripts Commission Reports, vol.v. (1909): Edmonstone Mss.
Pp.181–3: contain orders to Captain Sir Thomas Livingstone from Nelson, (14 October 1805).

1929. [Anonymous].
Report of a Committee appointed by the Admiralty to examine . . . the tactics employed by Nelson at Trafalgar.
House of Commons Parliamentary Paper; Cmnd. 1720. (1913).
    Includes extracts from the logs and journals; schedule of signals made; a plan and a bibliography. The signatures of the members of the Committee – Admiral Sir Cyprian Bridge, Admiral Sir Reginald Custance, Professor Charles H.Firth, and W.G.Perrin – are recorded in this work.

1930. [Anonymous].
La tattica di Nelson alla battaglia di Trafalgar.
Revista Marittima, vol.xlvi (1913), pp.243–257; map.

1931. [Anonymous].
Trafalgar. Final instructions issued by Admiral Villeneuve before the battle.
Naval Review, vol.xii (1924), p.589.

1932. [Anonymous].
The Trafalgar General Order Book of *HMS Mars*.
In: *The Mariner's Mirror*, vol.xxii (January 1936), pp.87–104.
    Her commander, Captain George Duff, was killed in the battle.

II. Home Waters, North Sea and the Baltic

1933. BEUTLICH, F.
Norges Sjøvaebning, 1750–1809.
Oslo; H.Aschehoug; 1935. 483pp. 8vo.
The greater part of this book is concerned with the first two years of the Swedes and Danes war with England, after the seizure of the Danish fleet in 1807.

1934. BRETT-JAMES, Anthony.
The Walcheren failure, 1809.
History Today, vols.xiii (1963), pp.811–820, & xiv (1964), pp.60–68.

1935. [CHAMBERS, *Surgeon* Charles].
The bombardment of Copenhagen, 1807 – Journal of Surgeon Charles Chambers of HM fireship *Prometheus*.
In: The Naval Miscellany, vol.iii, (Navy Records Society series, vol.lxiii; 1928), pp.367–466.
With an introductory note by W.H.Perrin.

1936. CHRISTIE, K.
The Walcheren expedition.
University of Dundee Ph.D thesis; (1972).

1937. CROOKES, Septimus.
Particulars of the expedition to Copenhagen, with an account of the siege and bombardment . . . in 1807 . . . including a list of the captured Fleet, ships names, rates, and when built . . .
By Septimus Crookes, Private in the Fourth, or King's Own Regiment.
Sheffield; Slater, Bacon; 1808. 24pp. 8vo.

1938. DALY, *Lieutenant-Commander* Robert W.
Operations of the Russian Navy during the reign of Napoleon I, 1801–1815.
The Mariner's Mirror, vol.xxxiv (July 1948), pp.169–183.

1939. GACHOT, Edouard.
Le projet de descente en Angleterre en 1804 . . .
Correspondent, vol.ccxvi (1904), pp.128–143.

1940. GLOVER, *Professor* Richard.
Britain at bay. Defence against Bonaparte, 1803–4.
London; Allen & Unwin/New York; Barnes & Noble; 1973. [x], 235pp. 8vo.

1941. GREY, Walter.
Proceedings on a motion for inquiry into the conduct and policy of the late expedition to the Scheldt . . .
London; A.Topping for J.Stratford; [1809]. 168pp.,; 1 map; 1 chart. 8vo.
Being the minutes of the evidence presented to the House of Commons, following the disastrous expedition to Walcheren in 1809.

1942. LAUGHTON, *Sir* John Knox, (1830–1915).
[editor].
[a]. Official correspondence relating to the seizure of Heligoland, 1807.
In: The Naval Miscellany, vol.i. (Navy Records Society series, vol.xx; 1902).
[b]. Operations in the Scheldt, 1809.
In: The Naval Miscellany, vol.ii. (Navy Records Society series, vol.xl; 1912).

1943. LÜTKEN, *Kapitän* Otto.
De Danske paa Schelden, (1809–1813).
Copenhagen; A.F.Høst; 1888. 154pp. 8vo.

1944. MALONE, Joseph J.
England and the Baltic naval stores trade in the seventeenth and eighteenth centuries.
The Mariner's Mirror, vol.lviii (November 1972), pp.375–395.

1945. MARSHALL, M.A.N.
The hired armed ships of Kent.
The Mariner's Mirror, vol.xliv (August 1958), pp.244–249.
Of the period ca. 1803–1815.

1946. McGUFFIE, T.H.
The Walcheren expedition and the Walcheren fever.
English Historical Review, vol.lxii (1947), p.191.

1947. MORTIMER, M.
Some naval problems of Scilly in Napoleonic times.
The Mariner's Mirror, vol.xlvii (November 1961), pp.291–295.

1948. RUSSELL, *Admiral* Thomas Macnamara.
(1743–1824).
The seizure of Heligoland, 1807.
In: The Naval Miscellany, vol.i. (Navy Records Society series; 1902).

1949. RYAN, Anthony N.
The British expedition to Copenhagen in 1807.
Julian Corbett Prize Essay; 1951.
Précis in: *IHRBull.*, vol.xxxv (November 1952), pp.231–2.

1950. RYAN, Anthony N.
The Navy at Copenhagen in 1807.
The Mariner's Mirror, vol.xxxix (August 1953),
pp.201–210.

1951. RYAN, Anthony N.
The causes of the British attack on Copenhagen in
1807.
English Historical Review, vol.lxviii (1953), pp.37–55.

1952. RYAN, Anthony N.
The defence of British trade with the Baltic, 1808–
1813.
English Historical Review, vol.lxxiv (1959), pp.443–
446.

1953. RYAN, Anthony N.
Trade with the enemy in the Scandinavian and
Baltic ports during the Napoleonic Wars; for and
against.
RHS Trans., 5th series, vol.xii (1962), pp.123–140.

1954. RYAN, Anthony N.
The melancholy fate of the Baltic ships in 1811.
The Mariner's Mirror, vol.l (February 1964), pp.123–
134; 1 map.

1955. [SAUMAREZ, *Admiral* James, KB, *First Baron
de Saumarez*, (1757–1836).
The Saumarez papers.
Selections from the Baltic correspondence of Vice-
Admiral Sir James Saumarez, 1808–1812. *edited* by
A.N.Ryan.
London; Navy Records Society series, vol.cx; 1968.
xxvi, 288pp.; plates & maps. 8vo.
    *After distinguished service – including two notable
actions off Algeçiras and Gibraltar in July 1801 –
Saumarez in 1808 was appointed to the Baltic
Squadron, which he commanded for the next five years.*

1956. SCHEEN, *Commander* Rolf.
A tale of the Norwegian and Danish sailors who
manned warships of Napoleon's Scheldt Navy.
Marine Academie Mededelingen, boek xvii (Antwerp;
1965), pp.123–139.

1957. [SCHELDT, The].
Naval State Papers relating to the Scheldt expedition,
1809–10.
In: Naval Chronicle, vol.xxiii (1810), pp.113–135;
200–241; and 301–9.

1958. SCHOPPEN, Werner.
Grossbritannien und die Ostsee, 1780 bis 1812.
Wissen und Wehr (1939), pp.713–720; 745–757.

1959. WARNER, Oliver.
The Sea and the Sword. The Baltic: 1630–1946.
London; Jonathan Cape; 1965. 320pp., illustr. 8vo.
    *Includes chapters on the importance of the Baltic in the
French Wars, 1803–1815.*

1960. [Anonymous].
Accounts of the proceedings at Copenhagen, 1807.
In: Naval Chronicle (1807), vols.xviii, pp.228–235;
247–266; 429–474 *and* xix, pp.66; 185; 191 & 492.

1961. [Anonymous].
Great Britain: Government Reports and Navy
Estimates.
1808: Papers relating to the Copenhagen expedition.
Account of transports employed on the Copenhagen
expedition. Declaration of His Majesty in
justification of the attack on Copenhagen.

1962. [Anonymous].
Copenhagen. The real state of the case respecting
the late expedition.
London; J.Ridgway; 1808. 17pp. 8vo.

1963. [Anonymous].
Naval papers respecting Copenhagen, Portugal and
the Dardanelles, presented to Parliament in 1808.
London; A.Strachan; 1809. 145pp. 8vo.
    *Includes official papers and reports on the expedition to
Copenhagen, 1807.*

1964. [Anonymous].
Letters from Flushing; containing an account of the
expedition to Walcheren, Beveland and the mouth
of the Scheldt, under the command of the Earl of
Chatham.
London; Richard Phillips; 1809. 286pp., pls. 8vo.

1965. [Anonymous].
Account of the expedition to the island of
Walcheren, 1809.
In: Naval Chronicle (1809), vols.xxii, pp.75, 133, 140
et seq., *and* xxiii, pp.77–83.

1966. [Anonymous].
A collection of Papers relating to the expedition to
the Scheldt, presented to Parliament in 1810.
London; A.Strachan; 1811. 792pp. 8vo.
    *A full account of the disastrous Walcheren expedition,
1809. Includes details of the preparation and operation of
the naval force; the subsequent statements by Lord
Chatham and the despatches and letters of Rear-Admiral
Sir Richard Strachan.*

1967. [Anonymous].
Recollections of Walcheren in 1809.
United Service Journal, no.vi (June 1829), pp.695–701.

1968. [Anonymous].
Expedition to Walcheren in 1809.
United Service Journal, nos.cxviii (September 1838),
pp.48–57 *and* cxix (October 1838), pp.182–192.

1969. [Anonymous].
British minor expeditions, 1746–1814.
London; HMSO; 1884. 91pp., numerous plans &
maps. 8vo.
 *Although chiefly a military survey, there is important
naval material in the account of the following expeditions:
to Copenhagen, 1807; to Walcheren, 1809; to Bergen-
op-Zoom, 1813–14.*

1970. [Anonymous].
With the expedition to Walcheren in 1809.
Blackwood's Magazine, vol.clxxxviii (1910), pp.287–
308.

III. The Mediterranean and the Peninsular War

1971. ANDERSON, *Dr.* Roger Charles.
Naval wars in the Levant, 1559–1853.
Liverpool; University Press; 1952. 619pp., pls &
plans. 8vo.
 *Includes a chapter on naval operations in the Levant
during the Napoleonic period.*

1972. [COLLINGWOOD, *Vice-Admiral* Cuthbert,
first Baron Collingwood, (1750–1810)].
The Private correspondence of Admiral Lord
Collingwood.
Edited by Edward Hughes.
London; Navy Records Society; 1957. [Society
series, vol.xcviii]. xiv, 348 + [6]pp. 8vo.
 *With much material during his command in the
Mediterranean.*

1973. DAVIN, Emmanuel.
La Proserpine et le combat naval des Sablettes, (28
Fevrier 1809).
Neptunia, vol.xxxiii (January 1954), pp.9–13.
 The frigate PROSERPINE, *32, was becalmed south of
Toulon and then intercepted and taken by the French 40-
gun frigates* PÉNÉLOPE, PAULINE *and* POMONE.

1974. DEGOUY, *Amiral* —.
Quel role la marine aurait elle pu jouer à la fin de la
campagne de Portugal en 1808?
La Revue Maritime, no.cxlvi, (February 1932), p.145.

1975. DOUGHTY, Katharine Frances.
The capture of Alexandria in 1807.
United Service Magazine, vol.clxxx (1919), pp.54–60.

1976. GWILLIAM, R.G.
The Dardanelles expedition of 1807.
University of Liverpool, MA thesis; 1955.

1977. [KALLISTOVA, *Lieutenant* H.D.].
ДѢЙСТВІЯ РУССКАГО ФЛОТА ВЬ ВОЙНѢ
СЪ ТУРЦІЕЙ ВЪ 1807 ГОДУ.
[The activities of the Russian Fleet in the War
against Turkey, 1807].
St. Petersburg; 1908–1912. In three parts; 43pp., 3
charts of the Dardanelles. 8vo.

1978. [KALLISTOVA . . .].
ПРОРЫВЪ ЧЕРЕЗЪ ДАРДАНЕЛЛЫ И
БОСФОРЪ И ВЗЯТІЕ КОНСТАНТИНОПО-
ЛЯ СЬ МОРЯ... ВОЙНЫ РОССІН СЬ
ТУРЦІЕЙ 1806–12 ГГ.

1978. [KALLISTOVA . . .], *continued*
[Studies of the Dardanelles, the Bosphorus and the
seizure of Constantinople by sea . . . in the War
between Russia and Turkey, 1806–1812].

1979. [KUMANIYA, H.M.].
ДѢЙСТВІЯ ЧЕРНОМОРСКАГО ФЛОТА ВЬ
ЦАРСТВОВАНІЕ ИМПЕРАТОРА АЛЕК-
САНДРА I-го СЬ 1801 ПО 1826 ГГ.
[The operations of the Black Sea Fleet in the reign
of Emperor Alexander I, 1801–1826].
St. Petersburg; 1900.
In: МОРСК СБОРН, pp.37–63; 51–79; 37–86.
bound. 8vo.

1980. MACFARLAN, P.C.
Commander in the Adriatic: Sir William Hoste,
1780–1828.
History Today, vol.xx (1970), pp.107–111.
    *Especially of his victory over the Franco–Venetian
squadron under Dubourdieu off Lissa Island on 13
March, 1811.*

1981. MACKESY, *Professor* Piers G.
British strategy in the Mediterranean, 1803–1810.
University of Oxford D.Phil thesis; 1953.
Précis in IHR Bull., no.xv (May 1954).

1982. MACKESY, *Professor* . . .
To rescue His Holiness – the mission of the *Alceste* in
1808.
The Mariner's Mirror, vol.xl (August 1954), pp.206–
211.

1983. MACKESY, *Professor* . . .
Collingwood and Ganteaume: the French offensive
in the Mediterranean, January to April 1808.
The Mariner's Mirror, vol.xli (February 1955),
pp.3–14; 137–148.

1984. MACKESY, *Professor* . . .
The War in the Mediterranean, 1803–1810.
London; Longmans; 1957. 430pp., appendices. 8vo.
    *An excellent study, being an expansion of his doctoral
thesis (see above). There are chapters on: Nelson's
command; the War of the Third Coalition; the struggle
between Collingwood and Gauteaume. The appendices
include details of British naval strength in the
Mediterranean, 1803–1810; distribution of the
Mediterranean Fleet, 8 March, 1808; and enemy naval
forces in Mediterranean ports, 1805–1810.*

1985. MACKESY, *Professor* . . .
Collingwood in the Mediterranean.
History Today, vol.x (1960), pp.202–210.

1986. MAGUIRE, T.Miller.
The British in the Iberian Peninsula, as illustrating
sea power, and strategy.
London; Aldershot Military Society; 1905. 77pp. 8vo.

1987. MARTIN, Harrison P.
The tragi-comedy of Corcubion.
USNIP, vol.lxviii (July 1942), pp.982–5.
    *About the abortive effort to succour Spanish guerillas,
operating on the NW coast of Galicia near Finisterre, in
1809.*

1988. MÄRZ, Josef.
Eine English–Italienische seeschlacht vor 125 jahren:
Lissa, 13 March 1811.
Marine Rundschau, vol.xli (April 1936), pp.190–1.
    See also entry no.1980.

1989. MONTANI, M.
Quelques notes sur le Rivoli au combat de Pirano.
Neptunia, vol.lxviii (April 1962), pp.19–23.
    *On 22 February 1812, there was an action between
HMS VICTORIOUS and WEASEL and the French frigate
RIVOLI off Pirano in the Adriatic.*

1990. MORRIS, N.
The *Constitution* off Tripoli in 1808.
USNIP, vol.lii (1926), pp.127–9; illustr.

1991. O'NEIL, *Lieutenant-Cmdr.* Thomas, RM.
A concise and accurate account of the proceedings
of the squadron under the command of Rear-
Admiral Sir Sydney Smith . . . in effecting the
escape of the Royal Family of Portugal to the
Brazils, on November 29, 1807 . . .
London; J.Barfield; 1810. 89pp., frontis. 8vo.

1992. RODGERS, Robert S.
Closing events of the war with Tripoli, 1804–1805.
USNIP, vol.xxxiv (1908), pp.889–916.

1993. ROSE, *Professor* John Holland, (1855–1942).
Sir John Duckworth's expedition to Constantinople.
Naval Review, vol.vii (1920), p.485.

1994. SAINSBURY, A.B.
Sir John Duckworth and the Dardanelles, 1807.
Julian Corbett prize essay: 1965.
Summarised in: IHR Bull., vol.xl (May 1967),
pp.112–114.

1995. SHORE, *Commander* Henry Noel, *5th Baron
Teignmouth*, (1847–1926).
The Navy in the Peninsular War.
The Navy and Wellington's army.

1995. SHORE, *continued*
The Navy and the lines of Torres Vedras.
United Service Magazine, vols.clxvi (1912) – clxx
(1914), *passim*.

1996. SHORE, *Commander* Henry Noel, *5th Baron
Teignmouth*, (1847–1926).
A famous sea fight in the last great war.
Chambers' Journal, series 7, vol.vii (1917), pp.333–336.
  *An account of the action between English and French
frigates in the Gulf of Salonica, 1808.*

1997. SHORE, *Commander* Henry Noel, *5th Baron
Teignmouth*, (1847–1926).
Briton and Turk in the Aegean Sea, 1807–1914.
RUSIJ, vol.lxiv (November 1919), p.660, *seq*.

1998. SPINNEY, David B.
The evacuation of Naples, 1806.
The Mariner's Mirror, vol.xvi, (January 1930),
pp.90–91 (n).

1999. USSHER, *Rear-Admiral Sir* Thomas, CB.
(1779–1848).
Narrative of the embarkation and conveyance of
Napoleon from Fréjus to Elba in the *Undaunted*
frigate, with personal anecdotes and opinions of the
ex-Emperor on the voyage and after his occupation
of that island.
United Service Journal, no.cxliii (October 1840),
pp.145–169.

2000. WARNER, Oliver.
Collingwood and Nelson.
History Today, vol.xvi (1966), pp.811–817.

2001. [Anonymous].
Great Britain: Parliamentary Reports & Navy
Estimates.
1808 [Cmnd. 129; 167–8].: Papers relative to the
Dardanelles expedition, 1807.
1815 [Cmnd. 55; 141].: Papers respecting naval
operations in the Adriatic.

2002. [Anonymous].
Naval papers respecting Copenhagen, Portugal and
the Dardanelles, presented to Parliament in 1808.
London; A.Strachan; 1809. 145pp. 8vo.
  *Includes papers and official reports on: the transport of
the expeditionary force to the Tagus, August 1806;
Duckworth's squadron and his operations in the
Dardanelles, end–1806/early 1807.*

2003. [Anonymous].
The loss of His Majesty's ship *Nautilus*, 1807.
Naval Review, vol.xxxvi (1948), pp.281–3.
  The sloop NAUTILUS *was wrecked in the Aegean on 3
January, 1807.*

IV. The Atlantic Ocean, coast of France and exile of Napoleon

2004. BROCK, *Lieutenant (now Rear-Admiral)* P.W.,
CB, DSO.
Lord Cochrane's secret plans.
The Mariner's Mirror, vol.xvi (April 1930), pp.157–
167.
  *Concerning a variety of proposals made by Cochrane
in 1812, including – combined operations to secure the
capture of islands off the French Atlantic coast; cutting
the enemy's coastal telegraphs; experimental mortar and
explosion ships.*

2005. [COCKBURN, *Admiral of the Fleet Sir*
George, (1772–1853)].
Extracts from the diary of Rear-Admiral Sir George
Cockburn, with particular reference to General
Napoleon Buonaparte on passage from England to
St. Helena in 1815, on board *HMS Northumberland*,
bearing the Rear-Admiral's flag.
London; Simpkin, Marshall; 1888. 96pp. 12mo.

2006. EMMANUEL-BROUSSE, Charles.
Les consignes secrètes données à la marine de guerre
anglaise pour la garde de Napoléon à Sainte Hélène.
Révue Études Napoleoniennes, vol.xxv (July 1936),
pp.56–64.

2007. GLOVER, J.R.
Napoléon à bord du *Northumberland*.
La Revue Maritime, nos.clxxi–clxxxiii (January–
March 1935), pp.3–39; 190–215; 325–355.

2008. INGRAM, *Sir* Bruce Stirling, (1877–1963).
The occupation of Tristan da Cunha.
The Mariner's Mirror, vol.xxi (January 1935), pp.31–2.
  'On the 2nd August, 1816, His Majesty's Ship
FALMOUTH *quitted St. Helena and on the 14th . . .
arrived off the Island of Tristan da Cunha, which
pursuant to orders from England, was to be taken
possession of in the King's name, and a garrison left on it,
consisting of officers and men belonging to the ship. . .'* .
[*From the Journal of Midshipman William Burnaby
Greene of* HMS FALMOUTH.]

2009. LEYLAND, John. [*editor*].
Dispatches and letters relating to the Blockade of
Brest, 1803–5.
London; Navy Records Society series, vols.xiv &
xxi; 1899–1902. 2 volumes.
i. lxvi, 369pp., map. ii. liv, 390pp., pls. 8vo.
  *An important source, with valuable introductions in
both volumes.*

2010. MAITLAND, *Rear-Admiral Sir* Frederick
Lewis, (1776–1839).
Narrative of the surrender of Buonaparte and of his
residence on board *HMS Bellerophon*; with a detail
of the principal events that occurred in that ship,
between the 24th of May and the 8th of August,
1815.
London; Henry Colburn; 1826. Second edition.
xvi; 248pp.,; map. 8vo.

2011. MAITLAND, *Rear-Admiral Sir* Frederick
Lewis, (1776–1839).
The surrender of Napoleon. Being the narrative of
the surrender of Buonaparte and of his residence on
board *HMS Bellerophon*, with a detail of the
principal events that occurred . . .
Edinburgh & London; Blackwood; 1904. lxxvii,
261pp.; pls. 8vo.

2012. [MAITLAND, *Rear-Admiral Sir* Frederick
Lewis, (1776–1839).].
Napoleon à bord du *Bellerophon*. Souvenirs du
Capitaine de vaisseau F.L.Maitland. Translated by
Henri Borjane.
La Revue Maritime, nos.clxvi–clxviii (October–
December 1933), pp.433–480; 616–652; & 773–806.

2013. McGUFFIE, T.H.
The Stone Ships expedition against Boulogne, 1804.
English Historical Review, vol.lxiv (October 1949),
pp.488–503.
   *Being the project to blockade the entrances to the port
and thereby hamper the French invasion plans.*

2014. McKAY, Derek.
Great Britain and Ireland in 1809.
The Mariner's Mirror, vol.lix (February 1973),
pp.85–95.

2015. QUINN, Dorothy M.
Napoleon on board the *Bellerophon*.
USNIP, vol.cxxxix (1953), pp.628–633.

2016. RODGERS, *Vice-Admiral* William Ledyard,
USN.
A study of attacks upon fortified harbours.
USNIP, vol.xxx (1904), pp.533–566.
   *Includes material on the attack on the French Fleet in
Basque and Aix Roads, and the Flushing expedition,
1809.*

2017. SHORTER, Clement. [*editor*].
Napoleon and his fellow travellers. Being a reprint
of certain narratives of the voyage of the dethroned
Emperor on the *Bellerophon* and the *Northumberland*
to exile in St. Helena . . .

London; Cassell; 1908. 332pp., pls. 8vo.
   *The narratives reproduced are those of: George Home;
Captain Ross; Lord Lyttelton and William Warden.*

2018. SIEGEL, Michael H.
Lord Cochrane's explosion vessels.
The Mariner's Mirror, vol.lvii (November 1971),
p.378.
   *Used at Basque & Aix Roads, April 1809. See also
entry no.2004 and below.*

2019. SILVESTRE, Pierre Jules.
Les brulôts anglais en rade de l'Île d'Aix.
Paris; 1912. xv, 252pp., map. 8vo.

2020. THORNTON, Michael John.
Napoleon after Waterloo. England and the St.
Helena decision.
Stanford, California; University Press; 1968. 241pp.
8vo.
   *'. . . mainly a day by day account of the two weeks
during July and August of 1815, that Napoleon spent on
board the British ships of war* BELLEROPHON *and*
NORTHUMBERLAND *off the English coast, while the
Cabinet debated his fate. . .'.*

2021. [USSHER, *Rear-Admiral Sir* Thomas, CB.
(1779–1848)].
Napoleon's last voyages. Being the diaries of
Admiral Sir Thomas Ussher, RN, KCB, (on board the
Undaunted) and John R.Glover, secretary to Rear-
Admiral Cockburn (on board the *Northumberland*).
New edition, with introduction and notes by
J.Holland Rose.
London; Unwin; 1906. 247pp. 8vo.

2022. WARDEN, *Surgeon* William.
Letters written on board His Majesty's Ship the
Northumberland, and at St. Helena; in which the
conduct and conversation of Napoleon Buonaparte
and his suite . . . are faithfully described and related
by William Warden, Surgeon on board the
Northumberland.
London; Richard Ackermann; [1816]. 215pp.,
frontis. 8vo.
   *A copy of the third edition of this work is also in the
Library.*

2023. [Anonymous].
Account of the destruction of the French fleet in
Basque Roads, April 11 1809, by Lord Cochrane.
Naval Chronicle, vol.xxi (1809), pp.315; 344–7;
368–75; 399; 403–7 & 412–14.
   *Part of this account derives from a journal kept by an
officer of* HMS VALIANT *at the time.*

I. Mayfield.   J. Ward.   J. Chesterman.   I. Fitzgerald.

J. Rowland.   T. Jones.   T. Crofs.   W. Cook.

C. White.   J. Collins.   J. Locker.   I. Cummins.

W. Hillier.   I. Dayley.

PORTRAITS of the MUTINEERS

PLATE XI: Portraits of the Mutineers. Frontispiece of: *The Trial of the Mutineers, late of His Majesty's Ship Temeraire . . . January 6, 1802*. London; 1802

SIR JAMES SAUMAREZ BAR.ᵗ

FIDELIS ET GENEROSUS

Rear Admiral of the Blue Squadron

PLATE XII: Admiral Sir James Saumarez, K.B. (1757–1836). From: *The Naval Chronicle, vol. vi. (July–December 1801)*. London; 1802

2024. [Anonymous].
The passage of the Gironde in 1815.
United Service Journal, no.cxlvi (January 1841),
pp.13–25.

2025. [Anonymous].
The blockade of Brest.
Edinburgh Review, vol.cxcvii (1903), pp.1–33.

V. North America and the West Indies: especially the War of 1812

2026. ADAMS, Reed M.E.
New Orleans and the war of 1812.
Louisiana Hist. Quart., vols.xvi (1933) *and* xvii (1934),
pp.169 *passim*.

2027. AINSWORTH, Walden Lee.
An amphibious operation that failed: the battle of
New Orleans.
USNIP, vol.lxxi (February 1945), pp.193–201.
   Towards the end of 1814 a British squadron under
Vice-Admiral Sir Alexander Cochrane, escorting an
expeditionary force, arrived at the mouth of the
Mississippi. An attack made on 14 December upon five
United States gunboats moored in the shallows of Lake
Borgne was fiercely resisted. The subsequent British
operations on land failed.

2028. AMME, Carl Henry.
Chesapeake versus *Shannon*.
USNIP, vol.lxxx (1954), pp.214–215.

2029. APGAR, Wilbur E.
William H.Allen and the *Chesapeake – Leopard* affair.
USNIP, vol.lxiii (1937), pp.115–116.

2030. BALDRIDGE, Harry Alexander.
How the *Constitution* escaped.
USNIP, vols.liii (1927), pp.623–9 *& liv, p.342.
   From a superior British force, 17 July 1812.

2031. BARNES, James.
Naval actions of the War of 1812.
New York; Harper; 1896. xiv, 263pp., pls. 8vo.
   There is also a copy of the 1897 English edition,
(London; Osgood McVaine), in the Library.

2032. BARNES, James.
Yankee ships and Yankee sailors: tales of 1812.
New York; Grosset & Dunlap; 1897. ix, 281pp.,
pls. 8vo.

2033. BAX, *Admiral* Robert N.
The epic of Diamond Rock, an extemporized naval
base of 1804.
RUSIJ, vol.lxxx (August 1935), pp.567–571.
   In January 1804 a party of men from the CENTAUR,
74, (Commodore Samuel Hood), seized the Diamond
Rock – a small precipitous islet lying ¾ mile SW of Fort
Royal, Martinique. Equipped with gun-batteries and a
garrison of 120 men, it was commissioned as HM sloop
of war DIAMOND ROCK.

2034. BIRD, Harrison.
Navies in the mountains. The battles on the waters
of Lake Champlain and Lake George, 1809–1814.
New York; Oxford University Press; 1962. xii,
361pp., plt & maps. 8vo.

2035. BOSWALL, *Captain* John Donaldson, RN.
Narrative of the capture of the Diamond Rock,
effected by Sir Samuel Hood in the *Centaur*.
United Service Journal, no.lv (June 1933), pp.210–215.
   See entries nos.: 2033, 2061, 2081, 2097.

2036. BRANNAN, John. [*editor*].
Official letters of the military and naval officers of
the United States, during the war with Great Britain
in the years 1812, 13, 14 & 15. With additional
letters and documents elucidating the history of that
period.
New York; Arno Press; 1971. 510pp. 8vo.
   A facsimile reprint of the 1823 Washington edition.

2037. BROWN, Wilbur S.
The amphibious campaign for West Florida and
Louisiana, 1814–1815. A critical review of strategy
and tactics at New Orleans.
Alabama; University Press; 1969. xii, 233pp., maps.
8vo.

2038. CHAPELLE, Howard I.
The ships of the American Navy in the War of 1812.
The Mariner's Mirror, vol.xviii (July 1932), pp.287–
302.

2039. COLES, Harry L.
The War of 1812.
Chicago/London; University of Chicago Press;
1965. ix, 298pp., pls. 2 maps. 8vo.

2040. CRUIKSHANK, Ernest Alex.
The contest for the command of Lake Ontario in
1812, 1813 and 1814.
Proc. & Trans. Royal Society of Canada (ser.3), vol.x
(1917), pp.161–223 *and Ontario Hist. Soc. Papers*,
vol.xxi (1924), pp.99–159.

2041. CRUIKSHANK, Ernest Alex.
An episode of the War of 1812. The story of the
schooner *Nancy*.
Ontario Hist. Soc. Papers, vol.ix (1910), pp.75–126.

2042. CUMBERLAND, Barlow.
The navies on Lake Ontario in the War of 1812 . . .
Ontario Hist. Soc. Papers, vol.viii (1907), pp.124–142;
illustr.

2043. DENNIS, D.L.
The action between the *Shannon* and the *Chesapeake*,
1 June 1813.
The Mariner's Mirror, vol.xlv (February 1959),
pp.36–45.

2044. DENT, K.S.
The British Navy in the Anglo–American War of
1812.
University of Leeds MA thesis; 1949.
Précis in IHR Bull., vol.x, part 2 (December 1948).

2045. DIETZ, Anthony G.
The use of cartel vessels during the war of 1812.
American Neptune, vol.xxviii (1968), pp.165–194.

2046. DOWLING, Christopher.
The convoy system and the West Indian trade,
1803–1815.
University of Oxford D.Phil thesis; 1965.
Précis in IHR Bull., vol.xxvii (May 1966).

2047. DUDLEY, C.E.S.
The *Leopard* incident, 1807.
History Today, vol.xix (1969), pp.468–474.
   About the encounter between the LEOPARD *and the*
   CHESAPEAKE *off the Virginia coast, 22 June 1807. See
   also entry no.2049.*

2048. DUNN, *Commander* Lucius C.
A chapter from the genesis of the War of 1812.
USNIP, vol.lxv (1939), pp.1574–1586.

2049. EMMERSON, John C.
The *Chesapeake* affair of 1807. An objective account
of the attack by *HMS Leopard* upon the US frigate
Chesapeake off Cape Henry, Virginia, on June 22
1807 . . . compiled from contemporary newspaper
accounts, official documents and other authoritative
sources.
Portsmouth, Virginia; 1954. 223pp., plates. 8vo.

2050. FISHER, Charles Willis.
The log of the *Constitution*, February 21–24, 1815.
USNIP, vol.xliii (1917), pp.227–232.

2051. FORESTER, Cecil Scott, (1899–1966).
The naval war of 1812.
London; Michael Joseph; 1957. 255pp., pls. &
maps. 8vo.

2052. GARBETT, *Captain* H.J.G.
The *Shannon* and the *Chesapeake*.
RUSIJ (1913), p.797.

2053. GOUGH, Barry M.
The Royal Navy and the Northwest coast of North America, 1810–1914: a study of British maritime ascendancy.
Vancouver; University of British Columbia Press; 1971. xvi, 294pp., pls. 8vo.
    Chapter i covers the period 1810–1818.

2054. GRAHAM, *Professor* Gerald Sandford.
Seapower and British North America, 1783–1820. A study in British colonial policy.
Cambridge, Mass.; Harvard U.P.; 1941. xii, 302pp.; maps. 8vo.

2055. HILL, Ada Winifred.
The naval history of Lake Ontario and Lake Erie in the War of 1812.
Proc. New York State Hist. Assoc., vol.xiii (1914), pp.377–388.

2056. HORSMAN, Reginald.
The War of 1812.
London; Eyre & Spottiswoode; 1969. xii, 286pp., pls. 8vo.

2057. JAMES, William. [*d.*1827].
A full and correct account of the chief Naval Occurrences of the late War between Great Britain and the United States of America . . .
London; Thomas Egerton; 1817. xv, 528pp. 8vo.

2058. JAMES, William. [*d.*1827].
An inquiry into the merits of the principal naval actions between Great Britain and the United States, comprising an account of all British and American Ships of War, reciprocally captured and destroyed since the 18th of June 1812 . . .
Halifax, Nova Scotia; Anthony H.Holland; 1816. 102pp. 8vo.
    For the author's five-volume: 'The Naval History of Great Britain . . . 1793 . . . to 1820' . . ., see under General Works.

2059. JENKINS, H.J.K.
The capture of *HMS Junon*, 1809.
The Mariner's Mirror, vol.lx (February 1974), pp.33–39, diagrs.

2060. JORDAN, *Lieutenant-Commander* Douglas S., USN.
Stephen Decatur at New London; a study in strategic frustration.
USNIP, vol.xciii (1967), pp.61–65.
    In the War of 1812, Decatur commanded the UNITED STATES *in her victory over the* MACEDONIAN (*25 October 1812*), *and likewise the* PRESIDENT *against the* ENDYMION (*15 January 1815*).

2061. KALKFUS, Edward Clifford.
British 'Sloop of war' *Diamond Rock*.
USNIP, vol.liii (1927), pp.1301–2.

2062. KEMBLE, Parker H.
The *USS Essex* versus *HMS Phoebe*. [28 March 1814].
USNIP, vol.lvii (1931), pp.199–202; illustr.

2063. LARSEN, Arthur.
Scapegoat of the *Chesapeake–Shannon* battle.
USNIP, vol.lxxix (1952), pp.528–531.

2064. LEWIS, Charles.
Powell Perry's victory on Lake Erie.
USNIP, vol.li (1925), pp.1473–9.

2065. LLOYD, John H.
The last cruise of the old *Trenton*.
USNIP, vol.liii, (1927), pp.1041–1044.

2066. LOSSING, B.J.
A naval victory one hundred years ago.
Harper's Magazine, vol.lxvi (1913), p.17.
    Of the battle of Lake Erie, 10th September 1813.

2067. MAHAN, *Rear-Admiral* Alfred Thayer, USN, (1840–1914).
Sea power in its relations to the War of 1812.
London; Sampson Low; 1905. 2 volumes. i. xxiv, 423pp., pls & maps. ii. xx, 456pp., pls & maps. 8vo.
    Still a prime authority for the subject.

2068. McCLELLAN, Edwin North.
The Navy at the battle of New Orleans.
USNIP, vol.l (1924), pp.2041–2059.

2069. McKEE, Linda.
Constitution versus *Guerrière*.
USNIP, vol.lxxxviii (1962), pp.72–79.

2070. [MILNE, *Admiral Sir* David, (1763–1845).]
Letters from Captain Sir David Milne to George Home, regarding the Royal Navy on the American and West Indies Stations, 1811–1818.
Historical Manuscripts Commission: Milne Home Mss. (London; 1902), pp.145–176.

2071. MORRIS, Ruth.
Joint military and naval operations upon the waters and shores of Lake Erie in 1813.
Western Reserve Univ. Bull., vol.xvii (1914), pp.68–79.

2072. MURDOCH, Richard K.
The battle of New Orleans and associated events.
History Today, vol.xxiv (1964), pp.172–182.

2073. MURDOCH, Richard K.
Intelligence reports of British agents in the Long
Island Sound area, 1814–1815.
American Neptune, vol.xxix (1969), pp.187–198.

2074. NEESER, Robert Wilden.
The battle of Lake Erie, September 10, 1813.
USNIP, vol.xxxiv (1913), pp.921–930; illustr.

2075. PADFIELD, Peter.
Broke and the *Shannon*.
London; Hodder & Stoughton; 1968. x, 246pp.,
pls. 8vo.

2076. POOLMAN, Kenneth.
Guns off Cape Ann. The story of the *Shannon* and
the *Chesapeake*.
London; Evans; 1961. 175pp., pls. 8vo.

2077. PRUDDEN, Theodore M.
Her thunder shook the mighty deep.
USNIP, vol.xc (1964), pp.74–83.
    This is about the remarkable Atlantic cruise of the
USS CONSTITUTION, *44, (Captain Charles Stewart,*
USN) *in 1815.*

2078. PULLEN, *Rear-Admiral* H.F., RCN.
The *Shannon* and the *Chesapeake*.
Toronto/Montreal; McClelland & Stewart; 1970.
xviii, 174pp., plans. large 8vo.

2079. ROOSEVELT, *President* Theodore. (1858–
1919).
The Naval War of 1812, or the history of the
United States Navy during the last war with Great
Britain; to which is appended an account of the
battle of New Orleans.
New York; Putnams; 1894. xxxviii, 549pp. 8vo.
    Theodore Roosevelt also wrote the chapter: 'The
War with the United States, 1812–1815', in vol.vi of
Laird Clowes [q.v.].

2080. ROSE, *Professor* John Holland, (1855–1942).
British West Indies commerce as a factor in the
Napoleonic War.
Cambridge Historical Journal, vol.iii, no.1 (1925), p.17.

2081. ROWBOTHAM, *Commander* W.B.
The British occupation of the Diamond Rock,
1804–5.
Naval Review, vols.xxxvii (1949), pp.385–395 *and*
xxxix (1950), pp.53–64; *and RUSIJ* (August 1956),
pp.396.

2082. SALAS, Eugenio Pereira.
First contacts: the glorious cruise of the frigate *Essex*.
USNIP, vol.lxvi (1940), pp.218–223.

2083. SHORE, *Commander* Henry Noel, *5th Baron
Teignmouth*, (1847–1926).
Sidelights on the naval war with the United States,
(1812–14).
United Service Magazine, vol.clxxiii (1916), pp.644–
656.

2084. SNIDER, C.H.J.
In the wake of the Eighteen-Twelvers. Fights and
flights of frigates and fore-'n-afters in the War of
1812–1815 on the Great Lakes.
London; John Lane; 1913. xxii, 292pp., pls. 8vo.

2085. SOLEY, *Professor* James Russell.
Frigate actions and the naval campaign of 1812.
USNIP, vol.vii (1881), pp.297–324.

2086. STACEY, C.P.
The ships of the British squadron on Lake Ontario,
1812–14.
Canadian Historical Review, (December 1953),
pp.311–323.

2087. STACEY, C.P.
Another look at the Battle of Lake Erie.
Cambridge Historical Review, (March 1958), pp.1–11.

2088. STEEL, Anthony.
More light on the *Chesapeake*.
The Mariner's Mirror, vol.xxxix (August 1953),
pp.243–265.
    In his article the author makes the point that whereas
everyone knows about the CHESAPEAKE *v.* SHANNON
duel, English readers are less familiar '. . . with the more
inglorious story of 22 June 1807, when the ill-fated
CHESAPEAKE *struck her flag for the first time to* HMS
LEOPARD. . . .'* .

2089. STEVENS, William Oliver.
The action between the *Prince de Neufchatel* and the
Endymion.
USNIP, vol.xli (1915), pp.25–32.
    In a desperate engagement off Nantucket on 11
October 1814, the American brigantine, which was
carrying goods to the value of $300,000 on board,
successfully repulsed an attack by ships' boats from the
British frigate ENDYMION, *40.*

2090. THAYER, Henry Otis.
The naval combat of the *Enterprise* and *Boxer*,
September 5, 1813.
Sprague's Journal of Marine History, vol.ii (1914),
pp.63–73.

2091. WASHBURN, Harold Connett.
The battle of Lake Champlain.
USNIP, vol.xl (1914), pp.1365–1385; plan.

2092. WHITE, Henry C.
The cruise of the *Tigress*.
USNIP, vol.i (1874), pp.39–57.

2093. WHITEHILL, Walter Muir.
New England blockaded in 1814. The journal of
Henry Edward Napier, lieutenant in *HMS Nymphe*.
Salem, Mass.; Peabody Museum; 1939. xxii, 88pp.,
pls. 8vo.

2094. WILSON, Herbert Wrigley, (1866–1940).
The War of 1812.
In: 'Cambridge Modern History', vol.vii: The
United States (Cambridge; 1903) – chap.x, pp.335–
348.

2095. WINTON-CLARE, C., [*i.e. Dr. R.C.
ANDERSON*].
A shipbuilders' war.
The Mariner's Mirror, vol.xxix, (July 1943), pp.139–
148.
   Describes the War of 1812 on the Great Lakes.

2096. ZASLOW, Morris.
The Defended Border: Upper Canada and the War
of 1812.
A collection of writings giving a comprehensive
picture of the War of 1812 in Upper Canada.
Toronto; Macmillan; 1964. xiv, 370pp., pls. 8vo.

2097. [Anonymous].
The loss of the Diamond Rock.
Naval Chronicle, vol.xvi, (1806), pp.123–136.

2098. [Anonymous].
The capture of the Danish islands St. Thomas, St.
John and their dependencies by Admiral Sir
Alexander Cochrane and General Bowyer,
December 1807.
Naval Chronicle, vol.xix (1808), pp.156–168.

2099. [Anonymous].
Accounts of the British naval squadrons in the
Chesapeake Bay and estuaries, 1813–14.
Naval Chronicle, vols.xxix (1813, *et seq.*), pp.501–
502; xxx, 162–8; 182–3; 243–6; 403; 438–9; xxxi,
246–9; xxxii, 247–251, 256, 503–9; & xxxiii, 160–
172; 434–7.

2100. [Anonymous].
Accounts of the attack made on Washington, D.C.,
by the British on August 24, 1814.
Naval Chronicle, vol.xxxii (1814), pp.247–251; 337–
348.

2101. [Anonymous].
Account of the operations against New Orleans by
the British, December 1814.
Naval Chronicle, vol.xxxiii (1815), pp.385–8; 470–2;
484–8; map.

2102. [Anonymous].
The Naval Monument; containing official and other
accounts of all the battles fought between the Navies
of the United States and Great Britain during the
late War★ . . .
Boston; A.Bowen; 1816. [318]pp., 25 engr. pls. 8vo.
   ★*That is the War of 1812. The appendices include a
tabulated list of the United States Navy's warships –
from Bainbridge's* INDEPENDENCE, *74, down to the* TOM
BOWLINE, *9.*

2103. [Anonymous].
Narrative of the naval operations in the Potomac,
by the squadron under the orders of Captain Sir
James A.Gordon in 1814.
United Service Journal, no.liii (April 1833), pp.469–
481.

2104. [Anonymous].
Recollections of the expedition to the Chesapeake
and against New Orleans, in the years 1814–1815.
United Service Journal, nos.cxxxvii (April 1840),
pp.443–456; cxxxviii (May 1840), pp.25–36;
cxxxix (June 1840), pp.182–195 *and* cxl (July 1840),
pp.337–352.

2105. [Anonymous].
Naval recollections of the late American War.
United Service Journal, nos.cxlix (April 1841),
pp.455–467; & cl (May 1841), pp.13–23.

2106. [Anonymous].
The British *Shannon* and the American *Chesapeake*.
United Service Journal, no.ccl (August 1849), pp.50–
68.

2107. [Anonymous].
American vessels captured by the British during the
Revolution and War of 1812; the records of the
Vice-Admiralty Court at Halifax, Nova Scotia.
Salem, Mass.; 1911. 166pp. 8vo.

2108. [Anonymous].
Notes on Commander Barclay's account of the
Battle of Lake Erie.
Journal of American History, vol.viii (1914), pp.123–
128.

2109. [Anonymous].
The capture of *La Topaze*, 1809.
Naval Review, vol.x (1922), p.346.

2109. [Anonymous], *continued*
After an action with HMS JASON, 38; CLEOPATRA, 32 *and* HAZARD, 18, *the large French frigate* LA TOPAZE, 40, *was captured off Pointe Noire, Guadeloupe on 22 January, 1809.*

2110. [Anonymous].
The causes of the War of 1812.
Naval Review, vol.xvii (1929), p.76.

VI. Events and operations elsewhere

2111. BRIDGE, *Admiral Sir* Cyprian Arthur George, (1839–1924).
The capture of Mauritius in 1810.
Cornhill Magazine, n.s., vol.xxix (1910), pp.521–526.
In July 1810 a British maritime expeditionary force landed and took possession of Mauritius (French: Île de France) and Réunion (French: Île de Bourbon).

2112. BROWNE, Douglas Gordon.
A forgotten battle: a study in obscure naval history.
Blackwood's Magazine, vol.cxcii (1912), pp.63–80.
About the British attack on Mauritius in July 1800; see the preceding entry.

2113. COLGATE, H.A.
Trincomalee and the East Indies squadron, 1746 & 1844.
University of London MA thesis; (1959).

2114. COSTA, Ernestina, *Baroness de Nieuwburgh.*
The English invasion of the River Plate, [1806–1807].
Buenos Aires; Guillermo Kraft; 1937. 167pp., pls.; chart. 8vo.
Describes the costly and abortive British naval and military expedition against Buenos Aires and Montevideo, 1806–7, which ended with General Whitelock's humiliating evacuation in July 1807. The part of the Royal Navy (against whom no criticism was made) in the River Plate operations was discharged in 1806 by forces under Commodore Sir Home Riggs Popham and in 1807 by Rear-Admiral Charles Stirling.

2115. DICKINS, Bruce.
Merchantmen of war in Nelson's day.
The Mariner's Mirror, vol.liii (February 1967), pp.33–38.
An account of Sir Nathaniel Dance's remarkable triumph, with a convoy of East Indiamen, over a superior French squadron under Linois, off Pulo Auro (or Aor) in the Malacca Straits, 14 February, 1804.

2116. FIELD, Arthur G.
The expedition to Mauritius in 1810 and the establishment of British control.
University of London MA thesis; 1931–2.

2117. FIGUEIREDO, Fidelino de.
Os Ingleses uo Rio de la Plata, 1806–1807.
Junta Historica de America Boletino, vol.x (1937), pp.171–185.

2118. GILLESPIE, *Colonel* R.St.J.
Sir Nathaniel Dance's battle off Pulo Auro.
The Mariner's Mirror, vol.xxi (April 1935), pp.163–
186.
See entry no.2115, above.

2119. GRAHAM, *Professor* Gerald Sanford. [*editor*].
The Navy and South America, 1807–1823. Correspondence of the commanders-in-chief on the South American station.
Edited by Gerald S.Graham . . . and R.A. Humphreys.
London; Navy Records Society; 1962. xxxiv; 394pp. 8vo.

2120. LEYLAND, John.
Decaen and Linois.
The Mariner's Mirror, vol.i (March 1911), pp.68–71.
About the French expedition to Pondicherry and Île de France (Mauritius) in 1813.

2121. LLOYD, *Professor* Christopher.
The mutiny of the *Nereide*.
The Mariner's Mirror, vol.liv (August 1968), pp.245–251.
The mutiny on board the frigate NEREIDE, 36, *took place on 8 January 1809 off Madagascar.*

2122. METHLEY, V.M.
The Ceylon expedition of 1813.
RHS Trans., 4th series, vol.i (1918).

2123. PARKINSON, *Professor* Cyril Northcote.
Trade and war in the eastern seas, 1803–1810.
University of London, Ph.D thesis; 1935.

2124. PARKINSON, *Professor* Cyril Northcote.
Trade in the eastern seas, 1793–1813.
Cambridge; University Press; 1937. 453pp., pls. 8vo.

2125. PARKINSON, *Professor* Cyril Northcote.
War in the eastern seas, 1793–1815.
London; Allen & Unwin; 1954. 477pp., pls. 8vo.

2126. PENDLE, George.
Defeat at Buenos Aires, 1806–1807.
History Today (1952), pp.400–405.
See also entry no.2130.

2127. PERRIN, Walter Gordon, (1874–1931).
[*editor*].
The second capture of the Cape of Good Hope, 1806.
In: The Naval Miscellany, vol.iii; 1928.
[Navy Records Society series, vol.lxiii].

2128. [POPHAM, *Rear-Admiral Sir* Home Riggs, (1762–1820)].
Letters by Rear-Admiral Sir Home Riggs Popham relating to the capture of the Cape of Good Hope, 1806.
In: The Naval Miscellany, vol.iii, 1928. [Navy Records Society, series, vol.lxiii.]

2129. RAINBOW, S.G.
English expeditions to the Dutch East Indies during the Revolutionary and Napoleonic Wars.
University of London MA thesis; 1934.
Précis in: IHR Bull., vol.xi (February 1934), pp.192–5.

2130. ROBERTO, Carlos.
Los invasiones inglesas del Rio de la Plata, 1806–1807.
Buenos Aires; J.Penser; 1938.
xxix; 458pp., illustr., maps & plans. 8vo.

2131. ROSE, *Professor* John Holland, (1855–1942).
The French East Indian expedition at the Cape in 1803.
English Historical Review, vol.xiv (1899), pp.129–132.

2132. SAENZ VALIENTE, José Maria.
Los Alcades de Buenos Aires en 1806, su actuacion durante la primera invasion inglesa.
Instit. Historicas Bolétim, vol.xviii (1934), pp.98–141.

2133. TREGONNING, K.G.
A forgotten naval battle.
The Mariner's Mirror, vol.xlvi, (May 1961), pp.214–215 (n).
On the action between HMS GREYHOUND and HARRIER and four Dutch frigates and corvettes in the Java Sea, 27 July 1806.

2134. [WALTERS, *Lieutenant* Samuel, RN. (1778–1834)].
The memoirs of Samuel Walters, Lieutenant, RN: edited by C.N.Parkinson.
Liverpool; University Press; 1950. 154pp. 8vo.
Between 1805–1810, Walters took part in the expedition to the Cape and to the River Plate and served in the Indian Ocean.

2135. WURTZBURG, C.E.
Who planned the sea route of the Java expedition in 1811?
The Mariner's Mirror, vol.xxxvii (April 1951), pp.104–8.

2136. [Anonymous].
The attack on the forts of Boolukumba by *HMS Cornwallis* in 1809.

2136. [Anonymous], *continued*
United Service Journal, no.ccxxi (April 1847),
pp.531–7.
   During operations against Dutch settlements in the
East Indies, which culminated in the capture of
Amboyna, February 1810.

2137. [Anonymous].
The destruction of Dutch men of war off Grisee,
Java, in 1807.
Naval Review, vol.xxvi (1938), pp.99–103.

VII. General works of the period, including administration and policy

2138. BONNEL, Ulane.
La France, Les États-Unis et la guerre de course,
(1797–1815).
Paris; Nouvelles Éditions Latines; 1961. 489pp.,
pls. & charts. 8vo.
   The appendices include lists of privateers captured and
their captors.

2139. BRENTON, *Captain* Edward Pelham, RN.
(1774–1839).
The naval history of Great Britain from the year
MDCCLXXXIII to MDCCCXXII.
London; C.Rice; 1823–1825. 5 volumes. pls. &
diagrs. 8vo.
   There is also a set of the revised edition, [2 volumes;
London; Charles Colburn; 1837], in the Library.

2140. CAMENER, Clyde Bradley.
The naval surgeon afloat during Nelson's time.
USNIP, vol.lxi, (1935), pp.1804–1810; 1 plate.

2141. CASTEX, Raoul Victor Patrice.
Reflexions sur la stratégie des operations combinées.
La Revue Maritime, nos.lxxvii (May 1926), pp.595–
626; lxxviii (June 1926), pp.734–767; lxxix (July
1926), pp.62–79.

2142. CHEVALIER, *Capitaine* Louis Edmond.
Historie de la Marine Française sous le Consulat et
l'Empire.
Paris; Hachette; 1886. 439pp., pls. 8vo.

2143. CLAESSON, Carl-Erik.
Några synpunkter på Napoleons sjöstrategi.
Skriften Utgivna av Sjöhistoriska Samfundet, no.6
(Uppsala, 1945), pp.120–126.

2144. CLOWES, *Sir* William Laird (1856–1905),
et alia.
The Royal Navy. A History from the earliest times
to the present.
London; Sampson, Low, Marston & Co.,; 1897–
1903. 7 volumes. 4to.
   Volume 5, (623pp), is entirely devoted to the period
1803–1815 and comprises the following parts: Major
operations, Minor operations, Civil history of the Royal
Navy – and comprehensive appendices, which include
details of ships lost or captured in the British, French,
Spanish, Dutch, Danish, Russian, Turkish and United
States' navies during the period.

2145. CONTE, Pierre le.
Napoleon et les appelations des bâtiments de guerre.
La Revue Maritime, no.xclv (November 1927), pp.613–632.

2146. COOPER, *Lieutenant* Guy E., RN.
The methods of blockade and observation employed during the Revolutionary and Napoleonic Wars.
RUSIJ, vol.lxi (1916), p.523 *and Naval Review*, vol.iv (1916), p.7.

2147. CRIMMIN, Patricia K.
Admiralty administration, 1783–1806.
University of London M.Phil thesis; 1967.
There is a précis in IHR Bull., no.xxix (May 1968), part i.

2148. CRIMMIN, Patricia K.
Admiralty relations with the Treasury, 1783–1806: the preparation of naval estimates and the beginnings of Treasury control.
The Mariner's Mirror, vol.liii (February 1967), pp.63–72.

2149. CRIMMIN, Patricia K.
The financial and clerical establishment of the Admiralty Office, 1783–1806.
The Mariner's Mirror, vol.lv (August 1969), pp.299–309.

2150. EKINS, *Admiral Sir* Charles, GCB. (1768–1855).
Naval battles from 1744 to the Peace in 1814, critically reviewed and illustrated.
London; Baldwin, Cradock & Jay; 1824. xxix, 425pp., diagrs. & plans. 4to.
Includes numerous battle-plans.

2151. FOX, *Lieutenant* H.C.
A discussion of the problems of naval administration arising from the period covered by the Barham papers.
Naval Review, vol.xxiii (1935), pp.758–773.

2152. GARBETT, *Commander* H., RN.
The Seamen of the Guard, 1803–1815.
RUSIJ, vol.xl (1896), pp.59, 165.
A translation of the article by Lieutenant Émile Bertrant, which originally appeared in: La Revue Maritime et Coloniale.

2153. GRAHAM, *Professor* Gerald Sandford.
Seapower and British North America, 1783–1820.
Cambridge, Mass.; Harvard University Press; 1941. xii, 302pp., pls. & maps. 8vo.

2154. GRIEVE, J.S.Mackenzie.
The observation and blockade of the French fleets during the Revolutionary and Napoleonic Wars, (1793–1815).
United Service Magazine, (April–June 1916).

2155. GUERIN, Léon.
Histoire de la Marine contemporaire de France, depuis 1784 jusqu'à 1848.
Paris; Adolphe Delahaye; 1855. 730pp., pls. & maps. large 8vo.

2156. HANNAY, David, (1853–1934).
Napoleon and Nelson.
Cornhill Magazine, vol.ix (n.s.). (1905).

2157. HENDERSON, James.
The Frigates. An account of the lesser warships of the wars from 1793 to 1815.
London; Adlard Coles; 1970. 192pp., pls. & diagrs. 8vo.

2158. JAMES, William, (d.1827).
The Naval History of Great Britain from the declaration of war by France . . . 1793, to the accession of George IV . . . 1820, with an account of the origin and progressive increase of the British Navy; illustrated, from the commencement of the year 1793, by a series of tabular abstracts.
London; 1822–1824. 5 volumes. 8vo. First edition.
A standard contemporary authority for detailed naval events of the period. Although criticised on the grounds of prejudice, still invaluable as a work of reference. There were numerous later editions, of which there are also copies in the Library, viz: Second edition. With additions & notes, 1826. Third edition. With continuation by Captain Frederick Chamier, 6 vols.; 1837. Fourth edition. With portraits & index by C.T.Wilson. 6 vols.; 1847. Fifth edition. With preface by T.W.Cole. 6 vols.; 1859, reprinted 1864. Sixth edition. With corrigenda. 1877. Seventh edition. With additions by Professor York Powell. 6 vols. 1886; reprinted 1902.
Note, too, the one-volume epitome by R.O'Byrne (London, 1888) and the Index to James' Naval History (1886 edition), compiled by Toogood and Brassey, in the Navy Records Society series (vol.iv; 1895).

2159. [JENKINS, James].
The naval achievements of Great Britain from the year 1793 to 1817.
London; James Jenkins; [1817]. 164pp., 55 cold. engr. pls. large 4to.
A second London edition appeared in 1818, published by L.Harrison.

2160. JURIEN DE LA GRAVIÈRE, *Vice-Amiral*
Jean P.E. (1812–1892).
Les guerres maritimes sous la République et
L'Empire.
Paris; G.Charpentier; 1847. 2 vols. 380; 428pp.,
foldg. maps. 8vo.

2161. LEWIS, *Professor* Michael.
A Social History of the Navy, 1793–1815.
London; Allen & Unwin; 1960. 467pp., pls. 8vo.
   A brilliant study.

2162. LOBBAN, Robert Dalziel.
Nelson's navy and the French Wars.
London; University of London Press; 1968. 64pp.,
pls. 8vo.

2163. MAHAN, *Rear-Admiral* Alfred Thayer, USN.
(1840–1914).
The Influence of Sea Power upon the French
Revolution and Empire, 1793–1812 . . .
London; Sampson Low, Marston; 1892. 2 vols.
380; 428pp., maps & plans. 8vo.

2164. MARCUS, Geoffrey.
A Naval History of England.
Volume two: The Age of Nelson.
London; Allen & Unwin; 1971. 532pp., maps. 8vo.

2165. MASEFIELD. John. (1878–1967).
Sea life in Nelson's time.
London; Methuen; 1905. xii, 225pp., pls. 8vo.

2166. MAXWELL, John Irving.
Reports of the Commissioner of Naval Inquiry for
the year 1804 . . . with notes and a copious appendix,
containing selections from the most important
documents upon which the reports are founded.
London; H.D.Symonds; 1805. xxxii; 400; 253pp.
8vo.

2167. McCORD, Norman.
The impress service in North East England during
the Napoleonic War.
The Mariner's Mirror, vol.liv (May 1968), pp.163–
180.

2168. MEAD, *Commander* Hilary Poland, RN.
The Admiralty telegraphs and semaphores.
The Mariner's Mirror, vol.xxiv (April 1938), pp.184–
203, pls., diagrs.

2169. MURACCIOLE, José.
Napoleon et l'artillerie navale.
La Revue Maritime, no.ccxliii (May 1967), pp.607–
614.

2170. NORIE, John William, (1772–1843).
The Naval Gazetteer, Biographer and Chronologist;
containing a history of the late wars . . . 1793 . . .
1801, and from their recommencement in 1803 to
their final conclusion in 1815 . . .
London; Norie; 1827. xii; 586pp. 12mo.
   *There is also a copy of the 1842 edition of this work in
the Library.*

2171. POOL, Bernard.
Navy contracts in the last years of the Navy Board,
(1780–1832).
The Mariner's Mirror, vol.l (August 1964), pp.161–
176.

2172. RALFE, James.(*fl.* 1820–1829).
The Naval Chronology of Great Britain; or, an
historical account of naval and maritime events,
from the commencement of the War in 1803, to the
end of the year 1816 . . .
London; Whitmore & Fenn; 1820. 3 vols. 288; 284;
318pp., numerous engravings. 4to.

2173. RODGER, Alexander Bankier.
The War of the Second Coalition: a strategic
commentary.
Edited with a concluding chapter by Christopher
Duffy.
Oxford; Clarendon Press; 1964. 312pp. 8vo.
   An important study.

2174. ROSE, *Professor* John Holland, (1855–1942).
Napoleon and sea power.
Cambridge Historical Journal, vol.ii (1924), pp.138–
157.

2175. SELEMENT, George.
Impressment and the American merchant marine,
1782–1812; an American view.
The Mariner's Mirror, vol.lix (November 1973),
pp.409–418.

2176. STEEL, David.
Steel's Naval Chronologist of the late war . . .
including also a copious description of Lord Nelson's
victory off Cape Trafalgar in 1805.
London; Steel; 1806. civ, 122pp., plans & diagrs.
small 8vo.

2177. TALBOT, M.F.
A sketch of fleet maintenance in Nelson's day.
USNIP, vol.lxv (July 1939), pp.958–960.

2178. THOMAZI, *Capitaine* A.
Les idées maritimes de Napoleon.
Neptunia, vol.xxxvii (January 1958), pp.21–25.

2179. TURNER, Eunice H.
The naval medical service, 1793–1815.
The Mariner's Mirror, vol.xlvii (May 1961), pp.119–133

2180. WILKIN, W.H.
The Admiralty telegraph to Plymouth, 1805–1814.
Devon & Cornwall Notes and Queries, vol.xix (January 1929), pp.202–4.

2181. WILSON, Herbert Wrigley, (1866–1940).
The command of the sea, 1803–1815.
In: Cambridge Modern History, vol.x: 'Napoleon,' chap.viii, pp.208–243.

2182. YORKE, H.R. *and* STEVENSON, W.
British naval achievements; being an accurate account of the lives and actions of British seamen from 1780 to . . . 1816 . . .
London; C.J.Barrington; 1822. 2 vols. 552; 389pp., engr. pls. 8vo.
  There is also a copy of the 1823 edition – contents unchanged – in the Library.

2183. [Anonymous].
Naval anecdotes; or, a new key to the proceedings of the late naval administration.
London; C.&R.Baldwin; 1807. xvi, 190pp. 8vo.

2184. [Anonymous].
Chronological sketches of the most remarkable events of the years 1807 . . . to 1815.
In the: Naval Chronicle, (1808–1816).
vols.xix, pp.127–9; xxi, pp.47–50; xxiii, pp.62–65; xxv, pp.51–54; xxvii, pp.35–39; xxix, pp.134–157; xxxi, pp.58–59; xxxiii, pp.61–65; & xxxv, pp.77–79.

2185. [Anonymous].
An inquiry into the present state of the British Navy. Together with reflections on the late war with America; its probable consequences . . .
London; C.Chapple; 1815. xvi, 166pp. 8vo.

PART FIVE

General Works

General Works

[*Note. The following general works on Naval History comprise those which span the whole, or a great part, of the period surveyed in this volume. For general works referring to a particular century – or an aspect of it – see the relevant section under that heading.*]

2186. ADAMS, W.H.Davenport.
England on the Sea; or the story of the British Navy.
London; White; 1885. 2 vols. 244; 259pp. 8vo.

2187. ALBION, Robert Greenhalgh.
Forests and Sea Power. The timber problem of the Royal Navy, 1652–1862.
Cambridge, Mass.,; Harvard University Press; 1926. xv; 485pp. 8vo.
An original study, stressing the Navy's growing dependence on imported raw materials for shipbuilding.

2188. ALLEN, Joseph. (1810–1864).
Battles of the British Navy.
London; H.G.Bohn; 1852. 2 vols. 527; 604pp. 8vo.
There is also a copy of the 1853 edition in the Library.

2189. ANDERSON, *Dr.* Roger Charles.
Naval wars in the Baltic during the sailing ship epoch, 1522–1850.
London; C.Gilbert-Wood; 1910. 423pp.; pls. 8vo.

2190. ANDERSON . . .
Naval wars in the Levant, 1559–1853.
Liverpool; University Press; 1952. 619pp., pls., & plans. 8vo.

2191. BÄCKSTRÖM, P.O.
Svenska Flottans Historia.
Stockholm; P.A.Norstedt; 1884. 513pp. 8vo.

2192. BALLARD, *Admiral* George Alexander. (1862–1948).
The influence of the sea on the political history of Japan.
London; John Murray; 1921. xix; 311pp. 8vo.

2193. BALLARD . . .
America and the Atlantic.
London; Duckworth; 1923. vii, 351pp., maps. 8vo.
A general survey of American maritime history, from Columbus to the end of the 19th century.

2194. BAMFORD, Paul Walden.
Forests and French seapower, 1660–1789.
Toronto; University Press; 1956. xi; 240pp. 8vo.

2195. BARROW, *Sir* John. (1764–1848).
The Naval History of Great Britain; with the lives of the most illustrious Admirals and Commanders from the reign of Queen Elizabeth . . .
London; Rivington & Fletcher; 1758. 4 vols.: 272; 311; 293; 432pp. 8vo.
A copy of the second edition (1776) is also in the Library.

2196. BERCKMAN, Evelyn.
Creators and destroyers of the English Navy as related by the State Papers Domestic.
London; Hamish Hamilton; 1974. xii; 212pp., pls. 8vo.

2197. BERKLEY, *Captain* George, RN (*d.*1746).
The Naval History of Britain, from the earliest periods of which there are accounts in history, to the conclusion of the year MDCCLVI . . .
London; T.Osborne; 1756. 708pp., pls. & maps. 8vo.

2198. BLEVENETS, P.E.
The needs and development of the Navy and its importance in Russian history.
St. Petersburg; 1909. Russian text. 282pp., pls. 4to.

2199. BOWEN, Frank Charles, (1894–1957).
Wooden walls in action.
London; Halton; 1951. viii; 144pp.,; pls. 8vo.

2200. BRADFORD, Ernle D.S.
Wall of England; the Channel's two thousand years of history.
London; Country Life; 1966. 112pp., pls. 8vo.

2201. BRADFORD . . .
The Mediterranean; portrait of a sea.
London; Hodder & Stoughton; 1971. 575pp., pls. 8vo.

2202. BRAGADIN, Marc'Antonio.
Repubbliche Italiane sul Mare.
Milan; Gazanti; 1951. 278pp., illustr. 8vo.

2203. BRIDGE, *Admiral Sir* Cyprian A.G. (1839–1924).
Sea power and other studies.
London; Smith Elder; 1910. 311pp. 8vo.

2204. BRUN, V.
Guerres maritimes de la France . . .
Paris; Plon; 1861. 2 vols. 560; 684pp. 8vo.

2205. BURCHETT, Josiah.
A complete History of the most remarkable transactions at sea, from the earliest accounts of time to the conclusion of the last war with France . . . In five books.

2205. BURCHETT, *continued*
London; J.Walthoe; 1720. 800pp. large 4to.
The survey concludes with Queen Anne's War,
(1702–1713).

2206. BUSCH, Fritz Otto & RAMLOW, *Dr.*
Gerhard.
Deutsche seekriegsgeschichte.
Berlin; Bertelsmann; [*n.d.*]. 864pp. 8vo.

2207. CALLENDER, *Sir* Geoffrey R.R. (1875–
1946).
The Naval side of British history.
London; Christophers; 1924. 305pp., pls. 8vo.

2208. CAMPBELL, John. (1708–1775).
Lives of the admirals, and other eminent British
seamen . . . including a new and accurate naval
history from the earliest account of time . . .
London; J. & M.Pemberton; 1742. 4 vols. 8vo.
Copies of all the later editions, (1785; 1812–17; 1818;
1841 and 1873), are also in the Library.

2209. CANNON, Richard.
Historical record of the Marine Corps, containing
an account of their formation and services from
1664–1748 . . .
London; [*ca.*1840]. xxxiv; 56pp. 8vo.

2210. CARRISON, Daniel J.
The United States Navy.
New York; Praeger; 1968. 262pp.; pls. 8vo.

2211. CHATTERTON, Edward Keble. (1878–
1944).
The story of the British Navy from the earliest times
to the present day.
London; Mills & Boon; 1911. 371pp., pls. 8vo.

2212. CHATTERTON . . .
Battles by Sea.
London; Sidgwick & Jackson; 1925. 271pp., pls.
8vo.

2213. CHEVALIER, Louis Edouard.
Histoire de la Marine Française, depuis les débuts de
la Monarchie jusqu'au traité de la paix, 1763.
Paris; Hachette; 1886–1902. 3 vols. 517; 439;
438pp. 8vo.
The above is the title of the first volume. The sequels
cover the period 1763–1814 and 1815–1870, respectively.

2214. CIPOLLA, *Professor* Carlo M.
Guns and sails in the early phase of European
expansion, 1400–1700.
London; Collins; 1966. 192pp., pls. 8vo.

2215. CLARKE, *Sir* George S. (1848–1933).
Russia's sea power past and present, or the rise of the
Russian Navy.
London; John Murray; 1898. 202pp., pls. 8vo.

2216. CLOWES, *Sir* William Laird (1856–1905),
et alia.
The Royal Navy, a history from the earliest times to
the death of Queen Victoria.
London; Sampson Low, Marston; 1897–1903.
7 vols. 4to.

2217. COLLIBER, Samuel. (*fl.*1718–1737).
Columna Rostrata; or, a critical history of the
English sea-affairs . . .
London; R.Robinson; 1727. 312pp. 8vo.
A copy of the 1739 edition is also in the Library.

2218. COLOMB, *Rear-Admiral* Philip Howard.
(1831–1899).
Naval warfare; its ruling principles and practice
historically treated.
London; W.H.Allen; 1891. 448pp., pls. & maps.
8vo.

2219. CORBETT, *Professor Sir* Julian S. (1854–
1922). [*editor*].
Fighting Instructions, 1530–1816.
London; Navy Records Society series, vol.xxix;
1905. 366pp. 8vo.

2220. CRESSE, A.J.B.de.
Histoire de la Marine de tous les peuples . . .
Paris; Aimé André; 1824. 2 vols. 558; 576pp. 8vo.

2221. CRESWELL, *Captain* John, RN.
Generals and Admirals. The story of amphibious
command.
London; Longmans Green; 1952. 192pp., maps. 8vo.

2222. CUSTANCE, *Admiral Sir* Richard N. (1847–
1935).
A study of war.
London; Constable; 1924. 214pp., maps. 8vo.

2223. DAVIS, *Professor* Ralph.
Rise of the English Shipping Industry in the 17th
and 18th centuries.
Newton Abbot; David & Charles; 1972. 440pp.,
pls. 8vo.
A masterly study.

2224. DERRICK, Charles.
Memoirs of the rise and progress of the Royal Navy.
London; Blacks & Parry; 1806. 309pp. 4to.

2225. DIRKS, J.J.Backer.
De Nederlandsche Zeemagt in hare verschillende
tijdperken geschetst . . .
Rotterdam; H.Nijgh; 1865–76. 4 vols. 8vo.

2226. DURO, Cesareo Fernandez.
Armada Española desde la union de los Reinos de
Castilla y de Leon.
Madrid; Rivadeneyra; 1895–1903. 9 vols. ca.4,000pp.
8vo.
 *The standard history of the Spanish navy and
maritime affairs. A monumental work, drawing upon a
wealth of detail and the use of original sources.*

2227. EARDLEY-WILMOT, *Rear-Admiral Sir*
S.M. (1847–1929).
Our Navy for a thousand years . . .
London; Sampson Low; 1899. 395pp., pls. 8vo.

2228. ELDRIDGE, Frank Burgess.
The background of eastern sea power.
Melbourne; 1945. 386pp., pls. 8vo.
 *A general history of the development of seapower in
the Pacific and Indian Oceans.*

2229. ENTICK, John.
A new Naval History, or, compleat view of the
British marine. In which the Royal Navy and the
merchant's service are traced through all their
periods and different branches . . . including the
most considerable naval expeditions and sea-fights . . .
London; R.Manby; 1757. lxii; 888pp., pls. folio.

2230. FIELD, *Colonel* Cyril, RMLI.
Britain's sea soldiers. A history of the Royal Marines
and their predecessors and of their services in action,
ashore and afloat.
Liverpool; Lyceum Press; 1924. 2 vols.: 324;
357pp., pls. 8vo.

2231. FOSTER, Thomas.
The pictorial history of sea battles.
London; Marshall Cavendish; 1974. 128pp., illustr.
8vo.

2232. FRASER, Edward.
Famous fighters of the Fleet. Glimpses through the
cannon smoke in the days of the Old Navy.
London; Macmillan; 1904. xvi; 323pp., pls. 8vo.
 A copy of the 1907 edition is also in the Library.

2233. FRASER . . .
Champions of the Fleet; captains and men of war in
days that helped to make the Empire.
London; J.Lane; 1908. 299pp., pls. 8vo.

2234. FRASER . . .
The romance of the King's Navy.
London; Hodder & Stoughton; 1908. viii; 312pp.,
pls. 8vo.

2235. FRASER . . .
The fighting fame of the King's ships. Dreadnoughts
and captains of renown.
London; Hutchinson; 1910. xii; 348pp., pls. 8vo.

2236. GARDE, *Captain* H.G.
Efterretninger om den Danske og Norske sømagt.
Copenhagen; J.D.Qvist; 1832–3. 3 vols. small 8vo.

2237. GIBSON, Charles E.
The clash of fleets. The stories of ten great sea battles.
London & New York; Abelard-Schuman; 1962.
256pp., pls. 8vo.

2238. GIFFARD, Edward.
Deeds of naval daring. Anecdotes of the British
Navy.
London; John Murray; 1910. 410pp. 8vo.

2239. GOLDSMITH, *Captain* William.
The Naval history of Great Britain from the earliest
period . . .
London; Jacques & Wright; 1824. 808pp., pls. 8vo.

2240. GRAHAM, *Professor* Gerald S.
Empire of the North Atlantic: the maritime struggle
for North America.
Toronto; University Press/Oxford; University
Press; 1958. 338pp., 8vo.
 *An important book, emphasizing the strategic aspects
during the period 1689–1815.*

2241. GUGLIELMOTTI, P. Alberto.
Storia della Marina Pontifica.
Rome; Tipografia Vaticana; 1886–93. 9 vols. 8vo.

2242. GUERIN, Léon.
Histoire maritime de France depuis la fondation de
Marseille jusqu'à nos jours.
Paris; Ledoux; 1843. 2 vols. 8vo.

2243. GYLLENGRANAT, C.A.
Sveriges sjökrigs-historia.
Carlskrona; Ameen; 1840. 2 vols. 8vo.

2244. HALE, John Richard.
Famous sea fights from Salamis to Tsu-Shima.
London; Methuen; 1919. xii; 350pp. pls., 8vo.
 First published in 1911.

2245. HANNAY, David. (1853–1934).
A short history of the Royal Navy, 1217–1815.
London; Methuen; 1897–1909. 2 vols.: 474; 524pp.,
9vo.
   A second edition of volume i was published in 1911.

2246. HANNAY . . .
The Navy and seapower.
London & New York; Williams & Norgate/Henry
Holt; [*ca.*1913]. 256pp. 8vo.

2247. HARGREAVES, Reginald.
The Narrow Seas: a history of the English Channel,
400 BC – 1945 AD.
London; Sidgwick & Jackson; 1959. 517pp. 8vo.

2248. HEARNSHAW, *Professor* F.J.C.
Sea power and Empire.
London; Harrap; 1940. 291pp. 8vo.
   *Based on lectures delivered in the University of
London, 1939.*

2249. HERVEY, Frederic.
The Naval History of Great Britain, including the
lives of the admirals and other illustrious
commanders and navigators . . .
London; Adlard; 1779–80. 5 vols. 8vo.

2250. HILL, F.S.
The Romance of the American Navy . . . 1775–1909.
New York & London; Putnam; 1910. xxxi;
394pp., pls. 8vo.

2251. HODGES, H.W. *and* HUGHES, E.A.
[*editors*].
Select Naval Documents.
Cambridge; University Press; 1922. xii; 227pp., 8vo.

2252. HOWARTH, David.
Sovereign of the Seas. The story of British seapower.
London; Collins; 1974. 382pp., pls. 8vo.

2253. HURD, *Sir* Archibald S. (*d.*1959).
Our Navy.
London; Frederick Warne; 1914. 270pp., 8vo.
   *A general History of the Royal Navy up to the out-
break of World War I.*

2254. HURD . . .
Sea Power.
London; Constable; 1916. 94pp. 8vo.

2255. JAMES, *Admiral Sir* William M.
The influence of sea power on the history of the
British people.
Cambridge; University Press; 1948. 71pp. 8vo.

2256. JANE, Fred T. (*d.*1916).
The Imperial Russian Navy; its past, present and
future.
London; Thacker; 1899. 755pp., pls. 4to.
   *There is also a copy of the 1904 edition in the
Library.*

2257. JANE . . .
Heresies of sea power.
London; Longmans Green; 1906. 341pp., pls. &
maps. 8vo.

2258. JANE . . .
The British Battle Fleet; its inception and growth
throughout the centuries.
London; Partridge; 1914. 406pp., pls. 8vo.

2259. JONGE, J.C.de.
Geschiedenis van het Nederlandsche Zeewezen.
Haarlem; A.C.Kruseman; 1858–62. 5 vols. 4to.

2260. JENKINS, E.H.
A History of the French Navy from its beginnings
to the present day.
London; Macdonald & Janes; 1973. 364pp., pls. 8vo.

2261. [KHALIFEH, Haji].
The history of the maritime wars of the Turks,
translated by . . . James Mitchell.
London; 1831. 80pp. 4to.

2262. KEMP, *Lieutenant Commander* Peter K.
[*editor*], *et alia.*
History of the Royal Navy.
London; Arthur Barker; 1969. 304pp., pls. & maps.
4to.

2263. KIRCHHOFF, *Vice-Admiral* D.
Seemacht in der Ostsee. Ihre einwirkung auf die
geschichte der Ostseeländer im 17, 18 und 19
jahrhunderts.
Kiel; Robert Cordes; 1907–8. 2 vols.: 481; 340pp.,
charts & plans. 8vo.

2264. LAUGHTON, *Sir* John Knox. (1830–1915).
Studies in naval history.
London; Longmans; 1887. 469pp. 8vo.

2265. LAUGHTON, . . .
Sea fights and adventures.
London; George Allen; 1901. 294pp., pls. 8vo.

2266. LEDIARD, Thomas. (1685–1743).
The Naval history of England, in all its branches;
from the Norman Conquest in the year 1066 to the
conclusion of 1734 . . .

2266. LEDIARD, *continued*
London; John Wilcox; 1735. 2 vols. in one. 933pp.,
pls. folio.
 A French translation was published in 1751.

2267. LEWIS, *Professor* Michael A. (1890–1970).
The Navy of Britain. A historical portrait.
London; Allen & Unwin; 1948. 660pp., illustr. 8vo.

2268. LEWIS . . .
The History of the British Navy.
London; Allen and Unwin; 1959. 260pp. 8vo.

2269. LEYLAND, John.
The Royal Navy; its influence in English history
and in the growth of Empire.
Cambridge; University Press; 1914. 167pp. 8vo.

2270. LLOYD, *Professor* Christopher C.
The Nation and the Navy; a history of naval life and
policy.
London; Cresset Press; 1954. xiii; 287pp., pls. 8vo.
 *A copy of the second edition, (1961), is also in the
Library.*

2271. LLOYD . . .
Sea fights under sail.
London; Collins; 1970. 128pp., pls. 8vo.

2272. LOIR, *Lieutenant* Maurice.
La Marine Française.
Paris; Hachette; 1893. 620pp., pls. large 4to.

2273. LOW, *Lieutenant* Charles Rathbone, RIN.
History of the Indian Navy, 1613–1863.
London; Richard Bentley; 1877. 2 vols.: 541:
596pp. 8vo.

2274. MACLAY, Edgar Stanton.
A History of the United States Navy from 1755 to
1901 . . .
New York; Appleton; 1901. 3 vols.: 660; 559;
499pp., pls. 8vo.

2275. MAHAN, *Rear-Admiral* Alfred Thayer,
(1840–1914).
The Influence of seapower upon history, 1660–1783.
London; Sampson Low; 1889. 557pp., maps and
plans. 8vo.
 *The classic work. Copies of the 1890; 1893; 1915
and 1918 editions are also in the Library. For Mahan's
studies of the French Revolutionary, Napoleonic and
1812 Wars, see under the appropriate sections.*

2276. MAHAN . . .
Naval administration and warfare. Some general
principles, with other essays.
London; Sampson Low; 1908. 409pp., 1 map. 8vo.

2277. MARCUS, *Dr.* Geoffrey J.
A Naval History of England:
vol.1.: The Formative Centuries.
London; Longmans; 1961. 494pp., maps. 8vo.
vol.2.: The Age of Nelson.
London; Allen & Unwin; 1971. 532pp., maps. 8vo.

2278. MOLLEMA, J.C.
Geschiedenis van Nederland ter Zee.
Amsterdam; van den Vondel; 1939. 4 vols. 8vo.

2279. MONASTEREV, N. *and* TERESCHENKO,
S.
Histoire de la Marine Russe.
Translated from the Russian by Lieutenant Jean
Perceau.
Paris; Payot; 1932. 349pp. 8vo.

2280. MORDAL, Jacques.
Twenty-five centuries of sea warfare.
Translated by Len Ortzen.
London; Souvenir Press; 1965. 420pp., pls. 8vo.

2281. MURRAY, *Sir* Oswyn A.R. (1873–1936).
The Admiralty.
The Mariner's Mirror, vols.xxiii (1937), pp.13–35;
129–147; 316–331; xxiv (1938), pp.101–104; 204–
225; 329–352; 458–478; & xxv (1939), pp.89–111;
216–228; 328–338.
 An important series of articles.

2282. NAVARRETE, Adolfo.
Historia maritima militar de España . . .
With an introduction by D.C.Fernandez Duro.
Madrid; Rivadeneyra; 1901. xi; 452pp. 8vo.

2283. PACK, *Captain* S.W.C.
Sea power in the Mediterranean. A study of the
struggle for sea power . . . from the seventeenth
century to the present day.
London; Arthur Barker; 1971. 260pp., pls. & maps.
8vo.

2284. PROTHEROE, Ernest.
The British Navy; its making and its meaning.
London; Routledge; [*ca*.1914]. 694pp.; pls. 8vo.

2285. QUINTELLA, Ignacio da Costa.
Annales da Marinha Portugueza.
Lisbon; Typografia da Mesma Académia; 1839-40.
2 vols.: 525; 354pp. 8vo.

2286. RICHMOND, *Admiral Sir* Herbert W.
(1871–1946).
National policy and naval strength, and other
essays . . .
London; Longmans; 1928. xvii; 355pp. 8vo.

2287. RICHMOND . . .
Naval warfare.
London; Benn; 1930. 96pp. small 4to.
  *Based on two lectures delivered at King's College,
Cambridge, in 1926.*

2288. RICHMOND . . .
The Navy and its records, from the Armada to
Trafalgar.
The Mariner's Mirror, vol.xxiv (January 1938),
pp.68–80.

2289. RICHMOND . . .
Amphibious warfare in British history.
Exeter; 1941. [Historical Association Pamphlet,
no.119.]. 31pp. 8vo.

2290. RICHMOND . . .
The objects and elements of sea power in history.
History, vol.xxviii (March 1943), pp.1–16.

2291. RICHMOND . . .
Statesmen and Sea Power . . .
Based on the Ford Lectures delivered in the
University of Oxford . . . 1943.
Oxford; Clarendon Press; 1946. xi; 369pp., 8vo.

2292. RICHMOND . . .
The Navy as an instrument of policy, 1558–1727.
Edited by E.A.Hughes.
Cambridge; University Press; 1953. 404pp. 8vo.
  Published seven years after Admiral Richmond's death.

2293. RITTMEYER, Rudolph.
Seekriege und seekriegswesen in ihrer weltgeschicht-
lichen entwicklung . . .
Berlin; 1907. xxi; 642pp., pls. 4to.

2294. ROBINSON, *Commander* Charles Napier.
The British Fleet. The growth, achievements and
duties of the Navy of the Empire.
London; Bell; 1894. 560pp., pls. 8vo.
  A copy of the 1895 edition is also in the Library.

2295. RONCIÈRE, Charles G.M.B.de la.
Histoire de la Marine Française . . .
Paris; Plon; 1899–1932. 6 vols. 8vo.
  *Volumes, which with the works of Chevalier [q.v.],
offer a good introduction to the study of French naval
history.*

2296. ROSSI, Ettore.
Storia della Marina dell'Ordine di S.Giovanni di
Gerusalemme, di Rodi e di Malta.
Rome & Milan; 1926. 256pp., pls. 8vo.

2297. SCHOMBERG, *Captain* Isaac, RN. (1753–
1813).
Naval Chronology; or, an historical summary of
naval and maritime events, from the time of the
Romans, to the Treaty of Peace, 1802.
London; Thomas Egerton; 1802. 5 vols. 8vo.
  *A detailed and comprehensive work, with numerous
appendices.*

2298. SELANDER, Einar.
En bok om vår flotta.
Stockholm; Gebers; 1907. 235pp., pls. 8vo.

2299. SOUTHWORTH, John van Duyn.
The age of sails. The story of naval warfare under
sail, 1213–1853.
New York; Twayne; 1968. 468pp., pls. 8vo.

2300. SPEARS, John R.
History of the United States Navy, from its origin
to the present day, 1775–1897.
London; Bickers; 1898. 4 vols.; illustr. 8vo.

2301. STENZEL, Alfred.
Seekriegsgeschichte in ihren wichtigsten
abschnitten . . .
Hanover & Leipzig; 1907–11. 5 vols., pls. & charts.
8vo.
  *There are many folding battle-plans and charts at the
end of each volume.*

2302. SUE, Eugène.
Histoire de la Marine Française.
Paris; Felix Bonnaire; 1835. 5 vols., pls. & charts.
8vo.

2303. SVENSSON, S.Artur. [*editor*].
Svenska Flottans Historia . . .
Malmo; A.B.Allhems; 1942–5. 3 vols., pls. &
charts. 4to.

2304. SZYMANSKI, Hans.
Brandenburg-Preussen zur see, 1605–1815. Ein
beitrag zur frühgeschichte der Deutschen Marine.
Leipzig; Koehler & Amelang; [1939]. 200pp., pls.
8vo.

2305. TRAMOND, Joannes.
Manuel d'Histoire Maritime de la France.
Paris; Augustin Challamel; 1916. 911pp., charts. 8vo.

2306. TROUDE, O.
Batailles navales de France.
Paris; Augustin Challamel; 1867–8. 4 vols. 8vo.

2307. TUXEN, J.C.
Den Danske og Norske sømagt fra de aeldste tider
indtil vore dage.
Copenhagen; P.G.Philipsens; 1875. 674pp., pls. 8vo.
    *This is a general naval history of Denmark and
Norway.*

2308. VAUGHAN, *Lieutenant-Commander* H.R.H.,
RN.
Comparative table for use in the study of naval
history.
Naval Review, (November 1922), pp.525–547.

2309. VESELAGO, A.O.
A Short History of the Russian Navy.
St. Petersburg; 1875. Russian text. 652pp., pls. &
plans. 4to.

2310. WARNER, Oliver.
Great Sea Battles.
London; Weidenfeld & Nicolson; 1963. 304pp.,
pls. & charts. folio.

2311. WARNER...
Great Battle Fleets.
London; Hamlyn; 1973. 240pp., pls. 4to.

2312. WARNER...
The Navy.
Harmondsworth, Mx.; Penguin Books; 1968.
218pp., pls. 12mo.

2313. WILKINSON, Norman *and* SWINBURNE,
H.L.
The Royal Navy.
London; 1907. 378pp., pls. 8vo.

2314. WILLIAMS, Hamilton.
Britain's naval power; a short history of the growth
of the British Navy from the earliest times to
Trafalgar...
London; Macmillan; 1898. 265pp., illustr. 8vo.

2315. YONGE, Charles Duke.
The History of the British Navy from the earliest
period to the present time.
London; Richard Bentley; 1863. 2 vols.: 716;
809pp., plans. 8vo.
    A copy of the second edition (1869) is in the Library.

2316. [Anonymous].
Britannia Triumphant: or, an account of the sea-
fights and victories of the English nation from the
earliest times, down to the conclusion of the late
war...
London; R.James; 1766. The second edition.
frontis.,; 224pp., pls. 8vo.
    *Ends with the Seven Years' War (1756–63). The
Library also has a copy of the new (or third) edition of
276pp., published by R.James in 1777.*

2317. [Anonymous].
The Field of Mars: being an alphabetical digestion
of the principal naval and military engagements, in
Europe, Asia, Africa, and America, particularly of
Great Britain and her allies, from the ninth century
to the present period...
London; J.Macgowan; 1781. 2 vols., pls. 4to.

2318. [Anonymous].
Judicio critico sobre la Marina Militar de España.
Madrid; Miguel de Burgos; 1814. 6 parts in 2 vols.
12mo.

Index

Printed in England for Her Majesty's Stationery Office by W. & J. Mackay Limited, Chatham Dd 288830 K12 8/76